Contributions to Economics

www.springer.com/series/1262

Further volumes of this series can be found at our homepage.

Sugata Marjit, Rajat Acharyya
International Trade, Wage Inequality and the Developing Economy
2003. ISBN 3-7908-0031-7

Francesco C. Billari/Alexia Prskawetz (Eds.)
Agent-Based Computational Demography
2003. ISBN 3-7908-1550-0

Georg Bol/Gholamreza Nakhaeizadeh/ Svetlozar T. Rachev/Thomas Ridder/ Karl-Heinz Vollmer (Eds.)
Credit Risk
2003. ISBN 3-7908-0054-6

Christian Müller
Money Demand in Europe
2003. ISBN 3-7908-0064-3

Cristina Nardi Spiller
The Dynamics of the Price Structure and the Business Cycle
2003. ISBN 3-7908-0063-5

Michael Bräuninger
Public Debt and Endogenous Growth
2003. ISBN 3-7908-0056-1

Brigitte Preissl/Laura Solimene
The Dynamics of Clusters and Innovation
2003. ISBN 3-7908-0077-5

Markus Gangl
Unemployment Dynamics in the United States and West Germany
2003. ISBN 3-7908-1533-0

Pablo Coto-Millán (Ed.)
Essays on Microeconomics and Industrial Organisation, 2nd Edition
2004. ISBN 3-7908-0104-6

Wendelin Schnedler
The Value of Signals in Hidden Action Models
2004. ISBN 3-7908-0173-9

Carsten Schröder
Variable Income Equivalence Scales
2004. ISBN 3-7908-0183-6

Wilhelm J. Meester
Locational Preferences of Entrepreneurs
2004. ISBN 3-7908-0178-X

Russel Cooper/Gary Madden (Eds.)
Frontiers of Broadband, Electronic and Mobile Commerce
2004. ISBN 3-7908-0087-1.5

Sardar M.N. Islam
Empirical Finance
2004. ISBN 3-7908-1551-9

Jan-Egbert Sturm/Timo Wollmershäuser (Eds.)
Ifo Survey Data in Business Cycle and Monetary Policy Analysis
2005. ISBN 3-7908-0174-7

Bernard Michael Gilroy/Thomas Gries/ Willem A. Naudé (Eds.)
Multinational Enterprises, Foreign Direct Investment and Growth in Africa
2005. ISBN 3-7908-0276-X

Günter S. Heiduk/Kar-yiu Wong (Eds.)
WTO and World Trade
2005. ISBN 3-7908-1579-9

Emilio Colombo/Luca Stanca
Financial Market Imperfections and Corporate Decisions
2006. ISBN 3-7908-1581-0

Birgit Mattil
Pension Systems
2006. ISBN 3-7908-1675-1.5

Francesco C. Billari et al. (Eds.)
Agent-Based Computational Modelling
2006. ISBN 3-7908-1640-X

Kerstin Press
A Life Cycle for Clusters?
2006. ISBN 3-7908-1710-4

Russel Cooper et al. (Eds.)
The Economics of Online Markets and ICT Networks
2006. ISBN 3-7908-1706-6

Renato Giannetti/Michelangelo Vasta (Eds.)
Evolution of Italian Enterprises in the 20th Century
2006. ISBN 3-7908-1711-2

Ralph Setzer
The Politics of Exchange Rates in Developing Countries
2006. ISBN 3-7908-1715-5

Dora Borbély
Trade Specialization in the Enlarged European Union
2006. ISBN 3-7908-1704-X

Iris A. Hauswirth
Effective and Efficient Organisations?
2006. ISBN 3-7908-1730-9

Marco Neuhaus
The Impact of FDI on Economic Growth
2006. ISBN 3-7908-1734-1

Nicola Jentzsch
The Economics and Regulation of Financial Privacy
2006. ISBN 3-7908-1737-6

Klaus Winkler
Negotiations with Asymmetrical Distribution of Power
2006. ISBN 7908-1743-0

Sasha Tsenkova · Zorica Nedović-Budić (Editors)

The Urban Mosaic of Post-Socialist Europe

Space, Institutions and Policy

With 77 Figures and 25 Tables

Physica-Verlag
A Springer Company

Series Editors
Werner A. Müller
Martina Bihn

Editors

Prof. Dr. Sasha Tsenkova
University of Calgary
Faculty of Environmental Design
2500 University Drive NW
Calgary, Alberta, Canada, T2N 1N4
tsenkova@ucalgary.ca

Ass. Prof. Dr. Zorica Nedović-Budić
University of Illinois at Urbana-Champaign
Department of Urban and Regional Planning
611 Taft Drive
Temple Bell Hall
Champaign, IL 61820, USA
budic@uiuc.edu

ISBN 10   3-7908-1726-0 Physica-Verlag Heidelberg New York
ISBN 13   978-3-7908-1726-3 Physica-Verlag Heidelberg New York

This work is subject to copyright. All rights are reserved, whether the whole or part of the material is concerned, specifically the rights of translation, reprinting, reuse of illustrations, recitation, broadcasting, reproduction on microfilm or in any other way, and storage in data banks. Duplication of this publication or parts thereof is permitted only under the provisions of the German Copyright Law of September 9, 1965, in its current version, and permission for use must always be obtained from Physica-Verlag. Violations are liable for prosecution under the German Copyright Law.

Physica-Verlag is a part of Springer Science+Business Media

springer.com

© Physica-Verlag Heidelberg 2006

The use of general descriptive names, registered names, trademarks, etc. in this publication does not imply, even in the absence of a specific statement, that such names are exempt from the relevant protective laws and regulations and therefore free for general use.

Typesetting: Camera ready by the author
Cover: Erich Kirchner, Heidelberg
Production: LE-TEX, Jelonek, Schmidt & Vöckler GbR, Leipzig

SPIN 11751601   Printed on acid-free paper – 88/3100 – 5 4 3 2 1 0

Acknowledgements

We are pleased to introduce these diverse contributions on post-socialist cities, which we believe will be of interest to policy makers and researchers in different countries. We hope that these compelling narratives on urban change in cities and comparative perspectives on the economic, social and spatial transformation will be both informative and intellectually stimulating.

The editors gratefully acknowledge the generous support of the Russian, East European, and Eurasian Centre at the University of Illinois at Urbana Champaign for the organization of a conference on post-socialist cities. The forum provided a stimulating environment for the development of the book. We acknowledge the financial contribution of the European Union Centre and Illinois Program for Research in the Humanities as well as the University of Calgary and Social Sciences and Humanities Research Council of Canada. Our special thanks to our reviewers Professor Larry Bourne, University of Toronto, Professor Christine Whitehead, London School of Economics and Kieran Donaghy, University of Illinois at Urbana Champaign, for their constructive input and ideas. Lynda Park, Dorothy Silvers, Stephanie Sanders and Brenda Deville provided valuable assistance with logistics, editing and preparation of the manuscript. We acknowledge the support of Springer-Verlag editors during the past two years—Katharina Wetzel-Vandai and Gabriele Keidel—who provided much-appreciated feedback on earlier drafts of the book. Finally, we wish to thank the authors for their contribution to this volume and wish them successful and productive work in the future.

May 2006

Dr. Sasha Tsenkova
Dr. Zorica Nedović-Budic

Contents

Acknowledgements — v

PART I
The Driving Forces of Post-socialist Change

1 **The urban mosaic of post-socialist Europe**
Zorica Nedović-Budić and Sasha Tsenkova with Peter Marcuse — 3

2 **Beyond transitions: Understanding urban change in post-socialist cities**
Sasha Tsenkova — 21

3 **Institutional and spatial change**
Tuna Taşan-Kok — 51

4 **Wall and mall: A metaphor for metamorphosis**
Gregory Andrusz — 71

5 **The spatial structures of Central and Eastern European cities**
Alain Bertaud — 91

PART II
Urban Processes and Spatial Change

6 **The changing spatial structure of post-socialist Sofia**
Sonia Hirt and Atanass Kovachev — 113

7 **Spatial restructuring in post-socialist Budapest**
Iván Tosics — 131

8 **Poverty and inequality in Greater Tirana: The reality of peri-urban areas**
Luan Deda and Sasha Tsenkova — 151

PART III
Urban Functions: Housing and Retail

9   Urban housing markets in transition: New instruments to assist the poor
    Robert M. Buckley and Sasha Tsenkova — 173

10 Conquering the inner-city: Urban redevelopment and gentrification in Moscow
    Oleg Golubchikov and Anna Badyina — 195

11 The role of property rights reforms in Warsaw's housing market
    Annette M. Kim — 213

12 The retail revolution in post-socialist Central Europe and its lessons
    Yaakov Garb with Tomasz Dybicz — 231

13 Spatial imprints of urban consumption: large-scale retail development in Warsaw
    Karina Kreja — 253

PART IV
Urban Planning and Policy Responses

14 Planning and societal context – The case of Belgrade, Serbia
    Miodrag Vujošević and Zorica Nedović-Budić — 275

15 Entrepreneurial governance and the urban restructuring of a Slovakian town
    Brian Schwegler — 295

16 Urban redevelopment programmes in Kazan, Russia
    Nadir Kinossian — 319

17 Urban policies and the politics of public space in Bucharest
    Augustin Ioan — 337

18 The post-socialist urban world
    Sasha Tsenkova with Zorica Nedović-Budić — 349

List of figures	367
List of tables	370
Contributors	371
Index	375

PART I

THE DRIVING FORCES OF POST-SOCIALIST CHANGE

1 The urban mosaic of post-socialist Europe

Zorica Nedović-Budić and Sasha Tsenkova with Peter Marcuse

Introduction

In 1989, European socialist countries crossed into a new ideological category of post-socialism. Fifteen years have elapsed since the overthrow of state socialism in the Soviet Union and Central and Eastern Europe (CEE). Post-socialist cities have gained new authority and functions since the political and fiscal decentralization shifted power and responsibilities to local governments. Substantial changes have occurred in the nature, role and functioning of government and of other institutions involved in spatial development and urban policy. Most notable is the move from government to governance, reflected in new structures based on interaction among a multitude of local and regional actors.

In the new context of governance, the policies affecting urban areas – land development, neighbourhood and central area revitalization, housing, transportation and provision of infrastructure – have major ramifications for both the economic efficiency and the social well-being of local communities. The urban planning and policy responses of localities have been quite diverse, reacting to specific and often dramatic conditions: political democratization, reintroduction of market principles, the state's fiscal crisis, massive privatization, commercialization, discontinuation of "welfare state" programs, and intensified international financial transactions and investments in urban areas. The new circumstances have prompted not only new institutions but also a "new notion of planning" that strives to regain its legitimacy, become more flexible, and adapt to the new economic and political mechanisms (Kornai 1997; Maier 1994). In those dynamics, an idiosyncratic mix of old, new and innovative practices shapes the transformed reality.

We view cities in post-socialist societies as entities where the societal processes are most visible and significant. The cities are the foci of dominant political, economic, and cultural activities in those societies. Post-socialist cities in the 1990s accounted for as much as four-fifths of their nations' gross domestic product (GDP). At the same time, their concentrations of socially deprived population and rising poverty have been major concerns (Tsenkova 2003). The recent political, social and economic transformations have left a powerful imprint on the urban spatial structure, as have also such institutional transformations as privatization of urban land and housing, and the commercialization of infrastructure and urban space (Nedovic-Budic 2001). Thus urban space may be seen as both manifesting and mediating the societal processes of economic production and consumption, technological innovation, cultural diversity and poverty (Lefebvre 1991). Moreover, the abrupt changes in post-socialist cities also reveal the effects of globalization in an intensified form (Bodnár 2001). Some of the highly dynamic CEE urban spaces have started to integrate into the global economy, becoming new nodes in the global network of cities (Sassen 2000; Hamilton et al. 2005).

A few books published over the past decade have dealt with the theme of post-socialist cities and change in the former Soviet Union and in Central and Eastern Europe. Publications on the transforming societal context and its effect on urban conditions and policy are relatively scarce, as compared to the proliferating literature on such other aspects of the transition as privatization, politics, and the economy. Most of the published accounts focus on a particular country and address only specific issues of urban policy and planning.

Several recent publications from major presses have begun to fill that gap, including Andrusz et al. (1996) on cities and urbanization before and after socialism; Enyedi (1998) on social change and urban restructuring in Central Europe; Bodnár (2001) on urban transformation in Budapest; Strong et al. (1996) on transitions in land and housing in the Czech Republic, Poland, and Bulgaria; Tsenkova and Lowe (2003) on housing change in Eastern Europe; Pickvance (2003) on Hungarian local environmental regulation; and Hamilton et al. (2005) on Central and Eastern European cities in the context of globalization.

The present book offers a timely examination of what has changed in cities and what new trends have emerged there during the 'transition to markets and democracy.' The case studies here are valuable snapshots of post-socialist urban reality – its protagonists, actions, and outcomes. The book emphasizes the diversity of urban experiences, policy and planning in the post-socialist world of cities. By focusing on the societal and institutional dynamics of the cities that emerged from state socialism, the book contributes to the shaping of theoretical frameworks on cities and societal change. The information presented here on the latest urban trends and issues in that area should enrich the international exchange of planning and policy ideas and the development of new policies functionally adapted to local circumstances and needs. For an appreciation of the context in which policy and planning are applied in Central and Eastern European cities is essential if those cities are to adjust successfully to the new conditions and arrive at innovative and sustainable institutional arrangements (Nedovic-Budic 2001).

1.1 Conceptual framework

Through the urban lens, this book examines the processes of economic, societal, institutional and spatial change, with a focus on the implications for urban planning and policy in post-socialist CEE. The discussions of the recent dynamics of post-socialist cities are organized around a framework (Fig. 1.1.) that encompasses: (1) the context, including political, socio-economic, and institutional structures and forces; (2) spatial / urban change manifested in the variety of spatial forms of urban functions (e.g., housing, production, commerce, infrastructure services, and amenities); (3) the evolution of urban planning and policy as a system responding to and guiding urban development dynamics; and (4) key qualifiers characterizing the processes and interactions among the context, urban space, and urban planning. We suggest that the following four qualifiers are the most prominent in defining current, post-socialist, urban phenomena: the processes of transition and transformation; property rights and markets; the diversity of urban landscapes, conditions, and experiences; and the competition engendered by the pressures for new economic positioning and connectivity at both global and regional levels.

The relationship among the contextual influences and structures, planning and policy, and the processes of urban change is complex and not easy to untangle in terms of either its extent or its direction. While this book cannot resolve that complexity, it does explore particular circumstances and manifestations of spatial change and examines the policy instruments affecting that change.

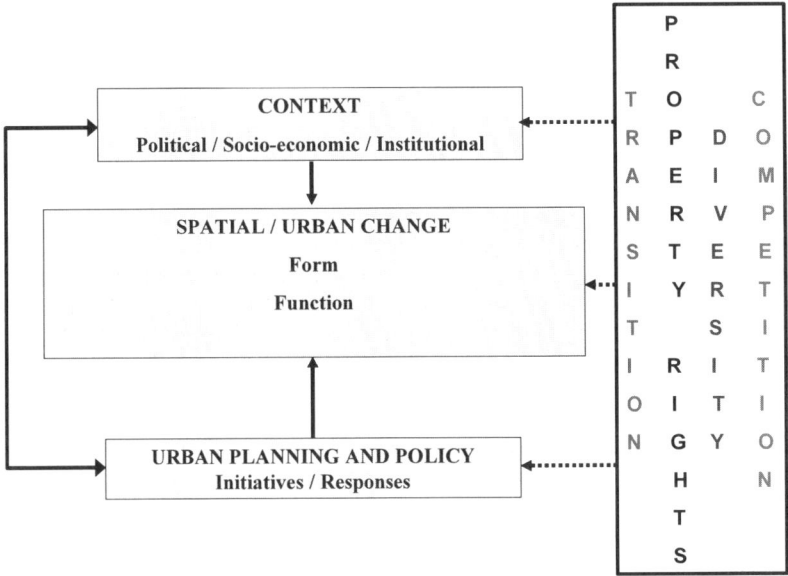

Fig. 1.1. Conceptual framework

1.1.1 The context

The most basic contextual elements affecting how post-socialist cities develop are the political regime and the level of societal development. The shift from a communist political regime and a centrally planned economy to a pluralistic society and a market economy was the defining moment that precipitated all other changes in post-socialist countries and their cities. These shifts are accompanied by institutional changes (Taşan-Kok 2004) and the creation of new formal and informal institutions. Institutions matter: they shape economic behavior and economic performance, and provide an incentive structure for the development of political and social organizations (North 1990; 1994). They also help to stabilize the range of collective economic practices in a particular territory (Amin and Thrift 1994; Taşan-Kok 2004). In post-socialist cities, the institutional change fostered the privatization of property, as well as the relaxation of controls over spatial development so that a multitude of investors could access urban property markets more easily. Webster and Lai (2003) consider the reduction of transaction and cooperation costs to be the main motive driving the creation of new or the restructuring of old institutions.

The institutional change in many post-socialist cities mimics the general trends in their Western European counterparts, including a transition from government to governance.[1] In policy terms, 'governance' should enable the divergent views and preferences of citizens to be expressed and translated into effective policy. It amounts to a transformation of the plurality of societal interests into unitary action taken in compliance of social actors (Kohler-Koch and Eising 1999). The transformation from government to governance is compatible with the new demands put upon urban planning and policy. First, urban planning has to abide with the principles of good governance: legitimacy and voice (participation and consensus building); strategic direction and vision; performance (responsiveness, efficiency and effectiveness); accountability and transparency; and fairness (equity and the rule of law) (Graham et al. 2003; Banachowicz and Danielewicz 2004). Second, the new circumstances press post-socialist cities to compete at the regional and global levels for foreign and domestic investments and the accumulation of capital. The shift from 'managerial government' to a 'participatory governance system' places the municipal government as the key player among many other agents in promoting local advantages, negotiating investments in urban development, and implementing urban plans and policies (Taşan-Kok 2004).

Institutional functional analysis and urban regime theory are two approaches that are useful for exploring the emerging institutional dynamics. Institutional functional analysis looks at the relationships between the actors in property development and at the rules set to organize those relationships. While the 'old institutionalism' replaces neoclassical economic rationality with a social, political and cultural contextual view, the 'new institutionalism' extends formal, neoclassical economics with a broader set of factors (Rutherford 1995).

---

[1] According to Stewart (2003) the difference between government and governance is as follows:
"'Government' can be defined as the activity of the formal governmental system, conducted under clear procedural rules, involving statutory relationships between politicians, professionals and the public, taking place within specific territorial and administrative boundaries. It involves the exercise of powers and duties by formally elected or appointed bodies, and using public resources in a financially accountable way." Governance "is a much looser process often transcending geographical or administrative boundaries, conducted across public, private and voluntary / community sectors through networks and partnerships often ambiguous in their memberships, activities, relationships and accountabilities. It is a process of multi-stakeholder involvement, of multiple interest resolution, of compromise rather than confrontation, of negotiation rather than administrative fiat. Transaction costs are minimized, trust maximized, collaborative advantage extracted" (p. 76).

Regime theory offers agency – or actor – sensitive explanations of the transformation of governance (Ward 1998). A regime is established through inter-organizational relationships and structures linking market forces and political actors. An urban regime reflects the capacity of local leadership (in both public and private sectors) to develop a strategic vision and to coordinate their own and other stakeholders' actions through formal and informal coalitions and alliances (Stewart 2003). While the U.S. growth-machine regime model (Logan and Molotoch 1987; Lauria 1997) does not fully apply in the European context, some of its elements are becoming increasingly relevant, offering a useful point of departure for analyzing institutional transformation in the post-socialist cities.

With the main effect of globalization and neo-liberalism being to weaken local institutions, the localities have been pushed to be innovative in making alliances and negotiating the conditions for their future development. The presence of powerful global actors makes the participatory model of governance even more relevant and the involvement of local players more crucial to decision-making. As Keohane (2001) puts it, "[l]iberal-democratic institutions must meet standards of accountability and participation, and should foster persuasion rather than rely on coercion and interest-based bargaining. Effective institutions must rely on self-interest rather than altruism, yet both liberal-democratic legitimacy and the meaning of self-interest depend on people's values and beliefs" (p. 1). In addition to changes in the institutional nature and the context that are driven by economics and politics, influence on the models of governance and democratic processes arises from advances in information and communication technologies (ICTs) and their intensified use (Falch 2006).

1.1.2 Urban planning and policy

The transformation in the nature, role and functioning of both government and private-sector (i.e., market) institutions closely influences changes in urban planning and policy (Stewart 2003). Planning and policy making involve an interplay between market and government actions, and the balance between the two differentiates state socialism from democratic capitalism (Offe 1997). In fact, "[t]he central issue in the long debate between socialism and capitalism is often characterized as one of planning versus markets" (Hodgson 1998, p. 407). In state socialism, action is based on planning, scientific knowledge, and the party's monopoly on power and decision-making. Emancipatory goals are achieved with institutional means. In capitalist societies, markets prevail, exercising innovativeness, attention to the social consensus, and economic activity independent of collectively reached decisions and approvals. While the claim that overall social objectives are absent from pluralist democratic societies is debatable, capitalism is fundamentally driven by both micro planning at the individual company level and macro-level anarchy. The reverse is true of state-socialist societies; the socialist city is an incarnation of the political will of the state, the party, and the planner.

In the governance model increasingly followed in CEE, planning and policy-making involve of a wide range of organizations (actors) in deciding policy directions (Tasan-Kok 2004). Although central governments continue to be stakeholders intervening directly, usually to facilitate or obstruct large-scale projects, and often with a rigid managerial attitude preserved from the socialist past, such interventions have become scarce. In contrast to the state's interventions, local planning regulations have become more relaxed, ad-hoc, opportunity-led, and corrective mechanisms (McDermott 1998).

The decentralized model, however, is undermined by its lack of implementation power, particularly at the metropolitan level. Planning has become weakened, with informal decision-making dominate. Lacking the capacity to effectively coordinate urban development, planning produces incomplete solutions. Only a few, if any, city governments have achieved dominance over their constituent districts. In most cases, effective city or regional plans are missing (Thomas 1998). All this disarray faces the private sector's intensified role, both in urban development and in providing services and infrastructure (Lorrain and Stoker 1997). Thus it would seem that localities that want a strategic role in urban development may need to adopt a more centralized model. Given that their planning is driven by competition for resources (Stewart 2003) as they try to quickly gain entry into the global and regional economic systems, coordination is crucial for favorable positioning. The pressure for more local effectiveness has led to calls for the re-introduction of strong planning roles at the regional and state levels (Djordjević 2004).

The priority given to reshaping the economic system has left revamping of the spatial planning systems behind. What has been introduced, however, are significant enabling changes in land and property tenure. Even the new planning legislation has still not remodeled the institutional structure for planning to provide a planning framework that would support and regulate market operations effectively. The question then is how to change the planning systems to meet the new circumstances of operating in a market economy. Previously, the state had been the source of most development. Now investments originate mostly outside the state, necessitating the development of regulatory planning (Thomas 1998). The regulatory form implicitly recognizes the rights of autonomous agents to carry out development, but structures the rules and obligations that each agent must observe.

After fifteen years of diminished legitimacy, it is time for urban planning and policy to assume a stronger role in managing urban development. The decreasing role of government and the state challenges the possibilities of planning for sustainable cities and effectively implementing of local collective decisions and policies (Beauregard 2001). Moreover, European policies and guidance must be taken into account in developing local planning strategies, and those, while well intended and useful, present other daunting tasks (Williams 1995). In these dilemmas, Webster and Lai's (2003) view of coordination as the main mechanism for achieving both the public and the private sector's goals promises a more balanced resolution (or at least understanding) of the roles of planning and markets. The authors believe that "state and markets co-evolve, complementing each other and, by trial and error, discovering better ways of distributing responsibilities between private and public sectors and between private and collective action" (p. 2).

1.1.3 Spatial / urban change

Urban change is the central element of the book's framework. Spatial phenomena and processes are explored in the form and functions of urban areas. Drawing on Soja's (2000) concept of *human spatiality*, we see the urban form and functions as the "product of both human agency and environmental or contextual restructuring" (p. 6). Urban spaces are collectively produced and socially constructed by human actions, and people in turn relate to their surroundings and are affected by them in complex ways. Urban form (or built environment) is "expressed in physical structures (buildings, monuments, streets, parks, etc.) and also in the mappable patterning of land use, economic wealth, cultural identity, class differences, and the whole range of individual and collective attributes, relations, thoughts, and practices of urban inhabitants" (Soja 2000, p. 8). Urban functions refer to the various activities and interactions taking place in urban spaces, including housing, production (industry), consumption (commerce), and the provision of infrastructural services and amenities. Infrastructure services include roads for private and public transport as well as other modes of transportation; electric, water, sewer, and waste collection utilities; health; and education. Amenities include spaces and facilities for recreation (e.g., parks) and entertainment (e.g., cultural centers, museums, concert halls). All those activities are provided through either the public or the private realm, but increasingly through public-private partnerships. The book focuses on housing and retail as two examples of urban functions that, probably more than others, have undergone a dramatic transformation in post-socialist cities.

The urban form evolves through individual development actions at a variety of scales with guidance and incentives from formal planning documents and policies. During socialism, urban development was substantially centralized and had certain specific features (Andrusz et al. 1996), but whether the state-socialist cities fall into a category distinct from those developed in capitalist societies is widely debated. Bodnár (2001) identifies three treatments of the differences: exaggeration of the distinctiveness of socialism; focus on the quantitative differences in a universal, unilinear pattern of development; and explaining away socialist urban phenomena as simply continuations of patterns that had always been qualitatively different from those of the West.

Two of the most sharply opposed streams of the debate over socialist versus capitalist cities are the ecological and the historical schools (Bodnár 2001; Hirt 2006; Szelenyi 1996). The ecological school argues that urban form is the outcome of universal processes of urbanization and industrialization that cross the capitalist-socialist boundary, and that socialist cities represent a mildly distorted urban model (Enyedi 1996). Advocates of the historical approach believe that in minimizing private ownership of land, housing, and the means of production, socialism produced a truly unique urban model (Szelenyi 1996).

There is general agreement on certain points: socialist cities are more compact; they have large civic buildings, plazas, and parks; and their suburban development takes the form of housing estates. The state control over land markets and the provision of housing together with the commitment to an egalitarian society resulted in cities relatively less segregated by social status (Haussermann 1996; Musil 2005; Sykora 1999; Szelenyi 1996; Wezlawowicz 1998). Civic and retail uses were consolidated in a few selected locations: the city centre, the main boulevards, or the new town centres within the housing estates. The amount of space devoted to production was higher than in the capitalist cities, and retail and service land uses were underrepresented (Bertaud 2000; Sykora 1998).

The questions now concern the directions and ways in which the formerly socialist cities are changing socially, economically, and structurally. The consensus is that the post-socialist cities are converging to their capitalist counterparts and resuming the historical trajectories already established (or at least started) when centralized control and planning intervened. Market forces are likely to produce a variety of post-metropolis forms as suggested by Soja (2000): post-fordist industrial metropolis, global cities, dispersed and clustered urban landscapes – and also places of deep inequality and poverty. Discussions of the trends in the European metropolitan form increasingly mention the "diffused city" as well as the traditionally familiar "compact city" (Beauregard 2001). Concern about public spaces as quintessentially urban features (Lofland 1998) and as sites of collective consumption is intrinsic to any such discussions as public places become more privatised and segregated.

1.2 Qualifiers

1.2.1 Transition/transformation

It has been argued that the transition of societies and cities from socialist to post-socialist is not a unilinear process with respect to its contents, sequence or timescale (Harloe 1996). The transition process depends on—among other things—systems of local governance, legal and institutional frameworks, the manner in which privatized public assets are distributed and policy choices (Andusz et al. 1996). The idea of 'transition' also implies an identifiable starting point—perhaps a ubiquitous 'socialist city' as claimed by French and Hamilton (1979)—and an end point—a 'capitalist city' with some sort of evolution from one to the other. A discourse based on the idea of 'transition' might therefore be challenged by evidence that the concepts 'revolutionary change' and 'path dependency' increasingly map out diverging scenarios for the cities in the new system (Pickles and Smith 1998).

The theory of transition is rooted in the democratization theory that views transition as primarily a political process.[2] Transition specifically of urban phenomena

---

[2] The main features of transition theory are: 1) a comparative approach; 2) an emphasis on democratization (civil society, political society, rule of law and constitutionalism, state apparatus, economic society with an institutionalized market); 3) categorization of the pre-

and processes, too, is viewed as essentially political and economic, and perhaps not distinguishable from the transition in general (Holmes 1997; Wu 2003). If the cities are viewed as the means of accumulation in the material, functional and symbolic senses, then the bottom line of transition is the 'internal shift of the logic of production.' Moreover, the focus on transition tends to emphasize discontinuities rather than continuities, whereas, the latter emphasis views state socialism as part of European modernity, and the current transformation as part of the global restructuring of late modernity (Bodnár 2001). Marcuse and von Kempen (2000) also challenge the notion of a distinctive or new "spatial order" resulting from the transitional periods and processes.

An alternative transformation framework includes new economic order, new legal and constitutional order, and new rules of social integration (Offe 1997). During the transformation periods, institutional and organizational structures are under reconstruction, property markets are affected, and urban development may be disturbed (Taşan-Kok 2004). Path-dependency is evident primarily from the nature of the previous political regimes and the continuity of social relations, cultural practices and the built environment (Beauregard and Haila 1997; Wu 2003). From his examination of the recent transformations in twenty-one former communist European countries, Dostál (1998) concludes "that a successful early post-communist transformation means (1) a quick resumption of macroeconomic balance and economic growth resting on (2) genuine democratization and economic liberalization, and (3) higher levels of inherited modernization" (p. 281). Across CEE countries and cities, the process of transformation is at various stages, areas of action and levels of success and, as inherently constant, it is bound to continue through a series of incremental changes in diverse contents and scales.

1.2.2 Property rights and markets

Privatization of land and housing is probably the most radical aspect of the transition from state socialist systems to democratic and market systems. Property rights and markets lie at the heart of that process (Marcuse 1996). According to Webster and Lai (2003), "[i]nstitutions that protect private property are essential for market activity and economic growth" (p. 3). The authors differentiate between *economic rights* (the ability to derive direct or indirect income or welfare from a resource or attribute of a resource) and *legal rights*; and between formal and informal rights. Rights are exchanged by formal (legal) or informal contracts. The attributes or properties with unassigned rights are in the *public domain*, and as shared public

---

transition situation as authoritarian, totalitarian, post-totalitarian, sultanism; 4) the determining influence of the past on the path of transition (path dependency). The theory also includes a 'moment of discontinuity' defined as a period where the structure and function of a country or city does not correspond to the external environment with which it has to interact. Transition is the period, stage, process, or policy that encompasses this moment and leads from one period or situation to the next (Stark 1992; Thomas 1998).

goods are subject to competition for consumption. Property rights can be reallocated between the public and private sectors, and such reallocation has been happening on a massive scale in post-socialist CEE countries since the end of the communist political regime.

The bundle of rights associated with a property comprises the actual ownership of the property—usually divided between individuals and the government—and rights to use, build (or control building), sell, transfer or inherit it (Marcuse 1994). During the socialist period, the balance of ownership was tilted toward the state, particularly in urban areas, though substantial variation existed among the socialist countries.[3] By the mid-1990s, privatization of property and the re-institution of private property rights had occurred in most countries as one of the first steps in the transition to capitalism and markets. Both the earlier socialist move to state ownership of property and its reversal were accomplished through legal changes made up of the following components (Marcuse 1996):

- Pre-socialist legal forms
- Imposition of state socialism
- Reforms within state socialism
- Constitutional provisions in the transition
- Generalized legislation for destatification, including authorization for sales to private entities, decentralization of state ownership rights, and provisions for management of property continuing in state ownership
- Restitution to former owners
- Implementation of legislation, including technical facilitation of market transfers (transactions), differentiation according to types of property, differentiation according to types of owner / ownership entity; judicial procedures for enforcement of ownership rights
- Regulatory land-use and planning controls
- Comprehensive housing policy formulation (p. 169).

Though some privatization elements had been present before the 1990s, in most of the post-socialist CEE countries major legislative changes were established soon after the communists lost political power, through constitutional or special legal provisions. The legislation has produced a variety of results both expected and unexpected, including disincentives to assume ownership due to the financial burdens associated with it and has also substantially reduced provision of social housing. Privatisation of housing might have been the wrong answer to the housing problems of transitional economies. It makes housing more expensive, less secure, more segregated, and less socially equitable. Marcuse (2004) argues that its ideological underpinning (for the most part modelled after the western or Anglo-

---

[3] For example, in 1990 in Poland the state and cooperative ownership of housing stock amounted to 60%, with the remaining 40% individually owned; in the Russian Federation inheriting the pattern of the former USSR, however, individual ownership was only 26%, and the state owned 67% of the housing stock (Struyk 1996).

Saxon approach to property rights) is only one of many possible versions of "property rights," one that is often inadequate and politically biased.

The preoccupation with privatisation in post-socialist countries has introduced private ownership and profit motivation into the production of goods and services. Factories, shops, banks and retail services are privatized with the aim of increasing production, rationalizing distribution, and accelerating economic growth. However, the logic of privatization in the realm of production, whatever its merits, is quite different from that logic in the sphere of consumption. In the latter, the criterion of profit encounters criteria of use: it is recognized that for certain things, consumption is better done collectively than individually (parks, transportation, urbanity, for example). Moreover, in some matters issues of fairness, justice, and social responsibility may be more relevant than issues of efficiency or growth (for example, in dealing with children, the handicapped, and the homeless). The glib assumption that privatization is uniformly appropriate and that property rights apply alike to all possible objects of private ownership, conceals major cleavages of substance. That is particularly so in the realms of housing and urban amenities.

1.2.3 Diversity

Cities in Central and Eastern Europe have reacted differently to the transition from socialism to market-based economies and to the broad processes of globalization (see Tsenkova in this volume). The diversity, which arises from the interactions among local and global organizations, institutions, and circumstances, has concrete spatial consequences. The local reactions define the types of transformation in urban areas.[4] However, distinguishing among the complex realities of post-socialist countries and cities is difficult, since similar processes can lead to diverse outcomes. The same phenomena may be produced by different causes in different instances (Castells 1979; Pickvance 2001). Along those lines, Bodnár (2001) questions even the uniqueness of state socialism. For example, he argues that the oft-cited distinguishing characteristics of socialist versus capitalist cities: restricted private ownership of land, state role in planning, financing, construction and distribution of housing (French and Hamilton 1979, Szelenyi 1993) may be affected by factors other than the political system and ideology alone.

To demonstrate the diversity of post-socialist experiences, Offe (1997) attempts a typology of the post-communist states by classifying six countries into three groups and comparing them across seventeen criteria: duration of transition or breakdown, mode of transition, geo-strategic location, industrial output per capita before 1989, level of "nationalist" integration, level of repressiveness, elite continuity before/after 1989; institutional change of the economic system, prospects for integration into the European Union, nature of ethnic minority conflict, record of

---

[4] See Offe (1997) for a typology of transitional processes (p. 139) with three types represented by i) Czechoslovakia and the German Democratic Republic; ii) Hungary and Poland; and iii) Bulgaria and Romania.

economic reforms, record of internal opposition, constitutional development after 1989, size of private sector, religious structure, international crises, and prevailing mode of societal integration. Offe's three categories of countries represent a commendable effort to find commonalities between some states, but the effort probably required overlooking many of the differences and neglecting all local contextual characteristics and uniqueness.

Since 1989, the cities of Central and Eastern Europe have seemingly been subjected to the unifying and homogenizing forces of European integration and globalization. Those forces are not, however, unidirectional; they are more likely to create tensions and localized reactions than a unified response (Beauregard 2001). In fact, many cities strive to distinguish themselves from others, and their citizens refuse to relinquish their history and identity. Rather, cities have quickly realized that their uniqueness is what gives them an advantage in the global competition. Convergence, though fostered by mass communication and culture and the extensive flows of goods, capital and people, as well as by grand regional (pan-European) policies such as the European Spatial Development Perspective (Faludi 2002), remains more of an intellectual notion than a concrete reality. The built environment, in particular, changes only incrementally, since its design is geared toward local purposes and subsumed to local culture and politics. Beauregard (2001) finds that the "enduring differentiation indicates that convergence might not be as strong a force, at least as regards the intellectual production and the urban development that it represents, as the forces of globalization and the European regionalization imply" (p. 258). Hence, we believe that the reality of post-socialist CEE cities resembles more a mosaic than a homogeneous pattern.

1.2.4 Competition

Societal transformation and urban change are also influenced by external factors, including regional, international and sometimes global players and processes (Thomas 1998). Bodnár (2001) argues that the recent social and economic transformation of Central and Eastern Europe is part of an overall global restructuring. Like other major world centers, post-socialist cities represent nodes of global society and compete for places in the global and regional networks. The requirements and consequences of economic globalization shape cities' ability to compete by applying new strategies of urban governance, and their ability to capture international capital by financial deregulation (Tasan-Kok 2004).

It is this relatively new competitiveness that links urban form to globalization and neo-liberal capitalist ideology (Beauregard 2001). During socialism, a certain level of resources was assured through systematic state allocation; now, under the new circumstances, cities have to compete for resources and attract capital. The opening to, and the dependency on, both internal and external investments and financial markets require cities to adapt their planning and policies appropriately. Taşan-Kok (2004) notes the many innovative strategies being pursued: building an international image, urban entrepreneurialism, partnerships, and planning responsive to market forces. Those strategies are not unfamiliar to the cities' Western counterparts, who also rely on cultural policies, tourism and financial services and technology to attract investments and to promote their images (Beauregard 2001; Andersson 2001). Interestingly, in the process, the public spaces that are essential to local urban experience become an economic development tool as well, and acquire the characteristics of regional, if not global, commodity.

The rising wave of competition and competitiveness, along with other qualifiers—*transformation, property rights and markets, and diversity*—considerably affect the process of spatial / urban change. In turn, these spatial processes are embedded in the societal historical, political, economic and cultural context and guided with urban planning and policy. The outcome is a rich mosaic of urban landscapes and experiences, bustling with innovative practices and creative solutions aiming to achieve higher standards of urban development, urban sustainability, and improve the quality of life for their inhabitants.

1.3 Scope and contents of the book

The 'urban mosaic' metaphor expresses the complexity, diversity and uniqueness of the processes and spatial outcomes in post-socialist cities that this book explores. Its chapters examine the urban systems and the policy and planning frameworks that have resulted from the socio-economic, political, and institutional transformations after the fall of state socialism. The authors rely on conceptual expositions, narratives and quantitative indicators to illustrate the emerging urban phenomena with sensitivity to their historical themes and cultural issues, as well as noting the more immediate socialist legacy. As an edited volume, the book's individual contributions are organized in four parts around the following themes:

- The context and the driving forces of post-socialist change
- Urban processes and spatial change
- Urban functions: housing and retail
- Urban planning and policy responses.

Part I combines theoretical and methodological discussions with empirical insights to review the urban context and dynamics across post-socialist CEE countries. The section's three chapters focus on the issues of urbanization and urban growth, decentralization of political power and institutional change, economic restructuring, commercialization of the private and public social spheres, as well as on the relationships between spatial structures, and urban policy interventions. Tsenkova' s chapter presents comparative data on urbanization, unemployment, poverty, and the provision of urban services in 26 countries in Central and Eastern Europe and the Commonwealth of Independent States. The chapter's conclusion summarizes the major processes and drivers of change, and compares the outcomes in socialist and post-socialist cities. Taşan-Kok's chapter examines the change in planning institutions. Within the institutional transformation, urban planning is viewed as currently opportunity-led and too flexible to establish and enforce a functional urban regulatory framework. Andrusz's chapter turns to a powerful "wall and mall" metaphor to explore the multifaceted transformations in

CEE cities, illustrating them with examples from Moscow and St. Petersburg. The author emphasizes the emerging polarization, social stratification, marginalization, homelessness and ethnic conflicts.

Part II of the book considers the changes in urban space. Bertaud' s informative chapter introduces a system of indicators—population density, density gradients, land prices and proportion of industrial land—to compare and contrast European cities, both with each other and with cities from other continents. The main argument is that, despite the imprint of socialist political regimes and centralized planning, the urban structures of post-socialist cities resemble the traditional European model, and that context defies the influences of political ideology. Bertaud's comparative chapter is followed by case studies of three post-socialist capital cities: Sofia (Bulgaria) by Hirt and Kovachev; Budapest (Hungary) by Tosics; and Tirana (Albania) by Deda and Tsenkova. Hirt and Kovachev examine residential and commercial suburbanization and the privatization of green spaces. Tosics distinguishes three periods of post-communist urban development: vacuum, adaptation, and adjustment periods, and identifies structural changes and territorial conflicts across various zones of Budapest. Deda and Tsenkova focus on the problem of poverty in the peri-urban areas of Tirana, relating it to the systemic economic and social transformation. The chapters in this section highlight urban planning and policy solutions to address the socialist legacies and the negative consequences of the post-socialist transitions in different cities.

Part III of the book consists of five chapters addressing two highly dynamic urban functional areas—housing and retail. The three housing chapters explore the topics of housing markets and policy reforms, private housing development and gentrification. Buckley and Tsenkova provide a comprehensive comparative overview of housing reforms in a number of urban markets. Golubchikov and Badyina's chapter offers insights into the redevelopment of a prestigious neighbourhood in Moscow. Kim undertakes an institutional and functional analysis of the housing market in Warsaw. Garb and Dybicz, and Kreja turn attention to retail developments as the manifestations of new consumerism. In particular, Garb and Dybicz explore the effects of retail deconcentration (hypermarkets) on travel behaviour; Kreja looks at large-scale retail developments in Warsaw and their impact on city structure.

Part IV focuses on planning and policy responses to both old and new spatial problems in several cities. The case studies include Belgrade (Serbia and Montenegro), Komarno (Slovakia) and Bucharest (Romania). Vujošević and Nedović-Budić provide a critical overview of the legislative context for urban planning and its impact (process and contents) on the new master plan for Belgrade. Schwegler illustrates the struggle of local leadership in Komarno to market a new city image infusing competitiveness and economic success; Kinossian offers an institutional analysis of two programs in Kazan (Tatarstan Republic) in the Russian Federation: slum clearance and preservation of the historic center. Continuing the urban politics theme, Ioan tells the story of manoeuvring and a difficult post-socialist adjustment in the redevelopment of the city center in Bucharest.

Finally, drawing on the findings and the discussions in the comparative and case study sections, the concluding chapter identifies theoretical contributions and research needs, and recommends a policy/planning agenda that will improve understanding of the transition in post-socialist cities.

The authors gathered here have provided enduring and sound illustrations of the post-socialist urban experience as well as insightful contemplation of the future of these cities. Using a comparative approach informed by the 'urban mosaic' metaphor, a broad but rigorous conceptual framework, and fresh empirical evidence, we have aimed to contribute to discussions about the nature of post-socialism, its spatial manifestations and relevant urban policy issues. The book can be read with any of several purposes in mind—for the value of the individual case studies, for the comparative analysis of Central and Eastern European cities, for discussions on urban politics and planning, and for analyses of the processes of socio-economic and institutional change in cities.

References

Amin A, Thrift N (1994) Globalization, institutions, and regional development in Europe. Oxford University Press, Oxford

Andersson H (2001) New spaces of urban transformation: Conflicting 'growth areas' in the development of Finnish cities. In: Andersson H, Jorgensen G, Joye D, Ostendorf W (eds) Change and stability in urban Europe. Ashgate, Aldershot, pp 45-65

Andrusz G, Harloe M, Szelenyi I (eds) (1996) Cities after socialism - Urban and regional change and conflict in post-socialist societies. Blackwell Publishers, Oxford

Banachowicz B, Danielewic J (2004) Urban governance – The new concept of urban management: The case of Lodz, Poland. In: Nedović-Budić Z, Tsenkova S (eds) Winds of Societal Change: Remaking Post-communist Cities, conference proceedings. University of Illinois at Urbana-Champaign, Russian, East European and Eurasian Center, Champaign, Illinois, pp 155-169

Beauregard RA (2001) Epilogue: Globalization and the city. In: Andersson H, Jorgensen G, Joye D, Ostendorf W (eds) Change and stability in urban Europe. Ashgate, Aldershot, pp 251-262

Beauregard R, Haila A (1997) The unavoidable incompleteness of the city. American Behavioral Scientist 41: 327-341

Bertaud A (2000) The Costs of utopia: Brasilia, Johannesburg and Moscow. Paper presented to the European Network for Housing Research. Gävle, Sweden, June 2000

Bodnár J (2001) Fin de Millénaire Budapest – Metamorphoses of urban life. University of Minnesota Press, Minneapolis

Castells M (1979) The urban question. MIT Press, Cambridge, Massachusetts

Djordjević D (2004) "Decentralized Serbia" and its spatial development: Questions of tools and concepts (in Serbian). In: Milašin N, Spasić N, Vujošević M, Pucar M (eds) Održivi prostorni, urbani i ruralni razvoj Srbije [Sustainable spatial, urban and rural development of Serbia], Symposium Proceedings, pp. 3-6. Institut za arhitekturu i urbanizam Srbije - IAUS (Institute of Architecture and Urban Planning of Serbia), Belgrade

Dostál P (1998) Democratization, economic liberalization, and transformational slump: a cross-sectional analysis of twenty-one post communist countries. Environment and Planning C: Government and Policy 16:281-306

Enyedi G (1996) Urbanization under socialism. In: Andrusz G, Harloe M, Szelenyi I (eds) Cities under socialism - Urban and regional change and conflict in post-socialist societies. Blackwell, Oxford, pp 100-118

Enyedi G (eds) (1998) Social change and urban restructuring in Central Europe. Akadémiai Kiadó, Budapest

Falch M (2006) ICT and the future conditions for democratic governance. Telematics and Informatics 23:134-156

Faludi A (ed) (2002) European spatial planning. Lincoln Institute of Land Policy, Cambridge, Massachusetts

French RA, Hamilton IFE (1979) The socialist city: Spatial structure and urban policy. John Wiley & Sons, New York

Graham J, Amos B, Plumptre T (2003) Principles for good governance in the 21st Century. Policy Brief 15, Institute on Governance, Ottawa

Hamilton FEI, Dimitrovska Andrews K, Pichler-Milanović N (eds) (2005) Transformation of cities in Central and Eastern Europe: Toward globalization. United Nations University Press, Tokyo

Harloe M (1996) Cities in the transition. In: Andrusz G, Harloe M, Szelenyi I (eds) Cities after socialism -- Urban and regional change and conflict in post-socialist societies. Blackwell Publishers, Oxford, pp 1-29

Haussermann H (1996) From the socialist to the capitalist city: experiences from Germany. In: Andrusz G, Harloe M, Szelenyi I (eds) Cities after socialism -- Urban and regional change and conflict in post-socialist societies. Blackwell, Cambridge, MA and Oxford, UK, pp 214-231

Hirt S (forthcoming 2006) From the socialist to the post-socialist city: Transformations of built forms in Sofia, Bulgaria. Urban Studies 43

Hodgson GM (1998) Socialism against markets? A critique of two recent proposals. Economy and Society 27:407-433

Holmes L (1997) Post-communism: An introduction. Polity Press, Cambridge

Keohane RO (2001) Governance in a partially globalized world. American Political Science Review 95:1-13

Kohler-Koch B, Eising R (1999) The transformation of governance in the EU. Routledge, London

Kornai J (1997) Reforming the welfare state in postsocialist societies (editorial). World Development 25:1183-118

Lauria M (ed) (1997) Reconstructing urban regime theory: Regulating urban politics in a global economy. Sage Publication, Thousand Oaks, CA

Lefebvre H (1991) [1974] The production of space. (Translated by Donald Nicholson-Smith) Blackwell, Oxford

Lofland L (1998) The public realm: Exploring the city's quintessential social territory. Aldine de Gruyter, New York

Logan JR, Molotch HL (1987) Urban fortunes: The political economy of space. University of California Press, Berkeley, CA

Lorrain D, Stoker G (eds) (1997) The privatization of urban services in Europe. Pinter, Herndon, Virginia

Maier K (1994) Planning and education in planning in the Czech Republic. Journal of Planning Education and Research 13: 263-269

Marcuse P (2004) The fallacies of "property rights" approaches to housing and tenure. In: Nedović-Budić Z, Tsenkova S (eds) Winds of societal change: Remaking post-communist cities, conference proceedings. University of Illinois at Urbana-Champaign, Russian, East European and Eurasian Center, Champaign, IL, pp 103-108

Marcuse P, van Kempen R (2000) Globalizing cities: A new spatial order? Blackwell, Oxford

Marcuse P (1996) Privatization and its discontents: Property rights in land and housing in the transition in Eastern Europe. In: Andrusz G, Harloe M, Szelenyi I (eds) Cities after socialism – Urban and regional change and conflict in post-socialist societies. Blackwell, Oxford, pp 119-191

Marcuse P (1994) Privatization, tenure, and property rights: towards clarity in concepts. In: Danermark B, Elander I (eds) Social rented housing in Europe: policy, tenure and design. Delft University Press, Delft, pp 21-36

McDermott P (1998) Positioning planning in a market economy. Environment and Planning A 30: 631-646

Medvedkov O (1990) Soviet urbanisation. Routledge, New York

Musil J (2005) City development in Central and Eastern Europe before 1990: Historical context and socialist legacies. In: Hamilton FEI, Dimitrovska Andrews K, Pichler-Milanović N (eds) (2005) Transformation of cities in Central and Eastern Europe: Toward globalization. United Nations University Press, Tokyo, pp 22-43

Nedović-Budić Z (2001) Adjustment of planning practice to the new Eastern and Central European context. Journal of the American Planning Association 67:38-52

North D (1990) Institutions, institutional change and economic performance. Cambridge University Press, Cambridge.

Offe C (1997) Varieties of transition – The East European and East German experience. The MIT Press, Cambridge, Massachusetts

Pickles J, Smith A (eds) (1998) Theorising transition: The political economy of post-communist transformations. Routledge, London

Pickvance CG (2003) Local environmental regulation in post-socialism: A Hungarian case study. Ashgate Publishing Limited, Aldershot, UK

Pickvance CG (2001) Four varieties of comparative analysis. Journal of Housing and the Built Environment 16:7-28

Rutherford M (1995) The old and the new institutionalism: Can bridges be built? Journal of Economic Issues 29: 443-451

Sassen S (2000) Cities in the world economy, 2nd Edition. Pine Forge Press, Thousand Oaks, CA

Soja EW (2000) Postmetropolis. Blackwell, Oxford

Stark D (1992) The great transformation? Social change in Eastern Europe. Contemporary Sociology 21:299-304

Stewart M (2003) Towards collaborative capacity. In: Boddy M (ed) Urban transformation and urban governance – Shaping the competitive city of the future. The Policy Press, Bristol, UK, pp 76-89

Strong A, Reiner L, Szyrmer J (1996) Transitions in land and housing: Bulgaria, the Czech Republic and Poland. St. Martin's Press, New York

Struyk RJ (1996) Housing privatization in the former Soviet Bloc to 1995. In: Andrusz G, Harloe M, Szelenyi I (eds) Cities after socialism – Urban and regional change and conflict in post-socialist socieities. Blackwell Publishers, Oxford, pp 192-213

Sýkora L (1998) Commercial property development in Budapest, Prague and Warsaw. In: Enyedi G (ed) Social change and urban restructuring in Central Europe. Academia Kiado, Budapest, pp 109-136

Sýkora L (1999) Transition states of East Central Europe. In: Balchin P, Sýkora L, Bull G (eds) Regional policy and planning in Europe. Routledge, London, pp 161-192

Szelenyi I (1993) East European socialist cities: How different are they? In: Guldin G, Southall A (eds) Urban anthropology in China. E.J. Brill, Leiden, The Netherlands, pp 41-64

Szelenyi I (1996) Cities under socialism—and after. In: Andrusz G, Harloe M, Szelenyi I (eds) Cities after socialism -- urban and regional change and conflict in post-socialist societies. Blackwell, Cambridge, MA and Oxford, UK, pp 286-317

Taşan-Kok T (2004) Budapest, Istanbul, and Warsaw – Institutional and spatial change. Eburon, Delft, The Netherlands

Thomas M (1998) Thinking about planning in the transitional countries of Central and Eastern Europe. International planning studies 3:321-333

Tsenkova S (2003) Post-socialist cities in a globalizing world. PLANUM, pp 1-20, http://www.planum.net/topics/east-tsenkova.html

Tsenkova S, Lowe S (eds) (2003) Housing change in Central and Eastern Europe. Ashgate Publishing Limited, Aldershot, UK

Ward, SV (1998) Place marketing: A historical comparison of Britain and North America. In: Hubbard P, Hall T (eds) The entrepreneurial city: Geographies of politics, regime, and representation. John Wiley & Sons, New York, pp 31-54

Webster C, Lai LWC (2003) Property rights, planning and markets – Managing spontaneous cities. Edward Elgar, Cheltenham, UK

Węzławowicz G (1998) Social polarization in postsocialist cities: Budapest, Prague and Warsaw. In: Enyedi G (ed.) Social change and urban restructuring in Central Europe. Academia Kiado, Budapest, pp 55-66

Williams RH (1995) European spatial strategies and local development in central Europe. European Spatial Research and Policy 2:49-61

Wu F (2003) Transitional cities (Commentary). Environment and Planning A 35:1331-1338

2 Beyond transitions: Understanding urban change in post-socialist cities

Sasha Tsenkova

Introduction

In the last fifteen years, transition economies in Central and Eastern Europe (CEE) and the Commonwealth of Independent States (CIS) have experienced highly dramatic change in political, economic and social terms. Studies have pointed out the sharp divide between countries in CEE and CIS (UNECE 2003; World Bank 2002). In the west of the region, most countries have become functioning market economies, have come close to or exceeded the level of economic output of the early 1990s, and have moved to decentralized political and administrative power. Some have joined the European Union. In the eastern part of the region, changes on both the economic and the political front have been more moderate, and progress uneven (EBRD 2004). In all countries of the region, inequality and poverty are much greater than during socialism, and region-wide the number of the poor had risen to 100 million by 2001. The pursuit of private-sector-driven growth as well as macroeconomic and social reforms has delivered mixed results with respect to economic performance, provision of basic services, and the effectiveness of social safety nets, particularly in the urban areas where most of the region's people work and live.

These important manifestations embedded in the overall process of economic, social and political change influence profoundly the spatial adaptation and repositioning of post-socialist cities. The transition from a centrally planned to a market-based economy offered significant opportunities to increase the economic prosperity and social well-being of urban residents through more democratic governance. Fifteen years later, the cities with transition economies have remained centres of economic growth, service expansion, technological innovation and cultural diversity. However, they have also experienced rapid social polarization, poverty and environmental degradation.

This research focuses on the process of urban change in post-socialist cities in the countries of Central and Eastern Europe and the Commonwealth of Independent States. It draws much-needed attention to an important set of urban policy issues with wide implications for the success of the transition process in the region. The study has the following objectives:

- To explore the links between the transition to democracy, markets and decentralized governance, and related processes of change in post-socialist cities; and

- To highlight the most salient characteristics of these multilayered transformations, noting differences and similarities.

The research uses data from government reports, national and regional assessments and key-person interviews with local government officials in several capital cities. At the city level, the geographic scope of the study is limited to the capital cities in the 14 countries in the region included in the UN-HABITAT survey in 2001.[1] The choice of countries is driven by the premise that the region is very diverse and it is important to reflect that. The transition process has different starting points for the individual countries, but is also affected by the policy choices of governments at the national level. While the socialist legacy is no doubt an important determinant of 'path dependency' in the institutional behaviour and spatial organization of post-socialist cities, it is argued that notions of convergence are not really applicable to the analysis of urban issues in the context of transition (Tsenkova 2003). The general hypothesis is that within the context of regional diversity, differences in national-level performance as well as in the way cities are planned, managed and developed are expected to map increasingly divergent scenarios. That hypothesis is explored here using comparable data at the national and city levels.

The paper has four parts. The first part presents the conceptual framework for the comparative analysis. Second, differences in capital cities, levels of urbanization and concentration across transition economies are examined to highlight the current importance of post-socialist cities and their diverging patterns of urbanization. Third, major outcomes at the national level of the transitions—to democracy, markets and decentralized governance—are examined with reference to their effects on the capital cities. The analysis focuses on the most salient characteristics of the transitions at the city level and their manifestations in the economic, social and governance domains. Fourth, the chapter highlights some of the spatial manifestations of change in post-socialist cities, with particular reference to spaces for production and consumption. The concluding comments first recognize the need for more effective policy solutions to urban challenges and then map a trajectory for the urban change seen in the region.

2.1 A conceptual framework for analysis of urban change

While it may be too early to develop a convincing theoretical account of the transition process in post-socialist cities, insights from different countries and cities across the region may nonetheless test the capacity of theoretical concepts to generate explanations of concrete situations, and may provide empirical material for further theoretical development.

---

[1] Data on selected urban indicators were collected by local experts in 18 cities in the region under the overall supervision of the Metropolitan Research Institute in Budapest.

It is important to position the post-socialist urban experience in the framework of overall institutional transformation on the one hand, and in the context of rapid economic and political system change on the other. This undeniable complexity creates unique challenges for planning and urban policy making. The conceptual framework draws on approaches in the urban literature that explore recent trends in national urban systems and their implications for policy and planning. Free of ideological bias these studies recognize new sources of difference in highly urbanized societies and use a country's urban system as the analytical construct through which to measure and interpret such trends. It is argued that the urban system serves as the primary channel linking the national economy to the system of global cities (Beaverstock et al. 2000; Yates and Cheng 2002), embodying all the forces at work: economic, social, and political (Bourne and Simmons 2003; Greyer 2002). Cities are a component of the large urban system linking local realities to national and indeed global trends and processes of change. Such research approaches view development through the urban lens, recognizing that cities are not simply products of the market and/or patterns of consumption, but are also public sector constructs (Bourne and Simmons 2003; Marcuse and van Kempen 2000).

The present study's conceptual framework uses the urban system as the analytical construct that mirrors some of the unique development and transformation challenges in post-socialist cities. In particular, it explicitly links the changes in the external environment (national and global), which are much more dramatic and revolutionary, to changes in the internal environment (the urban system and the city itself), by emphasizing the nature of the ongoing transformation, reciprocity and diversity. The transformations are associated with three aspects of the transitions process that are particularly important for post-socialist cities (see Fig. 2.1.). Two of these transitions — to democracy (systemic political change) and to markets (systemic economic change)—and their impact on the diverse cluster of post-socialist countries have attracted considerable attention (Buckley and Mini 2000; van Kempen et al. 2005; World Bank 2000b; 2003). However, most of such evaluations so far have centred on national (country-level) performance and lacked any explicit focus on how cities have been affected. Indeed, very few studies (Adair et al. 1999; Buckley and Tsenkova 2001; Hamilton et al. 2005) have acknowledged the diversity in the outcomes of this dual 'transition' across post-socialist cities.

In addition to systemic political and economic change, another, less known aspect of the transition—'the quiet revolution' of decentralization and the devolution of power and responsibility to local governments—significantly affects the performance of post-socialist cities. New intergovernmental institutions and new fiscal relations devolve many responsibilities from the central to the local level without ensuring adequate fiscal capacity there to deliver urban services and cope with the problems of post-socialist cities (Tsenkova 2005a; van Kempen et al. 2005). These transitions to democracy, to markets and to a decentralized system of governance are major drivers of urban change. Similarly, the local responses to these drivers of change as well as global pressures (competition for markets, trade, etc.) and policy reforms at the national level (privatization of industry, deregulation of real estate markets, trade, social policy reforms, etc.) set the framework for specific changes in the economic, social, institutional and spatial structure of the city. Finally, since post-socialist cities are increasingly drawn into a system of global relations, the positioning of their respective nation-states within the global economic system also exercises considerable influence. Therefore the conceptual framework here highlights the important differences in the performance of nation-states with respect to the three major transitions: to democracy, markets and decentralized governance.

The model relates the transitions to processes of urban change in four domains: 1) economic change (reindustrialisation, growth vs. decline, effects of globalization); 2) social change (demographic transition, income polarization, poverty); 3) changes in urban governance (new role of the state, central-local relationships, provision of services, urban planning); and 4) spatial change (emerging trends in spaces of production and consumption).

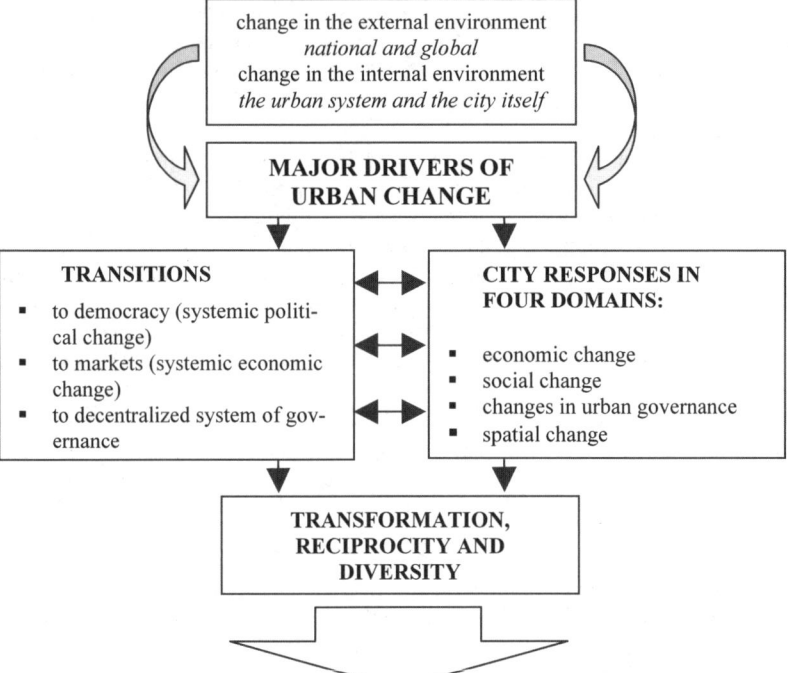

Fig. 2.1. Conceptual framework for analysis of urban change in post-socialist cities

The impact of these transitions on cities may trigger the rise or fall of certain cities within the national urban system, in addition to specific responses to processes of change in the four domains. While some trends and directions of that change are clear, uncertainty about the choices made by governments, organizations, businesses and individuals in the turbulent environment of post-socialist cities challenges observers of the process (Nedovic-Budic 2001). The internal environment also is in a state of flux, with the rapid adjustment of the physical, economic, social, and political structures of the city itself (Musil 1993; Sykora 1994). Although national differences are a powerful determinant of diversity and of the transformation path of post-socialist cities, different cities within the urban system will nevertheless have a variety of trajectories. What the conceptual framework recognizes is the critical link between national-level policies and types of responses at the local level. Such an approach can capture the pace of change and the multi-layered nature of the transformations. The end point is not necessarily 'a capitalist city' or 'a post-fordist city,' if there is one; rather the focus is on the process of change in the city's economy, society, system of governance and spaces of production and consumption.

2.2 Urbanization and urban growth in post-socialist countries

With 67% of the region's population (close to 300 million) living in cities, the levels of urbanization in post-socialist countries are close to those in Western Europe and North America. Russia, though with a per capita income about 1/10 that of the United States, has the same level of urbanization: 74%, up from only 17% in the late 1920s. Similarly in many countries in the CEE region, the traditional relationship between income growth and urbanization clearly does not hold (Buckley and Mini 2000; UNECE 1997). The emphasis on industrialization and urbanization during socialism has caused the dual imbalance of 'overindustrialization' and 'over-urbanization' that affects much of the region today. With some exceptions, notably countries from CIS, transition economies today face urban problems closer to those of Western Europe during the 1980s' deindustrialization, but without their wealth and institutions.

Fig. 2.2. presents the relationship between urbanization and income in market-oriented and in socialist economies. In the 1990s, at the beginning of the transition, the average levels of urbanization and income (purchasing power parity 1990 US$) in the region were 64% and $5,300 respectively (point A). On the 'market economies' line (point B), the level of urbanization corresponding to a $5,300 per capita income is 52%—12 percentage points lower than the level in the region. The per capita income on the 'market economies' line that corresponds to a 64% urbanization level is $8,700 (point C); thus, at that level of urbanization, the per capita income achieved in transition countries is only 60% of such a benchmark.

It is important to note the significant differences not only across cities, but across countries in the group, as well. Some countries, as Fig. 2.2. demonstrates, followed the socialist urbanization pattern; others did not (e.g., Albania, Moldova, Romania). For example, before 1990 the Kyrgyz Republic within the former Soviet Union had a planned economy with a high degree of economic specialization and industrialization along with low levels of urbanization. Albania, the country

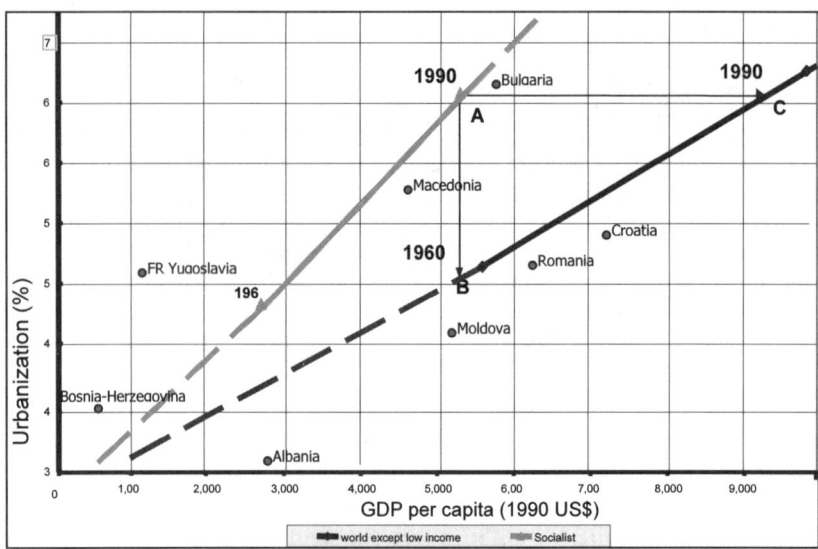

Fig. 2.2. Patterns of urbanization and growth in socialist and middle income market economies, 1960-1990

Source: Adapted from Buckley and Tsenkova 2004

that began the transition with the region's lowest per capita income, had certainly functioned with an economic system disparate from that of the former Soviet Union. Its urbanization and industrialization patterns were quite similar to those of a typical developing country.

The literature on recent urbanization in the region indicates that countries are highly urbanized with the urban populations have, on average, being 64-76% (see Fig. 2.3.).[2] Most of those patterns are a legacy of socialist development: most of the 28 post-socialist countries had very low or even negative population growth in the previous fifteen years. The islands of urbanization in CEE are low, and limited to a few smaller nation-states in the Balkans; in CIS, Tajikistan and Uzbekistan stand out with urban shares of population only 27% and 37%, respectively. Levels of urbanization are higher, for example, in Belarus, Ukraine and the Baltic States, but their income calculated at purchasing power parities is lower than in most CEE countries. Correspondingly, countries such as Poland, with high employment in agriculture and less urbanization, have higher per capita incomes. Finally, 'the goulash type of communism' in Hungary or the emphasis in Slovenia and the Czech Republic on dispersed spatial development through networks of cities,

---

[2] For an in-depth discussion of urbanization trends and their effects on urban change, see Strong et al. (1996); Szelenyi (1996), Tosics, 2005 and UNCHS (2001).

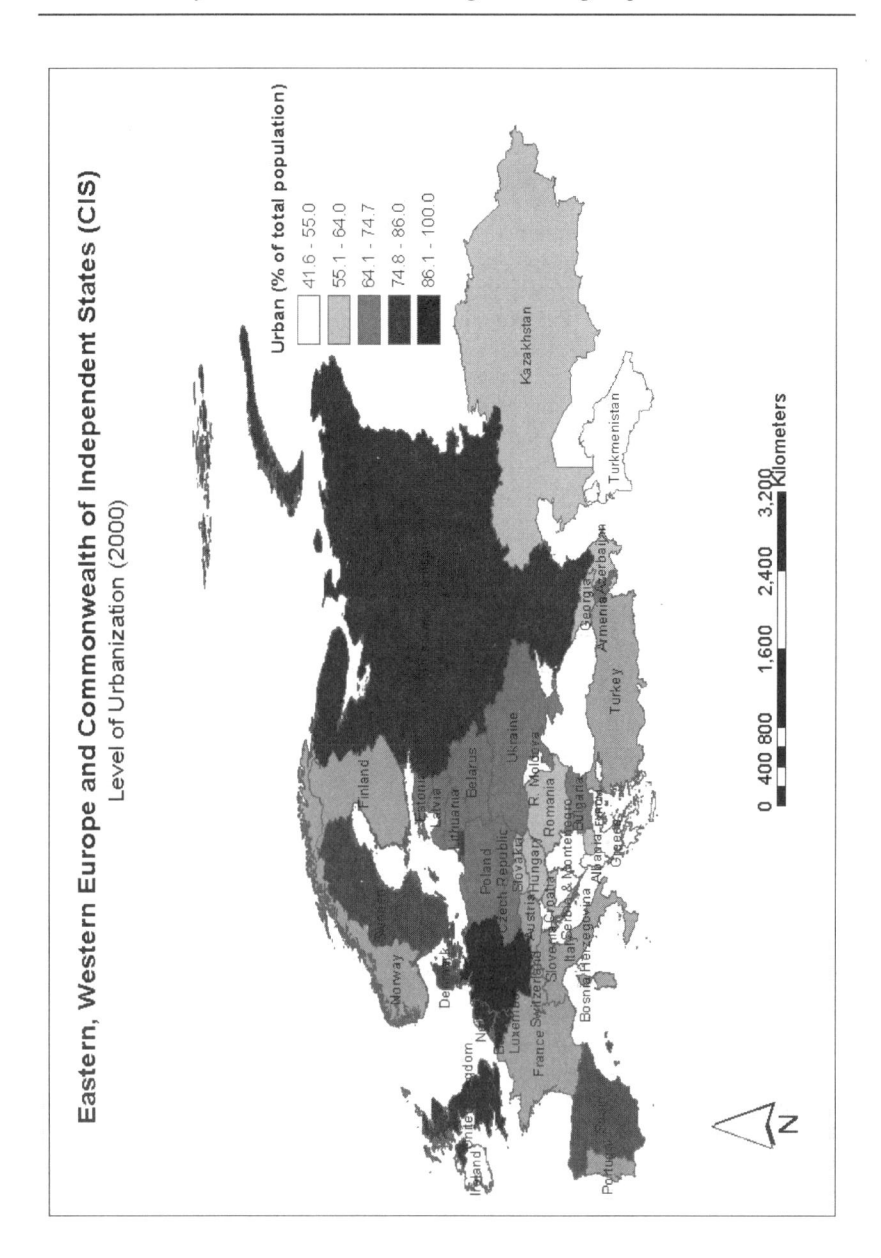

2 Beyond transitions: Understanding urban change in post-socialist cities   27

Fig. 2.3. Urbanization patterns in 2000

Source: Data from United Nations Department of Economic and Social Affairs (2002)

towns and rural communities may explain their lower urbanization rates despite higher income levels.

In summary, state socialism's legacy of centrally directed urbanization driven by industrial growth has had powerful consequences for the transition. The socialist policies created a highly urbanized economic system across the region, which is much more vulnerable to external shocks and, given the relatively low per capita income, is difficult to maintain. Over-industrialized cities were hit badly by the massive closures of unproductive state enterprises. Unemployment and poverty escalated. Not surprisingly, urban poverty is a much more significant and persistent phenomenon in the region than anywhere else (World Bank 2000b). On the other hand, some countries in the region have economies much more dependent on agriculture and resource-based industries, with low levels of urbanization (e.g., Albania, Bosnia & Herzegovina, Moldova and Azerbaijan). Two aspects of these observations have particular significance for the future: 1) countries in the region that have been 'over-industrialized' and 'over-urbanized' may have more severe economic shifts affecting their urban areas, and 2) countries with less urbanization and less economic development may face migration to urban areas and rapidly rising urban poverty.

It should be noted that overall urban growth across the region became less pronounced in the 1990s. Data indicate that projected annual urban population growth in most countries will be lower than 1% till 2015 (see Table 2.1.). Estonia and Latvia notably are expected to have negative population growth, in the range of 0.7/0.8% per year for the same period. Countries in CIS with lower levels of urbanization, however, are projected to have annual growth rates almost three times the sub-regional average. In CEE, similar trends are shown for Albania and Bosnia and Herzegovina, where rapid urbanization was triggered by the transitions to markets and democracy.

Concentration of the population in large urban agglomerations is another characteristic feature of the region. The United Nations population statistics for 2001 reveal that the region has 45 metropolitan agglomerations with populations in excess of one million, mostly in the Russian Federation, for a total of 95 million inhabitants (UN-HABITAT 2001). Moscow and St Petersburg are the largest cities in the region with respectively, 9 and 5 million inhabitants. In CEE, large metropolitan centres—Warsaw, Bucharest and Budapest—each have over 2 million, followed by Prague, Lodz and Sofia with over 1.2 million. In CIS a large share of the urban population (61%) lives in cities with over 100,000 people, while in CEE this share is much smaller, 46%. The concentrations of urban population in the capital cities are higher in Latvia, Estonia, Armenia and Belarus, as the data in Table 2.1. demonstrate.

Table 2.1. Major urban indicators in selected CEE countries

	Level of Urbanization (% Population) 2000	Urban Population, Millions 2000	Projected Annual Growth (%) 2000-2015 [a]	Capital City	Urban Share of Population (%)
CEE Countries					
Albania	41.2	1.2	2.1	Tirana	43[b]
Bosnia & Herzegovina	43	1.7	1.8	Sarajevo	23[b]
Bulgaria	69.6	5.7	-0.1	Sofia	21
Croatia	57.7	2.5	0.5	Zagreb	16
Czech Republic	74.7	7.6	0.0	Prague	16
Estonia	68.6	0.9	-0.8	Tallinn	44[b]
Hungary	64	6.4	0.0	Budapest	28
Latvia	69	1.6	-0.7	Riga	47[b]
Lithuania	68.4	2.5	0.0	Vilnius	22[b]
FYROM[c]	62	1.2	...	Skopje	42[b]
Poland	65.6	25.4	0.5	Warsaw	9
Romania	56.2	12.5	0.3	Bucharest	16
Slovakia	57.4	3.0	0.6	Bratislava	15[b]
Slovenia	50.4	1.0	0.5	Ljubliana	50[b]
Serbia & Montenegro	52.2	5.5	0.8	Belgrade	27
CIS Countries					
Armenia	70	2.4	1.0	Yerevan	52
Azerbaijan	57.3	4.4	1.6	Baku	44
Belarus	71.2	7.2	0.3	Minsk	24
Georgia	60.1	3.0	0.9	Tbilisi	18
Kazakhstan	56.4	9.1	0.8	Alma-Ata	14
Republic of Moldova	46.1	2.0	0.7	Chishnau	35[b]
Russian Federation	77.7	114.1	0.2	Moscow	8
Tajikistan	27.5	1.7	2.0	Dushanbe	33[b]
Turkmenistan	44.8	1.9	2.2	Ashgabat	32[b]
Ukraine	68	34.3	0.5	Kiev	8
Uzbekistan	36.9	8.9	1.7	Tashkent	24

Sources: Columns 1-3: World Bank 2003a; Columns 4-8: UNCHS 2001.
Notes:
a. Estimates of UN Population Division; b. Author's estimates; c. FYROM-Former Yugoslav Republic of Macedonia.

2.3 The transition to democracy – political and institutional change

The hallmark of the political transition is the move to democracy and multiparty elections. The transition to democracy has resulted in the break-up of two federations and the creation of 28 independent states. Many regional urban centres—Riga, Tallinn, Vilnius, Zagreb, Ljubliana, Bratislava, Sarajevo, to name a few—were reinvented as national capitals, which signalled major transformations in their economies and urban structure.

Though the political landscape is very diverse, most commentators on the process of establishing democratic societies in the post-socialist world seem to divide countries into two groups. Competitive democracies, which are underpinned by widespread political rights to participate in multiparty elections and an extensive range of civil liberties, have taken root in nearly all the CEE countries. In contrast, limitations on rights to participate in elections and constraints on civil liberties during at least some period of the transition have concentrated political power in many countries in the CIS and South East Europe. The concentration of power has been associated with diminished state performance in implementing regulatory reforms and providing public goods due to corruption and weak public sector management.

Moreover, the civil wars in South East Europe at the close of the twentieth century brought political and social instability. In the largest refugee crisis in Europe since World War II, by 1995 the sub-region had suffered the displacement of more than 2 million people and faced unique housing crises. Declining living standards as well as refugees, border disputes and security concerns are still major barriers to the economic development of the South East Europe countries (Tsenkova 2005a).

Across transition economies, political regimes have moved from right to left and then back again, with various nuances of the neo-liberal agenda for economic and social change. In some countries the economic shocks have produced 'reform fatigue,' making the population resistant to further changes. Although both right-wing and left-wing governments have followed an economic path of measures to increase competition, market liberalization and de-regulation, their social policies tend to differ. These differences no doubt create a diverse framework for implementation of urban policy at the local level.

Within cities, however, some of the most visible manifestations of the transition to democracy appear in the local politics surrounding municipal elections. The post-socialist cities have a variety of political structures ranging from single-tier to multi-tier governments. In local government elections, which are not as dramatic as the national ones, parties negotiate representation and their 'quotas' of municipal council seats, creating multi-party coalitions. Council members often broker different political interests, making consensus difficult. Most countries lack national urban policies, and the frequent changes in political regimes no doubt lead to a lack of consistency in party politics at the city as well as the national levels. (See van Kempen 2005 for discussion of these issues in the European Union accession countries.) These national changes have made urban politics less predictable, and also socially and economically more conservative compared to those of socialist times. Even without explicit urban policies in most countries, however, social redistribution policies, investment strategies, privatisation and trade liberalisation policies, among others, increasingly affect localities and influence private sector investment in cities. Local governments have an important role in shaping these outcomes through strategic planning, land use planning and city marketing (Adair et al. 1999; City Development Authority of Prague 2000; City Development Department 2001). In addition, the path-dependent nature of local institutions helps to explain the variety of local responses in the post-socialist world of cities and the new sources of difference depending on cities' localities, competitive positions, and ability to manage change (see Tasan-Kok and Schwegler in this volume).

2.4 The transition to markets - economic change

In addition to global pressures for change, cities in the region are being profoundly transformed by the transition from centrally planned to market-based economies. The years of economic stress and market volatility have had contrasting consequences across the region. The transition countries in the first wave have pushed ahead with the more challenging structural and institutional changes and have been able to maintain macroeconomic stability (UNECE 2003). In fact, some of the fastest growing economies in Europe and Central Asia in 2002 had had the worst overall performance in the previous decade. Fig. 2.4. shows that while the rates of gross domestic product (GDP) growth across Western Europe have been in the range of 1%, with high economic performance in Greece and Ireland (3.3%), the fastest growing economies have been Turkmenistan (15%), Azerbaijan (8%) and Kazakhstan (7%). After years of economic recession, most CEE countries have exceeded their pre-transition GDP. In CIS, however, the average GDP has remained at 68% of its 1990 level; see Tsenkova 2005a for an overview of these trends.

In South East Europe the economic recessions in the last decade were particularly severe. For example, GDP per capita of Serbia & Montenegro before the war was estimated at about US$3,500; it is believed to have fallen to about half of that. The share taken by the informal economy in these countries continues to be high, at 30 to 40% of their GDP (Tsenkova 2005b). These circles of informality have a major impact on cities, where much of the informal sector appears to be concentrated. Some of the visible manifestations are the growing importance of street retail (flea markets) and/or the investment in informal housing settlements in many large cities in South East Europe.

Further economic and social divisions in post-socialist societies are reflected in the differences of economic wealth, an important factor influencing urban consumption and production patterns. The economic wealth, measured in purchasing

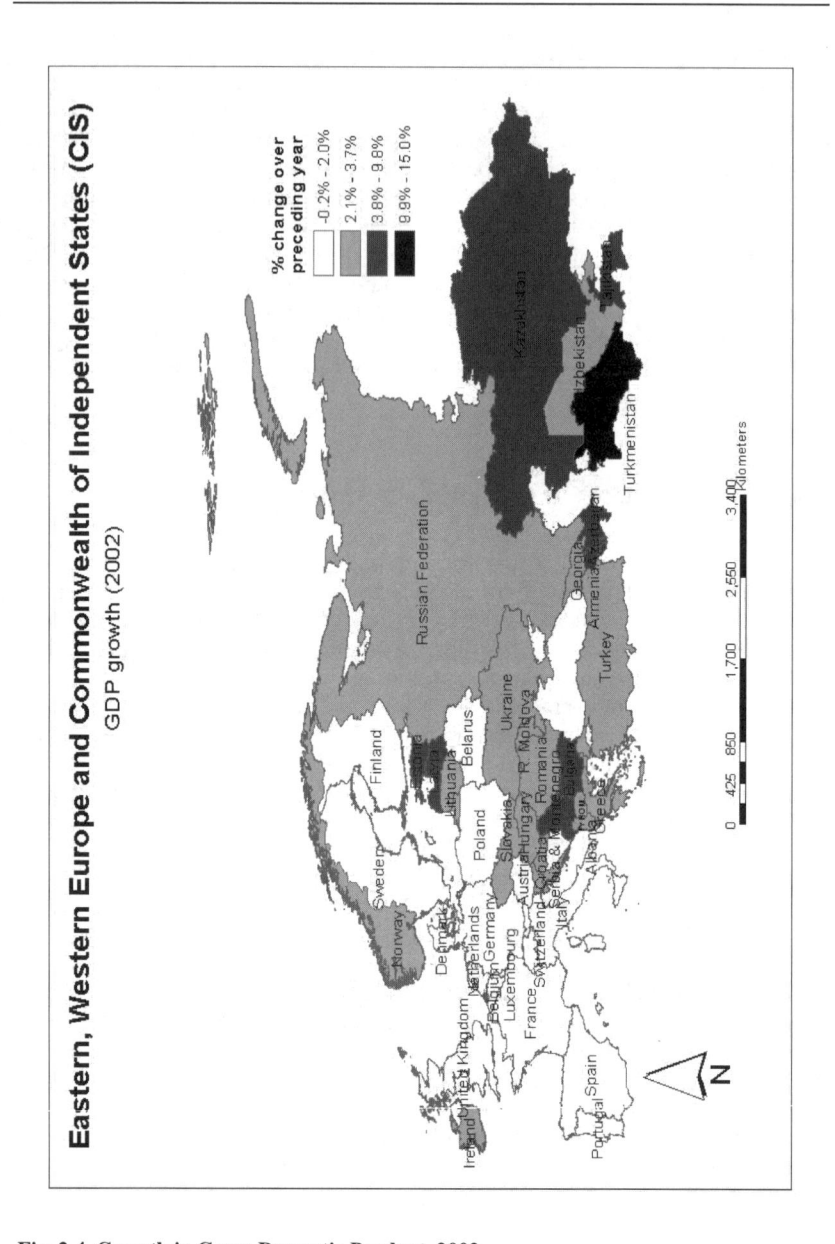

Fig. 2.4. Growth in Gross Domestic Product, 2002

Source: Based on data from United Nations Department of Economic and Social Affairs (2002)

power parity, in CEE is in the range of US$11,000, notably higher than the levels in CIS of US$2,500 (see Table 2.2.).[3] Residents of the poorest country in the region (Tajikistan) have 17 times less average annual income than do the residents of the most affluent one (Slovenia). Per capita incomes in the three wealthiest countries in the first wave of European Union accession, in 2002, were still only 68% of the European Union average for Slovenia, 59% for the Czech Republic, and 49% for Hungary.

Another important factor affecting economic change in cities is the level of foreign direct investment, which has advanced steadily over the past decade in line with the countries' progress in transition and macroeconomic stabilization. Foreign investment has provided a major boost to market economies, particularly in the Czech Republic, Estonia and Hungary, where more liberal and stable environments have attracted strategic investors to enterprise restructuring and technology transfer. The region's cumulative investment flows per capita for 1990-1999 demonstrate significant variations, with the Czech Republic and Hungary taking the lion's share: US$2,745 and US$2,386, respectively. The Balkans, not surprisingly given the political turmoil are at the bottom of this ranking, with levels in Serbia and Montenegro and Bosnia and Herzegovina close to US$108 per capita. The winners of foreign investment in CIS are clearly the resource-rich economies of Azerbaijan and Kazakhstan, where levels of foreign direct investment hover around the average for CEE (see Table 2.2.).

Profound structural reforms across the region are constituted by changing economic structures and labour market adjustments. Shifting large numbers of employees into new firms, restructuring state enterprises and services, closing down or privatizing inefficient state industries and reducing state subsidies clearly resulted not only in lower GDP per capita, but also in major shifts in its composition. Most CEE countries today have service-based economies, with the service sector accounting for close to 55% of the GDP in 2000.[4] The Russian Federation, and surprisingly, Tajikistan are the only two CIS countries with similar GDP sector breakdowns (refer to Table 2.2.). The decline of industrial employment and production has been more pronounced in CEE, particularly in the early years of the transition (UNECE 1997; EBRD 2004). The growth of services in the regional economy has been almost universal, the most noticeable increase being in the Baltic States and Hungary. Within the service economy, the capital cities across the region are regaining their position as financial, business and administrative centres of the nation-state. Some (Prague, Budapest, Warsaw, Vilnius) clearly state their ambitions to become the springboard for international investors; others market themselves as the regional centres of command and control for head offices and servicing operations in resource-rich countries and other regional sub-markets

---

[3] The transition economies started reforms with an extreme range of initial conditions. 1989 per capita income varied by more than six times, from $9,200 in 1989 dollars in Slovenia to $1,400 in Albania. Some countries are proximate to Western European markets, with good transport connections; others are isolated from such markets.

[4] For comparison, in 1992 32.8% of the European Union economy was based on industry and 60.9% on services; the corresponding figures in the USA were 26.2% and 70.9%.

Table 2.2. Economic and social indicators in post-socialist countries

Countries	PPP Gross National Income Per Capita, in US$, 2000	FDI/US$[a]	Gross Domestic Product Value added as % of GDP		Unemployment, 2001	Gini coefficient[b]		Population living on less than $2 a day (%)[c]	
			Industry, 2000	Services, 2000		Gini	Survey year		Survey year
CEE Countries									
Albania	3500	213.9	28	17	14.5	...	...	...	...
Bosnia & Herzegovina	...	108.5	...	...	39.9	...	...	...	...
Bulgaria	5530	466.8	24	62	17.9	26.4	1997	21.9	1997
Croatia	7780	1441.5	32	59	23.1	29	1998	<2	1998
Czech Republic	13610	2745.6	43	53	8.9	25.4	1996	<2	1996
Estonia	9050	1935.8	28	66	7.7	37.6	1998	5.2	1998
Hungary	12060	2386.9	34	61	8	24.4	1998	7.3	1998
Latvia	6960	1067.9	26	71	7.7	32.4	1998	8.3	1998
Lithuania	6960	781.7	32	59	12.9	32.4	1996	7.8	1996
FYROM	4960	368.9	35	53	42	...	...	...	...
Poland	9030	912.8	32	65	17.5	31.6	1998	<2	1998
Romania	6380	341.3	30	55	8.8	28.2	1994	27.5	1994
Slovakia	11000	1100.8	32	64	18.6	19.5	1992	<2	1992
Slovenia	17390	1044.2	38	58	11.8	28.4	1998	<2	1998
Serbia & Montenegro	...	107.9	...	...	27.9	...	...	...	...

Table 2.2. (cont.)

Countries	PPP Gross National Income Per Capita, in US$, 2000	FDI/US$[a]	Gross Domestic Product Value added as % of GDP - Industry, 2000	Gross Domestic Product Value added as % of GDP - Services, 2000	Unemployment, 2001	Gini coefficient[b] - Gini	Gini coefficient[b] - Survey year	Population living on less than $2 a day (%)[c]	Survey year
CIS Countries									
Armenia	2570	162.9	33	39	9.8	44.4	1996	34	1996
Azerbaijan	2760	508.6	43	36	1.3	36	1995	9.6	1995
Belarus	7550	137.6	42	45	2.3	21.7	1998	<2	1998
Georgia	2470	152.9	13	52	...	37.1	1996	<2	1996
Kazakhstan	5490	623.4	30	60	2.8	35.4	1996	15.3	1996
Kyrgyzstan	...	83.4	...	...	3.1	...	...	...	...
Republic of Moldova	2240	145.9	22	53	1.7	40.6	1997	38.4	1997
Russian Federation	8030	166.4	38	56	8.7	48.7	1998	25.1	1998
Tajikistan	1060	23.7	25	57	2.6	...	...	...	...
Turkmenistan	4040	155.1	45	28	...	40.8	1998	59	1993
Ukraine	3710	217.6	40	47	3.7	29	1999	31	1999
Uzbekistan	2380	30.3	24	43	...	33.3	1993	26.5	1993

Sources: Column 1,3,5 & 6: World Bank 2003a. Column 2: Author's estimates based on UNECE 2003 data. Column 4: UNECE 2003.
Notes:
a. Cumulative Foreign Direct Investment (FDI) per capita in US$ (1990-2001); b. Gini Coefficient ranges from 0 to 1, where 0 means perfect equality and 1 perfect inequality. c. International Poverty Line is equivalent $2(1993 PPP in US$). d. FYROM-Former Yugoslav Republic of Macedonia

(Adair et al. 1999; General Council for St Petersburg 1998; Ghanbari-Parsa and Moatazed-Keivani 1999).

While economic growth prospects in the region have been acclaimed, the social effects of the transition process present a major challenge of the transition to market economies (UNECE 1997; Tsenkova 2001). Unemployment has increased rapidly in most countries as a result of macroeconomic change and continues to be excessively high in Bulgaria, Poland, Slovakia and the countries affected by civil war (see Table 2.2.). Structural adjustment policies, economic restructuring and the 'shock therapy' have created serious difficulties for particular groups, e.g., as the long-term unemployed, unskilled labour and youth. By contrast, in CIS unemployment has remained low, in the range of 2-3%; Armenia and to some extent Russia appear to be the only exceptions.[5] CIS countries have sheltered their economies and labour markets from privatization, but have had to restructure social expenditures to make them more affordable to the state budget (World Bank 2002).

The region's urban economies have responded differently to the changes in macroeconomic conditions. The market-based restructuring of urban systems responds to a parallel process of integration in the global economic hierarchy of cities. New challenges are due to the pressures of national and international economic forces, and the opening up of previously sheltered markets. The consequent rapid adjustment of industries, services and other economic activities has crucial effects on the direction of growth and change, on future specialization in cities' economic bases, on their mix of traditional manufacturing industries and advanced services. Empirical evidence suggests that in most cities the economic diversification associated with the transition from industrial to service-oriented, information-based urban economies has increased.[6] During the transition, individual urban areas have undergone differentiated development, with some losing and others gaining economic attractiveness. Capital cities and large urban centres have been privileged in that respect, attracting a large share of the regional investment in banking, retail and information-based technologies.[7] Their economies have managed to sustain a more stable labour market sheltered from high unemployment, as indicated by the most recent available data, presented in Fig. 2.5. Methodological differ-

---

[5] Russia's GDP in 2000 was 66% of its value in 1990, and 20% of its population was under the poverty line, but it has been growing steadily ever since, and the pace of restructuring in different sectors is picking up tempo. In contrast, Turkmenistan, another resource-rich country, made minimal steps towards a market-based economy, conserving as many of the old ways as could be financed by commodity exports. The population was not subjected to shocks and losses, but neither has its welfare changed much for the better. This is particularly felt in the countryside, which is mired in poverty (World Bank 2002).

[6] In the case of Sofia, 80% of the city's GDP in 2002 was generated by services; in Vilnius this share is close to 70% (Tsenkova 2005a).

[7] For example, in 1998 Prague's GDP per capita was 85% of the European Union average, while in northern Bohemia and northern Moravia, it was half of that.

ences notwithstanding, country-specific studies have confirmed these trends for the 1990s (van Kempen et al. 2004; Hamilton et al. 2005).

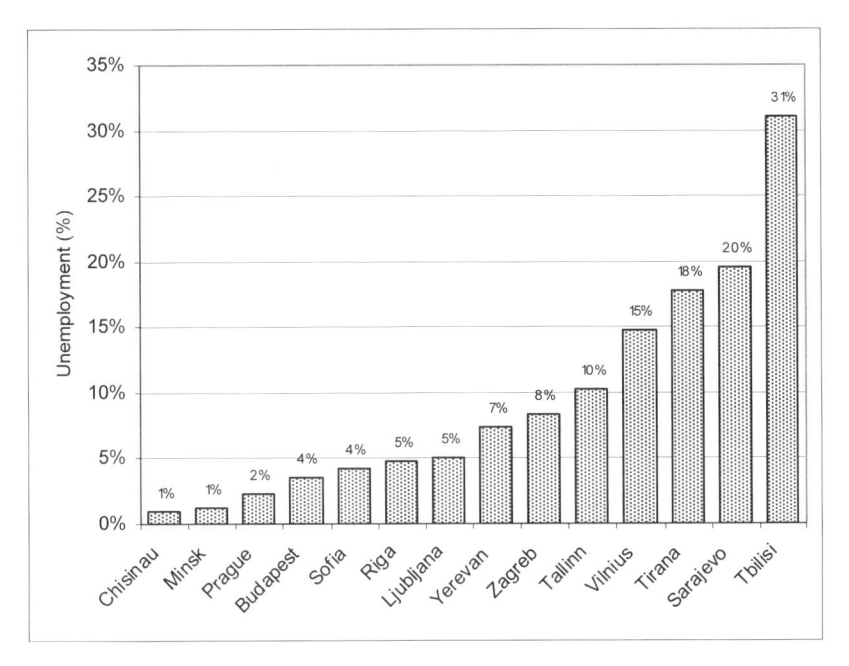

Fig. 2.5. Unemployment in capital cities in selected transition economies, 2000

Source: Based on UNCHS 2000

2.5 The social change

As a result of 'over-industrialization' and 'over-urbanization' under the socialist regime, in some cities in the region poverty has rapidly increased as public enterprises collapsed, particularly because of the absence of an effective social safety net. It is not surprising that many of the cities in the CIS, with the old regime's emphasis on industrialization, have become home to large concentrations of poor and/or unemployed people, particularly where heavy industry had been located.[8]

---

[8] While in Central Europe rural poverty is more pervasive than urban poverty, the overall level is lower than in the rest of the region. The post-war Balkan countries show a relatively even picture between rural and urban poverty. In contrast, the extent of urban poverty in the former Soviet Union is a significant concern. Tajikistan, a predominantly rural country, has poverty concentrated in medium sized, secondary cities, where its incidence is about twice as high as in rural areas; similar findings exist for Bulgaria, Romania and several other countries (Jones and Revenga 2000).

These developments should be evaluated against the background of rising income inequality, social distress and growing insecurity across the transition economies. The socialist system had a more egalitarian income distribution than market economies have (see Milanovic 1992). It also tolerated lower economic growth for the sake of avoiding income inequality (especially in its later stages, when qualitative deficiencies outweighed the initial quantitative successes). Not surprisingly, an attribute of the transition process was income polarization, with important implications for social safety nets and access to housing and urban services. The available data on income inequality for CIS countries show that the ratio between the lowest and the highest income quintile has increased from 0.27 in the early 1990s to 0.42 in 1999, while in the CEE countries it has grown from 0.24 to 0.31. In both sub-regions the Gini coefficient has increased, but the increase in the CIS countries is twice as large as that in CEE (Buckley and Mini 2000).

The patterns of income inequality continue, as data in Table 2.2. demonstrate. Income inequality measured by the Gini coefficient is highest in the Russian Federation (47.8%) and Armenia (44.4%), closely followed by Moldova and Turkmenistan (40%). Further, the percentage of the population living on less than US$2 per day has increased dramatically. It is alarmingly high in some CIS countries: Turkmenistan (59%), Moldova (38%) and Armenia (34%). This sub-region has the highest percentage in the region of people living in absolute poverty. Capital cities, however, have poverty rates below the national average. For example, the 1998 survey data in 14 large cities in the region showed poverty rates lower than 5 percent.[9] Vilnius and Belgrade had higher concentrations of poor people, exceeding 15% (UNCHS 2000).

The high rates of income inequality, particularly in the urban areas, have broad impacts on social well being, such as the inability of some citizens to participate in society and in activities leading to improved health and educational attainment. The urban poor are especially vulnerable to economic shocks, since they lack access to services, safety nets, and political representation (World Bank 2002). Groups at risk are the long-term unemployed, large or one-parent families, people with low education, and, increasingly, ethnic minorities. There are particularly deep poverty pockets among Roma communities.

Demographic changes across the region, while not as dramatic as the increases in poverty and inequality, include declining birth rates in most countries, rapid ageing of the population (due also to emigration), and growing numbers of single-person and non-family households (UNECE 1997, World Bank 2003a).

In summary, the region's countries have increasingly divergent social experiences, with 'advanced policy reformers' moving towards European Union standards—and the rest lagging behind. The move towards market economy and democracy has not delivered uniform benefits to all countries in transition not to all social groups. It is widely acknowledged that the second generation of policy reforms is driven by sober reflection that market failures should be addressed in

---

[9] Poverty rates are measured as the percentage of households with incomes below the officially established poverty line in the country.

more effectively, and that the social protection of vulnerable groups is perhaps the most important aspect of public policy intervention. The urban application of this new agenda is indeed important, given the high level of urbanization in the post-socialist world.

2.6 The transition to decentralized forms of governance – changes in planning and service delivery

Political, fiscal, and administrative decentralization has taken place across the region during the past decade in an effort to make governments both more democratic and more efficient. The original impetus for strong decentralization was a reaction to the centralized socialist system and a demand for greater autonomy. However, studies have pointed out that decentralization has resulted in excessive fragmentation (e.g., the Czech Republic, Hungary and Latvia) that has left most local governments too small to operate basic services independently (van Kempen et al. 2005). Most countries are finding themselves with a very large number of small municipalities lacking the mechanisms for necessary co-ordination and economies of scale.[10] At the city level, this situation has led to confusing and contested areas of responsibility and authority among central, local and regional levels of government. In some cases (e.g., Russia, Uzbekistan, Kyrgystan) self-governing bodies have become important in local governance.[11]

Within the region's framework of institutional change, central governments have enhanced local autonomy by decentralizing power and responsibilities. Local governments have become principally responsible for urban planning and management. They also have retained statutory responsibility for providing and maintaining technical infrastructure and urban social services. In most cases, municipalities have acquired ownership of the fixed assets of water and sewerage companies, district central heating systems and public housing (Mitric 1999). At the same time, however, inflation, subsidy restructuring and significant budget cuts have raised the cost of urban services dramatically. Running schools, hospitals, social care homes and other social facilities has raised the local governments' public expenditures.[12] Hungarian and Polish local governments have found themselves in the premier league of European spenders, along with the Scandinavian

---

[10] For example, the Czech Republic has 6,196 municipalities with an average population of 1,666 residents; close to 70% of Latvia's municipalities have less than 2,000 residents.

[11] Local governments in Uzbekistan have acquired important functions and now retain about 60% of all government revenues. The mahallas, official self-governing bodies in each neighbourhood, have emerged as important institutions administering social assistance and community economic development projects.

[12] It should be acknowledged that there is a considerable diversity with respect to provision of urban social services. In Hungary, local governments have the primary responsibility for primary and secondary education, hospital health care, social services and part of the social security system. In Poland, secondary education, health and social care were transferred to cities in 1996 (Davey 1999).

countries. The newly expanded local budgets have increased the dependency on intergovernmental transfers, since the scale of resources needed far exceeds the potential of any local tax base. A study by Buckley and Tsenkova (2001) estimated that locally controlled revenue as a percentage of total local government revenue in most CEE countries was less than 25%.[13] Poland and the Czech Republic had shares as high as 35%, but in Lithuania it was 5%. Overall, fiscal decentralization has not enhanced the ability of local governments to raise resources locally and achieve a sustainable tax base (UNECE 1997). Rather, it has led to a growing number of unfunded mandates, particularly in the realm of social responsibilities, with unhappy long-term implications for residents of the 'have' vs. those of the 'have not' cities (see van Kempen et al. 2005 for comparative perspectives).

The decentralization of governance has been labelled 'the quiet revolution', but it is one that handed over critical tasks to the local level, creating a triple challenge: 1) provision of adequate infrastructure; 2) management of transport; and 3) land use planning (Tsenkova 2005a). Limited progress has been made in upgrading the region's infrastructure, and most of what has been done has been carried by increasing private sector involvement and foreign participation. The lack of adequate funding has eroded the quality of urban services and transportation. Cash-constrained local governments have often resorted to privatizing land, buildings and other municipal assets. Privatisation of infrastructure is under way in many countries, mostly through concessions and/or competitive contracting of services, however, tariff reforms continue to be undermined by weak enforcement of payments (Mitric 1999).

Although both access to drinking water and sanitation in the region are reportedly adequate, urban–rural inequalities are still visible. Despite some progress in most post-socialist cities since the 1990s, urban water supply and sanitation remain problematic in Azerbaijan, the Kyrgyz Republic, Romania, Tajikistan and Turkmenistan [14] (Tsenkova 2005a). High connection rates—over 90%—in urban areas do not necessarily mean good quality of piped water. Regularity of supply is also a problem in a number of countries: Armenia, Belarus, Georgia, Moldova and Ukraine (World Bank 2003b) and the poor quality of the existing sewage networks is a growing environmental concern. Although most of the population in the capital cities is connected to sewers as well as piped water (if septic tanks are included), the systems are often poorly maintained, with frequent leakages. The system of financial management to recover the cost of services from the users also needs improvement As indicated in Fig. 2.6., in Sofia, Vilnius and Belgrade, only half of the generated wastewater is treated; in Tirana and Bishkek this share is almost non-existent.

---

[13] Own revenue excludes shared taxes and taxes which local governments have no authority to determine; data refer to 1998.

[14] The official data are not consistent with observations on the ground. For example, substantial problems are known to exist in water supply provision in Albania, Moldova and Ukraine, yet official data for these countries report delivery rates higher than 97%. Likewise for sanitation: figures of 100% for Georgia and the Kyrgyz Republic do not reflect experience on the ground (World Bank 2003b).

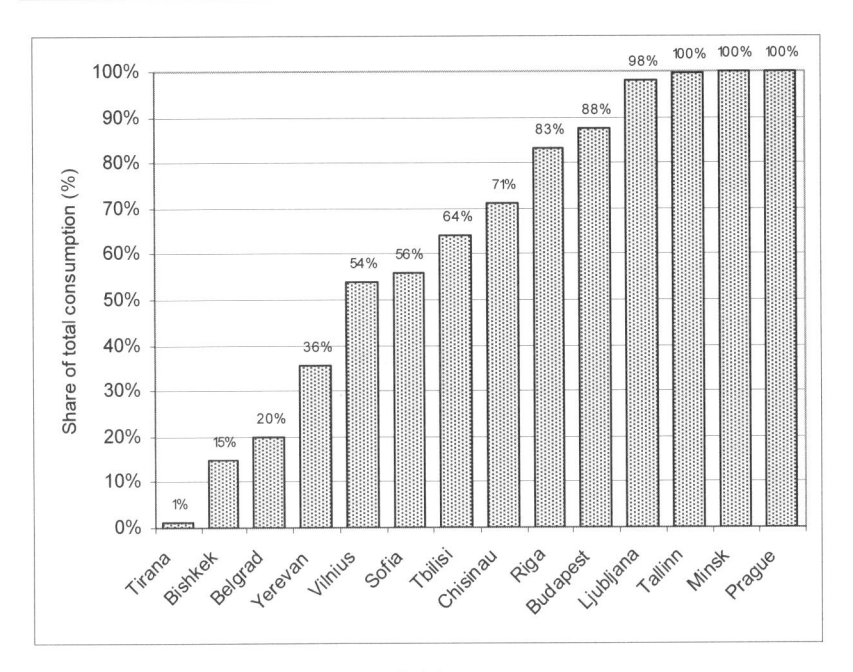

Fig. 2.6. Waste water treatment, selected cities

Source: Based on UNCHS 2000

In addition to water and sewer services, local governments in post-socialist cities are under pressure to maintain the level of public transit, while also investing in infrastructure to accommodate the rapid growth in vehicle use. In most transition economies vehicle ownership has increased at unprecedented annual rates, ranging from 10-15% in the Czech Republic and Moldova to 120-130% in Romania, Russia and Lithuania. The growth in motorization has been significantly lower in CIS and even negative in Georgia and Armenia (UNECE 2004). Data for individual cities are sparse, but confirm the observation that cities foster motorization. For example, car ownership increased by 106% in Warsaw and by 85% in Prague from 1990 to 1998. The rates in Moscow (196%) and St. Petersburg (207%) for the same period were even higher. The consequences of higher rates of car ownership, especially more commuting by private car, have major implications for intracity travel patterns and behaviour.

It is interesting to note that despite rapidly rising car ownership across the region, data from recent transportation surveys indicate that in most capital cities in CEE almost 70% of trips to work use buses, trams, or trolleys (EAUE 2003). Public transit is still very important in post-socialist cities, but the fiscal constraints have made it particularly challenging for local governments to provide adequate and affordable services. In some cases, (Prague, Sofia) local governments have gone to the capital markets and issued bonds to secure funding, but the funding problems go beyond the localities' capacity. Responses to the fiscal crisis have varied widely among countries, cities and public transport companies, depending on the initial conditions, the nature of the reform process, and each city's capacity to adapt and take political risks. Warsaw adopted 'shock-therapy' that achieved 70% cost recovery from riders for use of public transportation. Budapest raised fares in the metro and suburban rail systems substantially, which achieved 35% cost recovery from riders and maintained service levels. At the opposite extreme, urban bus companies in Russia and Central Asia faced progressive immobilization of their fleets. For example, the Tbilisi Metro could operate only intermittently because of electricity shortages (World Bank 2002).

With respect to changes in land use planning in the region, studies have found that the new, market-oriented regimes do not necessarily follow a coherent ideology, but rather have adopted a *laissez-faire* approach to planning, resulting in uneven urban development. The changed institutional structures in post-socialist cities have given rise to market-friendly organizations and the promotion of the 'entrepreneurial city' (Golubchikov 2004; Jaakson 2000). The new institutional actors often confront old planning rules, legislation and policies. Notable, the powerful socialist legacy in land use planning, of sectoral infrastructure planning and financial management, remains embedded in the planning legislation and planning practice (Bertaud and Renaud 1997; Meier 1994). Planning institutions have struggled to redefine their mandate in the new and more economically and politically diverse institutional mosaic, and to respond to the forces reshaping post-socialist cities.

2.7 Bringing it together: Urban spatial change

The last domain in which to explore the transitions to market economies, democracy and new forms of governance is spatial change in post-socialist cities. The transition to market-oriented forms of economic development, industrial production and technological advancement is reflected in a series of changes in the urban fabric. The existing industrial zones are being more intensively developed to accommodate the many new private firms, warehouses and offices. The continued growth of service sector industries has made areas with good exposure and transportation accessibility, more attractive to private sector investors. Some of the industrial zones, particularly associated with manufacturing and heavy industries, have declined. In some cities, the large state enterprises, a legacy of the socialist past, have gone bankrupt and the industrial landscape is dominated by abandoned complexes of industrial and administrative buildings. These 'ghost cites' will need to be recycled and allocated for more profitable land uses (Buckley and Tsenkova 2001). Shifts in technology and communications have established office functions, particularly in banking and finance, as a significant component in the economic base of capital cities. These trends have resulted in dynamic property development of office space and top prices in buoyant office markets (e.g. Budapest, Prague, and Warsaw). The retail sector also has experienced dynamic growth, particularly of private businesses (Sykora 1994; Tosics 2005; Weclawowicz 1992).

Fig. 2.7. Small scale retail in Sofia's pedestrian zone

Existing retail space is being restructured to accommodate a diverse retail sector, and unprofitable and under-utilized shopping centres at undergoing redevelopment. Especially in the inner cities, strip retailing has established itself as the principal retail activity, usually with exclusive shops, boutiques and retail spaces that cater to the affluent consumer.

Other forces driving the changes in spatial structure are land reforms, property market differentiation, and fragmentation of investment flows (Strong et al.1996). With the new market orientation urban development has ridden a wave of investment in those land uses offering the highest returns, and selective redevelopment by the private sector (Tsenkova 2000). Studies indicate that the region's investment and wealth accumulation through housing, other real estate, productive and infrastructure assets are concentrated in its cities (Adair et al. 1999; Ghanbari-Parsa and Moatazed-Keivani 1999). Firms locate in the capital cities to benefit from agglomeration economies, a diverse labour force and more access to information and technology.

While the trends outlined here can define the direction of change in the spaces of production, the transformation of housing areas, both inner city and suburban, is less uniform. Typically, new housing construction has gentrified attractive inner city neighbourhoods or has transformed the urban fringe with single family developments. However, the situation of post-socialist cities is uniquely characterized

44   Sasha Tsenkova

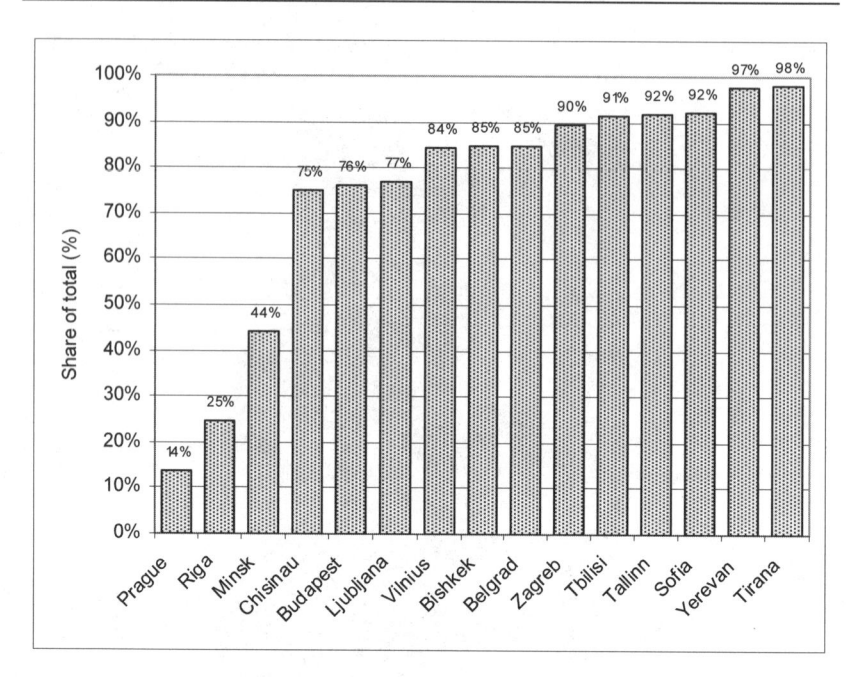

Fig. 2.8. Home ownership in CEE and CIS capital cities

Source: Based on UNCHS 2000

by another element: the housing estates in their urban structure. The legacy of socialist planning and housing provision has created a high-density urban periphery in the socialist world of cities (see Bertaud and Renaud 1997) characterized by system-built housing with accompanying basic social services such as schools and medical care. Those areas, however, lack retail and employment opportunities, so residents make long commuting trips to centres of employment and have high transportation costs (Tsenkova 2001). Mass produced housing in the peripheral housing estates is home to 50% of the residents of Sofia, Riga and Vilnius. In some cities that percentage rises to 80% (Bucharest); in others, such as Ljubljana, it is as low as 20%. By comparison, in Western European cities fewer than 7% of the people live in housing estates (EAUE, 2003).[15] At the same time, another characteristic feature of post-socialist cities is the high proportions of home ownership. Available data are presented in Fig. 2.8. In most of the capital cities in the region home ownership exceeds 75%; places such as Tirana and Yerevan reach 97-98%.

---

[15] Conditions in different countries under socialism were not equal, which has had long-term repercussions within the system of owner-occupied housing. The levels of home ownership in cities across the region are the legacy of socialist housing systems as well as different privatisation strategies with respect to public housing (Marcuse 1996; Pishler-Milanovich 1994; Tsenkova 2000).

While Riga and Prague have been the exceptions, creeping privatization in the last five years has transferred another 50% of Riga's stock into private hands. Given the nature of the housing stock, the rising utility costs and poverty, post-socialist cities face a serious challenge to sustain the value of their existing housing assets (see Buckley and Tsenkova in this volume).

Concluding comments: The trajectory of urban change

While it may be too early for a convincing theoretical account of the transition process in post-socialist cities, this chapter suggests a conceptual framework for understanding urban change in the post-socialist cities. The rich tapestry of urban experiences discussed here displays some of the unique development and transformation challenges in the transition economies. The chapter's conceptual framework links the changes in the external environment (national and global), which are notably dramatic and revolutionary, explicitly to changes in the internal environment: the urban system and the city itself. Three aspects of the transition that are particularly important for post-socialist cities are explored: the transitions to democracy (systemic political change), to market economies (systemic economic change), and to decentralized systems of local governance. These transitions are major drivers of change at the city level in four domains: 1) economic change; 2) social change; 3) changes in urban governance; and 4) spatial change (transformation of production and consumption spaces).

The application of this framework maps critical differences between CEE and CIS transition economies in terms of both national and urban transformation during the last fifteen years. Although national differences are powerful determinants of diversity and of post-socialist cities' transformation paths, the cities themselves also shape their own trajectory in the national urban system. What the chapter's conceptual framework recognizes is the critical link between national policies and the types of responses at the local level, thus capturing the multi-layered nature of transformations in the four domains. The main point of departure is perhaps the ideal model of a 'socialist' city. That important legacy affects a city's economy, its social structure, the spatial distribution of its production and consumption activities, and the quality of urban services. How 'socialist' cities actually were under state socialism is an important question to debate. Notwithstanding sub-regional and country-specific differences, however, one can distinguish the salient characteristics of the 'socialist' city model, extensively discussed in the literature (see, e.g., Andrusz et al. 1996; Hamilton et al. 2005; UNECE 1997). The matrix presented in Table 2.3. links those characteristics to the four domains of urban change explored in the chapter. While the end point of the transition is not necessarily 'a capitalist city' or 'a post-fordist city', the matrix summarises the trajectory of change and highlights the major outcomes discussed here. It looks at the process of transition from 'socialist' to post-socialist city as a sequence of phases or stages in which both national and local differences increasingly map a diversified trajectory. The focus is on differences in outcomes and a multi-layered process of urban change. It is argued that such process will multiply differences in the post-socialist world, leading to the rise or fall of certain cities within the national and indeed within the regional urban system.

The matrix creates a framework for the analysis of urban change in the post-socialist world. Despite the importance of cities in the overall process of economic and social transition, there has been limited research on the underlying forces driving urban change or on the impact on cities and urban communities of policy reforms such as structural adjustment and fiscal decentralization. A few studies have argued that policy responses to transition imperatives can best be integrated within an urban policy agenda (Buckley and Mini 2000; Simpson and Chapman 1999). The future of post-socialist cities is critical for more than two-thirds of the people in transition economies. That focus also offers an opportunity to influence policy dialogues on national poverty reduction, economic competitiveness and environmental improvement. Cities do matter.

The analysis in this chapter demonstrates the need to view future development in the post-socialist world through an urban lens. One reason is that problems with high unemployment, growing poverty, and ethnic tensions appear to be much more pronounced in urban areas, and particularly in larger industrial centres affected by massive closing of state enterprises. Secondly, changing intergovernmental relations have devolved major responsibilities in the area of economic development, education, health care and social assistance to local governments. Local governments in urban areas are now seen as crisis managers charged with myriad responsibilities, but without adequate resources to manage them. Finally, successful change at the urban level hinges on strengthening public sector institutions, as well as on securing popular support for costly restructuring.

Table 2.3. The trajectory of urban change in post-socialist cities

\multicolumn{3}{c}{**MAJOR DRIVERS OF URBAN CHANGE:** Transition to Democracy (Systemic Political Change), Markets (Systemic Economic Change), Decentralized System of Local Governance}
Domain	From 'socialist' city: Outcomes	To 'post-socialist' or to 'capitalist' city?: Outcomes
National urban system	Centrally planned population growth, investment, economic development and job creation; Stable increases in the level of urbanization, sustained concentration in large metropolitan areas – economies of scale in production	Market-based restructuring of the urban system, integration in the global economic hierarchy of cities, service-led growth, core vs. periphery; Selective growth of cities, population decline in most urban centres.
Urban economic change	Macroeconomic control through central planning, regulation, collective bargaining and control of markets through income and price policies	Deregulation of markets, *laissez faire* approaches to economic development, growing competition, decline of manufacturing, unemployment, opening up of sheltered markets
Urban social change	Stronger welfare state, universal subsidies, moderate (controlled) urban growth, relatively homogeneous social structure, egalitarian income distribution	Retrenchment of the welfare state, socially polarized societies, poverty, marginalization, declining and aging population, high economic dependency
Change in urban governance & provision of urban services	Dominated by central government decision-making, appointed officials; little autonomy; Relative uniformity, provided by the state, largely funded by central governments, universal access to education and healthcare, investment in water, and sewer networks, strong emphasis on public transport	Democratically elected, decentralized, fragmented structure, fiscally dependent on central transfers, entrepreneurial approaches to planning and city marketing; Privatisation and marketisation in the provision of urban services, unfunded social mandates, growing inequalities in provision of water, sewer and public transport
Urban spatial change: production	Dominated by manufacturing and responsive to the needs of large-scale state producers, located in urban areas according to planning norms;	Growing percentage of obsolete manufacturing facilities, new spaces for private small and medium production, suburbanization of offices and retail;
Urban spatial change: consumption	Relatively uniform, social housing provision allocated by state institutions, universally affordable, built according to planning norms, mix of tenure types	Increasingly polarized social areas and housing markets, gentrified housing enclaves vs. problematic housing estates, predominantly owner-occupied

References

Andrusz G, Harloe M, Szelenyi, I (eds) (1996) Cities after Socialism, Blackwell Publishers Inc., Oxford

Adair A, Berry J, McGreal S, Sykora A, Ghanbari Parsa A, Redding B (1999) Globalization of Real Estate Markets in Central Europe. European Planning Studies, 7: 295-305

Beaverstock J, Smith R, Taylor P (2000) Globalization and World Cities. Bulletin 5, GaWC Research Programme, Louborough, UK
http:/www.lboro.ac.k/gawc/publicat.html, accessed July 2005

Bertaud A, Renaud B (1997) Socialist Cities Without Land Markets. J of Urban Economics, 41: 137-151

Bourne L, Simmons J (2003) Conceptualization and Analysis of Urban Systems: A North American Perspective. In Champion A, Hugo G (eds), Beyond the Urban-Rural Dichotomy. Ashgate Publishing Limited. Aldershot

Buckley R, Mini F (2000) From Commissars to Mayors: Cities in the Transition Economies. The World Bank, Washington, D.C.

Buckley, R and S. Tsenkova (2001) Sofia City Development Strategy: Preliminary Assessment, pp. 77, World Bank/Sofia Municipality
http://www.worldbank.bg/data/strategy/english.html, accessed July 2005

Buckley R, Tsenkova S (2004) Housing Policy in Transition Cities: The Unfinished Agenda. In Tsenkova, S. and Z. Budic-Nedovic (eds) (2004), Winds of Societal Change: Remaking Post-communist Cities. University of Illinois Urbana Champaign: Russian and East European Centre, pp. 83-102

City Development Authority of Prague (2000) Strategic Plan for Prague. City Development Authority, Prague

City Development Department (2001) A Strategy for Vilnius. City Development Department, Vilnius

Davey, K. (1999) Local Government Reform in Central and Eastern Europe, paper presented at Public Administration and Development Conference, Oxford University, April 1999

European Academy of the Urban Environment (EAUE) (2003) Twelve Candidate Countries Overview Report on Sustainable Urban Management, Sustainable Urban Transport, Sustainable Urban Design and Sustainable Construction. EAUE Berlin

European Bank for Reconstruction and Development (2004) Transition Report 2004. EBRD, London

General Council for St. Petersburg (1998) Strategic Plan for St. Petersburg. General Council for the Strategic Plan, St Petersburg

Ghanbari-Parsa A, Moatazed-Keivani, R (1999). Development of real estate markets in Central Europe: the case of Prague, Warsaw, and Budapest. Environment and Planning A, 31:1383-1399

Greyer HS (2002) International Handbook of Urban Systems. Edgar Publishing, Northhampton MA

Golubchkov O (2004) Urban planning in Russia: Towards the market. European Planning Studies, vol. 12 (2): 229-247

Hamilton F, Dimitrowska-Andrews K, Pichler-Milanovic N (eds)(2005) Transformation of Cities in Central and Eastern Europe. Towards Globalization. United Nations University Press, Tokyo

Jaakson R (2000) Supra-national spatial planning of the Baltic Sea region and competing narratives for tourism. European Planning Studies, 8: 565-579

Jones C, Revenga A (2000) Making Transition Work for Everyone: Poverty and Inequality in Europe and Central Asia, World Bank, Washington D.C.

Maier K. (1994). Planning and Education in Planning in the Czech Republic. J of Planning Education and Research, 13: 263-69.

Marcuse P. (1996) Privatisation and its Discontents, in Andrusz, G.; M. Harloe and Szelenyi, I. (eds), Cities after Socialism, Blackwell Publishers Inc., Oxford

Marcuse P, van Kempen R (2000) Globalizing Cities: A New Spatial Order? Blackwell, Oxford

Milanovic B(1992) Income distribution in late socialism: Poland, Hungary, Czechoslovakia, Yugoslavia and Bulgaria compared. World Bank Research Project "Income Distribution during the Transition," working paper no. 1, World Bank, Washington D.C.

Mitric S. (1999) Price and Subsidy Policies For Urban Public Transport and Water Utilities in Transition Economies. Discussion Paper, Infrastructure Unit, Europe and Central Asia Department, World Bank, Washington, D.C.

Musil J. (1993). Changing Urban Systems in Post-socialist Societies in Central Europe: Analysis and Prediction. Urban Studies, 30: 899-905

Nedovic-Budic Z. (2001). Adjustment of Planning Practice to the New Eastern and Central European Context. J of the American Planning Association, 67:38-52

Pichler-Milanovich N. (1994). The Role of Housing Policy in the Transformation Process of Central-East European Cities. Urban Studies, 31: 1097-115

Riga City (1996) Riga City Official Plan. 1995 – 2005. Riga City Development Department, Riga

Simpson F, Chapman M (1999). Comparison of Urban Governance and Planning Policy: East Looking West. Cities, 16: 353-364

Smith D. (1989) Urban Inequality under Socialism: Case Studies from Eastern Europe and the Soviet Union, Cambridge University Press, Cambridge

Strong A, Reiner LT, Szyrmer J (1996). Transitions in Land and Housing: Bulgaria, the Czech Republic and Poland. St. Martin's Press, New York

Sykora L. (1994) Local urban restructuring as a mirror of globalization processes: Prague in the 1990s, Urban Studies, 31(7): 1149-1166

Szelenyi I. (1996) Cities under Socialism - and After, in Andrusz, G.; M. Harloe and Szelenyi, I. (eds), Cities after Socialism, Blackwell Publishers Inc., Oxford

Tosics I. (2005) City Development in Central and Eastern Europe Since 1990: the Impact of Internal Forces, in K. Dimitrowska-Andrews and F. Hamilton, (eds.), Globalization and Transformations in Eastern and Central European Cities. The United Nations University, Tokyo

Tsenkova S (2000) Housing in Transition and the Transition in Housing: Experiences of Central and Eastern Europe. Kapital Reclama, Sofia

Tsenkova S. (2001) Cities in Transition: Challenges for Urban Governance, Urban Policy Futures. Stockholm: Ministry of Urban Development and Environmental Protection, pp. 1-13

Tsenkova S. (2003) The Reform Path in Central and Eastern Europe: Policy Convergence? In Tsenkova, S. and Lowe, S. (eds.), Housing and Social Change in Central and Eastern Europe., pp.312-328, Ashgate Publishing Limited. Aldershot.

Tsenkova S (2005a) Urban Sustainability in Europe and North America. University of Calgary, Faculty of Environmental Design, Calgary

Tsenkova S (2005b) Trends and Progress in Housing Reforms in South East Europe. Council of Europe Development Bank, Paris

United Nations Centre for Human Settlements – HABITAT (UNCHS) (2000) Global Urban Indicators Database for Istanbul+5. Nairobi: Habitat

United Nations Centre for Human Settlements - HABITAT (UNCHS) (2001) Cities in a Globalising World. Global Report on Human Settlements 2001. Earthscan Publications Ltd., London

United Nations Department of Economic and Social Affairs (2002) World Economic and Social Survey 2002. Trends and Policies in the World Economy. United Nations, New York

United Nations, Economic Commission for Europe (UNECE) (1997) Human Settlement Developments in the Transition Economies of Central and Eastern Europe. Geneva, New York: UNECE

United Nations, Economic Commission for Europe (UNECE) (2003) Economic Survey of Europe 2003, No 1. New York, Geneva: UNECE

United Nations Economic Commission for Europe (UNECE) (2004) Trends in Europe and North America. Statistical Yearbook. United Nations, Geneva and New York

van Kempen R; Vermeulen M, Baan, A (eds) (2005) Urban Issues and Urban Policies in the New EU Countries. Ashgate Publishing Limited, Aldershot

Weclawowicz, G. (1992) The socio-spatial structure of the socialist cities in East-Central Europe: the case of Poland, Czechoslovakia and Hungary, in: F. Lando (ed.) Urban and Rural Geography. Venezia: Cafoscarina, pp. 129-140

World Bank (2000a) Making Transition Work for Everyone. Poverty and Inequality in Europe and Central Asia. Washington, DC: The World Bank

World Bank (2000b) Cities in Transition. The World Bank Urban and Local Government Strategy. The International Bank for Reconstruction and Development/ The World Bank, Washington, D.C.

World Bank (2002) Transition – the First Ten Years: Analysis and Lessons for Eastern Europe and the Former Soviet Union. Europe and Central Asia Regional Department, The World Bank. Washington, D.C.

World Bank (2003a) World Bank Development Indicators Database. The World Bank, Washington, D.C.

World Bank (2003b) Meeting the Environment Millennium Development Goal in Europe and Central Asia. June, The World Bank, Washington DC,
www.worldbank.org/eca/environment, accessed in September 2004

Yates M, Cheng W (2002) North American Markets: Predicting Metropolitan Growth, Research Report No2002-01. Centre for the Study of Commercial Activity, Ryerson University, Toronto

3 Institutional and spatial change

Tuna Taşan-Kok

Introduction

After more than a decade of neo-liberal transition in economy, politics, and society, post-socialist cities are becoming important nodes of investment for international capital. In response to the forces of globalization that are taking precedence in these urban economies, their institutional and political structures have been decentralized and deregulated to capture increasingly mobile capital. Beset by these highly dynamic processes and changes, urban governments[1] and planning institutions have had to redefine their responsibilities. The resulting political and economic contingencies at both the local and national levels have influenced the degree to which post-socialist cities join global economic processes.

The realignments in their institutional structures have had pronounced spatial consequences in post-socialist cities. By the mid-1990s, those consequences had become more visible in their urban landscapes. The new patterns had been preceded by changes in urban governance, planning, and financial regimes as related to property markets. Cities had turned to private sector investment in new urban development projects to augment funds for much-needed improvement of their social, economic, and physical conditions. Those urban development projects have been driven by the increased presence of financial companies and their employees and customers, who require such supporting services as luxurious housing, shopping malls, and international entertainment centres. Spatial redevelopment also was stimulated by new financial regulations that eased the entry of foreign investment in national and urban economies. The international investors filled the capital gap in urban investment where public or private domestic capital fell short.

This chapter explores how neo-liberal institutional changes affected the spatial transformations in post-socialist cities, by focusing on urban government and planning institutions. How did the urban development actors in post-socialist cities, and especially in urban governments, reinvent themselves within an entrepreneurial urban economy? To what extent has there been a shift from 'managerial government' to 'participatory governance?' How have governing and urban planning institutions reflected the neo-liberal market conditions?

Offering empirical evidence from Budapest and Warsaw, this chapter illustrates how urban governments became one of the many players in urban development, and how their characteristics inherited from the socialist era challenged participa-

---

[1] "Urban government" is used here as the general term for urban administrations. Throughout the chapter, the higher tier of urban government (at the metropolitan/city level) is referred to as the "municipality," and the lower tier as the "district."

tory processes.[2] We argue that the new spatial elements that emerge in the urban landscapes of post-socialist cities, such as shopping malls, hypermarkets, entertainment centres, office plazas, and skyscrapers, though similar to those in the advanced capitalist countries, tend to appear through different institutional processes and dynamics. This thesis is explored from two perspectives:

1. Conceptually, urban government systems were re-oriented from a managerial to a participatory model of urban politics and from a passive to an entrepreneurial attitude-one that promotes competitive capitalism, accumulation and speculative mobilization of resources (Hubbard and Hall 1998). It is presumed that urban governments have become more innovative and aggressive in establishing coalitions and public-private partnerships (PPP) with other actors in urban development. We propose that *the entrepreneurialism in urban governments of post-socialist cities is influenced by characteristics inherited from the previous system of urban government.*
2. While struggling to carry out the institutional transformation, urban governments of post-socialist cities have faced increasing demand from international property companies to invest in the property markets and develop projects, and many other private actors also have become involved, while regulatory restructuring of the planning regime was still incomplete. The resulting pressures have led urban governments to adopt 'flexible' strategies and weak enforcement of planning regulations. It might be argued that *urban planning institutions have become opportunity-led mechanisms of the neo-liberal transformation.*

The material for this chapter was collected during dissertation research from 2001 to 2004.[3] Semi-structured interviews were conducted with key informants in Budapest and Warsaw to reveal the institutional dynamics and transformations behind urban spatial change. Analysis of the interviews brought to light the opportunities and restrictions created by the neo-liberal transformation processes. The field survey was conducted at two levels: at the macro level, general observations and literature search; at the micro level, interviews with selected actors engaged in project development, property investment, urban development or government. The field survey, which focused on the property markets of those two cities, elicited information on how the actors reacted to contingencies and on how their reactions affected urban development in general and commercial property development in particular.

The case studies of commercial developments in Budapest and Warsaw demon-

---

[2] Until the beginning of 2000s Warsaw had a complex urban government structure. There were eleven boroughs (GMINAs, which were clusters of districts), including the Warsaw Central Borough, and districts that existed only within the central borough (Warsaw Central Borough was divided into seven individual districts). With the Act of 2002 boroughs have been terminated. The urban government structure is now divided into 18 districts under the single authority of the Warsaw Municipality. In Hungary urban governments have a two-tiered system, consisting of the municipality at the metropolitan level and twenty-three districts. There are no hierarchical relations between the two tiers.

[3] See Taşan-Kok, T., (2004), Budapest, Istanbul, and Warsaw: Institutional and spatial change, Eburon, Delft

strate how planning became opportunity-led, and how divergent planning traditions have created conventional, corrective, or innovative practices within the organizations for spatial control. The opportunities and restrictions created by the planning legacies can be seen in urban development in the strong role of private actors and the flexibility and weakness of the planning system. With private property investors and developers mostly defining the path of urban development, the urban governments' role has been reduced to encouragement and permissiveness in the absence of adequate planning strategies.

3.1 Institutional and spatial change in Budapest and Warsaw

The institutionalist approach is an effective instrument for analyzing spatial transformations in post-socialist cities. Institutions set the rules that define the choices individuals can make (North 1990). Institutional structures pertain to organizations at all levels from national to individual, and apply to both formal organizations and informal conventions, habits, and routines (Amin and Thrift 1994). Inherited institutional structures may obstruct efforts to adapt to new circumstances (Eraydın 1999). Although the countries subscribing to centrally planned state-socialism followed similar institutional paths, those were implemented somewhat differently. Correspondingly, both similarities and differences have now affected the transition from socialist to market principles. Through local contingencies and characteristics, the inherited structures have shaped the choices available to individuals and organizations and thus how the new rules of urban development in post-socialist cities have been framed.

In the context of hyperactivity of capital, spatial developments are highly linked to property market dynamics. The increased international and domestic accumulation of capital in property investment together with institutional reforms of the investment process, have brought new groups of actors into urban development. The administrative decision-makers at urban government and state levels and the property investors and developers are the two main groups. The relationships among them are defined by administrative, financial, and spatial control regulations (Fig. 3.1.). Besides those two groups of actors, others who facilitate investment and development are property finance organizations, intermediaries (e.g. dealmakers, real estate agents, and consultants), landowners, end users, property-related services and consultants, architects, and building firms.

In an opportunity-led environment, the realization of projects depends greatly on the quality of the institutional relations. Major complexities in the establishment, functioning and effectiveness of such relations are generated by both formal institutional arrangements (e.g. laws, decrees, and regulations) and the informal relationships defined by political and economic interests, which influence the extent of involvement of individuals and organizations in the property market (Fig.

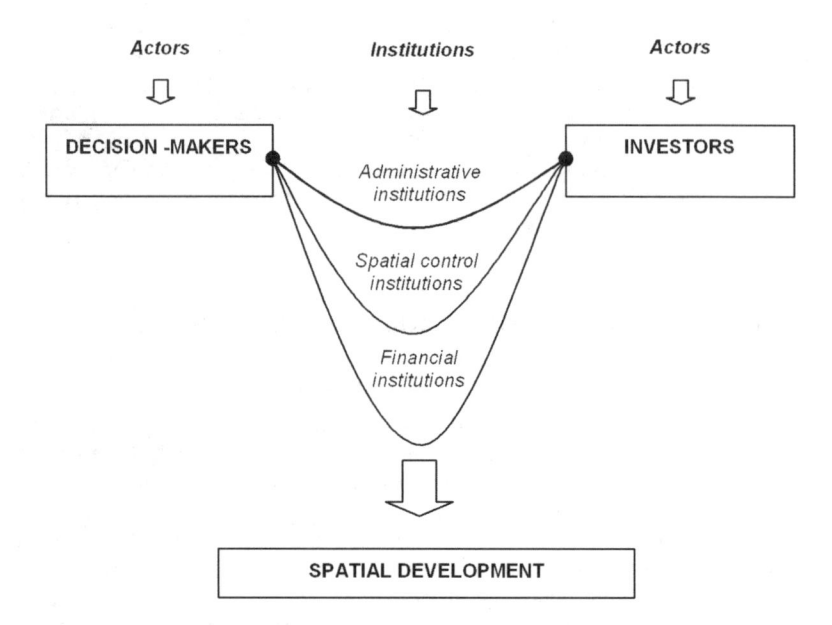

Fig. 3.1. Institutions, actors, and spatial development

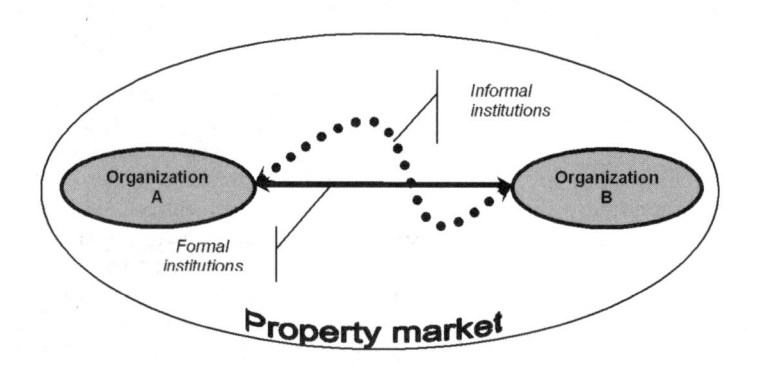

Fig. 3.2. Organizations, institutions, and property market

3.2.). Despite such complexities, in the 1990s the expectations of high speculative gains attracted many investors to the post-socialist property markets. Those markets started to resemble the ones in advanced capitalist countries in their competitiveness and the prospects for maximum return on investment capital concentrated in a particular project at a particular location (Ball et al. 1998). The post-socialist cities offered attractive possibilities for new investments with low risk and high liquidity. Before the 1990s, investments there would have had low liquidity and been considered less important than other of debt and equity commitments (Fainstein 1994). It was the shift in the property investment environment in the 1990s that accelerated the development of large-scale commercial projects in cities undergoing the post-socialist transformation.

Fig. 3.3. Distribution of commercial complexes in Budapest (2002)

In Budapest and Warsaw, as in other post-socialist cities, the decentralized structure of urban government and the competitive capitalist economic environment facilitated capital accumulation through investment in property. Both municipalities attempted to create an attractive investment environment and a new international image appropriate for prestigious projects. The property markets of Budapest and Warsaw since the early 1990s can be characterized as having these common trends:

- International capital has been eager to gain access to local property markets, and relatively easy access has brought in substantial investments in urban areas;

- The number of new non-governmental and non-local players in urban property markets has been rising;
- Imitation of "western" styles and speculation in urban property development has been increasing.

The demand for new kinds of land uses, particularly commercial, has grown. The spatial distribution of large-scale commercial complexes in the urban landscapes of Budapest and Warsaw is depicted in Fig. 3.3. and 3.4.

Fig. 3.4. Distribution of commercial complexes in Warsaw (2002)

3.2 Urban governments as entrepreneurs

Governance refers to the self-organizing of inter-organizational relations (Jessop 1997), involving quantitative and qualitative shifts in the relationships between organizations. The transformation from government to governance in post-socialist cities has been abrupt. While in urban policy they began to follow a direction similar to that of advanced capitalist countries, these cities did not go through a similar development to coordinate sophisticated organizational systems. Their shift from a managerial to a participatory system of government was based simply on financial, rather than organizational arrangements. Such a shift was made possible by the rapid introduction, but mostly ineffective implementation, of new regulations. The cities' diminished dependence on the state , greater autonomy for economic and spatial growth policies, and yet limited resources drove them to entrepreneurial pursuits. The property-based channelling of economic growth has been the most obvious manifestation of that new entrepreneurialism (Taşan-Kok 2005). The urban governments drew on their previous experiences with economic initiatives as they embarked on learning about entrepreneurial strategies and becoming entrepreneurs (Painter 1998).

In post-socialist cities, the urban government, financing, and planning systems resemble those in advanced capitalist cities. Moreover, despite difference in the development models and institutional settings, even the new spatial elements on the peripheries of post-socialist cities are similar to, perhaps even copies of those in advanced capitalist countries. In further emulation, urban governments have become more innovative and aggressive in establishing links with other private and public organizations along the lines of PPPs - probably in order to sustain their capital accumulation and political strength. Nonetheless, despite those evident similarities, the institutional and organizational relationships inherited from socialism, and the local contingencies: institutional arrangements, traditions, values, and power relations have shaped the shift toward the participatory governance systems and entrepreneurialism in post-socialist cities. In the institutional transformations, similar patterns, motivations, and dynamics have been realized through different implementation mechanisms.

In post-socialist cities the rising number of organizations and the tendency towards networking among them are challenging the state's entrenched, institutional regulatory culture. In these countries, the increase in private companies is most visible. The number of non-governmental organizations, pressure groups, and social movements also has been rising, but with only limited roles in decisions about urban policy, planning, development and management. Networking is based primarily on the country's traditions and cultural habits, which are mostly informal and unsophisticated, and works mainly with two organizations on either the demand or the supply side: the urban government (municipal or district level) and the developer. The most common form of these relationships is a project-based PPP (Taşan-Kok 2004; ING Real Estate-Warsaw 2002; Skanska-Warsaw 2001; Buzcek 1997). Alongside the new actors, the nation-state still has an important role in the economic and political transition.

Previous research has highlighted the factors that affect entrepreneurialism in post-socialist cities, by constructing a profile of government regulation (Taşan-Kok 2004). Even though entrepreneurialism is setting the political agendas of the urban governments, its efforts would not have been successful without certain facilitating factors. The following factors are identified:

- An open networking capacity, which eases development of any kind of extraordinary (innovative) urban project
- Urban governments' independence in decision-making
- Entrepreneurial actors with innovative ideas on urban development, both at national and urban levels.

If hindering factors are more dominant, the entrepreneuralization trend is distorted, particularly by the following factors:

- The presence of hierarchy and bureaucracy, which slow down urban development, especially under the dynamic conditions of the property market;
- Political instability, which affects decision-making at both national and urban levels;
- The intervention of the state organizations in urban development, which tends to relegate urban governments to simply administering the development.

1. Networking capacity
2. Independence
3. Local entrepreneurial actors
4. Hierarchy and bureaucracy
5. Political instability
6. Central government intervention

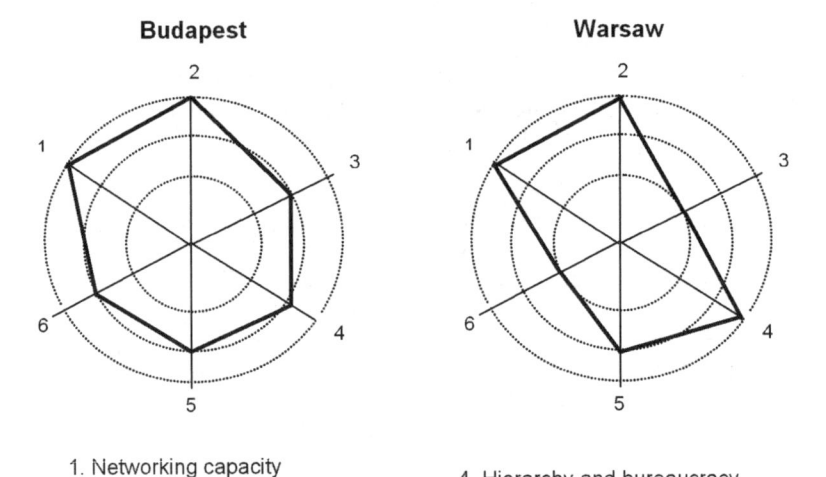

Fig. 3.5. Entrepreneurial capacity of municipal government systems in Budapest and Warsaw

The entrepreneurial capacity in Budapest and in Warsaw is compared in the following diagrams (Fig. 3.5.) according to the six factors mentioned above. The high score on each axis (4) indicates the highest capacity. Lines in the upper half of the circle represent facilitating factors; those in the lower half of the circle represent hindering factors. Thus, the fuller the coverage in the upper half of the circle (1 to 3), the more capacity for entrepreneurialism the urban government system shows; the fuller the coverage in the lower half of the circle (4 to 6), the more obstacles for entrepreneurialism the urban governments have.

According to those six factors, Budapest has a higher entrepreneurial capacity than Warsaw. Perhaps the relative eagerness of the urban governments to welcome foreign investment and international capital plays an important role. To examine the experiences of the urban governments of Budapest and Warsaw, the following questions arise: Are urban governments becoming entrepreneurial actors in post-socialist cities? If so, how do they create coalitions for new projects and initiatives? Is the state completely withdrawn from urban development? And how do the inherited political circumstances influence the establishment of the new governance systems? These questions lead to elaboration of the following aspects: the emergence and functioning of urban coalitions in these cities as an indication of entrepreneurship and multi-actor urban governance; state involvement contrary to the urban governments' expectation of independence; and local political characteristics that influence the execution of governance policies.

One of the distinctive characteristics of the new urban governance is a more visible role for urban coalitions, or PPPs, in urban development (McNeill and While 2001). PPP arrangements arise primarily because public funds are inadequate to cover investment needs, but also with the aim of improving the quality and efficiency of public services. In advanced capitalist cities, private sector involvement in PPP schemes provides additional capital, alternative management and implementation skills, value added services to the consumer and the public at large, and optimal use of resources that fit the identified needs (EU Commission 2003). In post-socialist cities these functions are allocated differently. Coalition formation runs into difficulties as local contingencies affect the institutional transformation. Moreover, communication among the layers of government does not run smoothly. This means that a limited number of governmental and non-governmental organizations are involved in the coalitions. Although the coalitions are expected to be formed through participatory processes, in actuality they merely focus on those actors that can provide financial resources to urban governments. Ultimately, the negotiating power that this situation gives the private parties allows them to define the location, function, and conditions of projects.

Other externalities also influence coalition formation in these two cities. Two examples are: 1) the state's intervention in urban development, and 2) inept coordination among urban government and state organizations. The political shifts when the political party taking power has different political interests from the party replaced also affect the functioning of urban governance systems and the formation of urban coalitions. In Warsaw some difficulties were encountered in the formation of coalitions and in urban governments taking a minor role in partnerships (Buzcek 1993). Although some urban governments were active in initiating projects, generally they were passive and thus constrained development. They usually provided the land in exchange for 20% share of ownership. Otherwise they simply sold the land and then were lenient in issuing building permissions (Skanska-Warsaw 2001; ING Real Estate-Warsaw 2002). Moreover, projects encountered administrative delays and protracted financial arrangements for to PPPs because the reforms dividing the Warsaw Municipality into districts had not been finalized. Another obstacle was the delay in providing infrastructure due to weak institutional connections between the organizations involved and unsynchronized public works (Taşan-Kok 2004).

Similar experiences in Budapest resulted from government fragmentation: each district has its own investment and development agenda, and the Budapest Municipality has only a weak management role. Districts, though autonomous, still depend on state subsidies slightly more than the Budapest Municipality. They usually have difficulty raising money unless they are in advantageous central locations. Each district tries to attract investors to its area, since they all depend financially on large-scale commercial property developments. Often the peripheral districts try to attract property investors by offering better tax conditions than in the districts with central locations. As a result, scattered large-scale commercial projects have mushroomed at peripheral locations. The districts' independent attitudes and eagerness to attract projects tends to create conflicts with the Budapest Municipality. PPPs are less popular in Budapest than in Warsaw. However, Warsaw and Budapest are similar in the passivity of their districts towards forming coalitions (Duna Plaza 2001; ECE-Budapest 2001; ECE 2002; Ecorys 2001; Mammut 2001).

State organizations are evidently involved, either actively or passively in urban development in post-socialist cities. The state's power to influence urban development is determined by several conditions: 1) state land ownership as a power base; 2) a key state role in entrepreneurial initiatives; 3) the state's longstanding tradition of ruling and exerting authority; 4) involvement of state politicians exerting political pressure in urban development; 5) the state's power to issue regulations; and 6) the leverage balanced against the urban governments.

However, state organizations' role is limited and fragmented, since they intervene only in prestigious or large-scale projects. They are not involved in the policies and decisions that shape the city structure and control urban development. Nonetheless, the spatial consequences of their project-led attitude are evident in both Budapest and Warsaw.

The influence of the Hungarian state on urban development was suppressed by the neo-liberal policies of the early 1990s. From being the sole investor during the socialist period, the state has moved to the more entrepreneurial functions of negotiation, debate, and competition. One area in which the state took the initiative was the effort to reinforce the national and international political importance of Budapest by enhancing the city's image. Although the implementation of those initiatives was fraught with political power struggles between Budapest Municipality and the state organizations, many projects have been completed, as among them the Millennium City Centre (district IX-Pest side), Millenáris Park (district II-Buda side), and Infopark (district XI-Buda side).

In Warsaw, since the beginning of the 1990s, state organizations have taken a passive stance toward urban development. Their inflexible decision-making processes, slow bureaucratic procedures and lack of entrepreneurialism have presented obstacles, as illustrated in the redevelopment of the area around the Warsaw Central Railway Station. The tender for the redevelopment of the station area has not yet been finalized, even though the station was opened in 1999. The station marks the centre of the city, together with the Palace of Culture (Pałac Kultury) and Złote Tarasy, a large commercial project. However, coordination among the Warsaw Municipality and Polish State Railways has been lacking. Moreover, approval of the purchase of the property or the transfer of ownership rights has involved several different agencies: the Treasury Ministry, the Transport Ministry, and later the Ministry of Infrastructure. Those impediments have coincided with a partial planning approach and a lack of metropolitan planning control. Most significantly, state organizations have neither the flexibility nor the knowledge to act as a partner with private parties and international developers.

The last point we intend to underline is the power of local contingencies, namely political conflicts and informalities, to affect entrepreneurialization urban governments' entrepreneurial capacities. When the different political interests represented in the state and the urban governments are in conflict, the resulting general disagreement means malfunctioning urban services and the misuse of political advantages. In both Budapest and Warsaw, the division of responsibilities among different levels of urban governments is not transparent, and conflicts over development are common (Keresztély 2002). Moreover, in Budapest, no hierarchy has been established between the two tiers of urban government (the municipality and districts). Projects are often cancelled, delayed, or changed. Large-scale projects are approved by the urban governments only unwillingly, for they have to provide the infrastructure. The level of these conflicts varies between the two cities, as the responsibilities and financial relationships between the municipalities and districts are defined differently.

In Hungary, the common political party orientation of urban governments and the state from 1994-1998 and also since 2002 facilitated large-scale urban investment schemes. The conservative party brought into office in 1998 cancelled many of the planned projects and changed the nature of strategic investments. For example, the Hungarian National Theatre, which was supposed to be located downtown, was shifted to the southern part of Pest at the Millennium City Centre because of a conflict between the Budapest Municipality and the state authorities (Budapest Sun 1998). Whenever such conflicts occurred, the state organizations turned to the districts for a quick solution. Using a location where it owned the land, it acted in the old 'state-socialist manner', investing without consulting other organizations. Lacking cooperation among districts, Budapest Municipality and the state, many other projects were delayed or changed.[4]

---

[4] This was the case with the WestEnd City Center project, which was originally supposed to be developed jointly by the French Telecom Company and MÁV (Hungarian Railways). That joint venture collapsed, and the project was eventually bought out by private investors.

Polish state organizations, too, are neither flexible, open, nor liberal enough to carry out large-scale urban projects of strategic importance for the internationalization of cities. In Warsaw, corruption and informalities are ingrained in the state organizations, which are less entrepreneurial and innovative in urban areas than are their Hungarian counterparts. The most striking example of their shortcomings is the delayed expansion of Okęcie Airport, due to the informal arrangements, fraud, and inter-organizational problems that intruded on the tender process. Upgrading the old terminal and building a new one would increase the airport's capacity to about 14.3 million passengers a year (Eurobuild 2002). The plans also included the expansion of the cargo terminal and construction of new access roads, a rail line, a hotel, office buildings, and a multi-level car-parking structure. The first stage of the tender was completed by September 2001; however, the rest of the project is still pending.

3.3 Opportunity-led planning

The concept of opportunity-led planning describes the shift in planning from controlling urban development to enabling piecemeal development that – notably - benefits urban governments financially. The result has been the spatial fragmentation and disorder that ensued in post-socialist cities from the early 1990s. The planning agencies there now serve as corrective rather than innovative forces. Under corrective planning, plans are adapted to demands, rather than guiding and overseeing urban development through comprehensive planning strategies established by public organizations (Buzcek 1997; Soóki-Tóth 2000). Private actors became increasingly powerful in urban development while the regulatory and institutional restructuring of planning was still incomplete. Thus, urban governments were forced to adopt 'flexible' strategies with very few restrictions on size, function or location, or the choice of urban development projects. Weak enforcement of planning regulations and manipulation of planning by market demands prevailed. Many post-socialist cities, in order to meet the expectations of the new actors in property markets, implicitly and sometimes explicitly eased the administrative plan approval and implementation procedures. That flexibility was used to revise existing plans so as to allow large commercial property projects that were important in creating of the new international image, or for financial reasons. Projects were usually approved whether or not they were in harmony with the existing spatial pattern (Soóki-Tóth 2000; Buczek 2001). In many cases, planning was reduced to a matter of negotiation between the property owners, the developers and the urban government actors. Indeed, many large-scale projects that have noticeably changed the urban landscape of post-socialist cities were the initiatives of private developers.

In post-socialist cities, government policy has trouble balancing public and private interests. Early in the transformation period, international and sometimes domestic property investors sought urban development opportunities (Sykora 1998; Buczek 2001). Even from the early 1980s, international (mainly German, Austrian, Dutch, and French) investors, developers, and retailers found relatively easy access to urban land in Hungary and Poland. For them, planning has been simply a procedural hurdle of obtaining building permits, which until recently was a formality with urban governments enthused about having large-scale projects within their boundaries. Both parties foresaw benefits.

Previous research has profiled of the planning regimes in Budapest and Warsaw (Taşan-Kok 2004). A package of hindering factors creates conditions for fragmented spatial development, e.g., large-scale projects spread out across the city in an uncoordinated way, with private property development as the main driving force. The three hindering factors are:

- Incomplete planning deregulation, which is open to interferences and informalities
- Unclear authority for plan approval, due to organizational and institutional conflicts
- Informalities, corruption, and bureaucracy, which foster undesired development.

Facilitating factors support controlled development based on concrete and formal cooperation between the public and private actors. The three facilitating factors are:

- Concrete and clear planning strategy, which allows a coordinated application of planning regulations
- Flexibility to adapt to new situations, negotiate, make quick decisions, and evaluate the consequences of the decisions in coordination with related actors
- An active and autonomous role for planning organizations.

The following diagram compares the profiles of the planning systems in Budapest and in Warsaw (Fig. 3.6.). The upper half of the circle (1 to 3) represents the facilitating factors listed above; the lower half of the circle (4 to 6) represents the hindering factors. Thus, the fuller the upper circle, the less likely it is for the planning system to lead to fragmentation; the fuller the lower circle, the more difficult it is for the planning system to avoid fragmentation.

Though the differences between the cities are not great, in Warsaw the hindering and facilitating factors seem more balanced. This means that the city has a moderately opportunity-led planning regime. Budapest Municipality, on the other hand, lacks a concrete urban strategy and has a high degree of flexibility in decision-making, marking an entrepreneurial attitude on the part of the urban government.

In both Hungary and Poland, opportunity-led planning arises for two reasons. First of all, public administration is completely decentralized, since the actions of the districts are not coordinated by the municipality. Secondly, metropolitan planning strategy is often weakly formulated or non-existent, and therefore simply cannot control development. The unclear planning strategy and the lack of coordination between plans at various scales create opportunities for private developers to steer the development to their advantage. The consequences of the opportunity-led planning regime can be illustrated by the development of two commercial axes extending from central business districts (CBD): Váci út in Budapest and Aleja Janna Pawła II in Warsaw. In both cases, large-scale projects were either initiated or led by private initiatives and partial plans played a major role. In other words, both commercial corridors were shaped primarily by individual initiatives and by fragmented decisions taken by districts on the basis of partial land-use plans.

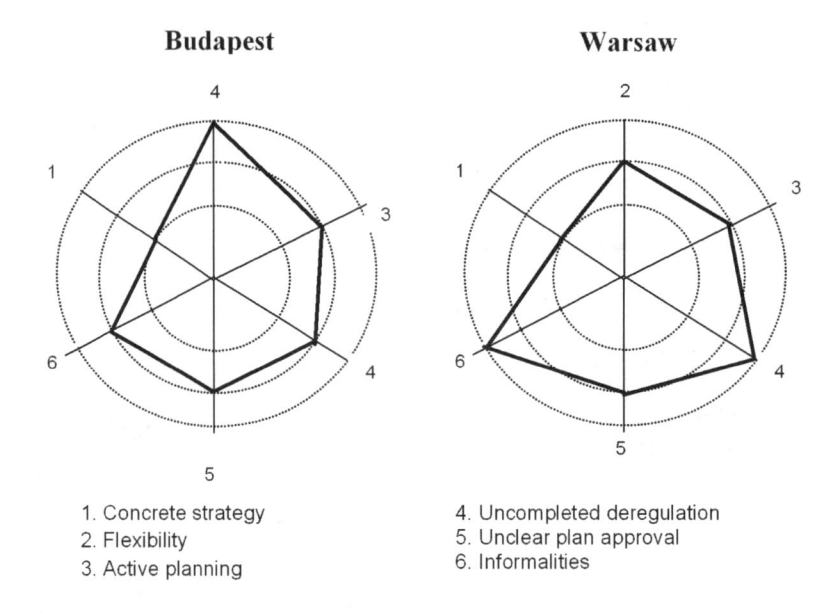

1. Concrete strategy
2. Flexibility
3. Active planning
4. Uncompleted deregulation
5. Unclear plan approval
6. Informalities

Fig. 3.6. Profiles of changing planning regimes in Budapest and Warsaw

Váci út is located on the Pest side of the city, starting from the Nyugati Railway Station and running parallel to the Danube River to Árpád híd (*Árpád bridge*). The axis, which runs through districts IV, XIII and VI, was a late nineteenth-century industrial zone developed by manufacturing activities. In several cases, there had now been a direct conversion from industrial use to office and retail, and later on to residential uses. For instance, Duna Plaza, which was the first shopping centre located on Váci út, replaced a boiler works owned by the company that developed the mall (Dingsdale 1999). Another important development was the WestEnd City Centre project. This large-scale shopping, entertainment, office and hotel complex has not only upgraded the area around Nyugati Railway Station, but has also made Váci út even more attractive to developers. International capital has now turned the zone between WestEnd City Centre and Duna Plaza into the new CBD extension, with no effort needed by Budapest Municipality. Municipalities evaluated the projects, gave their view, and left all the practicalities to the district governments. Since the decisions were made project-by-project, new developments along the axis vary significantly in their function, size, and building procedures. Further redevelopment is occurring not only along Váci út, but also along parallel streets, mostly as up-scale residential projects, for example in Teve utca in the early 2000s.

Warsaw's urban landscape was changed dramatically from the mid-1980s by an investment boom. However, at the time, local plans were too restrictive for the new commercial projects. Although some of the new developments adhered to the logic of the existing controls many others pressed for a new approach. The decentralization of the urban governments coincided with this demand for more flexibility. Like Budapest, Warsaw has taken an opportunity-led approach to development. As in Budapest, districts were closely involved in property development, and at the metropolitan level, Warsaw Municipality, lost its power to control urban development.

Aleja Jana Pawła II is one of the main axes in Warsaw, crossing Aleja Jerozolimskie and connecting two important roundabouts. The development along Aleja Jerozolimskie to the west is impressive, with high-rise office buildings, hypermarkets and other large-scale retail facilities having sprung up. Centrally located Aleja Jana Pawła II became the main magnet for international investors within the CBD. The city's first and only five-star Marriott Hotel was the first high-rise to be built across from the Palace of Culture, followed by a Holiday Inn in the vicinity.

Since the intention of the Warsaw Central Borough has been to develop CBD functions in this area, they paid special attention to strategic investors. The Swedish firm Skanska was the leading developer in the joint-venture project with Wola District (one of the districts within the body of the Central Borough at the time) to develop five towers along the axis. Other prestigious high-rise buildings, mostly built by international capital, have further shaped the commercial corridor. Other large office buildings that have opened along the avenue include Kaskada, the Ilmet Complex, and Les Tours BRC. Although all these projects were undertaken in accordance with the zoning plans approved by the boroughs, the administration was particularly generous in defining their compatibility: By law, building plans (detailed plans for individual projects) have to be compatible with zoning plans. However, the administration insisted only on the compatibility of a planned project with the local urban development plan, which was a framework plan that displayed the general land-uses in larger areas. Compatibility, which can be a subjective criterion was a prerequisite; the plan could be revised if the project went beyond the limits of the local urban development plan. However, to change the plan was the privilege of the Borough Council and was subject to its discretionary decision-making. Until 2000, many large-scale developments in Warsaw took shape under such procedures. Since then, new regulations have been adopted to provide a stricter and controlled framework for planning procedures.

Conclusion

This chapter examined the impact of the transitional characteristics of urban governments and planning institutions on the formation of post-socialist urban landscapes. We pointed out how the institutional processes and dynamics behind the spatial transformations are affected by local contingencies, so that neo-liberal institutional changes proceed in ways specific to the contexts of post-socialist cities. We hypothesized that the entrepreneurialism of urban governments and the formation of multi-layered participatory governance systems in post-socialist cities has been influenced not only by characteristics inherited from the previous system based on centralized management, but also by the uncertainties of the transitional period. Certain patterns were traced: 1) how urban coalitions in post-socialist cities were driven by private investments; lacked effective participation by citizens, NGOs and other interest groups; and included passive urban governments; 2) how the role of state organizations in urban development shifted though did not completely diminish in post-socialist cities; 3) how local political conflicts, competition, and informalities shaped the entrepreneurial approaches of urban governments. We conclude that the shift from top-down to bottom-up approaches was too rapid, so that the transformation of institutional structures to develop participatory, bottom-up, and entrepreneurial approaches was incomplete, especially at the beginning of the transitional period. Now, slowly but surely institutional and legislative transformations are being completed and bottom-up approaches also are slowly developing, adapted to local conditions. It has been a learning process not only for the urban governments, but also for the citizens of the post-socialist cities (Kovács 2000; Tosics 2005; Buczek 2001, Węcławowicz 2002).

Our second point was that the financial problems urban governments faced under the post-socialist reforms, and the increasing pressure from international property companies to invest in these property markets, motivated urban governments to adopt 'flexible' planning implementation strategies. That means that urban planning institutions have become opportunity-led mechanisms. The eagerness of governments in post-socialist cities to attract international capital and the increased demand from international investors for urban properties suitable for commercial development, coincided with the neo-liberal institutional change that began in the early 1990s. That transformation of urban government and planning institutions, however, differs from mainstream Western European practices.

Through analysis of large-scale commercial projects in Budapest and Warsaw, the chapter offers several generalizations about the nature of urban government, planning, and property market institutions in post-socialist cities (Table 3.1.).

Based on the empirical research from Budapest and Warsaw, the following five points highlight specific characteristics of the institutions and organizations involved in urban governance and development:

1. Urban coalitions function project-by-project, focusing on financial instruments and stimulating piecemeal spatial development.
2. Despite the independence of urban governments, the state still intervenes in urban development in several ways, especially when large-scale developments

are pursued. Its intervention may either facilitate or hinder the development, depending on the development's type, objectives, and structural background.
3. The informalities, political instability, and conflicts within the urban administration disrupt the continuity of the development process and result in fragmented spatial development.
4. In an opportunity-led planning context, private property investors act spontaneously, embarking on large-scale projects without seeking cooperation from other actors in urban development. In cities where the deregulation of the planning regime is incomplete and implementation is flexible, crucial decisions on urban development are made under pressure from the private-sector actors. As a result, the urban patterns are shaped by the decisions of property developers and investors.
5. With flexibilities in the planning practice, private interests can put pressure on urban governments and override public interests. Such uncontrolled development, whether small or large in scale, may have unintended spatial consequences and patterns.

Beyond these general characteristics, particular circumstances were found in each city that affected the course of urban government reform and differentiated the entrepreneurialism of the urban governments. The experiences of Budapest and Warsaw in urban governance reform proved to be different, because of the local contingencies affecting the entrepreneurial transformation in each city.

Table 3.1. Analysis of post-socialist urban government, planning and property market institutions

Urban governance	Planning	Property markets
Municipal governments as passive partners in urban coalitions (eager for projects but not taking initiatives or having a minor role)	Weak power of planning organizations and vague implementation processes due to incomplete regulatory reform	New and temporary actors in the market
Active role of central government organizations in city marketing of large-scale projects (that enhance the city's image – nationally and internationally)	Shift to strategic and flexible planning approach only to define the general guidelines for development, without efficient and effective instruments	Investment agendas of major private (mainly international) developers define urban developments and general urban strategies
Informalities and inherited political conflicts between central and municipal organizations hinder development	Development by partial (zoning) plans, without binding power at the metropolitan planning level	Old (local) actors adjust their attitudes and development approaches towards the international market conditions

Governance requires the self-involvement of a wide range of organizations (actors) in the production of policy outcomes. As Rhodes (1997) states, governance displays interdependence between organizations, continuing interactions between network members, game-like interactions, and a significant degree of autonomy from the state. From this perspective, we can observe that despite the increase in the number of non-governmental organizations in post-socialist cities, their interaction with governmental organizations is rare and not formally organized. Therefore, their actions are uncoordinated, in many cases opportunity-led, and sometimes ineffective.

The case studies showed that one of the most significant outcomes of the neoliberal transformation is the increasing financial autonomy of urban governments; to a certain extent, entrepreneurialism is also a significant outcome. The associated outcome is that more public and private stakeholders are involved in the urban development process, and that urban governments are impelled to reinvent their role as one of the stakeholders in urban development. The record of advanced capitalist countries suggests that state and private organizations, NGOs, interest groups, and citizens first define themselves as stakeholders and subsequently participate in decision-making. However, divergent political interests and conflicts can disrupt communication and thwart coalition formation. In post-socialist cities, the number of stakeholders in urban development has increased considerably, and the actors have different roles than they did in the past. Nonetheless, their participation in governance is still very limited. In fact, the case studies demonstrated that participation in governance is often limited to two main actors: urban governments and property investors. It is worth noting that as the number of participants rises, the chance of project success diminishes.

The experience of post-socialist cities in urban planning is also interesting and revealing of the formative and transitional nature of their planning institutions and regimes. As the property market became the major source of income for urban governments and they met increasing pressure by private-sector investors, the planning regulations were relaxed and the planning regime became an ad-hoc, opportunity-led, corrective mechanism. The power to coordinate development in cities was eroded through incomplete planning regulations and a predominance of informal decision-making.

The experiences of both Budapest and Warsaw show that the government lost most of its control over urban development, and planning was considered an old habit of the communist regime. While opportunity-led development appeals as a way for urban governments to sustain the inflow and accumulation of capital, a more centralized model of planning is needed if government is to play a strategic role in urban development.

In short, the weakening of public control over urban spatial development is closely related to the increasing role of the private sector. When planning regulations had to facilitate large-scale commercial property development and respond quickly to the investors' initiatives, urban administrations responded by allowing development to go ahead and making the necessary corrections in urban plans afterwards. Planning became a corrective mechanism rather than a guideline for development; opportunity-led planning enabled private developers to act freely within only the limitations of the property market. These behaviors produced urban spatial patterns like commercial axes and zones. The long-term consequences of these projects were ignored due to their scale, location, and socio-economic characteristics.

The case studies revealed that underlying this planning flexibility is a lack of metropolitan planning strategies and implementation power. The opportunistic planning gave private investors the chance to realize their potential and pursue their goals, but the process neglected the public interest.

References

Amin A, Thrift N (1994) Globalization, institutions, and regional development in Europe. Oxford University Press, Oxford

Ball M, Lizieri M, Macgregor BD (1998) The economics of commercial property markets. Routledge, London

Buczek G (1993) Some aspects of public and private sector cooperation, communal land development and investing in property: Case study of Commune Wola – district of Warsaw. (Unpublished expert report, Warsaw)

Buczek G (1997) The Atrium Business Centre: The example of the good practice. Press release, Atrium Business Centre

Buczek G (2001) Urban strategy and governance: The strategic and physical planning of Warsaw. World Bank- Urban and City Management Course, Budapest, August-September, 2001

Budapest Sun (1998) A stage for political point scoring. Budapest Sun, 7, 44, p. 1

Dingsdale A (1999) Budapest's built environment in transition. GeoJournal 49:63-78

Duna Plaza (2001) Anonymous interview with the developer by author (Tape recording, Budapest, 28.11.2001)

ECE Projektmanagement G.m.b.H. & Co. KG - Budapest (2001) Anonymous interview with the developer by author (Tape recording, Budapest, 27.11.2001)

ECE Projektmanagement G.m.b.H. & Co. KG (2002). Anonymous interview with the management by author (Monaco, 25.04.2002)

Ecorys (2001) Interview by author (Tape recording, Budapest, 18.10.2001)

Eraydin A (1999) Forming and bursting bubbles in Tokyo: Global cities under the pressure of global forces and the local regulation systems. (VRF Series, no, 332, Tokyo)

European Union Commission (2003) Guidelines for successful public-private partnerships. Regional Policy Report, European Union Commission, Brussels

Eurobuild (2002) Okęcie airport tender extended again. Online issue. Retrieved January 25, 2002 from http://www.eurobuild.com

Fainstein S (1994) The city builders: Property, politics and planning in London and New York. Blackwell, Oxford

Hubbard P, Hall T (1998) Introduction. In: Hubbard P, Hall T (eds) The Entrepreneurial city: Geographies of politics, regime and representation. John Wiley & Sons, Chichester, pp 1-27

ING Real Estate-Warsaw (2002) Interview by author (Tape recording, Warsaw, 21.05.2002)

Jessop B (1997) A neo-Gramscian approach to the regulation of urban regimes: accumulation strategies, hegemonic projects and governance. In: Lauria, M (ed) Reconstructing urban regime theory: Regulating urban politics in a global economy. Sage, London, pp 51-73

Keresztély K (2002) The role of the central government in the urban development of Budapest. Unpublished research report. SOROS Research Support Scheme Program, RSS No: 359/1999

Kovács Z (2000) Hungary at the threshold of the new millennium: The human geography of transition. In Kovács Z (ed) Hungary towards the 21st century: The human geography of transition. HAS (Geographical Research Institute), Budapest, pp 11-27

Mammut (2001) Interview by author (Tape recording, Budapest, 29.11.2001)

McNeill D, While A (2001) The new urban economies. In: Paddison R (ed) Handbook of urban studies. Sage, London, pp 296-308

North D (1990) Institutions, institutional change and economic performance. Cambridge University, Cambridge

Painter J (1998) Entrepreneurs are made, not born: Learning and urban regimes in the production of entrepreneurial cities. In: Hubbard P, Hall T (eds) The Entrepreneurial city: Geographies of politics, regime and representation. John Wiley & Sons, Chichester, pp 259-274

Rhodes R (1997) Understanding governance. Open University Press, Buckingham

Skanska-Warsaw (2001) Interview by author (Tape recording, Warsaw, 22.05.2001)

Soóki-Tóth G (2000) Planning regulation in Hungary. Unpublished study paper, Budapest Techincal University, Budapest

Sykora L (1998) Commercial property development in Budapest, Prague and Warsaw. In: Enyedi G (ed) Social change and urban restructuring in Central Europe. Akadémiai Kiadó, Budapest, pp 109-136

Taşan-Kok T (2004) Budapest, Istanbul, and Warsaw: Institutional and spatial change. Eburon, Delft

Taşan-Kok T (2005) Opportunity-led planning in Budapest, Istanbul and Warsaw. Unpublished Conference Paper, AESOP Conference, Vienna, 13-14 July 2005

Tosics I (2005) City development in Central and Eastern Europe since 1990: The impact of internal forces. In: Hamilton FEI, Dimitrowska-Andrews K, Pichler-Milanović N (eds), Transformations of cities in Central and Eastern Europe: Toward globalization. United Nations University Press, Tokyo, New York, Paris, pp 44-78

Węcławowicz G (2002) From egalitarian cities in theory to non-egalitarian cities in practice: the changing social and spatial patterns in Polish cities. In: Marcuse, P, van Kempen, R (eds) Of states and cities: Partitioning of urban space. Oxford University Press, Oxford, pp 183-199

4 Wall and mall: A metaphor for metamorphosis

Gregory Andrusz

Introduction

A metropolitan city—understood by Leach "as a 'mother city', a substantial conurbation, which exceeds the scale of the traditional city" (Leach 2002)—is the distillery of society's contradictions and conflicts and contains in hypertrophied form what is found in regional capitals as well as, to a much lesser extent, in many other cities. Metropolitan cities are home to the cultural avant-garde, including a new 'creative class' (Florida 2002); social and political misfits; and the largest concentrations of immigrants, beggars and homeless persons. As the locus for the concentration of private wealth and capital investment, they are the testing grounds for the quintessential form of contemporary consumerism—the Mall. The latter, by blurring the boundaries between shopping (buying goods), entertainment and browsing as a leisure activity, can become in its multi-functionality a public space like a piazza (Jameson 2003)–not, however, in the highly supervised post-socialist city.

The Berlin Wall was the ultimate *Festung* of socialism's actuality in Europe. In the eyes of the regime, it was a *cordon sanitaire* defending the system from ideological 'pollution' and insidious invasion from the capitalist West; from the West, the Wall was a grotesque symbol of state repression. 'Repression' meant a lack of political and economic choice. Indeed, the notion of 'choice' lay at the center of the Washington consensus: the choice of investors to place their capital wherever they wish; the choice of individuals to belong (or not to belong) to trade unions; the ability of citizens to choose their future pension or healthcare provider, or in some cases a private school to which to send their children. The Western view was that individual citizens and households would be "empowered" in a more democratic system to decide how to spend their money and how to maximise their welfare. Now, in the new order, the security that life behind the Wall provided has been exchanged (or surrendered) for the choices offered by the Mall.

Much has been written in recent years on Moscow, its post-socialist development and its claim to the status of a world city (Brade and Rudolph 2004; Golubchikov 2004; Gritsai and van der Wusten 2000). Although the focus of this chapter is the specific social changes occurring in Moscow, and to a lesser extent in St. Petersburg, the generalizations made here about trends apply in varying degrees to socialist and post-socialist cities in all those countries that adopted Soviet-type regimes after 1945. The chapter begins by detailing the defining features of socialist societies, which together with the pre-socialist buildings and city layouts set the parameters within which socialist cities evolved. The chapter then examines particular consequences of the abandonment of that legacy that have delivered unprecedented social polarization: the flight into gated communities and also homelessness. That polarity is the product of the privatization of housing and a land market. In contrast to the rising numbers of marginalised population, and the emergence of ethnic segregation – both symptoms of conflicts within society – is the arrival of the shopping mall, which epitomizes the blossoming of an ethos of merry consumerism. The chapter concludes by suggesting that monuments and place names and uses of space can be understood as ways in which the new regime is seeking to legitimize the changes described.

4.1 From socialist to post-socialist city in the Soviet Union

The defining characteristic of the Soviet Union its the enactment of legislation abolishing the private ownership of property, thereby concentrating most economic resources in the hands of the state and political power in the hands of a "vanguard party." The abolition of private property also meant the nationalization of land, which allowed the state to allocate land free of charge to publicly-owned enterprises and institutions, which had the right to use the land but not to sell or exchange it, not even if surplus to their requirements.

A consequence of these fundamental acts was that in Soviet-type social systems *money* played an extremely small role. The principal services—health, education, housing—were almost completely de-commoditised, as were many leisure activities, since employers had their own cinemas, clubs and sporting facilities, and gave their employees and families passes and travel warrants to go to a holiday resort or sanatorium.[1] In such a de-monetised economy, there was hardly any need for credit and financial institutions. The state savings bank (*Sberbank*) enabled individuals and households to accumulate small stocks of money for special occasions (marriage, celebrations and 'spending money' on holidays), the purchase of consumer durables, clothes and, for a small minority, the deposit for a housing co-operative apartment.

Thus money was not the basis of privilege, and neither was private wealth, since no one could own more than one flat or house and a country cottage (*dacha*). Nonetheless, some people were distinctly better off than others and enjoyed a variety of privileges, depending on their position in the country's economic and political structures. That there were income differentials and that certain groups enjoyed more privileges than others was never denied, but the causes and outcomes of social stratification were radically different from those seen today (Matthews 1978; Yanowitch 1977).

The Soviet Union was for ideological, geo-political and cultural reasons a militarized society, which meant that it exercised close control over the population's

---

[1] Furthermore, a high proportion of the population took their meals in the office, institute or factory canteen (stolovaya), where the food was highly subsidised.

mobility. The internal passport (*propiska*) system enabled the state to regulate population flows into metropolitan and other large cities and to control their demographic and ethnic composition (Matthews 1979). Despite such regulations, large numbers of people found unofficial employment, constituting a cohort known as *limitchiki*.

In order to suppress potential threats to political stability, the state pursued policies to preserve harmonious relationships between the various nationalities and ethnic groups within its boundaries. The spatial outcomes were, firstly, highly stable communities that secondly, were overwhelmingly socially and ethnically *integrated* spaces; and thirdly, towns classified as "closed" and governed by specific legislation, known by the acronym ZATO.[2] Cities in that category, closed in the sense that entry into and residence in them were restricted (and forbidden to foreigners), had nuclear facilities or were of strategic military importance or situated on or near state borders; many of them were not to be found on maps or were given false names.

The socialist city in the Soviet Union was a concept as well as a reality. Although new technologies, cost considerations and institutional capabilities conditioned town building, ultimately the choices made were driven by political ideology. During the socialist period, when households moved between cities, within the framework of the *propiska*, they did so not just for higher incomes but for the non-monetary benefits found in a particular industrial (or town-forming) sector, such as better accommodation and child-care facilities. A city's administrative ranking, which determined the volume and quality of services, including the range of educational institutions and consumer goods available, was another important factor (Vasil'ev et al. 1988; Domanski 1997). Inhabitants of the largest cities were invariably better provided for than those elsewhere. The general image of the socialist city, consisting of modern, high-rise housing of different heights and of schools, hospitals, research centers, and factories built according to a standard design, conformed to the ideal of socialist reality. Nevertheless, even by the end of the socialist period, low-rise, wooden housing covered large tracts of land within cities and on their outskirts, unconnected to the utility networks, except for electricity.

Alongside the range of monotonous multi-story tower blocks that are part of the spatial legacy of the socialist city stand the workers' palaces of culture, the ornately decorated railway stations built during the Stalin era and the large squares with their statues of political actors, artistic prodigies and military heroes. Whatever its faults, this broad legacy was at least constructive in being intended to raise the material standard of living and to foster positive attitudes and social relationships.

Another part of the socialist legacy, however, was avowedly destructive: Soviet leaders, especially Stalin and Khrushchev, and many local activists assiduously removed vestiges of the tsarist past, particularly by demolishing churches.

---

[2] This stands for Zakrytye Administrativno-Territorial'nye Obrazovaniia, which translates literally as "Closed administrative-territorial formations."

In periods of national, political and economic crisis, alternatives to the status quo emerge. Thus, when he came to power in 1985, Mr. Gorbachev described the previous decade as one of "stagnation" and announced his intention to initiate a programme of restructuring (*perestroika*) (Gorbachev 1987). The revolutionary period of 1986-1990 witnessed a serious attempt to move away, albeit very gradually, from the administrative-command economy towards some scope for individual decision making.

That "moment of transition," however, triggered a total transformation of the economic and political system. The term "transition" was employed to underline the teleological nature of the changes: socialist regimes and societies were "in transition" to capitalism. As an indication of their benevolence, Western countries would provide them with "technical assistance" (on how to become "like us"). Moreover, since allowing capital to flow unhindered was the foundation stone of globalisation (capitalism), reform of the socialist system through gradual reform and a "third way" would not be countenanced. The re-commoditisation of services and the *privatization* of publicly owned assets – capital, housing and natural resources – was the cornerstone of economic reform and its ideological and political premise. State expropriation and nationalization of land had helped to determine the development of the *socialist city*, but the *post-socialist city* is being more determinedly shaped by the return of land and property to private ownership.

The privatization of public housing, reduced funding of new building and curtailed size of subsidized social housing tenure were the *sine qua non* for the slow emergence of a mortgage and banking system geared to private housing finance. Class and status accordingly became based on the possession of money and private wealth. These changes were the precondition for a small, more affluent middle class to buy cars and speed off to the green-field suburbs. At the same time, socialist and pre-socialist accommodation in the inner city is being modernized and blocks are being gentrified. Concurrently, a boom in cafes and restaurants caters to the new elites, who also have substituted the private, urban fitness club for the Party or trade union sanatorium in a pre-socialist spa such as Kislovodsk or Karlovy Vary.

These privatization processes coincide with the loss of manufacturing jobs in cities, whose space is taken over by companies in the tertiary sector: information technology, finance, advertising and media, which employ fewer people. The low-income jobs being created to serve this sector – for example, cafes, restaurants, bars, and clubs - are usually taken by migrants from the countryside[3] and by immigrants, who also comprise a high proportion of those providing the sweat for the construction boom. Tajiks, Uzbeks and Azeris, work on hotel and other construction sites in Moscow, returning after work are by buses to their dormitories. According to the Federal Migration Service, an estimated 3 million unregistered foreigners, engaged and exploited by ruthless gang-masters, work illegally in Moscow (Krasinets 2003).

---

[3] According to one academic, Russia remains to a large extent a rural country, with most urban residents retaining deep rural roots, preferences and emotional attachments (Pivovarov 2001).

4.2 The housing market: a source of social polarization and marginalisation

The class polarisation of Russian society and its conspicuousness in Moscow are well documented. At one extreme are the superlatively rich, whose extravagant display of wealth, revealed in both Russian and English language magazines is already legendary (Самокат 2002; The Sunday Times 2004). Disclosures of this sumptuous life style and the ways in which the wealth has been accumulated have provoked severe criticism (Goldman 2003) and undermine the legitimacy of the new economic and political system. At the other extreme, 22 percent of the Russian population (30 million people) live on incomes below the official poverty line; the World Bank puts the figure at 25 percent, and pollsters at 25-40 percent (Ovcharova 2004). The income of the richest 10 percent is 19-20 times greater than that of the poorest 10 percent, compared with a ratio of 14:1 in the United States and 3:1 in Finland.

One cause of this *rapid* social polarisation and a root cause of stratification more generally was the law passed in 1991 allowing state-owned housing, with few exceptions, to be privatized. The trend was further encouraged by the dramatic reduction in construction of new house by the state. The scale of the change may be judged by the fact that in 1991, 67 percent of the total housing stock was state owned, and 90 percent in the largest cities. By 2003, 69.4 percent of the housing stock was in private ownership. Other legal and policy reforms aimed at restructuring the system of subsidies and social benefits and transferring the costs of housing, utilities and urban services to consumers (Ovcharova 2002, 2004). In 2004 the Government announced its decision to abolish its extensive system of 'privileges' (*l'goty*) and to consolidate benefits to be distributed instead as a graduated monetary payment. In early 2005, the monetisation of benefits caused the largest anti-government demonstrations, led largely by pensioners, of the past decade.

Social polarization in post-socialist Russia has a spatial concomitant. People who are superlatively rich buy their properties outright and tend to live segregated from others in high-security, gated communities outside the city or in a renovated house or flat in the city itself (Fig. 4.1.). Their houses, extravagant by any standard, particularly in Moscow, are typically in one of the capital's suburbs within a walled compound as part of an *usad'ba* (country estate) (Kishkovsky 2003). Many of these housing developments meet the desire of the *nouveaux riches* to emulate the pre-revolutionary aristocracy. The principal residence can include "a guesthouse and separate quarters for servants and bodyguards. Guests at one estate leave their Mercedes-Benzes at the gate and ride to the house by horse and carriage;" another estate has its own stables and church (Kishkovsky 2003). A magazine industry has emerged to cater to the consumers and the admirers of this ostentatious life-style. The promotional literature for a condominium complex, which will have a formal garden based on Peter the Great's Peterhof and have Bach piped into the parking garage, refers to the complex as a "XXI century aristocratic estate" whose residents, paying up to €1 million for a flat (90 percent of which

Fig. 4.1. Datchas in Moscow

have been sold), can justly call themselves the "new aristocrats."

But not all those who constitute this super-wealthy class are rushing to re-brand themselves as the landed gentry. As Moscow transforms itself into a modern metropolis, with luxury hotels, shopping malls and office complexes, other members of this super-rich bourgeoisie and *rentier* class prefer to live in gentrified houses in the historic core and adjacent districts (Fig. 4.2.). They seek out buildings with ornate, sometimes neo-classical facades and high ceilings that were erected in city center locations before 1917 or were built for members of the Soviet élites in the 1930s and in the decade after 1945 (Nivat 2004). In theory any new construction within the city's historical core is rigorously vetted to ensure that it complies with zoning laws and environmental-impact regulations, In practice, however, many old houses and other buildings that merit restoring are demolished to provide car parking, office space and new or gentrified accommodation, preserving perhaps only their facades (O'Flynn 2004).

The outcome of protests by residents follows a familiar pattern. Initially, a well-presented petition succeeds in persuading the local authorities to adhere to their own zoning and development plans. But as real estate prices, especially in the capitals, continue to climb, developers working in "close collaboration" with local officials, after a brief delay out of respect for planning regulations and local opposition, achieve their objective: to modernize and refurbish a single building or block for residential or commercial use and displace the original population (Bater 2002).

The new bourgeoisie is trailed and admired by a much less prosperous, aspirant middle class, whose members, having already exercised their 'right to privatize' and become the owners of their previously rented state accommodation, strive to emulate the exceedingly rich by taking part in the game of "home improvements." Just as the very rich emulate the tsarist aristocracy, an unknown proportion of this more humble class revels in a nostalgia for the tsarist past or engages in "retro-socialist chic;" in either case, the outcome is an emblematic assertion of a design and architectural style with a nationalist hue. Though nostalgia will no doubt yield

Fig. 4.2. Waiting to be gentrified – St Petersburg

to Italian and Ikea designer furnishing, the process could be slower than optimists would like. One rigorous analysis of social stratification in Russia confirmed that the economic reforms, rather than expanding the size of the middle class and making the distribution of economic wealth oval shaped, during 1990s the proportion of population with income 2.5 – 4.5 times greater than the official subsistence minimum, declined from over 40 percent to 20 percent in 1994 and to ten percent in 1998 (Bogomolova and Taplina 2001).

The group seeking home ownership contains an emerging small landlord class, composed of both foreigners and natives, who are interested in restoring and then renting out their properties in selective, gentrified areas. One of three attics acquired by a foreign interior designer in a 19th-century building in St. Petersburg's historic center was converted into a two-bedroom loft space, with exposed wooden beams and brickwork, and rented out. While the right to reclaim such derelict spaces conforms to the government's policy of increasing the housing stock, this sort of gentrification generates envy and litigation over titles to property, part of which is communally owned.

It is towards this small, but growing cohort of would-be home owners and small landlords that the developing mortgage market is oriented. The development of mortgage institutions and of a culture of long-term borrowing is firmly on the Russian President's policy agenda. It was given further impetus in 2005 when he proposed allocating funds from the state's "stabilisation fund" for this purpose.

However, Mr. Putin's constituency is far from limited to the emerging middle class and their need for better access to home loans and a more efficient mortgage system. His broader challenge is to improve accommodations for the majority of the population, who live in flats that are small, but heated throughout the cold season and supplied most of the time with running water, gas and electricity. For the many residents of flats the cost of accommodation, its quality and servicing remain a constant and aggravating problem. It was this group that Putin addressed in a television broadcast in June 2003, when he stated that, for the first time in a decade, considerably more funding would be allocated to the housing sector from the state budget, particularly for those living in dilapidated accommodation and needing to be re-housed (Putin 2003). However, there are two groups will not be affected by this additional funding: those living in communal flats (*kommunalki*) and the literally homeless.

The communal flat is a legacy of the socialist Revolution in 1917, when housing policy in the socialist city consisted of redistributing existing space by crowding a number of families (without accommodation) into single family dwellings that mainly, but not only, had belonged to the aristocracy and upper middle class. The government presumes that the functioning of the market system (developers aided by bribe-seeking, local officials) will, through a "natural process" of gentrification, gradually eliminate this type of tenure, although it may take longer in St. Petersburg, where an estimated one-fifth of all households continue to live in *kommunalki* (Utekhin 2001).

But neither the market nor the state will come to the aid of homeless people (*бездомные – БОМЖИ*), who are widely regarded as the undeserving poor and part of the underclass. At the beginning of the millennium, according to a study by the Russian Academy of Sciences, in the country as a whole, 3.3 million people were homeless (Gutov and Nazarov 2001), of whom 30,000 live in Moscow. Only 14 percent of those are actually from Moscow and the Moscow region, with 45 percent from other parts of Russia and the remaining 41 percent from the former Soviet Republics.

One of the main causes for the exponential growth in homelessness was the reform of the housing system (Fig. 4.3.). The 1990s witnessed huge increases in the price of housing, especially in Moscow, accompanied, as noted, by a precipitous reduction in the funding of new construction from the state budget. Tenants and those on official housing-waiting lists reacted to this crisis in various ways, ranging from squatting and the setting up for a few months in 1991 of a 'cardboard city' between Hotel Rossiya and Red Square, on the one hand, to the formation of organizations for homeless people and the foundation of an International Tenants' Union, on the other. Such grass-roots initiatives, in a broad and amorphous housing movement, were among the first indications of the evolution of civil society in Russia.

To conclude this short section on the housing system, it is worth recording that in 2004, the vice-chairman of *Gosstroi*, the Russian government's Department of Construction, noted that all the laws adopted in this sector have been worked out by two Russian foundations: the Urban Economy Institute and the Centre for Strategic Research, both of which are funded principally by the American government and lobby members of the Duma and senior civil servants to accept their legislative proposals. He also credited the work of those organizations for the policy now adopted by the Russian government to monetize the various benefits for veterans, invalids and pensioners (Rosbalt 2004).

Fig. 4.3. Cardboard city in Moscow

4.3 Homelessness, marginality and space in post-socialist Russia

Contrary to some idealised accounts of the socialist city, urban marginality did exist prior to 1990, and today few scholars and specialists would deny that homelessness, drug addiction, serious crime, delinquent behaviour and other social problems could be found in socialist cities (Gabani 1987).[4] Indeed, as far as homelessness is concerned, it would be a travesty to say that neither begging (*poproshainichestvo*) nor vagrants (*brodyachii*) were to be found in socialist cities; but to the extent that they did exist, their presence was regarded as a vestige of capitalism and as such excluded from public discourse. Therefore, although sanctions had been introduced against beggars in the 1930s, it was not until 1960 that they came to be covered by the Criminal Code for evading socially useful work and leading an anti-social, parasitical way of life.

The ideology of socialism required that a formal, public silence should be maintained about such matters; it contained them quantitatively but did not eradi-

---

[4] According to Gabani, who was head of the Sociology Department of the Georgian Ministry of Internal Affairs, the ministry had in 1967 set up an interdepartmental committee to study and combat drug addiction.

cate them altogether. For similar reasons, the socialist regime also hid the prosperous and powerful behind grey, urban facades or banished them to sylvan retreats. In contrast to the post-socialist city, which is a transparent city, such antithetical but undesirable phenomena as homelessness and substantial privilege were ideologically unacceptable. It is a key imperative of capitalism that the homeless and other marginalized groups should be visible, and that the rich should parade their wealth; the capital city of post-socialist Russia is the stage on which these glaring disparities are most flagrantly displayed.

The number of people who became homeless unquestionably rose in the late 1980s, and not only because state and society recognized and did not criminalise them. In 1992 the head of a Russian charity estimated that there were 150,000 homeless people in Moscow and the Moscow oblast (Tret'yakov 1992). Various factors account for the increase: the collapse of the Soviet Union gave rise to refugees and forced migrants (Grafova 2002a)[5]; restructuring caused unemployment, rising rates of alcoholism and drug addiction; and a dramatic decline in the number of new social housing units.[6] The privatization and commoditisation of accommodation, *The Law on Privatisation (of housing)* tempted some people to use criminal or unethical ways of gaining "vacant possession." In 1998, it was estimated that apartment fraud was responsible for 30 percent of those made homeless in St. Petersburg in 1996 (Varoli 1998).[7] In the post-socialist Russian city the emergence of a speculative real estate market correlates to increased housing hardship and, in extreme cases, homelessness.

The homeless phenomenon is closely associated with another: "street children" (*besprizorniki*). Estimates of their number vary considerably. Recent official Russian data put the figure at between 1.1 and 1.3 million, while the Ministry of Internal Affairs estimates that it is 2 –2.5 million and the Council of the Federation places it as high as 3-4 million (Aref'ev 2003). In 2004 the city government estimated that about 40,000 children were living on Moscow's streets, compared with 25,000 in 1999, of whom 6 percent were from the city itself (Page 2004). The phenomenon of homelessness, especially of school-age children, is an enormous tragedy. It is also a catastrophe for the society and especially for city residents, because HIV is spreading from marginalised urban groups such as prostitutes and intravenous drug users into the mainstream population.

---

[5] Since the collapse of the Soviet Union, 8.6 million people have migrated to Russia, of whom only 1.6 million have the official status of 'refugee' or "forced migrant." See: Vserossiiskii chrezvychainyi s"yezd v zashchitu migrantov, Moscow, 20-21 June 2002 (Grafova 2002b)

[6] The proportion of all new units erected by the state and municipal authorities declined from 80 percent in 1990 to 20 percent in 1998.

[7] In 1994 the Moscow city government passed a resolution establishing a service to protect elderly tenants from being defrauded by individuals offering them a variety of medical and other services in exchange for the title to their flats.

4.4 Ethnicity, space, security and surveillance

Current birth and mortality rates mean that the country's population is declining by 700,000 a year and in some years by one million. At this rate, the average estimate is that on average, between 2000 and 2015 the population will decline by 13-14 million people (Rybakovskii et al. 2002). For the government and the military, the population decline fuels a real fear that national security is threatened; for the right wing the decline feeds for their xenophobia. Even as steps are now being taken to counter the decline in the native Russian population, the number of immigrants in the economy will continue to rise, especially among those ethnic groups whose birth rates are higher than the national average. Different sources cite wildly different figures on the number of illegal immigrants and refugees in Russia.

In March 2004 a UN report stated that 3.5 – 5.0 million illegal labour migrants, of whom 30-40 percent come from Central Asia, headed by Tajiks, were living in the country (UN 2004). Wage rate disparities, growing poverty and population surpluses in countries of origin mean that instituting mechanisms to restrict legal migration only fosters illegal migration wherever the demand for labour exists.

Although the 2002 Census revealed that 20.2 percent of the population of the Russian Federation (29.3 million) are non-Russian, the majority of the non-Russian population live in their own titular republics (Bashkorstan, Tatarstan, Chechnya). Significant numbers have, however, moved into Moscow, St. Petersburg and other regional capital cities, where many live alongside marginalized members of the indigenous population in dilapidated buildings within small neighbourhoods in the central districts of metropolitan areas, such as the Kolomna neighbourhood in the historic centre of St. Petersburg.

A large number of immigrants, particularly from the Caucasus but also from Central Asia, who own and are served by shops that meet their cultural needs, live in the neighborhood. However, the social background of its residents is beginning to change. Kolomna has become popular amongst artists, who have begun to squat in abandoned buildings. The decision by St. Petersburg's city council in December 2003 to redevelop the former industrial neighborhood by demolishing run-down housing, relocating the inhabitants and constructing a new retailing and entertainment complex on the 4.5-hectare site is a typical example of a gentrification project. The scene is set for classical class and ethnic conflict for space, mainly for living, but also for working.

It is within such neighbourhoods, but more often outside them in peripheral housing estates that a younger generation suffering actual poverty and perceiving itself to be relatively deprived, nurtures rage and searches for identity. In these conditions youth sub-culture groups form that describe themselves as skinheads (*britogolovy*) or nazis and claim that their aim is to "clean up" Russia from black people (*negri*) and people from the Caucasus and Central Asia (*churki*). The harassment that they see inflicted on members of minority groups by militiamen readily justifies their ethnic prejudices, extreme xenophobia and anti-semitism, acted out in hostile behaviour.

Whether they are internal migrants to the Russian Republic from Tartarstan or Chechnya (constituent republics of the Russian Federation), or cross-national migrants, in both instances they are considered to be "immigrants." The term carries a negative connotation that enables employers to pay them lower wages and to house them in less than standard accommodation (hostels, caravans, makeshift cabins and worse). Ironically, the lower wages then become another cause for resentment of migrants by the local population, who accuse them of undercutting wages and competing for their jobs. Conversely, the exploitation that some migrants experience, including even non-payment of wages, melds with perceptions of discrimination and identity dissonance to engender discontent that can translate into criminal or proscribed political behavior.

The division of cities by social class can be either highly visible or quite blurred. In either case, individuals from different classes but the same ethnic background share a broad common understanding of the material and cultural symbols of the spaces through which they pass and within which they interact. That cannot be said of cities that have ethnically heterogeneous populations: individual buildings, shops, eating places, the uses of public spaces, the real and symbolic meanings of religious membership all contribute to sustaining cultural identities.

In contrast to the socialist city, where space was permeated with reiterated images and ideological meanings that were shared (or, at least, understood) by all, the post-Soviet city is a shattered social and symbolic space that is no longer shared, but contested. The sanctioning and lauding of ethnic diversity locks individuals and the social groups into mental cells that reproduce self-images and inimical images of others that undermine solidarity.[8]

From the earliest research by the Chicago School, the presence of immigrant groups has always been found to affect the socio-spatial structure of the city. Today, in many of the major Russian and European cities the mosque is both a place of worship and a place of a distinct Muslim identity; it symbolizes the unity of the *ummah* and an Islamic way of life and is a place for celebrating Muslin events and festivals. Empirical research is needed to understand how mosques and Muslim communities are shaping the use of space in post-socialist cities.

Against the perceived danger posed by members of the city's underclass, immigrants and the marginalized (Trenin 2004) to those in gated housing and small enclaves of gentrified housing, and to those who visit the "entertainment" city, the state, private corporations and residents' associations are beginning to set up defences. Surveillance cameras supplement security guards who patrol both outside and inside buildings, fortifying post-socialist space in "the defence of luxury."

New surveillance technology has been imported into post-socialist cities to defend the population against that daily irritant, the graffiti sprayer, and to provide

---

[8] In Kazan, the capital of Tatarstan, which is a constituent republic of the Russian Federation, there is a trend among young people to adopt Muslim attire, including for women, headscarves, veils and ankle-length tunics. The interest in Islam is a new phenomenon, which is not confined to modes of dress, but also evident in an emerging demand for food prepared according to Islamic dietary procedures (Eckel 2005).

personal and public security against ordinary criminals. Now the defences are aimed against the growing threats presented by real local, and imaginary global, terrorists, who in contrast to their nineteenth century predecessors, are motivated by religious, not class reasons, thus deliberately or unconsciously exacerbating inter-ethnic tensions.

Technological capacity, the frequent use of siren-sounding emergency services and CCTV cameras, combined with a media-led denunciation of these three categories of felons: the graffiti artist, the thief and thug, and the terrorist generate a feeling amongst the population that their safety and well-being are under an omnipresent threat. This lays the foundation for a gradual acceptance by the public that their physical security requires higher levels of surveillance, including more police, para-military and military personnel.

For the inhabitants of the post-socialist city, security services and surveillance constitute customary fixtures of their environment and a normal part of their mental mapping of social life. Under the previous regime, however, these 'fixtures' had been integral to the social compact according to which, almost in return, citizens were assured social security from their cradles to their graves.

4.5 Consumerism in post-socialist Russia: The mall as a symbol of choice

Ultimately, changes to the world of work affect a city's character most. Small businesses are emerging, despite the obstacles they face; but too few are in the spheres of engineering and manufacturing technology. This imbalance is now generating fears of the *Walmartisation* of the region, for it is mainly in the service sector that small businesses are emerging and entrepreneurship is being demonstrated.

Apart from cafes, restaurants, small retailing outlets and estate agents, it is the information society that creates opportunities for an individuated workforce. Independent micro-economies operate in such fields as information technology (website designers), financial services (accountants, legal and business advisors) and culture and the arts (fashion design, film making) all of which are beginning to emerge in post-socialist, mainly capital, cities. This economic change has created a highly contested economic space for cities, with clearly identifiable losers and winners (see Tsenkova in this volume).

One cluster of cities—the closed military cities—has been particularly disadvantaged by economic change as well as by the end of the Cold War. Russia inherited 1,060 military-industrial complexes and 943 R&D and design institutions employing 6.5 million people. This employment number fell to 2.33 million in 1998 (Hartner 2002). At the same time, in 1993 the Russian government decided to reduce its armed forces by 1.5 million and required the demobilization of 425,000 commissioned officers by the end of 1994 (OECD 1993). Despite some efforts to retrain military officers (EU Tacis 1998), over 30 percent of the 109,000 former officers have failed to find a job. Another dispiriting outcome was that, despite their considerable stock of human capital, military cities experiencing demobilisation were becoming havens of the unemployed, the underemployed, the elderly and the disadvantaged (Szabo and Kitov 2001).

The demolition of the Wall can thus, perhaps, be seen as an act of Faustian proportions: those who once served the military-industrial complex surrendered to become "consumers" or producers for the consumer market; but, the manufacturing sectors in which they work and the incomes that they receive preclude the majority of them from engaging with the Mall – an institution which almost half-a-century after it opened in a suburb of Minneapolis in 1956 (Hardwich 2003), has made its debut in Moscow and in a few of the major cities in the region.

Incorporating small, specialist shops, department stores, supermarkets, restaurants, bars, cinemas and other forms of entertainment, the Mall has become a place where some entertainment or "cultural" event can create its own important source of added value to the city and to shopping itself (Bittner 2001). Funded by wealthy private investors in Russia the ideology of the Mall, as a high status palace of consumption, is never to aspire to catering for a mass market; that remains the task of the declining and prestige-losing city center department store, the shop located on the ground floor of a block of flats, the kiosk and the ethnically diverse bazaar and open-air market, which remain responsible for over 70 percent of Moscow's retail turnover.

Just as once, in the socialist past, families would visit the Exhibition for National Economic Achievements in Moscow, today many Muscovites have made shopping a popular weekend entertainment including a family visit to Ikea, the first of which opened in Moscow in March 2000. Ikea reached a turnover of €100 million in its first year against a projected income of €60 million after three years. In December 2001 a second store was opened, followed twelve months later by a 'mega-mall' containing a hyper-market, 250 shops, 2 km. of shop fronts, a skating rink and Russia's largest cinema complex, which expects to host 25-40 million visitors annually.

The dynamic growth in the retail sector is regarded as one of the most promising sectors of the country's economy, ranking Russia first in a 2004 Global Retail Development Index of the top 30 emerging markets worldwide (Necarsulmer 2005). Few would dispute the potential of the country's retail market or the high growth rates attainable. The Pharmacy Chain, *36.6,* which was established in 1999, is emblematic of the sector's rapid growth.

Although that chain currently has a network of 230 integrated health and beauty outlets across the country, Moscow generates three-quarters of the company's revenues, thus underscoring the primacy of the capital, which accounts for 27 percent of the country's total domestic retail turnover. Despite its commanding position, with an average of 506 square metres of retail space per 1,000 inhabitants early 2003, Moscow remains far behind western capitals in terms of retail space per capita (Necarsulmer 2005). That gap means that the construction boom, fuelled by a shortage of office and retail space and accommodation, will continue to refashion the geographical and architectural form of the capital and its social structure.

Retailing, however, is more than sets of statistics on the supply of commodities and consumer demand for them; it participates in a broader spectacle and fantasy about the city itself. Since modern cities compete with each other by means of images, both private companies and public authorities are expending more and more effort to produce and distribute images of what their cities have to offer. They have to promote and package their histories and traditions for tourists, affluent residents and talented individuals rich in human capital, to present themselves as unique and attractive places in which to live and work. Yet, paradoxically, their *uniqueness* has to be combined with modes of retailing and marketing which make them the *same* as their competitor cities and shopping-entertainment spaces. The investors who finance each new Mall face the same contradiction: While they insist that globally branded companies - Benetton, Mercedes, Visa - be integral to new retail entertainment projects, the designers and executives from the themed entertainment industry want the entertainment-based (re)development to strive at the same time for a marketable identity based on local culture, history and identity.

The Mall offers individuals an ever expanding variety of choices, including the purchase of mortgages, insurance and, soon, legal advice. It is also the location where visitors confront the opportunity to become credit card holders. Above all, the Mall stands as a self-conscious symbol of capitalism as opposed to socialism. The largest and best stocked department store in Moscow during the socialist period could not be compared with the Mall or post-socialist boutique arcade. It would have been inconceivable, for both economic and ideological reasons, to have read that "The Russian passion for all things luxurious is driving the world's big fashion labels and single-handedly rescuing the luxury-goods industry from its economic mire – they are now one of the most influential consumer groups in the world...In 1994 Versace opened in Moscow and Russia now accounts for ten percent of the total sales of the label (The Sunday Times 2004).

But the materialistic values that the Mall embodies cannot serve as the glue that binds shoppers to one another as citizens. Ultimately, although the Mall is open to all - unlike the 'closed shops' in the socialist city, which were open only to those with hard currency or who were 'privileged' - in reality it is not accessible to all, for the majority of the population routinely have to shop in open-air bazaars, street markets, kiosks and small shops.

4.6 New monuments and symbols

Monuments and museums, buildings and the names given to streets, squares and parks help to constitute the glue that binds society and legitimates political authority. Changes in architectural styles, the functions of a town's most impressive buildings and the manner in which public spaces are used are all sound barometers of the way in which historical events and subjects are viewed by politicians, the public and the media.

In the Soviet Union after 1917, and elsewhere in Eastern Europe after 1948, obelisks and marble memorials were erected in parks, squares and streets of towns and villages to commemorate the Red Army and partisan leaders who had taken part in the liberation of the country from fascism (and capitalism). In 1989, when socialist cities slipped across a boundary into a new, ideologically denominated zone, they shifted their vision of the future and embarked upon fabricating their own convenience histories (Hobsbawm 1983) to justify their apostasy. They did so by filling spaces with new symbolic meanings. In many post-socialist cities, the statues and memorials to individuals who forty years ago were heroes of socialism have been, if not destroyed, decapitated or mutilated, then banished from public view, in some instances to museums. (Lenin's mummified body in the mausoleum is under constant threat of removal by those who want to bury him, both actually and symbolically.) These acts highlight the transience not just of heroes, but also of the myths about the present inhabitants' past and even of the perceptions of whom they wish to be. The erection and removal of monuments and buildings—totems to the regime—are potent symbolic acts, which destroy—or create and sustain—myths about people and events.

In Moscow, the most recent and among the most remarkable of such changes was the rehabilitation of General Denikin, the leader of the White Army, whose remains were interned in October 2005 at a ceremony at the Donskoi Monastery in Moscow. According to Patriarch Alexei II, this act symbolized the reunification of the nation, and it was appropriate that 2005 also would be the first time that the new public holiday, National Unity Day, would be held on 4th November, replacing 7th November, when the October 1917 Revolution used to be commemorated. Denikin's restoration intensifies the pathos that surrounds the founding, in 1996, of the Kutuzov Centre for the Employment of Former Military Personnel, which is located in a huge war memorial and museum complex in Moscow. Whilst the museum honors those who had died "defending the motherland" during the second Great Patriotic War (1941-45), the demobilized officers today who undergo training there to develop marketable skills may be seen almost as unsung heroes, the victims of a non-combatant, ideological war.

As far as the Soviet Marxist state was concerned, the Orthodox church was as much an ideological enemy as was capitalism. The state therefore considered itself justified in robbing the Orthodox church of its riches, destroying the churches altogether or using them as warehouses. In 1932, the Soviet government turned the Cathedral of the Lady of Kazan in Saint Petersburg, into a Museum of the History of Religion and Atheism (Fig. 4.4.). Post-socialist leaders have been rushing to undo such devastation by their predecessors by re-building churches, and acknowledging that they serve as standards where non-believers as well as believers can, as Durkheim invoking his distinction between the sacred and the profane observed, reaffirm their belief in a set of values and historical reference points (religious and other public holidays and festivals) and their sense of group identity (Bigg 2005).

A number of themes touched upon in this essay come together in the phenomenon of Cathedral of Christ the Saviour in Moscow, which was first conceived of in 1812 (to mark the defeat of Napoleon), completed in 1881, dynamited in 1931 and

Fig. 4.4. Kazan Cathedral in 1992—the Museum for Religion and Atheism—as a backdrop for Salvation Army event in St. Petersburg

rebuilt in 2000. Today it can be interpreted as linking tourism and religion – a place to which visitors come either to search for their spiritual selves or to consume religion as spectacle. The cathedral as a tourist destination can be reconceptualized as part of the culture industry and thus integrated into government policy as a means of achieving economic growth. Indeed, a smaller church with a museum situated in its gallery lies behind the main cathedral. In keeping with the post-modern era, "the new cathedral was designed both as a holy place and as *tourist attraction*" capable of hosting 7,000 visitors at a time. "Apart from being a modern, fashionably-equipped building, it plays its main role as a holy place open to people of different faiths and *lifestyles*" (Anishyuk 2004). The church is thus both totem and tourist attraction.

Conclusion

Compared with socialist cities, which had more or less planned economic and administrative profiles as part of a grand schema for the state's allocation of resources and functions, each post-socialist city now has to compete with all other cities for inward capital investment, consumers and tourists. It falls to local governments to devise ways of presenting an appealing image of their city that can be transmitted on to the regional and world stages. If they are successful in projecting themselves as possessing an "aesthetically satisfying environment" for urban (and, as an additional bonus, cosmopolitan) elites, they survive and thrive. Moscow and St. Petersburg fall into this category, as do, in a more limited way, ancient cities such as Novgorod and Kostroma. The list can be extended to include cities that because of, say, unusual geographical features, are attractive places in which to invest and work or to visit. However, for many more cities, if re-imaging is the key to survival, their future is bleak.

The post-socialist city, to restate the obvious, is a product of post-socialist society. Certain of its features express the very essence of capitalism, for example, allowing the market through land pricing to determine the location of specific types of residences and financial institutions. Other aspects of the post-socialist city may be described as epi-phenomenal: monuments, museums and place names fall into this category. Their study can serve as a guide to understanding deeper processes, one of which is the 'mallification' of the post-socialist city. However, this manifestation of consumerism is itself an expression of an historical trend: At the same time as Red Square becomes a shadow of its former symbolic significance, churches and cathedrals rise in totemic importance, betokening a shift from a secular, militaristic, socialist internationalism to a capitalist nationalism resting on the religious bed of Russian Orthodoxy. That shift has already generated the conditions for class and ethnic conflict, visible in the contests over space in post-socialist cities.

References

Anishyuk A (2004) The Church of Christ the Saviour, Moscow. In: HERE, The Alfa Laval International Customer Magazine, No 11, March, http://here.alfalaval.com, accessed on 9/15/2005

Aref'ev A (2003) Besprizornye deti v Rossii. Sotsiologicheskie issledovaniya 9:61-72

Bater J (2002) Market reforms and the central city: Moscow and St. Petersburg. In van Dijk H (ed) The European metropolis 1920-2000. Centre of Comparative European History, Berlin, pp. 1-38

Bigg C (2005) Russia: Rights groups say country intolerant to minority religions. Radio Free Europe/Radio Liberty (RFE/RL), 19 May, Washington DC, http://www.rferl.org

Bittner R (2001) The city as an event. In: Bittner R (ed) Die stadt als event. Zur Konstruktion Urbaner Erlebnisraume (Event City), Frankfurt/New York, Campus Verlag Edition Bauhaus, pp. 357-364

Bogomolova T, Taplina V (2001) Ekonomicheskaya stratifikatsiya naseleniya Rossii v 90-e gody. Sotsiologicheskie issledovaniya 6:32-43

Brade I, Rudolph R (2004) Moscow, the global city? The position of the Russian capital within the European system of metropolitan areas. Area 36.1:69-80

Domanski B (1997) Industrial control over the socialist town: Benevolence or exploitation. Praeger, Westport, CT

Eckel M (2005) Russia's Tatars turning to Islamic roots. Associated Press, 26 August, http://www.muslimnews.co.uk

EU Technical Assistance to the CIS (Tacis) (1998) The integration of former military personnel into civil society. EDRUS 9705, European Union

Florida R (2002) The rise of the creative class, Basic Books, New York

Gabani A (1987) Narkomania: gor'kie plody sladkoi zhizni. Sotsiologicheskie issledovaniya 1:48-53

Goldman M (2003) The piratisation of Russia. Russian reform goes awry. Routledge, London
Golubchikov O (2004) Urban planning in Russia: Towards the market. European Planning Studies 12:229-247
Gorbachev M (1987) Perestroika. New thinking for our country and the world. William Collins, London
Grafova L (ed) (2002a) Zachem Rossii migranty. Sbornik luchshikh publikatsii zhurnalistov Informatsionnogo Agenstva 'Migratsiya.' Forum pereselencheskikh organizatsii, Moscow, 20-21 June
Grafova L (ed) (2002b) Vserossiiskii chrezvychainyi s"yezd v zashchitu migrantov. Sbornik luchshikh publikatsii zhurnalistov Informatsionnogo Agenstva 'Migratsiya,' Forum pereselencheskikh organizatsii, Moscow, 20-21 June
Gritsai O, van der Wusten H (2000) Moscow and St. Petersburg, a sequence of capitals, a tale of two cities. GeoJournal 51:33-45
Gutov R, Nazarov A (2001) Bezdomnye v Rossii: vzglyad na problemu. Narodonaselenie 4: pp. 117-121
Hartner S (2002) The military-industrial complex, technological change and the space industry. In: Lane D (ed) The legacy of state socialism and the future of transformation. Rowman and Littlefield, Oxford, pp. 147-169
Hobsbawn E, Ranger T (eds) (1983) The invention of tradition. Cambridge University Press, Cambridge, United Kingdom
Hardwich M (2003) Mall maker: Victor Gruen, architect of an American dream. University of Pennsylvania Press, Philadelphia
Jameson F (2003) Future City. New Left Review 21, Second Series, May-June, pp.22-31
Kishkovsky S (2003) The czar didn't sleep here. The New York Times, 9 January.
Krasinets E (2003) Nelegal'naya migratsiya v Rossii: faktory, posledstviya, problemy regulirovaniya. Narodonaslenie 3:77-87
Leach N (ed) (2002) The hieroglyphics of space. Reading and experiencing the modern metropolis. Routledge, London
Matthews M (1978) Privilege in the Soviet Union. Allen & Unwin, London
Matthews M (1979) The passport society: Controlling movements in Russia and the USSR. Westview Press, Boulder, CO
Necarsulmer P (2005) Russian retail sector experiencing powerful growth. BISNIS Bulletin, January/February, http://www.bisnis.doc.gov/bisnis/bulletin.cfm, accessed on 9/15/2005
Nivat A (2004) The view from the Vysotka: A portrait of Russia today through one of Moscow's most famous addresses, St. Martin's Press, New York (translated from French by Frances Forte)
Organisation for Economic Co-operation and Development (OECD) (1993) Russian officer conversion programme. OCDE/GD (93)9, Paris
O'Flynn K (2004) Fast-changing centre is squeezing out locals. The Moscow Times, 13 January, p.4
Ovcharova L (2002) Social policy in changing Russia. Independent Institute for Social Policy, Moscow
Ovcharova L (2004) Who's poor in Russia? Gateway to Russia, 27 April, http://eng.expert.ru/society/04-16bedn.htm
Page J (2004) Life on the edge for Moscow's 40,000 street children. The Times (UK), 14 February, pp.3-4

Pivovarov Y (2001) Urbanizatsiya Rossii v XX veke: predstavleniya i real'nost. Obshchestvennye nauki i sovremennost' 6:101-113

Putin V (2003) 20 June, http://www.kremlin.ru/eng/priorities/21844.shtml

Rybakovskii L, Zakharova O, Ivanova A, Demchnko T (2002) Demograficheskoe budushchee Rossii. Narodonaselenie 1:33-48

Самокат (2002) Kommercheskaya nedvizhimost' v Nizhnem Novgorode. Journal for self-made man, April, 3-4:4-9

Stiglitz J (2002) Globalisation and its discontents. Penguin Press, London

Szabo G, Kitov V (2001) Russia's closed cities are open and shut case. The Russian Journal, 16-22 November, http://beta.russiajournal.com/, accessed on 9/15/2005

Trenin D (2004) What you see is what you get. The World Today (UK), April, 60(4):13-15

Tret'yakov E (1992) Lyudi bez krova. Soprichasnost' 1: pp. 2-17

United Nations (UN) Office for the Coordination of Humanitarian Affairs (2004) Labour Migrants to Russia. United Nations, Moscow

Utekhin I (2001) Ocherki kommunal'nogo byta. O.G.I., Moscow

Varoli J (1998) St. Petersburg coming to grips with homeless problem. Radio Free Europe/Radio Liberty(RFE/RL), 18 February

Vasil'ev G, Sidorov D, Khanin S (1988) Vyyavlenie potrebitel'skikh predpochtenii v sfere rasseleniya. Vestnik Moskovskogo Universiteta, seria 5, geografia, 2, pp.41-47

Yanowitch M (1977) Social and economic inequality in the USSR. Martin Robertson, London

5 The spatial structures of Central and Eastern European cities

Alain Bertaud

Introduction

Central and Eastern European (CEE) cities have been under a centralized command economy for periods varying from 45 to 75 years. During those years, the forces shaping the spatial structure of CEE cities were very different from the ones transforming their western counterparts. What had the most pervasive effect on the structure of socialist cities was the absence of real estate markets. Densities and land allocation among different uses – mainly, industrial and residential – did not reflect demand for specific land use, but rather were based mostly on administrative decisions to minimize input, not maximize financial values.

However, throughout the socialist period CEE cities have maintained their European cultural identity – defined as prestigious centres with extensive, radial and concentric transit networks that reinforce the monocentric structure. Nearly every CEE city is built around a large historical core established many centuries before socialism. Although the absence of market mechanisms during the socialist interval has altered the shape of CEE cities, they have not completely diverged from the Western European mold. In this chapter we argue that CEE cities are more European than socialist. The analytical method used to compare their spatial structures draws on that developed by Bertaud and Malpezzi (2003) in their comparative assessment of 50 cities. The four spatial indicators used, which are directly linked to spatial policy issues, are average density, density profile, land price profile, and proportion of industrial land over built-up area. The analysis explores the differences and similarities between post-socialist cities and their Western European counterparts.

The chapters argue that despite the resiliency of pre-socialist structures, socialism has altered the CEE cities to some extent. Consequently, the transition from socialism requires a series of strategies to make them fully functional and culturally European. While embarked on similar market mechanisms, however, the CEE municipalities' policy and investment responses to face the liabilities of the past and the new challenges of markets have not always been coherent and consistent; they lack a clear model for dealing with the complexities of transition. For example, the planning regulatory environment has been slow in moving away from rigid master plans toward more market-friendly rules; lack of a clear policy concerning vehicle use, in particular the pricing of parking in central areas, exacerbates the congestion in central areas; nor has a clear strategy emerged for balancing suburban development to meet the demand for housing and commercial facilities while still maintaining and enhancing the historical city centres. Furthermore, environmental legislation has not always been effective in protecting exceptional natural assets. Post-socialist cities should adopt an urban planning strategy that deals resolutely with the liabilities left from the socialist era and that also reflects their European culture: a strong and prestigious historical centre served by transit, and large suburbs allowed to develop consistently with consumer demand and the unavoidable rise in vehicle ownership.

5.1 Theoretical framework

The framework applied in this research is articulated in the comparative study of Bertaud and Malpezzi (2003) that examined urban form characteristics *systematically* around the world, with special reference to transition economies of Central and Eastern Europe. The comparative work draws on studies of the spatial distribution of population by Alonso (1964), Muth (1969) and Mills (1972) as well as on related empirical literature on the distribution of real estate prices (Follain and Malpezzi 1981) and the distribution of wages and incomes over space (Eberts 1981). Much of this literature is ably surveyed by McDonald (1989). Broad reviews of the theoretical models behind this empirical work can be found in Straszheim (1987) and Arnott et al. (1998).

The measure of city form that has been most often studied by urban economists is the population density gradient from a negative exponential function, often associated with the pioneering work of Alonso, Muth and Mills. This 'standard urban model' predicts that population density gradients will fall in absolute value as incomes rise, the city grows, and transport costs fall. Extensions to the model permit gradients to change with location-specific amenities as well. For further discussion, see Follain and Malpezzi (1981), Wu (2002), and Brueckner et al. (1999).

The literature argues that *the efficiency of the 'standard urban model'* is axiomatic. That is, under certain simplifying assumptions about the functional forms of production and demand functions, an optimizing model of urban producers and consumers yields a negative exponential function for population density, with a dense centre falling off exponentially (steep at first, then flattening as one moves out). See also Mills and Hamilton (1993) for an especially comprehensive exposition of this model, and Fujita (1989) and Turnbull (1995) for some extensions.

Probably the most central assumption in the model is that all employment is located at the centre of the city. Many models have been developed that relax this strict monocentricity, including some that have two centres, some that have a centre and a beltline of employment, and others that have multiple nodes.[1] While

---

[1] It should be noted that even in extremely decentralized labor markets such as Los Angeles or Atlanta, population density still largely follows the negative exponential in market economies (Bertaud 2002; Bertaud and Malpezzi 2003).

there is a strong theoretical literature with some empirical support that the rough, monocentric, negative exponential model is an efficient form, the relationship between urban form and efficiency is still under study and debate (Crane 2000).

While theory tells us that under certain restrictive conditions the negative exponential will be optimal, there is much to be done in future to test this notion empirically. Mills and Tan's (1980) survey of population density in different cities is in many respects the most comprehensive in the literature so far. It incorporates findings from a wide range of studies, most using the negative exponential model, e.g., Mills and Ohta (1976), and Mills and Song (1979). Mills and Tan relate flattening gradients to rising incomes and growing cities, but in a somewhat qualitative, informal way. They present evidence that population density gradients fall over time, worldwide; and that the decline is further related to growth in incomes and the size of cities.

Bertaud and Malpezzi (2003) demonstrate that measures based on simple models of urban form – and sometimes measures of departures from that model – are a useful way to characterize cities. Using data on selected measures of urban form for about 50 metropolitan areas in 27 countries, the study shows that several key predictions of the so-called 'standard urban model' are confirmed: cities everywhere decentralize as their populations grow, their incomes rise, and transport costs fall, as the standard model predicts. In several respects, the empirical results confirm the findings from the study two decades earlier by Mills and Tan (1980). The negative exponential function is considered a useful framework for comparative assessment of urban form. Bertaud and Malpezzi (2003), however, use more data and a competing measure of dispersion and regulation to explore how other factors affect density—namely, natural constraints and the regulatory regime of the city.

5.2 The post-socialist city: The framework applied

From the 'standard urban model' one could advance the hypothesis that post-socialist cities will differ from their counterparts in market economies in such key characteristics as average population density, population dispersion and the shape of their population density gradient. Correspondingly, the relationship between price gradients and density gradients will be different or even non-existent, given the lack of land and real estate markets under state socialism. During the transition from socialism, these differences in the characteristics of urban form will affect transportation efficiency, housing costs and future planning policies. On the basis of work by Bertaud and Malpezzi (2003), Bertaud and Renaud (1997) and Buckley and Mini (2000), and earlier work by Renaud (1995 a, b), it can be argued that cities without land markets have significant differences and spatial distortions—a spatial legacy of empty and seriously misallocated land parcels, environmental costs, and underutilized central areas.

Important factors that explain some of these differences from cities with market economies, and the spatial legacy of socialism concern the development process and the nature of the regulatory system for real estate markets. In the prototypical socialist system, real estate development is undertaken by state *kombinats* or other entities whose objective function is typically to minimize costs to manage a budget allocation from the government. However, a further difficulty under central planning is that inputs may be significantly mispriced or even unpriced (Buckley et al. 2001; Kornai 1992). For example, in pre-*perestroika* Moscow, land was allocated purely according to planning decisions. A characteristic of market-oriented development is that because individuals and firms have property rights in land, and these rights can be alienated, there is an incentive to redevelop land as a city grows and the "highest and best" use changes. In a prototypical socialist city, such redevelopment rarely takes place. In the absence of a market for land or real estate, firms and households have no way to capture gains from permitting the redevelopment of their land; in fact, without such a market, no one quite knows what the gains from redevelopment might be. Without market reference, central planners in socialist economies would be at a loss for benchmarks for the efficient allocation of land, even if that were to be their main objective (Bertaud and Malpezzi 2003).

In market-driven cities and market-oriented economies, density patterns occur because of price differentials. Once the initial simplifying assumptions of constant returns per unit of land are relaxed (that is, once substitution between land and other factors of production is permitted), real estate developers (and indirectly consumers) economize on the use of land at more expensive locations. They do so by adding more capital per unit of land, e.g., by building multi-family units instead of single family, and by building the tallest units with the highest floor area ratios at the closest-in locations. In market-oriented cities, it is the price gradient that gives rise to the density gradient. The prices reflect willingness to pay for central locations, and are driven by savings in transportation costs.

Thus the paradox of a socialist city is as follows: In the prototypical socialist city, especially a city like Moscow with highly centralized employment, consumers valued close-in locations. Because socialist planners in such a market made location decisions without market benchmarks, however, they built more densely on the periphery, i.e. have invested the highest proportion of the capital stock where it is worth the least (World Bank 1995). As Bertaud and Renaud (1995) as well as Mozalin (1995) have shown, after *perestroika*, in the early 1990s Moscow underwent a period of "price discovery." The upshot is that in the prototypical socialist city, *density gradients and price gradients are not in line with each other.* That pattern is fundamentally different from market cities, where "form follows price."

Given the lack of markets or planning adjustments to market signals and demand, the land for industry, services and retail was allocated in accordance with spatial planning norms based on the number of people or the spatial requirements per unit of output. In contrast to industry, which was considered the backbone of the economy and received large amounts of land, land for services was systematically under-allocated. Of course, one reason for that was the absence of certain services from the socialist economy, e.g., banking, insurance, and real estate brokerage. Other services such as health, specialized education, retail and restaurants were often made available on the premises of industrial enterprises or government offices and therefore did not require land allocation.

The spatial planning of residential areas, too, was subject to those planning norms. In some CEE countries, enclaves of private housing were tolerated, as Buckley and Tsenkova (2001) have documented, but under strict controls: the housing had to be owner-occupied, for one family only, and the unit's floor space could not be above 120 m2. Thus even privately owned housing, particularly in urban areas, followed a set of spatial norms independent of its location in the city. In some cases in the older CEE cities, the areas and locations where private housing was allowed to survive were not so much the object of deliberate planning decisions as a historical accident by which an old system of tenure was kept on what was considered "residual land." Prefabricated panel systems, which had been used for housing in many CEE cities since the 1960s, allowed for building of higher blocks of apartments and reduced the normative land requirements (Lowe and Tsenkova 2003). In that case, the density of large apartment projects was not linked to their location within the city, to perceived demand, or to the price of land, but to the technology used at the time of construction (Buckley and Mini 2000).

In summary, CEE cities retain from their socialist past a number of spatial malformations that will be challenging to correct: a) large amounts of obsolete industrial land located close to city centres; b) lack of retail and service space in the city centre; c) residential estates of high-density panel housing located on the periphery.

5.3 Comparative spatial analysis of post-socialist cities

This section compares the spatial structure of post-socialist cities with their counterparts in Western Europe, using four spatial indicators: average density, density profile, land price profile, and proportion of industrial land.

5.3.1 Indicator 1: Average density

Average density is calculated by dividing the population of census tracts within the built-up area of the city by the built-up area itself. The built-up area is defined as the area with built structures, including residential, industrial and utility areas, and roads, but excluding airports. Parks and open spaces larger that 4 hectares, and water bodies are also excluded from the built-up area.[2]

---

[2] In many cases the built-up area expands significantly outside the municipal boundaries. However, the amount of built-up area is often smaller than the total area within municipal boundaries, because the area within the municipal boundaries typically includes undeveloped space, large parks and open space and in some cases water bodies. In many other studies, comparative density figures are obtained by dividing the population of a city by the

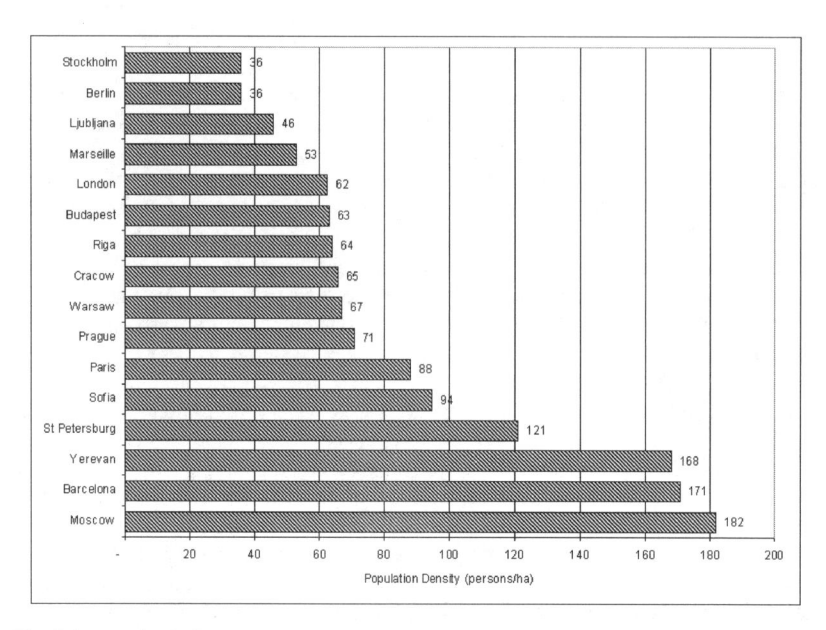

City	Population Density (persons/ha)
Stockholm	36
Berlin	36
Ljubljana	46
Marseille	53
London	62
Budapest	63
Riga	64
Cracow	65
Warsaw	67
Prague	71
Paris	88
Sofia	94
St Petersburg	121
Yerevan	168
Barcelona	171
Moscow	182

Fig. 5.1. Density in European cities

Average densities would be expected to be higher in post-socialist cities because of the way land had been allocated during the socialist period, and in particular, the ideologically motivated dominance of apartment buildings over individual housing. Working the other way, the over-allocation of land to industrial uses should tend to lower the densities. In fact, however, as compared to other cities, the density of CEE cities does not differ from the density of their market-economy counterparts (Fig. 5.1.). Average densities vary greatly among cities in various part of the world. The variations, however, are probably due more to cultural factors inherent in each region or continent than to economic and political systemic factors. Post-socialist cities in Europe have the same range of average densities – between 35 and 100 people per hectare – as their European market-economy counterparts. Moscow and St Petersburg are post-socialist outliers, with much higher densities, but Barcelona's density is similar to Moscow's.[3] It seems that for average density, i.e. consumption of land per person, regional location is more important than ideology. In CEE cities, being European is a more important predictor of densities than is being formerly socialist.

---

area within municipal boundaries. The gross municipal density figures obtained that way differ from the ones presented here.

[3] The similarity among the densities of Chinese, South Korean and Indian cities is remarkable (Bertaud and Malpezzi 2003).

5.3.2 Indicator 2: Density profile

The peculiarities of the socialist land allocation system described above should be identifiable on the density profile of cities (Fig. 5.2.). On the graphs, the distance from the city centre in intervals of 1 kilometre is represented horizontally; the density of built up areas within each one-kilometre ring is represented vertically. To facilitate the comparisons between cities, both horizontal scale and vertical scales are equal on all graphs and vary, respectively, from 0 to 30 km and from 0 to 300 people per hectare.

Cities are grouped into 3 categories: CEE cities that were for less than 40 years under socialist rule; cities that were for more than 40, but less than 70 years under socialist rule; and Western European cities with uninterrupted traditions of the market economy. With the exception of Budapest, CEE cities in the first category show a density profile that is negatively sloped but convex, with notable disturbance in the profile; cities in the second category tend to have a positively sloped profile; and cities in the third category show negatively sloped, concave exponential profile that conforms with the literature on density gradient in monocentric cities in market economies (Alonso 1964; Muth 1985; Mills 1970).

The comparison of density profiles confirms the hypothesis that CEE cities have a hybrid spatial structure, reflecting the time spent under different economic systems. The city development pattern under capitalism tends to shape densities along a negatively sloped exponential curve (example, Paris), while socialism tends to shape densities along a positively sloped curve (example, Moscow). The longer the time spent under socialism, the more positively sloped is the curve. Nonetheless, many CEE cities, with the exception of Moscow, have high density in the city centre, the resilient imprint of their capitalist past.

Fig. 5.2. shows a significant difference between the density patterns of Moscow and St. Petersburg and the densities of cities of Central Europe and the Baltics. In the Russian cities, density drops rapidly between 3km and 7km, corresponding to the industrial belt immediately adjacent to the historical core; the reduction in density is more gradual in Central European cities. The difference can be explained by the period in their history when these cities were transformed by industrialization and socialism. In the case of the cities in Russia, industrialization and socialism appeared nearly simultaneously, creating large industrial belts that are still visible today immediately around their historical cores. The cities of Central Europe, on the other hand, had already gone through initial industrialization when socialism was imposed on them. The locations and amounts of land used by industries had therefore already been allocated by markets. Cracow, with the creation of the Nova Huta steel mill, was an exception to this rule.

The density profile of Budapest is more puzzling, but is not inconsistent with the hypothesis of two superimposed spatial structures. The profile starts with a high density of 280 people per hectare in the centre (similar to Paris), then drops suddenly to around 60 at a distance of 4 km. The high density of Budapest's centre shows the imprint of its historical capitalist core, and the sudden drop in density is due to a wide industrial belt similar to those in St. Petersburg and Moscow. In the other CEE cities, the industrial areas are distributed along radial axes, and their

98 Alain Bertaud

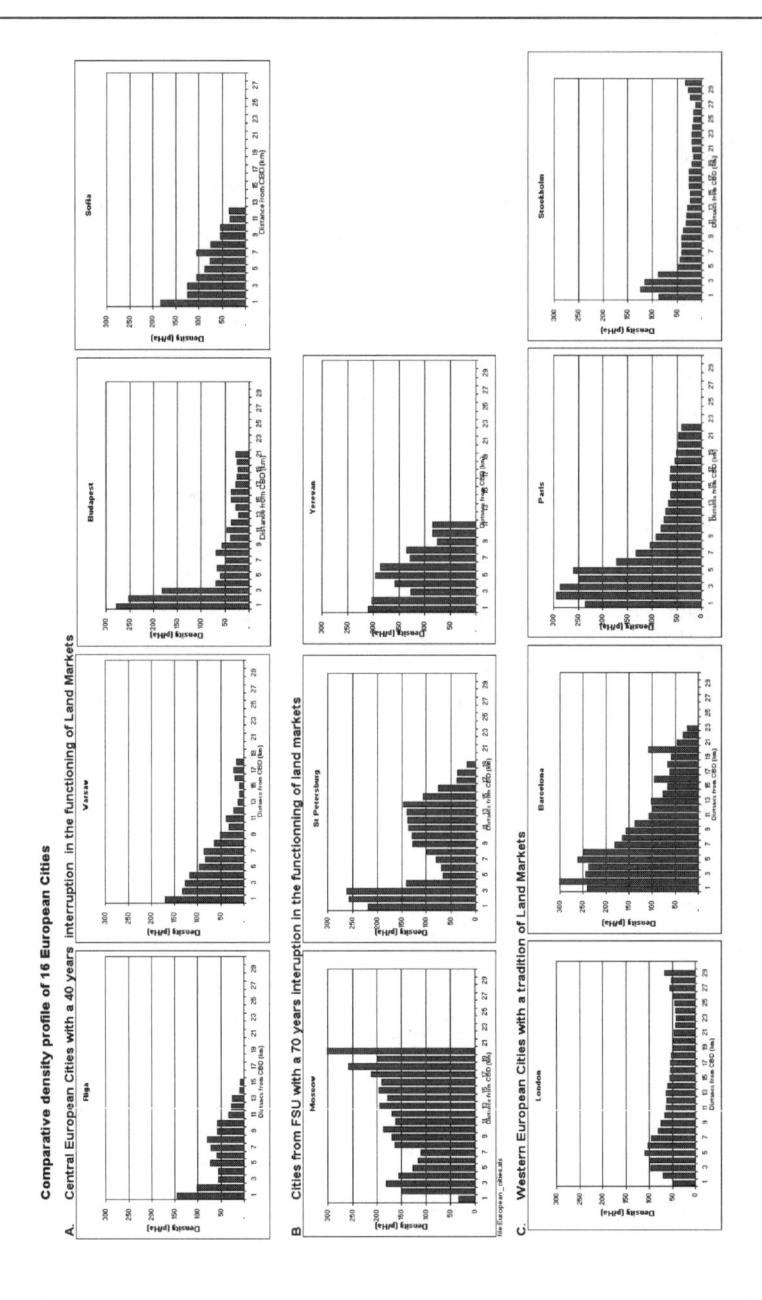

Fig. 5.2. Comparative density profile between CEE cities and Western European cities

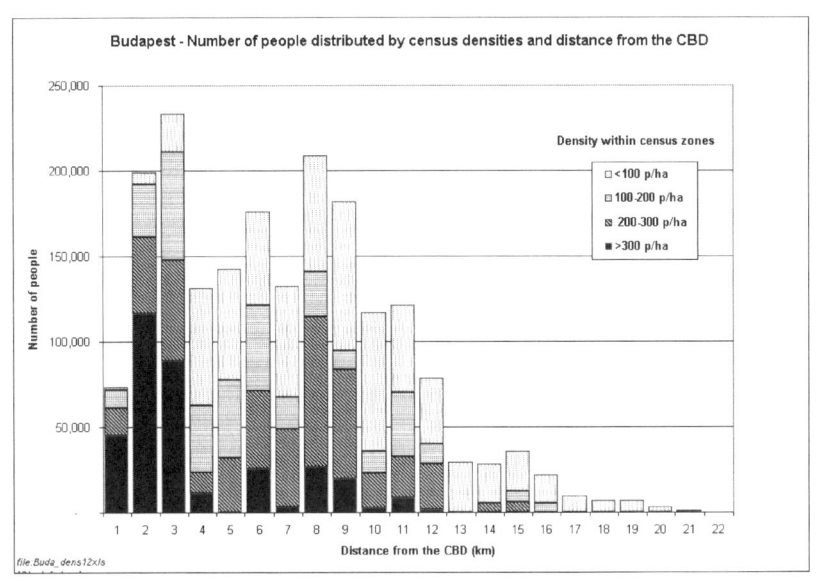

Fig. 5.3. Budapest: Distribution of people by distance from the centre and densities

densities tend to decrease more gradually (for instance in Warsaw, Sofia and Riga).

The density profile alone can be misleading in accounting for changes in densities with distance from the centre. In a socialist economy, within a given radius, a large proportion of the built-up area may be occupied by industries or low-density private housing, while the majority of the population lives in very high-density settlements. As a consequence, the average density may be rather low even in the areas with high-density residential projects. Fig. 5.3. shows that in Budapest, more people live in high-density neighbourhoods (more than 200 people per hectare) in 8-km and 9-km rings than in 4-km and 5-km rings. However, quite large numbers of people live in low-density neighbourhoods – often with private housing and controlled low density – near the city centre and probably close to or within industrial areas. More detailed analyses of densities by type and location are useful in describing socialist urban structure, which tends to display less homogeneity than does the capitalist urban structure.

5.3.3 Indicator 3: Land price profile

The monocentric city model of Alonso (1964), Muth (1985) and Mills (1970) suggests that there is a close correlation between density and land prices. In most market-economy cities that is usually confirmed by empirical evidence, – even if the cities are not dominantly monocentric. For instance, in Paris, the land price and density profiles follow the predictable negatively sloped exponential curve

(Fig. 5.4.), and both curves closely follow each other's inflections. The very steep decrease in price and density at a distance of about 4 km from the centre is typical of large European cities. It perhaps indicates that the high quality amenities and employment offered in the centre of the city are valued by high-income households.

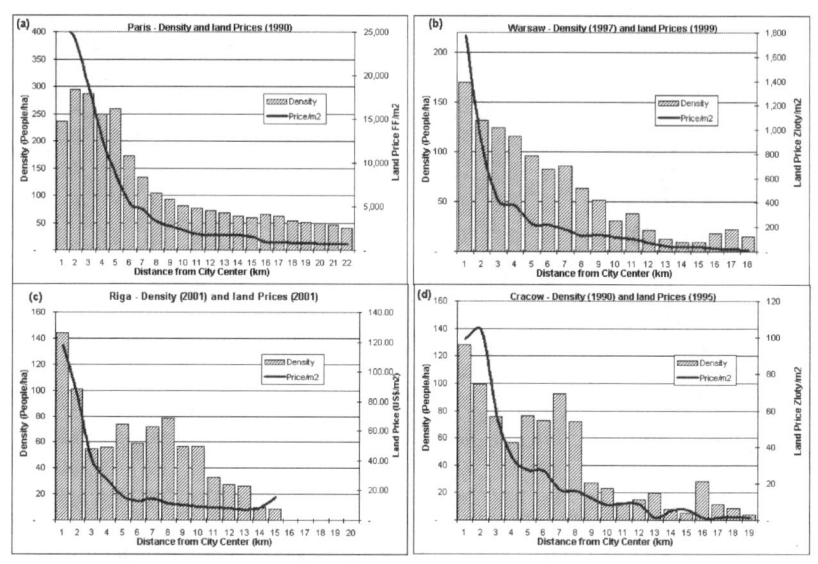

Fig. 5.4. Land price and density profile in CEE cities and in a market economy

In a socialist economy there was no land price profile, as land was distributed administratively. However, as soon as a market economy started to function in CEE cities, land bids aligned themselves along an exponential, negatively sloped curve (Brzeski and Dale-Johnson 2001) – as predicted by the monocentric model, while the density profile kept the shape it had acquired during the socialist period. There is therefore a discrepancy between prices and density in all CEE cities, as shown in Fig. 5.4., for Warsaw, Cracow and Riga, respectively. For instance, at the 5-km distance, in both Riga and Cracow land prices drop sharply while density increases.

In practical terms, does this discrepancy between price and density matter? It shows a mismatch between the existing supply of housing and the demand from households. On the ground, the mismatch is manifested in market rents that are often lower than maintenance cost, but more generally by capitalized market rents which are much lower than land prices combined with construction replacement costs. The low market value of a large part of the housing stock in CEE cities is not necessarily due to a temporary demand slump, but rather to a permanent spatial defect reflecting inefficient land allocation at the time of socialism. This raises important policy implications, which will be discussed below.

5.3.4 Indicator 4: Proportion of industrial land over built-up area

In market economy cities, industrial land developed during the industrial revolution and during the first part of the twentieth century has been progressively converted to other uses. This systematic and progressive conversion was due not to deliberate urban planning decisions, but rather to market forces. Industrial use is land-intensive and therefore requires higher investments of capital in the areas where land is expensive. In addition, the communication technology that allows for separate locations of production, design and management encourages movement of the production functions that are land-intensive to the locations where land is cheaper and retaining the design and management functions in the more expensive areas, often centrally located.

In CEE cities during the socialist period those market forces were not unleashed. The value of their real estate did not appear as assets in the accounts of industrial enterprises. In addition, the socialist ideology gave prestigious status to manufacturing, as can be seen on many propaganda posters including iconic smokestacks.

The land use map of St Petersburg illustrates how, in a post-socialism context, industrial land hinders urban growth (Fig. 5.5.). The industrial areas shown in dark offer very little employment and lie mostly under warehouses. For example, an area of more than 40 hectares in the first industrial belt directly to the south of the historic city centre was used in 2001 to store coal in bulk. The area is next to two subway stations, within a few minutes from Nevsky Prospekt. If the cost of capital represented by the market value of the land occupied by the coal depot were included in the price of coal distributed in St. Petersburg, it would certainly represent a sizable amount and would provide a strong incentive for its relocation. This suggests that the privatization of state-owned enterprises could improve land use efficiency quite effectively and affect future land-use plans.

The large percentage of the total built-up area that is given over to industry is a typical feature of CEE cities. In most market-economy cities, the industrial areas represent about 4% to 10 % of the total built-up areas. Fig. 5.6. shows the variations in the percentage of industrial area in total built-up areas in several CEE cities. The extensive under use of industrial land in CEE cities poses a major challenge to their modernization. In the absence of immediate conversion of land from industrial to other uses, new developments have to leap-frog derelict industrial waste land, increasing the cost of transport and of infrastructure development.

ST. PETERSBURG - INDUSTRIAL AREAS

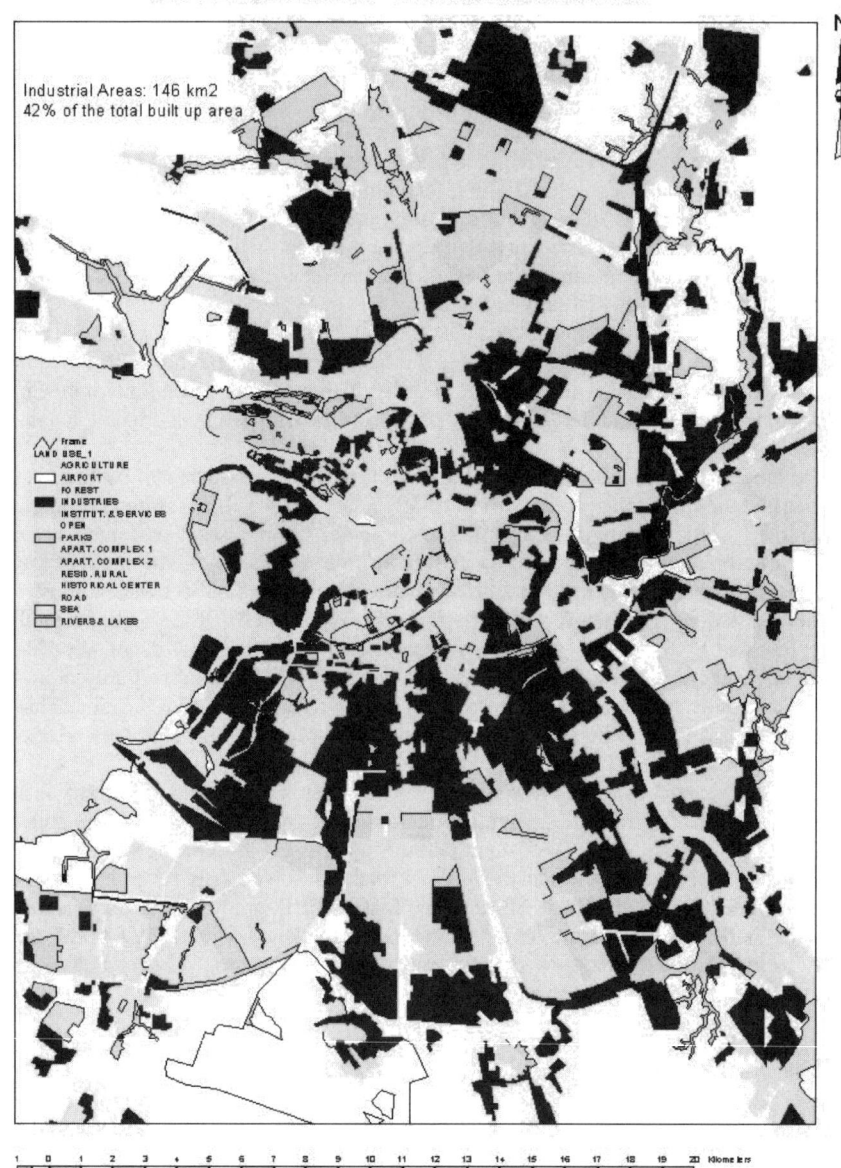

Fig. 5.5. St Petersburg. Map of industrial areas

Industrial Land In Built Up Areas (%):
- London: 4.7%
- Paris: 5.2%
- Prague: 13.4%
- Warsaw: 15.1%
- Sofia: 27.1%
- Ljubljana: 27.4%
- Cracow: 28.0%
- Moscow: 31.6%
- St Petersburg: 43.8%

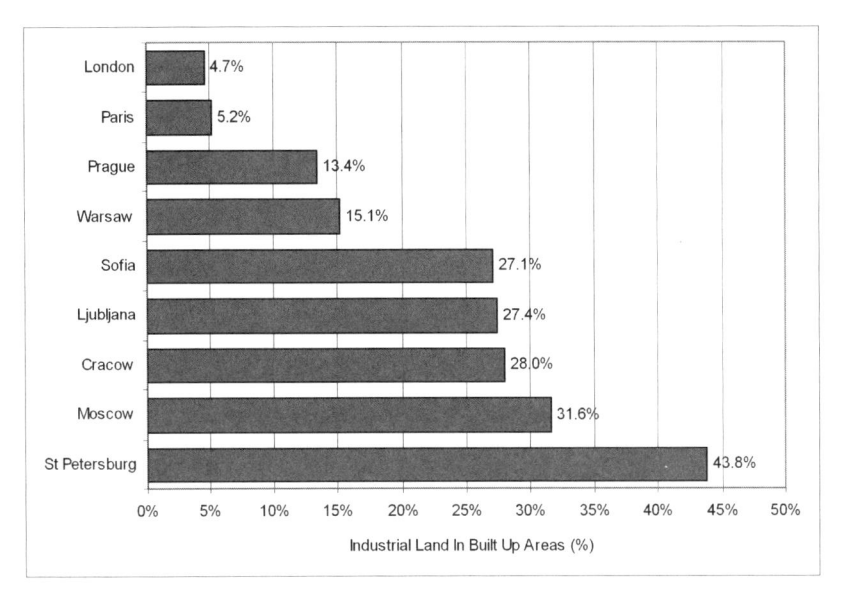

Fig. 5.6. Industrial land

5.4 Development of urban strategies for CEE cities

The policy responses of CEE municipalities to challenges posed by their socialist past and by the capitalist present have not always been coherent and consistent because of the lack of a clear model to deal with the transition and simply its pace. At the same time the declared development objectives of the post-socialist municipalities are remarkably similar to those of other European cities (Tsenkova 2005). For a more detailed analysis of these issues in the context of the city development strategies for Cracow, Budapest, Warsaw, Riga and Prague, see Bertaud 1999 (a) and (b), Bertaud and Bertaud 2000 (a) and (b), and Bertaud 2002. While the approaches might be similar, as Bertaud and Malpezzi (2003) have documented, this chapter will focus on four important thematic areas of planning policy that are directly related to the previous comparative analysis. They are:

- Reinforcing and preserving the historical character of the urban centre by maintaining a high level of economic activity and a mixed land use;
- Maintaining a high proportion of trips by transit and discouraging the use of private cars in the centre city;
- Maintaining a high level of employment – in particular in the city centre – by making cities attractive to business investments; and

- Developing density and land use policies to ensure the supply of affordable housing.

5.4.1 Reinforcing economic and cultural activities in city centres

To reinforce economic activities in the centre of CEE cities more freedom in land transactions and in land use changes is required. Much of the land or at least the floor space in the centre city of CEE cities is misallocated. Greater flexibility would progressively allow land use changes to serve the demand for new business, retail and commerce uses such as restaurants and cafés.

Planners in CEE, while recognizing the need for change, usually "design change" rather than letting market forces shape new land uses. For instance, the new master plan of St Petersburg in 1998 had already selected specific sites where respectively 2-star, 3-star and 4-star hotels should be located. It is of course much better to let the hotel operators propose how many and which types of hotels should be built on which sites. The city may then raise objections because of obvious externalities, or may negotiate an impact fee to compensate for additional off-site infrastructure that may be required. Micromanagement of land use is never successful, because urban planners do not have enough information about the demand for and the operational viability of e.g., hotels, barbershops or other businesses.

Many well-meaning regulations prevent land use conversions in downtown areas. For instance, in many centres of CEE cities, conversion of residential floor space into office space or even retail space is strictly controlled or even forbidden, to prevent the loss of housing stock. Restricting land use conversion in a downtown area for that purpose, however, is an ill conceived policy, as it helps to lessen the attractiveness of the centre and thus push modern commercial development in the suburbs, often in peripheral municipalities where regulations are more flexible (Bertaud 2000, 2002). Moreover, most apartments in CEE cities have been privatized, so the prices developers would pay for them are likely to be reinvested in newer, more modern apartments in the same city. Their conversion from residential use is therefore unlikely to result in a net loss of apartments.

Besides restrictive regulations, fuzzy property titles may hinder land use conversion. Uncertainty over property rights affects most particularly the older parts of towns, where overlapping titles and restitution claims have not yet been solved. Because it affects mostly the centre city, the problem of tenure uncertainty contributes to weakening the centre's economic activities, pushing toward the suburbs those activities that would have located in the centre if clear titles had been available.

The responsibility to maintain the historical character of city centres is often invoked to justify freezing land use there in its past, socialist state. That is a self-destructive policy, because historical buildings are expensive to maintain. Only high rents and high property taxes produced by prestigious economic activities can pay for the continuous maintenance of historical buildings.

To maintain a strong centre, the municipal government must make sizable investments in maintaining and renovating cultural and historic centres and even, in the European tradition, in subsidizing concert halls, operas and theaters.[4] Mixed land use—retail, services, institutional--should help to generate the taxes that make possible the subsidies for cultural activities. Culture and commerce reinforce each other. However, for that mix to happen, land transactions should be facilitated and regulations should allow changes in land use.

5.4.2 Maintaining a high level of transit trips

Most European cities are dominantly monocentric, having prestigious centres with high levels of amenities (Brueckner et al. 1999) and relatively high population densities around the centre. That creates very favourable conditions for operating an efficient transit network that is convenient for the consumer and successful for the operator. However, the reversal of those conditions – loss of economic activities in the centre, deterioration of amenities and reduced population densities – will reduce the number of transit trips. The municipal objective of maintaining a high level of transit trips therefore depends on land use policy at least as much as on the efficient operation of the transit network.

Maintaining a high level of transit trips depends on the conditions for the quality of the city centre as described in the preceding section. Land use regulations allowing land use change, a great flexibility in land use mix, and buoyant land transactions reinforce the use of transit. Deterioration of transit operations themselves and of the economic viability of the city centre reduce transit trips and increase the use of private cars. The policy toward the use of private cars, in particular road pricing and parking pricing, is key to spatial policy.

The high population density of the centres of European cities, ranging from 100 to 300 people per hectare, is possible only when an efficient transit system serves the high-density central area. But for the last 75 years, Western European cities have had to deal with the competition between cars and transit. The pricing of car access to the city centre that was recently imposed in London shows that the competition between cars and transit is still not over. Post-socialist cities need to maintain their higher transit ridership. It can contribute to the quality of the urban environment and strike a balance between transit and car access in the downtown area, while also preserving or creating large pedestrian areas.

In CEE cities the increase in car ownership and car use for commuting has been recent and rapid (Tsenkova 2005). Municipalities of CEE cities, confronting a flood of newly acquired cars, have a tendency to either enforce through regulations the building of new off-street parking or—even worse—subsidize the creation of municipal parking and under price on-street parking. The maintenance of a dense, dynamic centre, so characteristic of European cities is incompatible with subsidizing car access to the centre. Land in the centre of European cities is far too valuable to be used for free or subsidized parking. The price of land and its corresponding market rent should establish parking rates and, as a consequence, the number of cars that have access to the city centre. Rights of way of downtown streets should be used entirely for either pedestrian or car traffic, but be free of parked cars. Private developers should be free to build off-street car garages, provided they are built and operated without subsidies.

5.4.3 Maintaining or promoting high employment and recycling industrial land

Governments in CEE cities face the problem of high unemployment created by the closing of state-owned enterprises. While municipalities work to attract large foreign investments – say, a Volkswagen factory or a Coca-Cola bottling plant – they often ignore the land needs of small local businesses. Yet, in reality, most new jobs are created by small enterprises in the service and retail sector. Those sectors were grossly undeveloped under the past command economy. Now a major hurdle for newly created small enterprises in CEE cities is finding a place to operate their business.

Land is a major input in creating employment in urban areas. Because of the under-allocation of land during the socialist era, much of the land and floor space needed for creating new jobs is currently is being used, for industrial, residential, or even agricultural or governmental purposes. The creation of new jobs thus depends on the timely conversion of current obsolete land use and floor space to a new use for which there is demand. Unfortunately, the new zoning laws that have replaced the master plans of the earlier command economy often either prevent land use conversion or impose such high transaction costs that new businesses cannot afford the land.

Planners have converted the old master plans into "structural development plans" that usually include a new zoning plan similar to those in Western, market-economy cities. However, the new plans often perpetuate the old land uses. For some reason the notion of "nonconforming zoning," indispensable market economies, is not often included in the zoning legislation of CEE cities. For instance, the zoning plan of Prague established in 1998 has 68 zoning categories, representing the current land use. An entrepreneur who wants to start a new business is unlikely to find a ready seller in the zoning category corresponding to his/her new business in a compatible location. The entrepreneur will have therefore want a rezoning, which will be lengthy and costly if even possible.

Designing regulations which are consistent with markets is relatively easy in market economies, because zoning changes are usually preceded by public hearings where suppliers and consumers have a chance to express informed opinions. In former socialist economies the process is more difficult because, first, existing land use does not necessarily convey what "the market wants"; second, public participation in local government is still embryonic; and third, interest groups are much less organized and informed about technical issues such as zoning. In CEE cities the best approach to regulations could be the one used in Warsaw (Bertaud 2000). In Warsaw zoning areas are divided into 3 broad categories, *market driven areas*, covering about 48% of the municipal area; segregated *areas for noxious uses* (14%), containing heavy industries and utilities; and *protected areas* (37%), including historical areas, university areas, and green areas to be protected. Within these categories there of course are subcategories for more specific uses. The category of market-driven area is the most original feature of Warsaw's newly introduced zoning. In this category, regulations allow almost any mix of non-noxious use and relax the limit on density to far above the current one, encouraging developers to redevelop existing structures more intensively wherever there is demand for it. However, historical monuments and natural features such as the bluff dominating the Vistula River are fully protected. Prague zoning, by contrast, with its more than 68 zoning categories reflecting existing land use, provides much little incentive for developers and results in continuous zoning amendments that may be difficult to monitor.

5.4.4 Developing density and land use policies to increase the supply of affordable housing

Most CEE cities face falling populations over the next decades. Nevertheless, there is pressure on housing, because household size is also falling. Another problem is that many apartments in downtown areas have been transformed into offices or even torn down (as in Warsaw) to make room for office and commercial space. As incomes increase we can predict that the desire for more floor space per person will also fuel a demand for more housing. Many small apartments (outside panel housing) are being consolidated into larger ones, reducing the number of units. We have therefore paradox of a falling population and a concurrent housing shortage.

In some CEE cities the housing shortage has resulted in a sharp rise in housing prices, especially for modern and better standard constructions (Buckley and Tsenkova 2001). Understandably enough, municipal authorities are concerned about the rising housing prices. The best approach is, first, to facilitate land conversion from industrial or agricultural use to residential use; second, to allow the densities suggested by the market. Too often, because of popular rejection of large panel housing estates, regulators tend to over-regulate densities toward the low side. Regulations that systematically reduce densities to below the market demand cause the urban area to expand, creating more pressure on the natural environment. In the new zoning of Cracow, the low density set for areas adjacent to an electric tramway illustrates this point (Bertaud 1997). Urban planners should be reminded that higher residential density, if demand driven, reduces the foot print of the city and therefore reduces transport time and the pollution due to transport. Higher residential densities when there is a demand for them are therefore friendly to the environment.

The rehabilitation or progressive elimination of "panel" housing poses a particularly difficult problem. In many socialist cities, though most spectacularly in Moscow, a great deal has been invested in housing that is now worth very little, not only because of poor design and maintenance, but because of location. In many CEE cities, market rents in panel housing are below their maintenance costs, and panel housing apartments are trading much below replacement costs. That creates a conundrum for city managers. On the one hand, investing large sums to upgrade panel housing would be risky at best, given its locations. On the other hand, at least in some cities these units are such a large proportion of the stock that it will take years for the markets to build sufficient replacement stock to house the population. The best policy is probably to undertake some "minimum" maintenance, while accelerating the development of real estate markets that can fill the gap. This would include, but not be limited to, regulatory and planning environments conducive to market-driven infill and also some greenfield development.

Conclusions

In spite of the remnants of socialist land use, CEE cities have remained European because of their underlying spatial structure and the priorities expressed in their development plans. However, to maintain their European character, the land use patterns left from the socialist era have to be corrected. Improving the functioning of markets by allowing more transactions and reducing regulatory barriers and transaction costs is the best way to do so.

The reinforcement of the city centre with amenities and job concentration is an important objective that has many benefits: first, maintaining the dominantly monocentric character of the city increases the viability of the transit system and therefore reduces pollution; second, maintaining high densities in the centre reduces the pressure on the natural environment at the city fringe; and third, a prestigious centre maintains the cultural identity of the city.

The removal of the large industrial areas next to the historical centres is probably one of the highest priorities for maintaining the European character of CEE cities. Their removal is not always easy, as the soil is often polluted and has to be treated before another use is possible. Besides that, municipalities would have to invest considerable financial resources to create new streets and new infrastructure compatible with residential or business use.

Municipalities in CEE cities confront two apparently contradictory tasks: letting the market take the lead in allocating land and floor space between different uses in the city centres, while also taking investment initiatives in planning and building infrastructure to redevelop obsolete industrial areas. Private developers in CEE cities have neither the experience nor the access to financial resources to undertake the redevelopment of such large areas.

In the absence of strong municipal initiatives to reinforce the cultural and business character of the centre city and to invest in the redevelopment of industrial areas, the structure of CEE cities may be irreversibly damaged. The increase in vehicle use, combined with the difficulty of real estate transactions in the city centre will stimulate the growth of business and residential development in the suburbs, progressively marginalizing the historical city centre. If that scenario were to be realized, CEE cities would progressively lose their European character in spite of the stated objectives of their development plans.

Acknowledgement

The empirical research for this chapter has been supported by the World Bank. The author acknowledges the collaboration of Stephen Malpezzi and the Centre for Urban Land Economics Research, University of Wisconsin.

References

Alonso W (1964) Location and land use. Harvard University Press, Harvard
Arnott R, Anas A, Small K (1998) Urban spatial structure. J of Economic Literature 36: 236-241
Bertaud A (1999a) Cracow in the 21st century: Princes or merchants. World Bank Report
Bertaud A (1999b) The spatial development of Budapest. World Bank Report, World Bank, Washington DC
Bertaud A (2000) The costs of utopia: Brasilia, Johannesburg and Moscow. Paper presented to the European Network for Housing Research, Gävle, Sweden, 26-30 June 2000
Bertaud A (2002) Note on Riga spatial structure. World Bank Report, World Bank, Washington DC
Bertaud A, Bertaud M (2000a) Note on Prague city structure. World Bank Report, World Bank, Washington DC
Bertaud A, Bertaud M (2000b) The spatial development of Warsaw metropolitan area. World Bank Report, World Bank, Washington DC
Bertaud A, Malpezzi S (2003) The spatial distribution of population in 48 world cities: The role of markets, planning, and topography; and their implications for economies in transition. World Bank Report, World Bank, Washington DC
Bertaud A, Renaud B (1997) Socialist cities without land markets. J of Urban Economics 41:137-151
Brueckner J, Thisse JF, Zenou Y (1999) Why is central Paris rich and downtown Detroit poor? An amenity-based theory. European Economic Review 43:91-107
Buckley RM, Mini F (2000) From commissars to mayors: Cities in the transition economies. World Bank Report, World Bank, Washington DC
Buckley R, Ellis P, Hamilton E (2001) Urban housing and land market reforms in transition countries: Neither Marx nor market. World Bank Report, World Bank, Washington DC
Buckley RM, Tsenkova S (2001) Housing market systems in reforming socialist economies: Comparative indicators of performance and policy. European J of Housing Policy 1:257-89
Crane R (2000) The influence of urban form on travel: An interpretive review. J of Planning Literature 15:3-23
Dale-Johnson D, Brzeski JW (2001) Land value functions and land price indexes in Cracow, 1993-1999. J of Housing Economics 10:307-334
Eberts RW (1981) An empirical evaluation of intraurban wage gradients. J of Urban Economics 21:50-60
Follain JR, Malpezzi S (1981) The flight to the suburbs: Insight from an analysis of central city versus suburban housing costs. J of Urban Economics, 20:351-367
Fujita M (1989) Urban economic theory. Cambridge University Press, Cambridge

Kornai J (1992) The socialist system: The political economy of communism. Princeton University Press, Princeton

Lowe S, Tsenkova S (eds) (2003) Housing change in Central and Eastern Europe. Ashgate Publishing Limited, Aldershot

McDonald JF (1989) Econometric studies of urban population density: A survey. J of Urban Economics 26:361-385

Mills ES (1970) Urban density functions. Urban Studies 7:5-20

Mills ES (1972) Studies in the structure of the urban economy. Johns Hopkins University Press, Baltimore

Mills ES, Hamilton BW (1993) Urban economics. Fifth Edition, Harper Collins Publishers, New York

Mills ES, Ohta K (1976) Urbanization and urban problems. In: Patrick H, Rosovsky H (eds) Asia's new giant. Brookings, New York

Mills ES, Song BK (1979) Urbanization and urban problems. Harvard University Press, Harvard

Mills ES, Tan JP (1980) A comparison of urban population density functions in developed and developing countries. Urban Studies 17(3):313-321

Muth RF (1985) Models of land-use, housing, and rent: An evaluation. J of Regional Science 25:593-606

Renaud B (1995a) The real estate economy and the design of Russian housing reforms, Part I. Urban Studies 32:1247-1264

Renaud B (1995b) The real estate economy and the design of Russian housing reforms, Part II. Urban Studies 32:1437-1451

Straszheim MR (1987) The theory of urban residential structure. In: Mills ES (ed) Handbook of urban and regional economics. Volume 2, North Holland, Delft

Trumbull NS (1999) Transportation, urban form, and the environment in the transition economies: Challenges and opportunity. Transboundary Environmental Information Agency, St Petersburg

Tsenkova S (2005) Urban sustainability in Europe and North America. University of Calgary, Faculty of Environmental Design, Calgary

Wu J (2002) Environmental amenities, urban sprawl, and the economic landscape. Paper presented to the Lincoln Institute of Land Policy

PART II

URBAN PROCESSES AND SPATIAL CHANGE

6 The changing spatial structure of post-socialist Sofia

Sonia Hirt and Atanass Kovachev

Introduction

This chapter reviews spatial restructuring that has occurred in the Bulgarian capital of Sofia since the collapse of socialism in 1989.[1] It discusses the dimensions of the city's spatial restructuring that affect: 1) residential spaces; 2) commercial functional zones; and 3) open spaces in the urban neighbourhoods. Sofia is chosen as representative of Southeast European cities that have remained outside mainstream scholarly work on post-socialist, urban spatial change. Although such processes have been documented in Central East European cities (Sýkora 1999), and to a lesser extent in Russian (Rudolph and Brade 2005) and Baltic cities (Ruoppila 1998), Southeast European cities are severely understudied. In the case of Sofia, evidence of spatial restructuring has been fragmented and descriptive (Staddon and Mollov 2000).

Specifically, the chapter examines the following processes of restructuring: 1) in residential spaces: the loss of the compact urban form inherited from socialism and the growth of a lower-density, suburban periphery; 2) in commercial functional re-organization: the initial emergence of a strong commercial core and subsequent commercial developments at the periphery; and 3) in the organization of open space: loss of public green spaces and their fragmentation into explicitly private enclosures.

The three processes discussed here are critical aspects of the built environment that once distinguished the socialist city from its capitalist counterparts (Haussermann 1996; Szelenyi 1996). They have produced some the most visible shifts in the spatial character of the Bulgarian capital since 1989. In our view, they chronicle Sofia's spatial transition from a socialist back to a capitalist city.

The discussion of the changes in Sofia's spatial structure draws on a combination of primary and secondary sources. They sources include official data from the National Statistical Institute in Sofia; documentation available from the municipal government, local real estate firms, and scholarly and media publications; interviews with over three dozen key informants knowledgeable about Sofia's recent urban development (e.g., planners at the Municipal Directorate of Architecture

---

[1] Photos by Sonia Hirt unless otherwise stated. This chapter incorporates some material from an article entitled: "From the Socialist to the Post-socialist City: Transformations of Built Form in Sofia, Bulgaria" by Sonia Hirt, which is under review at Urban Studies.

and Urban Design and contributors to Sofia's latest comprehensive plan *Sofia 2020*); a photographic survey; and personal observation.

The following section briefly discusses characteristics of the spatial structure of socialist cities and is followed by a concise history of Sofia's development since the first settlement on its site. We then review the social, economic, and institutional aspects of the post-socialist period that underlie the current processes of spatial change. The next sections present the three processes of urban spatial restructuring that are the focus here, and the conclusion outlines the implications for urban planning.

6.1 Spatial structure of the socialist city

The term "socialist city" is a disputed one. There is no consensus in the literature that socialism brought about a truly distinctive urban model (Bodnar 2001; Szelenyi 1996). Some assert that urban form is the outcome of the universal processes of twentieth-century industrial urbanization, which cut across the capitalist-socialist boundary (Enyedi 1996). Others argue that by reducing the role of private ownership of land, housing and the means of production, socialism produced a truly unique urban category (Szelenyi 1996). The ongoing debate aside, however, most scholars agree that socialist cities had at least some distinctive characteristics.

Perhaps the most obvious difference between socialist and capitalist cities was in their overall spatial articulation, in particular of residential areas. Socialist cities were more compact than capitalist ones (Haussermann 1996; Sýkora 1999). Rings of low-density suburbs surrounded the capitalist cities. Socialist cities exhibited only state-controlled decentralization in the form of large housing estates that's unlike western suburbs, were high-density, marked a distinct urban edge, and did not lead to depopulation of the central city core (Tammaru 2001).

Key distinctions can be noted in the organization of the socialist city's commercial functions. Commercial activities, for instance, were grossly underrepresented, because the state's focus on heavy industry meant a permanent scarcity of consumer goods and consequently of outlets for their sale. Furthermore, most socialist countries had no privately owned, market-oriented businesses, although Yugoslavia, Czechoslovakia and Hungary permitted them to a limited extent. Hence, commercial spaces constituted only a small share of the socialist city. The paucity of commerce was equally pronounced in the peripheral urban zones, both the traditional ones and the new ones built under socialism auspices (the housing projects), and in the city centre (Dingsdale 1999; Sýkora 1998; Haussermann 1996; Szelenyi 1996). The city centre, unlike capitalist central business districts, was dominated by civic and residential uses.

Lastly, the scale and organization of public open spaces in the post-World-War-II urban neighbourhoods had a distinctively socialist imprint. As Szelenyi (1996) points out, socialist planners practiced "less economizing with space," i.e., socialist neighbourhoods were unusually well supplied with parks and other open public spaces. State control over most urban land facilitated generous provision of park and open spaces, unhindered by land prices or struggles over land ownership. Equally important was the symbolic underpinning for generous public spaces. Socialist ideology gave priority to collectivist social order and good and, monumental open public spaces expressed that (Crowley and Reid 2002). From the standpoint of socialist theorists, the pre-World-War-II city was an unfortunate collection of fragmented private spaces that reflected the conflicted capitalist society. The socialist city, in contrast, was intended to be the people's city, open to all.

6.2 Profile of pre-socialist and socialist Sofia

Sofia's remarkable history dates back to the Neolithic Age. It was an important regional node in pre-Roman, Roman and medieval times (Tashev 1972). However, most of the city's current fabric was built only after it became the Bulgarian capital in 1879, following independence from five hundred years of Ottoman rule. The city then grew rapidly, acquiring the basic structure of other early-to-mid-twentieth-century European cities. In 1880, it had only 20,000 residents, inhabiting an area of less than 3 sq km (Ishirkov 1928), but by 1934, the population had reached 400,000 and the total area approached 42 sq km (Labov 1979). In the late 19th and early 20th centuries a charming Art Nouveau downtown developed, comprising a vibrant mix of public buildings, shops, restaurants, cafes and trendy homes. Surrounding it were upscale neighbourhoods built according to European fashions. Beyond those spread the modest, chaotic areas housing workers and the refugees from several lost wars (Staddon and Mollov 2000).

In 1944, with the establishment of a communist-led government, Sofia's growth pattern changed. Land and real estate were nationalized in 1947-48. There followed several decades of steady urban growth. The population reached its present level of 1.2 million in 1985. A paradigm shift in city-building occurred in the 1960s with the adoption of industrialized building methods (Smolyanov 2000; Gugov 2000). Following the Soviet lead in building socialist "micro-regions" (Smith 1996), Sofia's post-World-War-II planners abandoned their initial focus on urban infill and pursued spatial expansion that brought the city's total area to 190 sq km. The urban core was encircled by large housing estates (e.g., Mladost, Nadezhda, Studentski Grad and Lyulin) that by the late 1990s housed 700,000 people or sixty percent of the city's population (Genova 2000).

The socialist period, therefore, brought notable changes in Sofia's spatial structure. The city, as noted, expanded dramatically. However, the spatial expansion was primarily due to substantial population growth. Unlike post-World-War-II capitalist cities, Sofia did not develop rings of low-density suburbs for its expanding population, but grew as a unified urban entity. As in other socialist cities, its housing projects defined a clear urban edge (Genov et al. 2000); their towers stood like a concrete wall dividing the dense urban fabric from the surrounding fields. Thus, socialist planning maintained Sofia's clear urban edge, and the city remained denser and more compact than European cities located to its north or west.[2]

The organization of commercial functions also changed markedly. As privately-owned retail firms and offices were put out of business, the proportion of commercial spaces in the city centre shrank. Government and civic uses took a much more prominent place, particularly after the construction of the *Largo* complex in the 1950s. The complex, which replaced several old city blocks, consisted of a massive group of neo-classic government buildings framing several monumental boulevards.

A similar functional monotony penetrated the newly built socialist housing estates. The estates were intended to be self-sufficient neighbourhood units, each with a full range of land uses and services, but in practice the residential buildings were built first and the other uses lagged behind (Staddon and Mollov 2000; Klassanov 1992). Apart from a general explanation that abundant retail spaces were hardly needed under socialism because of the scarcity of consumer goods, two other factors can be noted. The estates were built hastily, under great pressure to achieve the prescribed quantities. Once the planned number of residential units was reached, the most urgent goal had been met, and construction of the other spaces was postponed. Moreover, since the buildings were made of prefabricated panels allowing little flexibility in design, it was easier to repeat the same dwelling unit from top to bottom rather than modifying the panels to construct different spaces (e.g., for retail) on the ground floor.

Lastly, notable changes appeared in the organization of neighbourhood open spaces. Sofia's pre-World-War-II neighbourhoods followed a traditional scheme of buildings located along the street edges and surrounding a modest interior courtyard. In contrast, socialist neighbourhoods, particularly those built after 1960, were shaped according to modernist principles. The freestanding structures were set away from the street and far apart from each other, for several reasons: to allow the cranes that lifted the pre-fabricated panels space to manoeuvre; to achieve maximum exposure to sunlight; and, most importantly, to create grand open spaces (Smolyanov 2000; Lizon 1996). Private, enclosed spaces were deemed inappropriate in the socialist city, as the author of Sofia's first post-World-War-II master plan explained, "[I]t is the [private] yard that makes the bourgeois" (Tangurov 2000, p. 47).

---

[2] Sofia has a density of 57.5 persons per ha (Stolichna Obshtina 2003), higher than the 42.3 persons per ha in London, 46.6 in Paris, 48.8 in Amsterdam, and 53.1 in Stockholm (Kenworthy and Laube 1999). In the built-up areas of Sofia, density averages 105 persons per ha (Buckley and Tsenkova 2001: 16). Bertaud (2004) estimates it at 94 persons per ha. Even if the lower figure is correct, Sofia's built-up areas are nearly ten times denser than those of U.S. cities such as Atlanta or Houston.

6.3 Post-socialist institutional and socio-economic changes

Changes in Sofia's spatial structure can be understood only in the context of the radical institutional and socio-economic changes after the end of socialism. To begin with, a multi-party system replaced the political monopoly of the communist party. Simultaneously, state control over the economy and prices was relaxed. The heavily industrialized, state-run economy collapsed,[3] although now recovery signs are evident, with the GDP's recent annual growth reaching 5 percent. By 2000, 75 percent of all state assets had been privatized, including all agricultural land and production, over two-thirds of the service sector and half of the industrial facilities. The private sector's share of GDP increased from 9 percent in 1990 to 70 percent in 2003 (Yoveva et al. 2003). The building industry, in particular, underwent a major re-structuring. The public sector was almost entirely withdrawn from housing production and distribution. The large firms that had constructed the panel-built housing projects were broken into smaller entities and privatized. Consequently the construction of large housing estates ceased. As of 2000, 90 percent of all new dwelling units were privately built, and 92 percent of dwelling units were privately owned (Elbers and Tsenkova 2003).

Laws that enabled the restitution (return to pre-war owners) of extensive public lands and real estate were first passed in 1992. Although later amended, their essential meaning mandated the return of urban, rural and forest land, and also urban and rural real estate then owned by the state, municipalities or other public bodies to their pre-World-War-II owners. The nationalization laws from 1948 were thus reversed (Kovachev 2005). Land that had had no monetary value under socialism was abruptly transformed into a precious commodity. Thus, as we shall further discuss, the accessibility of land to the general public was sharply constrained.

Unfortunately, as in other post-socialist states, all the privatization reforms were carried out under controversial and sometimes corrupt conditions that led to the quick accumulation of great wealth by a very small group. A recent study claimed that the wealthiest 8 percent of Bulgaria's population has the spending power of the bottom 75 percent (Raichev at al. 2000 cf Buckley and Tsenkova 2001).

In Sofia, urban development is now led by private sector. This sector, however, is highly fragmented and financially weak. It includes mostly small-to-medium-size firms with fewer than ten employees, and individuals constructing their own homes (Buckley and Tsenkova 2001; Stolichna Obshtina 2003, 2002). Another prevailing urban trend is the rise of the service economy. From 1990 to 2000, the percentage of persons employed in the service sector in Sofia's region grew from 55 to 70 percent. In the city centre, that percentage is over 80 (Stolichna Obshtina

---

[3] Inflation ranged from 40 to 80 percent annually in the early to mid-nineties; GNP fell by a third (Andrusz 1996). Current data is more favourable, with recent inflation rates near the single digits. Still, GDP in Sofia is less than half that of Athens', and a tenth of Amsterdam's (Nacionalen Statisticheski Institut 2001).

2003). The rise in service jobs has accompanied the growth of small-to-medium local, private retail businesses, and most recently the entry of some large Western retail chains. In the meantime, poverty rates have risen sharply, reaching 37 percent in the mid-1990s (Buckley and Tsenkova 2001).

6.4 Residential restructuring: The growth of suburbia

From the changes in the context of urban development, several processes of spatial restructuring emerged. Perhaps the most notable is the growth of an upscale, low-density, residential suburbia of the type familiar from the recent history of western urbanization.

Demographic data for Sofia's administrative districts show that residential growth is occurring in the formerly rural areas beyond the urban edge established during the socialist period. While the population of metropolitan Sofia has declined by one percent from 1992 to 2001, five of its twenty-four districts have experienced double-digit growth in percentages of population (Nacionalen Statisticheski Institut 2001; 1993). Of those five, only one—Poduyane—lies within the bounds of what urban planning documents refer to as the "compact city" (i.e., areas bound by the socialist urban edge). The gain in Poduyane, however, occurred because of recent border re-drawing, which caused it to absorb population from neighbouring districts (Stolichna Obshtina 2003). All other high-growth districts—Bankya, Vrabnitsa, Ovcha Kupel and Vitosha—lie in the periphery.

Complementary evidence is provided by housing data. As Fig. 6.1. illustrates, the greatest positive changes (i.e., the darkest areas on the maps) have occurred in the outlying districts of Vitosha, Ovcha Kupel, Bankya, Pancharevo and Vrabnitsa (again with the exception of Poduyane). The peripheral district of Kremikovtsi is the only one that has lost population. That is because Kremikovtsi is home to Sofia's heaviest chemical industry, developed under socialism, and has severe ecological problems.

Among the fast-growing districts, Vitosha—named after the mountain in whose outskirts it is located—has become particularly famous as the home of the newly rich, or as some call them, the "Vitosha class" (Staddon and Mollov 2000). Since 1992 the number of dwelling units in Vitosha has increased by over 50 percent. It accounts for 15 percent of the increase in dwelling units in metro-Sofia from 1992 to 2001 (Nacionalen Statisticheski Institut 2001, 1993). Most of those new homes are along the so-called Vitosha Collar, which includes the neighbourhoods of Boyana, Knajevo, Dragalevtsi and Simeonovo.

Although the settlements in the Vitosha Collar were incorporated within the borders of metropolitan Sofia in 1938, they retained their rural character until they became part of the City of Sofia in the mid-1950s. At that time they were designated as "villa-zones," i.e., recreational districts suitable for the construction of low-density summer dwellings (Genov et al. 2000). Some of the areas, most notably Boyana as the official site of a large government complex, then attracted the interest of members of the communist elite who constructed luxurious villas there.

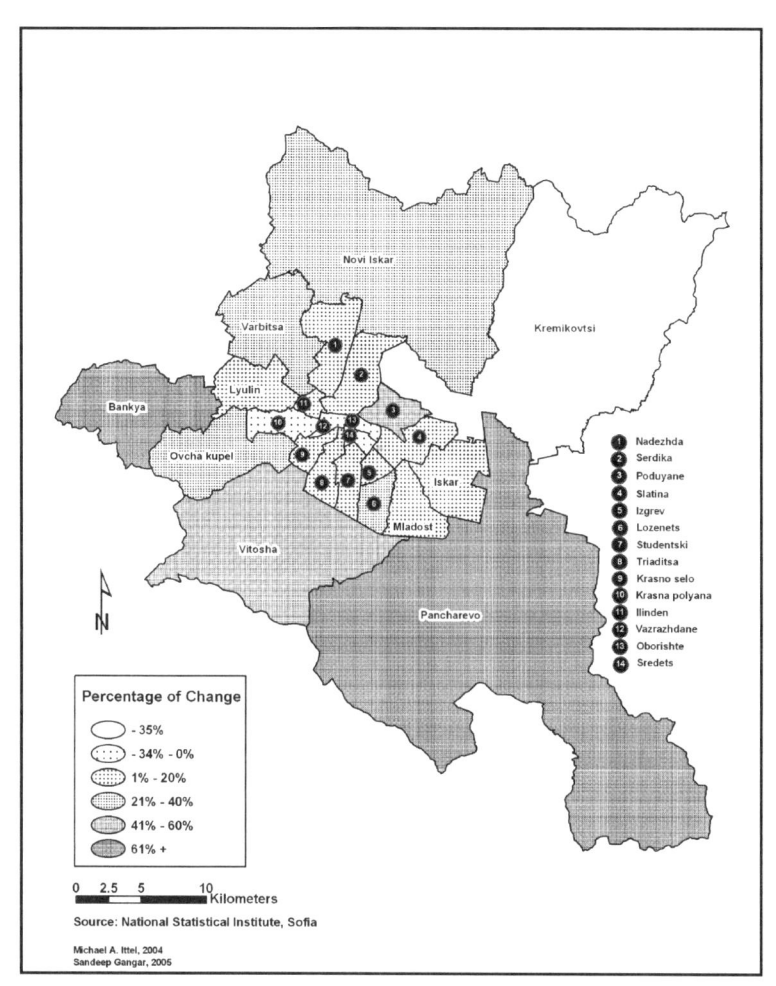

Fig. 6.1. Percentage change in dwelling units in the Municipality of Sofia by administrative district, 1992-2001.
Source: Stolicha Obshtina (2002)

Nevertheless, since the state investment in the rural infrastructure and civic amenities was insufficient, that development remained limited. Thus, until the late 1980s the urban fabric of socialist Sofia still ended abruptly with a high-density edge clearly marked by the last towers of the socialist estates (Mladost and Studentski on the south side; see Fig. 6.1.). The estates were clearly separated from the Vitosha outskirts by the city's Ring Road and by the flat farm fields flanking the road on both sides.

Since 1989, this picture has visibly changed: the dense urban fabric of Sofia and the lower-density fabric of the former villages near it have started to "crawl" toward each other. The once distinct, socialist urban edge is now partially blurred (Figs. 6.2. and 6.3.).

Fig. 6.2. A 1987 aerial image of "Vitosha Collar" in the outskirts of mountain Vitosha.

Fig. 6.3. An image of the same area in 2002: City and country have "crawled" toward each other.

Source: Datecs, Sofia

Fig. 6.4. Yet another imposing all-marble and gated residence in the Vitosha Collar.

The new residential growth in the urban periphery has a different character from that under socialism. In contrast to the massive towers of the socialist estates, the new residences are either small-to-medium-scale, multi-family buildings or single-family houses. Although there are no formal statistics on average yard sizes, interviewees from Sofia's planning department said that most vary around half an acre, so the density is much lower than in the socialist housing estates.

Data on the income levels of Vitosha's households also are unavailable, but their status is easy to guess by the granite fences and the marble balustrades adorning their homes (Fig. 6.4.). Near the new, five-star "Hrankov" hotel, for example, one finds the homes of two soccer stars, a former prime minister, a famous sculptor, the owner of a beer company, and others of less well-defined occupations.

The birth of the "Vitosha class" has also transformed some of the old village centres. In the 1980s, Dragalevtzi's centre, for instance, was a charming but nondescript square with a school, a post-office, a municipal building, a few modest stores and an open-air market. Today it boasts nearly a dozen posh hotels with pools and fitness clubs, and a similar number of fancy restaurants. At night, the once quiet square comes alive as scores of BMWs release their party-hungry owners.

6.5 Functional restructuring: The emergence of a commercial core and periphery

Like other socialist cities, before the 1990s Sofia had many fewer commercial spaces than did capitalist cities. That was true both of downtown, which still had a substantial population but lacked the bustling mix of retail and services that had made the pre-World-War-II "trading city," and for the socialist estates, which were closer to being "bedroom" communities than multi-functional neighbourhoods.

The post-socialist era is marked by a process of functional diversification or, more precisely, by a commercialization of the urban environment that reverses the lack of services during socialism. The commercialization tends to occur at the expense of residential and civic uses and is driven by several factors: the "unfreezing" of the land and real estate market, the liberalization of foreign trade, the quick rise of the post-socialist, tertiary sector, the growth of small-to-medium local private businesses, and most recently the entry of large-scale Western chains. The process has occurred across the city—in the first seven years of the transition, tripling the number of retail stores in Sofia (Dimov et al. 2000). But the most visible changes are in both the downtown and, more recently, the peripheral areas—in and between the socialist housing estates and the low-density suburban areas.

The demand for commercial space in the city centre at first was accommodated in existing buildings. In the early 1990s, there were only two large commercial renovation projects in the downtown area-- the former Central Department Store (*TSUM*) and the Central Halls grocery (*Halite*). Aside from those two, commercial demand targeted residential buildings. Many cash-strapped downtown dwellers welcomed the lucrative rents or buy-outs offered by private businesses, so during fewer than ten years 50,000 households left the centre; over 6,000 downtown apartments were being either rented or sold out annually (Stolichna Obshtina 2003, 2002). Fig. 6.1. illustrates the loss of dwelling units in the central areas. As residential uses were pushed out, ground floors, particularly along the main streets, were quickly remodelled for retail services unknown during socialism, from Brazilian restaurants to Belgian chocolate shops, all competing for clients' attention with their flashy windows. Office uses, as a rule, moved to the upper floors. Downtown buildings became a peculiar kaleidoscope of multiple uses, colours and signs. A stroll along the central streets could offer the perplexed visitor the sight of a single building in which one balcony might exhibit someone's laundry, while the balcony right above it might be decorated with a sign for a firm selling the laundry detergents.

By the late 1990s it became clear that existing buildings could not meet the demand for high-quality commercial space. The construction of new commercial buildings, particularly hi-tech offices, in the city centre accelerated after 1998, paralleling the recovery of the economy. According to property firms like Colliers International (2004a, 2004b), office space in Sofia now stands at nearly 600,000 sq m. Half of which was erected in the last five or years or so. In downtown, the largest new office centres include: *Bulgaria 2000* on Bulgaria Boulevard., *Business Centre T. Alexandrov* on Alexandrov Boulevard and *Soravia Centre* on Rousski Boulevard.

With space for new construction scarce, some of the new office buildings have replaced historic civic buildings, though not without public controversy. The *Soravia Centre*, for example, was constructed after the demolition of a historic building located right across from the National Parliament.

As the downtown was being established as a central business districts, commercial activities also spread in the periphery around the socialist housing estates and further in the low-density suburbia (see Fig. 6.5.). That trend started in the late 1990s, when several commercial functions that required large spaces to operate, such as warehouses, auto-body shops and car dealers, relocated from the dense urban areas to the outlying areas, particularly near the Ring Road (Stolichna Obshtina 2003; Dimov et al.2000; Staddon and Mollov 2000). In 1999, the first Western-chain hypermarket, the German *Metro*, opened in the outskirts of Sofia. Over the next five years, another 19 hypermarkets were built, all of them outside the central area, where space permitted such oversized construction. The largest are under German or Austrian ownership, such as *Billa* and *Hit*, followed by some smaller local, French, Turkish or Greek-owned superstores (e.g., Technopolis, Fantastico). As of 2005, another five Western hypermarkets are expected to enter the market, including the German *Kaufland and Lidl*. The overwhelming presence of large-scale Western operations led to a growing concentration of suburban retail businesses, which peaked in 2000 and has been on the decrease since (*Euromonitor* 2004).

Along with the other changes described, the distribution of office space has shifted from the city centre to the periphery. That occurred with the opening of the largest new office complex on the Balkan Peninsula, *Business Park Sofia*, with 300,000 sq m of office space at the edge of the housing estate Mladost. Thus, as of 2003, the ratio of high-quality office space in downtown to that near the outskirts of the city tilted in favour of the latter (Colliers International 2004a, 2004b).

Fig. 6.5. Location of Sofia's hypermarkets.

6.6 Open-space restructuring: Spatial fragmentation and privatization

The post-socialist changes—overwhelmingly, the aggressive post-1992 policy of restitution and the subsequent emergence of land as a market commodity—have substantially re-configured the open spaces in Sofia.

The roots of that reconfiguration can be traced to an unfortunate interpretation of the land restitution laws. The legal texts provided that land should be returned to its pre-World-War-II owners as long "the activity for which the land was expropriated [in 1948] had not been initiated" (Kovachev 2005). The word "activity" was commonly taken to mean the physical erection of buildings. Neither landscaping improvements, nor the presence of benches, fountains, gazebos or children's playgrounds typically counted as such an activity. As a result, large chunks of parks, common gardens, playgrounds and other green spaces vanished into private use. Restituted lands suitable for private development now comprise nearly 20 percent of the South Park, 10 percent of the West Park and 5 percent of the North Park (Kovachev 2005). The South Park, in particular, became the site of two vigorously protested projects, the massive Hilton Hotel and the four-hectare-wide complex of the American Embassy. Both were facilitated by the city government changing the open-space zoning for those sections of the park and turning them over to foreign investors.

Small public green spaces have been even more vulnerable, because developing the land between existing buildings requires no change in zoning. That loophole is a legacy of the socialist plans that placed entire city blocks in the vague category "residential-complex construction" without designating open spaces as a separate category. Because of the socialist generosity with space, city blocks were often built even below the permitted green-to-built-area ratios. Since restitution laws allowed the restitution of any reasonably sized plot of land as long as no buildings stood on it, neighbourhood open spaces became eligible for private development. In many parts of Mladost, for example, from 10 to 30 percent of the green spaces between buildings are under restitution claims (Kovachev 2005). Though residents were often shocked by the sight of the latest conversion of a playground to paid parking, the process was legal as long as green-to-built-area ratios were not exceeded.

Although there are no official data on exactly how much green space has been lost, preliminary results from an ongoing municipal survey that were recently leaked to the press, indicate that the loss amounts to 872 ha or 15 percent of all the public green space in the city, with another 20 percent awaiting the resolution of restitution claims (*Sofianets* 2004). In 2003, the fifteen-year-long process of destroying the green spaces was finally constrained by a moratorium on new construction in public parks. By then, the loss of green space had become a topic of heated public debate. Public opinion shifted sharply against aggressive restitution. The debate culminated in a roundtable organized by *Citizens for Green Sofia,* a coalition of 35 non-governmental organizations, which demanded that the process of building on common green spaces be stopped (*Dnevnik* 2004).

A recent survey found that 33 percent of respondents believed common green spaces between buildings should no longer be restituted under any circumstances; 50 percent believed that they could be restituted as long as some common spaces were retained; only 17 percent believed that restitution should continue regardless of the fate of common spaces. Furthermore, sixty percent of respondents believed that even those spaces that have already been restituted must be either bought back by the municipality or traded for spaces elsewhere (Kovachev 2005).

New neighbourhood open spaces are being created, but they are distinct from the spaces created under socialism. In the socialist housing estates, spaces between the buildings were oversized because: 1) socialist planners followed modernist urban planning doctrines that recommended placing freestanding buildings amid vast green fields available for the public; 2) the distances between the buildings were calculated to allow the movement of the large cranes lifting the pre-made panels; and 3) land had little monetary value. Since none of those rationales apply in the new capitalist era, spaces between buildings are organized quite differently.

Fig. 6.6. The gated entrance of "Green City"

Take, for instance, the new residential complex with the somewhat unimaginative name of "Green City" built at the southern edge of Sofia. Unlike the vast and amorphous spaces in the socialist estates, spaces in "Green City" are tightly shaped around gazebos, retro-looking fountains and seven tennis courts. The buildings are placed along the periphery of the lot to form an interior courtyard. Plans are under way to decorate the courtyard further with an artificial lake and even a church. Space does not flow freely; it is divided into smaller segments framed by buildings and exterior elements. This particular residential project is the companion to the four-star hotel "Olymp." The hotel offers such luxurious services as spas, fitness centres, private clubs, mini-markets, swimming pools and a cinema, available to "Green City" residents at a discount. The buildings of the residential complex are oriented distinctly inward. The complex is fenced on all sides, and outsiders' access is strictly restricted by "24-hour high-tech surveillance," as the marketing brochures proudly boast. Residents entering the residential complex need not step on a public street, since they can reach their homes directly from the garages. Once inside, they can find everything they need in the company of those like them, either in the residential complex or in the connected hotel. Outsiders, on the other hand, have few means or reasons to become part of the "Green City" world.

Restricted public access is a defining feature of the new suburban areas, as well there the predominant mode of construction is the single-family home. Boundaries are set in many ways, ferocious dogs, alarm systems, surveillance cameras and armed guards. They are set also through the re-birth of an old Balkan building tradition—the foot-wide and six-foot-tall stone fence. Although, during socialism many "villas" also were fenced, their fences were typically transparent, made of either tall bushes or light metal bars or nets. The post-socialist fence, however, is an imposing, solid structure that leaves little doubt that strangers are not welcome (Fig. 6.6.). Peculiarly, the building code allows only the bottom 60 cm of a fence around the front façade to be made of solid materials; the rest must be transparent. The code is obviously often violated, as any drive in the outskirts of Vitosha shows almost all new homes to be surrounded by tall and impermeable fences. If the growth of gated communities is indeed a global trend (Low 2003), then Sofia's suburbs are no exception.

6.7 Summary and implications for urban planning

Post-socialist conditions brought substantial urban re-structuring in the Bulgarian capital. The sharp edge that had marked the dense urban fabric of the socialist housing estates has been partially obliterated by the advent of a lower-density, suburban, and mostly upscale residential fabric. New functional nodes have emerged. Downtown has acquired a more commercial character and is now close to being a typical capitalist, central business district. Certain commercial functions, however, such as large-scale office parks and hypermarkets, have located outside the city centre, in and around the socialist housing estates and near the emerging suburbia.

Open spaces in the city have also undergone visible reorganization. Public spaces have dwindled. New types of open spaces—smaller, more intimate and more clearly defined, but also more fragmented and aggressively private—have emerged in the new post-socialist neighbourhoods.

Unfortunately, many of those processes have gone on unimpeded by active urban planning. As in other post-socialist countries, planning in Bulgaria suffered from a legitimacy crisis (Hirt and Slaev 2002a, 2002b). The aggressive application of restitution laws without much concern for the fate of public spaces is the clearest testimony to that. Recently, Sofia has prepared two important planning documents, a master plan and a development strategy (Stolichna Obshtina 2003; Buckley and Tsenkova 2001), which aim to deal in part with those neglected issues. Nevertheless, the new pattern of development seems to present a mixed bag of problems and opportunities whose effects have yet to be fully addressed.

As Nedovic-Budic (2001) argues, despite socialism's many flaws, from the urban planning point of view socialist cities had several positive characteristics that Western cities are now trying to recover: compact urban form, vital downtowns, less class segregation and better mass transit. With car ownership on the rise -- Sofia has more cars per person than Stockholm (National Statistical Institute 2001) -- and society stratifying, development of upscale residential suburbia there is inevitable. Yet a more coordinated investment in public infrastructure and more thoughtful restitution practices might directed that development to a few selected locations while keeping the rest of the peripheral land green. Currently, suburban settlements have sprung up on land that had been designated as public open space since the first master plan of Sofia was adopted in 1938 (Kovachev 2005).

Oddly, some professional planners see no problem. In fact, the team responsible for Sofia's latest master plan, *Sofia 2020,* aggressively advocated the "dispersed city model" and took the position that compact city form contradicts the principles of sustainable development. As the team leader explained in an interview:

> We want to encourage new types of dwellings, in a new type of environment of a totally different character, and encourage a lifestyle that is closer to nature, amid nature. People are totally fed up with this highly urbanized environment that is now offered in the compact city—an environment that contradicts the basic principles of sustainable development... Our people are craving for living amid nature... In socialist times, the government had interest in cramping people in high-density housing estates because this would save it money. But in a market economy, in an information-type society, in a democracy, the compact city is no longer the right choice (Interview, Division of the Master Plan 2002).

It is clear as well that the process of commercialization of urban structure will continue. One can easily view that as a positive development; the socialist downtown and housing estates indeed offered too few services. At the same time, it is crucial to put policies together to keep the city centre from resembling the after-working-hours emptiness of the downtowns we know in the U. S. It is also important for policy to address the growth of hypermarkets. At present there is no planning attention to that trend, in terms of either its effect on local businesses or its effect on the aesthetic character of the city. From the point of view of some interviewees, the hypermarkets are almost a point of pride.

One phenomenon that in fact has been recognized as a problem is the disappearance of public green space. Contrary to former restitution practices, the new master plan proposes that public green spaces with no buildings on them are considered as already developed and thus immune from restitution claims. Green spaces between the buildings in urban neighbourhoods will be marked on the maps and designated as such. Unfortunately, though, that recognition has come after many years of destroying the city greenery. The current efforts may amount to "too little, too late."

Lastly, it is hard to explain why the building code has not been enforced in the growing new areas. There is no reason why Sofia's streets or those of any other city should turn into dark passages flanked by fortress-looking six-meter walls. The core mission of urban planning is to defend the public interest and protect public space. That mission should be carried out even during this uncertain moment of history that we call post-socialism.

Acknowledgement

Sonia Hirt thanks the American Council for International Education and the Humanities Program and the Department of Interdisciplinary Studies at Virginia Polytechnic Institute and State University, for their financial support of her research on post-socialist urbanization.

References

Andrusz G (1996) Structural change and boundary instability. In: Andrusz G, Harloe M, Szelenyi I (eds) Cities after socialism: Urban and regional change and conflict in post-socialist societies. Blackwell Publishers, Malden, pp 30-69

Bertaud A (2004) The spatial structures of Central and European cities: More European than socialist? In: Tsenkova S, Nedović-Budić (eds) Winds of Societal Change – Remaking Post-communist Cities. Symposium proceedings, University of Illinois, Urbana-Champaign, June 17-19, 2004, pp. 45-64. Available on the web: http://alainbertaud.com/AB_Files/AB_Central%20European%20Spatial%20Structure_Figures_2.pdf, accessed October 1, 2005

Bodnar J (2001) Fin de Millenaire Budapest: Metamorphoses of urban life. University of Minnesota Press, Minneapolis and London

Buckley R, Tsenkova S (2001) Strategia za razvitie na grad Sofia: Predvaritelna ocenka. Sofia: Stolichna Obshtina, Direkcia po Arhitektura i Gradoustrojstvo (translated in Bulgarian)

Colliers International Bulgaria (2004a) Office Real Estate Market: 1st Half 2004 Report. http://www.colliers.com/Content/Repositories/Base/Markets/Bulgaria/English/Market_Report/PDFs/OfficeFirstHalf2005.pdf, accessed September 15, 2005

Colliers International Bulgaria (2004b) Office Real Estate Market: 2nd Half 2004 Report. http://www.colliers.com/Content/Repositories/Base/Markets/Bulgaria/English/Market_Report/PDFs/OfficeSecondHalf2005.pdf, accessed September 15, 2005.

Crowley D, Reid S (eds) (2002) Socialist spaces: Sites of everyday life in the Eastern Bloc. Oxford: Berg

Dimov N, Boyadjiev V, Ilieva M (2000) Stopanstvoto: Suvremenno sustojanie i prostranstvena struktura (in Bulgarian). In: Bulgarska Academia na Naukite, Sofia: 120 Godini Stolica. Akademichno Izdatelstvo Marin Drinov, Sofia, pp 90-98

Dingsdale A (1999) Budapest's built environment in transition. GeoJournal 49, pp. 63-78

Division of the Master Plan (2002) Interview. Directorate of Architecture and Urban Plannng, Municipality of Sofia, June 24

Dnevnik (2004) Citizen committees in Sofia: Municipality should return the seized green areas. 06-10-2004

Elbers A, Tsenkova S (2003) Housing a nation of home owners—reforms in Bulgaria. In: Lowe S and Tsenkova S (eds) Housing change in East and Central Europe: Integration or fragmentation. Ashgate, Aldershot, pp. 113-123

Enyedi G (1996) Urbanization under socialism. In: Andrusz G, Harloe M, Szelenyi I (eds) Cities after socialism: Urban and regional change and conflict in post-socialist societies. Blackwell Publishers, Malden, pp 100-118

Euromonitor (2004) Retailing in Bulgaria: Executive Summary. www.euromonitor.com/Retailing-in-Bulgaria, accessed March 10, 2005

Genova B (2000) Jilishtnata sreda v Sofia: sustojanie i perspektivi (in Bulgarian). In: Universitet po Arhitektura, Stroitelstvo i Geodezia. Godishnik na Universiteta po arhitektura, stroitelstvo i geodezia, Tom XL, Svituk I, Arhitektura: Istoria, tipologia, obrazovanie. Universitet po arhitektura, stroitelstvo i geodezia, Sofia, pp 126-145

Genov G, Slavejkov P, Ganev H (2000) Urbanizirani teritorii (in Bulgarian). In: Bulgaska Academia na Naukite, Sofia: 120 Godini Stolica. Akademichno Izdatelstvo Marin Drinov, Sofia, pp 83-90

Haussermann H (1996) From the socialist to the capitalist city: experiences from Germany. In: Andrusz G, Harloe M, Szelenyi I (eds) Cities after socialism: Urban and regional change and conflict in post-socialist societies. Blackwell Publishers, Malden, pp 214-231

Hirt S, Slaev A (2002a) Tradicii i praktiki v jilishtnite formi i gradskoto razvitie v Bulgaria i Suedinenite Shtati: Opit za sravnenie (in Bulgarian). Arhitektura 5-6: 70-73

Hirt S, Slaev A (2002b) Tradicii i praktiki v jilishtnite formi i gradskoto razvitie v Bulgaria i Suedinenite Shtati—Opit za sravnenie (in Bulgarian). Stritelstvo-Gradut 38:19; 39:19; 40:39; 41:19; 42:19; 43:25

Ishirkov A (1928) Naselenieto na Sofia (in Bulgarian). In: Komitet za Iztoriya na Sofia, Jubilejna Kniga na Grad Sofia. Knipegraph, Sofia, pp 65-78

Kenworthy J, Laube F (1999) An international sourcebook of automobile dependence in cities, 1960-1990. University of Colorado Press, Boulder

Klassanov M (1992) Totalitarizum, demokracia, arhitektura (in Bulgarian). Arhitektura 6:26-31

Kovachev A (2005) Zelenata sistema na Sofia: Urbanistichni aspekti. Pensoft (in Bulgarian), Sofia

Labov G (1979) Arhitekturata na Sofia (in Bulgarian). Tehnika, Sofia

Lizon P (1996) East Central Europe: The unhappy heritage of communist mass housing,. Journal of Architectural Education 50:104-114

Low S (2003) Behind the gates: Life, security and the pursuit of happiness in fortress America. New York: Routledge

Nacionalen Sattisticheski Institut (2001) Sofia v Cifri (in Bulgarian). Nacionalen Statisticheski Institut, Sofia

Nacionalen Sattisticheski Institut (1993) Statisticheski Sbornik—Sofia (in Bulgarian). Nacionalen Statisticheski Institut, Stolichno Teritorialno Bjuro, Sofia

Nedovic-Budic Z (2001) Adjustment of planning practice to the new Eastern and Central European context. Journal of the American Planning Association. 67, pp 38-52

Raichev A, Kolev K, Boundjoulov A, Dimova L (2000). Social stratification in Bulgaria. Social Democratic Institute, Sofia

Rudolph R, Brade I (2005) Moscow: Processes of restructuring in the post-Soviet periphery. Cities 22, pp 135-150

Ruoppila S (1998) The changing urban landscape of Tallinn. The Finish Journal of Urban Studies 35, pp. 36-43

Smith D (1996) The socialist city. In: Andrusz G, Harloe M, Szelenyi I (eds) Cities after socialism: Urban and regional change and conflict in post-socialist societies. Blackwell Publishers, Malden, pp 70-99

Smolyanov A (2000) Gradski jilishtni teritorii, 1944-1990 (in Bulgarian). Arhitektura 2, pp 49-52

Sofianets (2004) Zaradi opasnost ot izchezvane na gradinkite mejdu blokovete pravjat registri na zelenite ploshti (in Bulgarian). 28-06-2004, pp 1-2

Staddon C, Mollov B (2000) City profile: Sofia, Bulgaria. Cities 17: 379-387

Stolicha Obshtina (2003) Obsht Ustrojstven Plan na Grad Sofia i Stolichnata Obshtina: Sukraten Doklad (in Bulgarian). Stolichna Obshtibna, Direkcia po Arhitektura i Gradoustrojstvo, Sofia

Stolicha Obshtina (2002) Obsht Ustrojstven Plan: Obitavane i Jilishten Fond: Predvaritelen Proekt (in Bulgarian). Unpublished document available from Stolichna Obshtina, Sofia

Sýkora L (1999) Changes in the internal structure of post-communist Prague. GeoJournal 49, pp. 79-89

Sýkora L (1998) Commercial property development in Budapest, Prague and Warsaw. In: Enyedi G (ed) Social change and urban restructuring in Central Europe. Akademiai Kiado, Budapest, pp 109-136

Szelenyi I (1996) Cities under socialism—and after. In: Andrusz G, Harloe M, Szelenyi I (eds) Cities after socialism: Urban and regional change and conflict in post-socialist societies. Blackwell Publishers, Malden, pp 286-317

Tammaru T (2001) Suburban growth and suburbanization under central planning: The case of Soviet Estonia. Urban Studies 38, pp. 1341-1357

Tangurov J (2000) Modernata arhitektura 1944-1990 (in Bulgarian). Arhitektura 2000: 46-48

Tashev P (1972) Sofia. In: Gutkind E (ed) Urban development in Eastern Europe: Bulgaria, Romania and the U.S.S.R. (in Bulgarian). The Free Press, New York, pp 60-72

Yoveva A Dimitrov D, Dimitrova R (2003) Housing policy: the stepchild of the transition. In: Lux M (ed) Housing policy: An era or a new beginning. Open Society Institute, Local Government and Public Reform Initiative, Budapest, pp. 355-398

7 Spatial restructuring in post-socialist Budapest

Iván Tosics

Introduction

This chapter concentrates on the most visible aspect of post-socialist city development -- the spatial changes and their mutual links to urban planning and policy making. The turbulent last decade of the 20th century resulted in immense transformation of the spatial structure, appearance and functioning of the Central and Eastern European cities and their different zones. From analysis of the spatial changes in Budapest, the chapter focuses on the following questions about the post-socialist period:

- What are the main forces driving urban development in Budapest?
- To what extent is Budapest moving towards being a market-oriented city and losing its characteristics from the socialist period?
- Should any of these characteristics be preserved in the new phase of development?
- What role does the public sector (urban planning and policy) play in the subsequent stages of transition, the 'management' of spatial changes and control of market processes?

The conditions of spatial processes in the transition from central planning towards a market economy are determined by political, economic and institutional factors. According to Szelényi, "... societies with different socio-economic orders will produce qualitatively different urban conditions" (Szelényi 1996, p. 290). Urban development in Hungary was for 40-45 years influenced by the socialist political model, the system of planned economy. The public sector determined land use patterns; there were significant state ownership of the land and housing stock in cities (as a consequence of confiscation); administratively determined, controlled growth of major cities; and direct state control over the financial resources of the cities and thus over the decision-making process (Hegedüs and Tosics 1996). The "camel-back" anomaly in the density gradient of Hungarian cities (Bertaud and Buckley 1997; Bertaud and Malpezzi 2003) is a direct consequence of such an institutional environment.

During the socialist period, development in Budapest was dominated by the public sector as the owner of 2/3 of the housing stock and most urban land. The public sector controlled all aspects of urban development, and decision-making was centralised at the municipal level. Consequently, the most dynamically growing areas of the city were those where public investments were concentrated, e.g., the high-density housing estates at the periphery, which were built to alleviate housing shortages; and the high-quality housing zones in the green belt for the political and economic elites, which had been acquired through the nationalization of earlier elite districts and were developed by the government and by subsidized private investments. At the same time, the least supported or even restrained developments included the areas designated for demolition to make room for new housing estates; the publicly owned inner city areas whose stock of old buildings were deteriorating because of neglect of the confiscated or nationalized building stock and as a result of rent controls; and the transitional zone immediately outside the inner city dominated by large industry, storage, rail and other non-residential functions. Finally, private development occurred primarily in the agglomeration settlements, which grew rapidly with only a relatively low level of infrastructure provided, and which housed labour migrants from other parts of Hungary who could not move into the city because of administrative restrictions.[1]

According to Enyedi (1996), the principal agent of post-socialist change is the economy, with private households as the next most important factor. The main co-ordinators are the local governments. The transition to a market economy in Hungary had already begun before the communist system formally collapsed in 1989. Spatial changes preceded the political changes, as an early expression of the market orientation of the economy. The gradual move of economic policy towards the market-based system in the 1980s resulted in an upgrading of Budapest's central area by converting its inner city neighborhood into an area with international hotels and high-end retail on the first pedestrian street (Sármány and Parsons 1998), and by the construction of East-West Center, the first Budapest office complex adhering to international standards. These spatial transformations in the 1980s were complemented by the privatization of public housing initiated in 1986.

Even with this head start, it was in the period after 1989 that the most important spatial changes occurred: new shopping centers, office buildings, greenfield industrial and logistical structures, suburban and inner city housing, and urban redevelopment projects date to that period. Such developments required more fundamental change in the legal, administrative and financial systems. They were enabled by large-scale privatization in the productive sectors and in housing, by infrastructure development, and by the introduction of mortgage lending. The new investors first focused on the real estate sectors that were most in demand and least risk-prone, which in order of time were first petrol stations, then offices, retail/commercial establishments, hotels, and finally residential developments. These investments affected the spatial distribution of employment, created new patterns of commercial and service delivery and consumption, and also influenced the location and growth of the residential sector. Some of the further consequences that began to emerge were public spaces occupied by cars, an increasing disparity in the extent to which residential buildings were maintained, and social segregation evident in the shocking contrasts between the newly developed residential complexes and run-down areas of the inner city.

---

[1] The administrative restrictions specified that only people who had already lived or worked in the capital for at least five years could apply for new public housing.

In reviewing here the determinants of the spatial changes in Budapest during the transition, the post-socialist period is divided into several stages by distinguishing among basic political decision, detailed legal regulation and new public policies.

1. *Vacuum period*, between the basic political decisions and the introduction of detailed legal regulations: the early 1990s. The period was characterized by uncontrolled development triggered by massive privatization of the economy and the housing sector, by investors' focus on getting the best position in the urban restructuring process, and by contradiction laws - for example, the *Law on Prices* allowed the owner to determine the rent level, while the *Housing Law* still had very strict limitations on rent levels.
2. *Adaptation period*, from the introduction of new legislations till the emergence of public policies: the mid- to- late 1990s. The period was characterized by the initiation of new investments and planning instruments, the fragmentation of local governments used to the developers' advantage, and reliance on the infrastructure reserves. Within this framework the municipality of Budapest started to elaborate long-term plans such as the initially 3-, later 7-year forecast of financial revenues (Pallai 2003), and the Master Plan.
3. *Adjustment period*, marked by the emergence of national and local public policies: from the late 1990s on. The period has been characterized by continued investments, more regard to public sector plans, and emerging cooperation within the public sector. The end of this period is marked by fully functional and unconstrained market processes. For example, in Budapest the end of the transition was marked by – among others – the approval of the long-term strategic development strategy. That has been further developed into a medium-term development programme, approved in 2005.

The moves from one stage to the next depended on legal, administrative and political factors, while the content of each stage and the speed of its introduction and implementation were influenced primarily by economic forces. The combination of those factors created the playing field for households and firms making decisions about location and investment that influenced the overall urban development.

7.1 The urban development context

7.1.1 Political and administrative factors

Local governments' financial strengthening and decision-making independence are probably the most important institutional changes that accompanied the establishment of a democratic multi-party parliamentary system (Tosics 2005a). The "[s]ub-national governments ... were essentially deconcentrated units (or branch offices) of the central government and had little or no financial autonomy" (Bird et al. 1995, p. 1). By 1990 they had been replaced by self-governing units, and direct involvement of central government officers or politicians in local decision-making was no longer possible (Bennett 1998). Bird et al. (1995) suggest that the "[d]ecentralisation is ... a key dimension of the national transition from a command to a market economy. ... The total level of public sector activity must be dramatically reduced, but at the same time the new sub-national governments must be allowed to build staff and institutional capacities."

Local financial autonomy, however, is still limited because the central government is not very keen to allow local governments to become powerful political entities. Even when local taxation has been established, its magnitude is restricted, and local governments remain strongly dependent on central transfers. This suggests that decentralisation itself is limited (see Tsenkova in this volume). Although power sharing between the national and local levels changed substantially as compared to the socialist period, the central state managed to preserve a strong influence. The establishment of independent local governments "... has been accompanied by a higher degree of centralism than was first intended ... as a consequence of the fragmentation of the local level, the weakness (absence) of an intermediate level and as a result of the desire for efficiency and expediency in the context of economic transition" (Michalski and Saraceno 2000, page 19). Local governments were, however, important players in the urban and overall transition, the rules of which were determined at the central state level. Throughout the three transition stages—vacuum, adaptation and adjustment—local governments had to establish and implement their local strategies. Large cities, especially the capitals such as Budapest, usually had more room for manoeuvre in the development of their strategies, not only because of their size, but also because in the absence of strong regions they were the only potential alternative power centres to the central state.

The post-socialist administrative structure of Budapest's local government system, established in the 1990s (Tosics, 2005b), is based on the *Law on Local Governments*. The two-tier structure includes the municipal government, which became the owner of the public utilities and assumed the tasks related to all or large parts of the capital; and 23 district governments, which became owners of previously state-owned retail and commercial units, vacant land and public rental housing stock and which assumed all local public service functions (Bird et al. 1995). The municipality and the districts each acquired their own economic assets and taxation authority, and the right to establish their budgets independently. They share some revenues according to a special system for allocating financial resources.

The two-tier administrative structure was not very functional, since the two governments could successfully block each other's ideas, e.g., the municipality through its zoning authority and the district through its right to issue building permissions. The 1994 modification of the *Law on Local Governments* gave the municipal level somewhat more rights, especially in strategic planning issues with relevance for the whole city. None of the laws, however, dealt with regional government functions, or with the competencies related to urban development in large urban agglomerations like Budapest. In the course of the 1990s smaller settlements were favoured in the allocation of central government budget resources. That bias contributed to the fast development of the suburban area around Budapest, as local governments in Pest County completed major infrastructure development projects (gas, water lines, sewage, gymnasium, road construction, telephone lines). The county governments sought local economic development attractive to entrepreneurs, developers of shopping centres and industrial sites, and middle-class population. Settlements around Budapest used their increased power to re-zone large tracts in their jurisdictions from agricultural to residential, industrial or commercial use. They also took advantage of the tax authority given them by the *Law on Local Governments* to attract high-income households and economic investments by means of low local taxes.

In this very fragmented system the importance of the sub-national level was acknowledged in 1996 with the *Act XXI on Spatial Planning and Development*, which established development councils at the county and regional levels, such as the Budapest Agglomeration Development Council. However, the relations between the city and its surroundings remained problematic, as neither Pest County nor any other entity except the Parliament had any power to influence decisions made by the settlements. At the same time, given the lack of any formalized "agglomeration" structure, the individual settlements' positions are too weak to negotiate effectively with Budapest.

This brief overview of the institutional context of Budapest urban development points to how constrained and difficult the coordination of public policies beyond the district level can be, and to the practical impossibility of coordination between Budapest and the neighbouring settlements.

7.1.2 The economic factors

The public sector lost its previously dominant role in the economy very fast. Rapid cash privatization, the excellent geographical location of Budapest, and political stability all drew extensive Foreign Direct Investment (FDI). Between 1990 and 2003, 33.2 billion Euros of FDI was invested in Hungary (National Bank of Hungary 2005). According to the data from UNCTAD, the FDI stock in Hungary by the end of 2004 amounted to 48 billion Euros (Iceg-Corvinus 2005), with significantly higher FDI per capita than that of the Czech Republic, Slovakia or Poland. More than half of the FDI in the country came to Budapest, generating 35.1% of the country's GDP, a percentage more than double Budapest's share of the population (17%).

That phenomenon, the disproportionate role of the largest (usually capital) city in the accumulation of capital, is common among the post-socialist countries (Kovács 2002a). However, although the 2004 data on investment by firms shows a heavy concentration of 41% in the capital city, such dominance by Budapest is no longer stable. Since 1999 the investments in Hungary have been increasing each year by 3-7%, while investments in Budapest have fluctuated between a 10% decrease and a 9% increase.

The territorial and social consequences of transitional processes in Budapest and Hungary are very similar to the outcomes in other countries where "... economic restructuring that took part was largely left to market forces as the legacy of central planning had discredited top-down policies of economic and regional development. As a result of the transition, regional and social inequalities have risen substantially within Central and Eastern European countries" (Michalski and Saraceno 2000, p. 21). As a general rule, the largest cities came out as winners by gaining the most FDI and managing to carry out economic restructuring in the shortest time.

7.2 Spatial changes and restructuring in Budapest

To analyze the spatial change and distribution of investments in the post-socialist period, we distinguish between the following concentric zones in and around Budapest (Fig. 7.1.):

- "small Budapest" is the city within its pre-1950 border, containing the densely built city core and less dense mixed-use areas at the outer border, today with about 1 million residents;
- the "inner periphery" marking the rest of Budapest, annexed in 1950, today with about 700 thousand residents;
- the "agglomeration zone" defined since the mid-1990s, of 78 suburban settlements around the city, with about 700,000 residents with intensive connections to the city.
- the "outer periphery," the rest of Pest County, with about 400 thousand residents.

The four zones add up to the so-called Central Hungarian Region, one of the seven Hungarian planning and statistical regions, with over 2.8 million inhabitants.

Enyedi (1996) distinguishes three functional changes in the built environment that determine the development and structure of cities: expansion of commercial areas, transformation of industrial zones, and altered characteristics of housing. We present the spatial changes and restructuring in Budapest with respect to commercial developments, residential developments, and territorial conflicts.

7.2.1 Commercial developments

The development of Budapest after the political changes was dominated by foreign, mostly Austrian, real estate investments (Sármány-Parsons 1998). Almost all plots in the center of the city that had been empty since the Second World War were filled in with large office and bank buildings, built in standardized building envelopes to minimize risk and construction costs. In the late 1990s, the office

Fig. 7.1. The city of Budapest, the agglomeration zone, and the Central Hungarian Region
Notes:
1: the borders of Small Budapest (the city up till 1950); 2: the inner periphery; 3: the agglomeration zone (78 settlements); 4: the outer periphery (The total area of 1-4 is the CHR.)

boom continued along major connecting roads (mainly Váci út) and ringroads around the inner part of the city (Hungária körút).

Another visible manifestation of new urban investments was "ground floor capitalism"—the rapid establishment of shops. In this regard there was a definite difference between Prague and Budapest. In Prague, restitution of property to its former owners enabled the revival of family businesses in traditional form. The cash-privatization in Budapest stimulated an influx of foreign shopping chains and led to changes in the character and use of the shops (Kovács 2002b).

The real novelties, however, were the shopping centers and hypermarkets. Since 1994, the year of their first appearance, over one million square meters of new commercial investments have been built in and around Budapest. The commercial developments culminated in the second half of the 1990s, during the adaptation period. During the adjustment period commercial investments continue, although the figures show that Budapest is no longer the only place in Hungary to invest (Table 7.1.).

Table 7.1. New commercial investments in Budapest and its agglomeration, 1990-2004

Commercial development, new investments (in thousand square meters)	Vacuum period 1990-1995	Adaptation period 1996-2000	Adjustment period 2001-2004	Total 1990-2004 (percentage)	Total 1990-2004 ('000 sqm)
Small Budapest	31.1	45.1	64.7	51.0	531
Inner periphery	45.6	31.9	12.2	26.0	271
Agglomeration zone	23.3	22.9	23.1	23.0	240
Total (Budapest + agglomeration)	100.0	100.0	100.0	100.0	
Total in '000 sqm	103	554	385		1.042

Source: Statistical Yearbooks, own calculations

Table 7.1. shows the pattern of locational decisions of commercial investors. The share of new commercial investments outside Budapest has remained stable - below one quarter of all investments into the Budapest area. While the initial high share of the inner periphery decreased, the central areas of the city captured about 2/3 of all commercial investments in 2001-2005. The majority of these investments are located in the periphery of small Budapest, mostly in the transitional belt consisting mainly of brownfield areas.

Data show that the majority of new investments have remained within the city, and that the commercial investments have not become a driving force for urban sprawl. Another positive aspect is the partial revitalization of brownfield areas, as many of the large shopping centers have been built in abandoned areas of earlier industrial use. On the other hand, despite the relatively advantageous spatial pattern, the concentration of commercial activities into the large shopping centers and hypermarkets contributes to the collapse of traditional forms of commerce and to abandonment of many shopping streets in the inner part of the city.

The above chronology of commercial development in spatial terms reveals the public sector's challenges in regulating market processes. In the middle of the 1990s, Budapest local governments were unprepared for the investors, who could buy areas for commercial development with no restrictions. Only the zoning regulations had to be taken into account, and large developers could easily influence even those regulations by exploiting the conflicts of interest between local governments. Developers effectively used the loopholes in the two-tier local government system, searching for districts with less constraining conditions, or going out of Budapest to the neighboring settlements, where such big investments were more welcome. The first planning regulations limiting the size of shopping malls in dense built-up areas came out at the very end of the adaptation period. However, large scale commercial investments in the central areas of Budapest did not decrease after 2000, rather the contrary, which indicates the ineffectiveness of the new regulations and also that their appearance came late relative to the investors' purchases of suitable areas, made mostly before the regulations took effect.

7.2.2 Residential developments

The mass privatization of the housing stock, the increased income differentiation, and a major growth in private car ownership during the 1990s have all influenced the residential decisions of the population. The number of cars per 1,000 residents in Budapest increased from 241 in 1990 to 355 in 2004[2] (CSO 1991-2005). Residential mobility increased substantially, and along with it suburbanization began as the pursuit of social prestige. Real estate investment was gaining value in the developing suburban settlements, but was declining in many older urban areas.

Suburbanization is evident from the data on population change in Budapest, its urban agglomeration zone and Pest County (Table 7.2. and 7.3.). Like the population of Hungary, the population of Budapest has been decreasing since the 1980s, primarily because of the aging population. Although through the 1970s the natural loss of population was balanced by in-migration to Budapest, since 1993 the consolidated index of the changes of permanent and temporary residence between Budapest and the rest of the country has become negative for Budapest. In contrast to the rapidly declining population in Budapest, the population of the agglomeration zone has been increasing. Pest County is the only medium-level unit in the country to have rising population in the last few years.

Migration processes of the last one and a half decades show strong reorganization within the Budapest area: a quickly decreasing inner core and growing peripheral areas. It is interesting to note that the greater Budapest area, the Central Hungarian Region, was decreasing in population slightly faster than the national average. The reason for that could be the strong effect of the demographic loss of the former Budapest population.

The suburbanization process is evident in other post-socialist cities as well (Kovács 2002a). However, the migration loss in Budapest was higher than those in other Eastern and Central European capitals and has even increased since the beginning of the 21st century. Between 2001 and 2003 the yearly migration loss was 35 thousand in Budapest, compared to only five thousand in Prague, two thousand in Bratislava, and an annual gain of 15 thousand persons in Warsaw (CSO 2005).

---

[2] Motorization growth in other post-socialist capital cities was equally dramatic during the same period. For example, in Ljubljana these rates increased from 335/1,000 in 1990 to 420/1,000 in 2000, while in Prague motorization doubled from 277/1,000 to 520/1,000.

Table 7.2. Annual population change in and around Budapest, 1990-2003

Population change per year in thousand residents	Vacuum period 1990-1995	Adaptation period 1996-2000	Adjustment period 2001-2003
Small Budapest	-17	-20	-18
Inner periphery	0	-4	-12
Agglomeration zone	+4	+10	+22
Outer periphery	+1	+1	+1
Central Hungarian Region (total)	-12	-13	-7
(Hungary total)	(-20)	(-15)	(-11)

Table 7.3. Population in Budapest, the agglomeration zone, outer periphery and Hungary, 1990-2002*

Number of population, in '000	1990	2002	Change (2002/1990)
Budapest	2.017	1.719	85.2 %
Agglomeration zone	569	691	121.4 %
Outer periphery	381	414	108.7 %
Central Hungarian Region (total)	2.967	2.824	95.2%
(Hungary total)	(10.375)	(10.142)	(97.8 %)

Source: Budapest Statistical Yearbook 1990-2003
Note:
* at the end of the year.

A more detailed look, however, reveals an interesting fluctuation in the migration loss from Budapest to Pest County. From a relatively low level of yearly migration loss, the balance rose to 11-15 thousand per year in the second half of the 1990s and to 24-27 thousand persons per year in 2001 and 2002. However, in 2003 the intensity of suburbanization fell to the level of the late 1990s, and the predictions for 2005 show a further decline of migration loss, to the level of 5 thousand and most recently 2-3 thousand persons per year. These data suggest that *the peak of suburbanization is over in Budapest*: fewer families decide to move out from the capital, and some of them are even moving back.

The residential mobility is closely related to the changing transportation patterns. Although public transport in Budapest is comprehensive and still covers 60% of communications within the city, its share has shrunk substantially since the 1980s, when the modal split was 85 to 15. The sharp increase in the individual motorization rate and the suburbanization of Budapest are parallel processes. Even the most recent decline of the negative migration balance, since 2003, may be due to the worsening traffic situation. The capacity of the connecting and inner roads cannot be increased to match the rate of growth in car ownership and use. Consequently, the frequency and the intensity of traffic jams in the periphery as well as in the inner city areas are increasing.

Improvement of the public transport system is costly and therefore very slow. Enlargement of the "park and ride" capacity is limited, partly because it requires land acquisition and land costs are high. These are some of the reasons for suburbanization lessening as fewer and fewer households find the living circumstances outside Budapest to be superior enough to counterbalance the pains of commuting.

This overview of spatial mobility processes shows that in the case of Budapest the suburbanization of population, which was by far the largest among the Eastern and Central European capitals, seems not to be the consequence of the suburbanization of commercial or economic (employment creating) investments, as was the case for the new Lander of Germany (Herfert 1997). In the case of Budapest another type of "pull factor" operated: the increasing supply of land and built-for-sale housing in the surrounding settlements the intended effect of the large-scale rezoning there.

The residential and commercial market-based developments described above helped the country to recover from the economic collapse of the early 1990s. However, due to the dominance of the free market and the lag in developing mechanisms to protect the public, the inequalities between different strata of society, parts of the country, and areas of Budapest intensified at the same time. Similar social polarization and residential segregation is evident in other East and Central European countries (Enyedi 1996; Sármány and Parsons 1998). Many households are pushed into poverty, and the population living below the national poverty line is on the rise (see Tsenkova and Andrusz in this volume). Social exclusion, negative demographic trends, and deteriorating health situations all indicate growing social problems, particularly in remote rural areas and poor urban districts. The contrast between the poor and the rich is especially visible within Budapest, where both the most affluent areas and the most socially distressed areas are to be found. The difference in life expectancy between the "best" and the "worst" districts of Budapest is six years: the inhabitants of the Buda district II are on the level of Belgium, while the inhabitants of the Pest district X are on the level of Syria (Tosics 2005b).

7.2.3 Territorial conflicts

The post-socialist period of city development is dominated by the private sector, the privatised ownership of land, and a process of public decision-making decentralised to the district level. The most intensely growing areas of the city are those where the most financially well off want to live and where the office and retail developers want to invest.

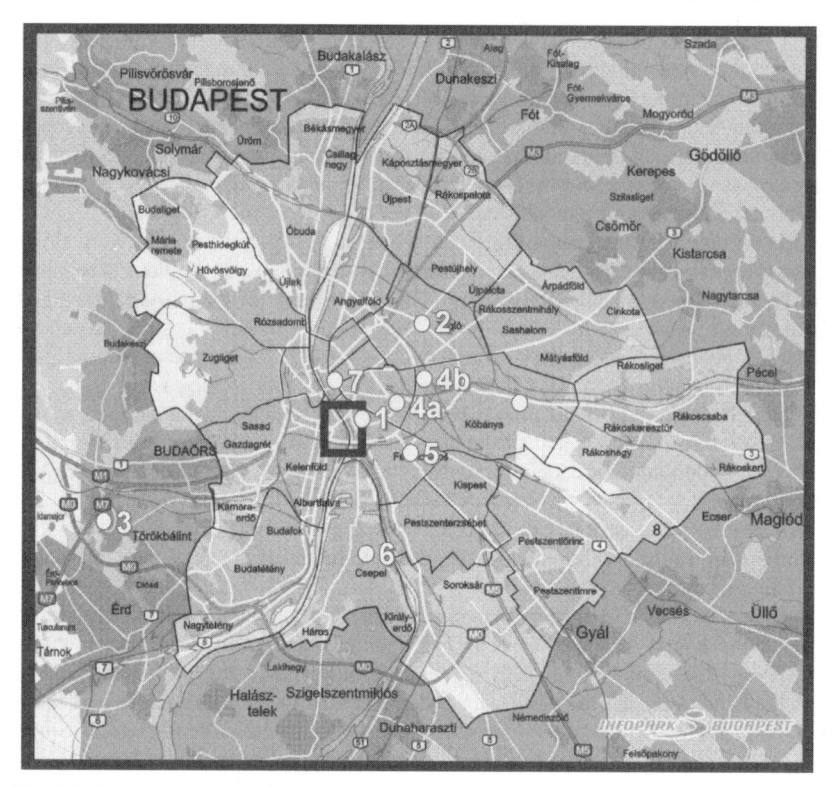

Fig. 7.2. Case study areas of territorial conflicts in Budapest
Notes:
1. Middle Ferencváros 2. Zugló 3. Törökbálint 4a: Magdolna quarter 4b: Hős street 5: Outer Ferencváros 6: Csepel housing estate 7: Central Business District

These areas include central parts of the inner city areas (central business district, CBD) with large office developments, scattered areas of gentrifying urban renewal at the edges of the inner city, some areas in the brownfield transition zone where new investments in shopping centers have concentrated, and agglomeration settlements that are sought by the suburbanizing middle classes. As a consequence of the pull of these dynamic areas, middle- and upper-class families have vacated certain parts of the housing stock, many of which have quickly deteriorated in the absence of public interventions at either the national, district or municipal level. Among the marginalized areas are the deteriorating, ghettoized areas at the edge of the inner-city that house minority ethnic groups and low income strata; some of the brownfield areas that are dominated by abandoned industrial buildings and are

Table 7.4. Conflicts in areas of newly acquired high prestige

The case	The process	The conflicts
1. Middle Ferencváros Urban renewal in an inner city housing area, on the border to the CBD	The decision of the district local government on area-based renewal preceded the law on Right to Buy and so exempted the area from compulsory privatization. It developed a well-elaborated, public-private partnership (PPP) strategy and with help from the Budapest municipal level successfully completed the project, with a relatively high share of public investments (some 20-30 % of total investments) and unavoidable partial gentrification (although with improvement in housing conditions).	Conflicts continue between the original residents and newcomers and with families relocated to other parts of the city (Tosics et al. 2003).
2. Zugló High-prestige, new housing development leading to densification of the garden-city-like, lower density, green-belt part of the inner city	In Zugló the densification is driven by market processes (single family or low density multi-family areas are rebuilt by developers into higher density residential areas).	From the point of view of the city as a whole, the densification of the residential areas at the edge of the inner city is appropriate and the best alternative to suburbanization. However, the rebuilding has triggered complaints from original residents regarding the spillover effects such as deteriorating parking situation, increasing traffic, and reduction of green areas. Also, the environmentalist groups attack the new higher density developments as giving priority to real estate investment interests against the environmental values of green-belt areas within the city.
3. Törökbálint Intense growth and densification of a suburban settlement illustrating uncontrolled metropolitan restructuring in the absence of strong medium-level (regional) government and with fragmented local government structure	The independent re-zoning decisions of settlements in the Budapest agglomeration result in an informal competition among these settlements to offer more land and investment possibilities for residential and commercial venture developers. In the short term this brings financial gain to the local government, as it gets paid by the developers for allowing the re-zoning of these areas, more than the cost of extending school, health and other services.	In the long run, however, the extension of the residential area is a loss, with costly management of the infrastructure and tax revenues collected from the new residents insufficient to bridge the gap between the demand for social infrastructure and the very limited supply. In addition, this development contributes to the loss of green space around Budapest. From the perspective of local environmental groups, there are no reasons to endorse the re-zoning, except for the personal interest of some of the council members who own land in the areas which gains in value as a consequence of re-zoning.

Table 7.4. (cont.)

Conflicts in areas of deterioration and decreasing prestige

The case	The process	The conflicts
4. Magdolna quarter and Hős street Emerging ghetto areas at the edge of the inner city.	Despite mixed housing tenure, the social structure becomes increasingly homogenized, leading to ghetto symptoms in the public schools (i.e., large number of segregated ethnic groups) and to the general feeling of insecurity. The district government is unable to change this trend under the conditions of fragmentated local government system and uncoordinated sectoral policies. Such physically and socially distressed areas could be tackled only by area-based interventions with the participation of district, municipal and central government agencies.	The usual signs of conflicts in ghettoizing areas, with high shares of all types of negative symptoms (low social status, ethnic segregation, criminality). As a typical ghetto symptom, a significant share of the population feels unsafe in their own neighbourhood.
5. Outer Ferencváros The deterioration of the transitional zone with numerous brownfield areas.	After its collapse, socialist industry left behind brownfield areas that are disproportionally larger than in the western cities. Considering the financial difficulties of the district local governments and the increasing supply of greenfield development options outside Budapest, it will be very difficult to transform these urban brownfields into functional new land uses. Their locational characteristics will probably play a role in the restructuring process.	The under-utilization of large areas in the inner periphery causes problems within these areas themselves (the remaining users are less and less able to maintain the infrastructure) and also with regard to the city as a whole (the large 'no-mans lands' are becoming gaps in the city structure).
6. Csepel housing estate Prefabricated housing estate in the inner periphery (district XXI)	A slowly deteriorating large housing complex, built during socialism, is experiencing the beginning of the downward trend. Since the early 1990s, the estates have acquired different positions in the new real-estate market hierarchy, depending on the extent of privatization, the demographic changes, and their location within the city.	Some parts of the estate are still dominated by publicly owned housing, usually full with families in arrears in paying their water or heating bills. Because further increase of arrears might endanger the service provision for paying families, conflicts between residents increase.

Conflicts in areas of competing development needs

The case	The process	The conflicts
7. CBD area of Budapest Structural changes from residential to non-residential functions	In the central business area of Budapest the dynamic spread of non-residential investments reduced the residential functions. The 'value gap' between residential functions and the new office and commercial functions was evident from the early stages of transition. The functional change proceeded without much public control, so the privatized flats could be converted into offices or commercial premises.	The restructuring has lead to mixed function buildings and neighborhoods. The residential use is in conflict with the new functions as well as regarding the use of public space (e.g. parking). These conflicts in the central city area are manifested in a substantial variability in the condition of areas in close geographical proximity.

unattractive to commercial investments because of their locations or heavy contamination; some of the large housing estates at remote locations that are difficult to access; and some of the suburban settlements at the edge of the agglomeration that offer cheap real-estate and draw 'social suburbanization,' i.e., families moving out from the expensive-to-run housing estates.

Examining the urban development conflicts over time, we find that the intensity of the territorial conflicts varies in different stages of transition. Most of such conflicts are sharper in the vacuum and adaptation stages, when control mechanisms are not yet developed and public policies to compensate the losers are weak or absent. In general, it also seems that it is easier to handle the conflicts in the upwardly mobile areas, where legal regulations may be sufficient in dealing with different interests, whereas in the deteriorating areas, substantial public investments would be needed to stop the downward spiral.

7.3 The role of the public sector in 'managing' the spatial restructuring

The public sector's role in urban planning and policy has changed substantially under the new circumstances. In the centralized planning system, the public sector determined the urban development processes from a dominant position, but now its task is to regulate the dominating market processes from a subordinate position. It clearly has not been easy for the public sector to perform competently in this new role, for several reasons: a limited capacity to deal with urban issues under market conditions, constrained authority and power relations, increased responsibilities, and persisting financial problems.

The financial problems resulted from cuts in central state funds and difficulties in extracting revenues from the private sector. During the vacuum period the private sector had windfall gains, but avoided paying its share of public revenue because of unclear regulations and lax enforcement. During the adaptation period either the private sector could not contribute or only a small portion of its contributions reached the local governments because the payments were collected and often used at other levels of government. During the adjustment stage and under established social and financial policy, the public sector had only small assets remaining; public goods and services had already been privatized.

In the new century, as the entire transition process comes to an end, the Budapest municipality is attempting to establish control over the market-led urban development. The municipality promotes urban renewal through a limited action-area approach and aims to apply "integrated" solutions to the challenges of urban development by combining economic, environmental and social interventions. The municipality has completed the first steps in strategic planning: approval of the Budapest Strategic Development Concept in 2003 and the launching of the medium-term, integrated development programme in 2005. Even ideas about regional governance have started to emerge, to deal with the difficulties in controlling and guiding regional development under the present legal and administrative set-up.

Compared to the richer and more powerful public sectors of western European cities, Budapest, like most other post-socialist cities, lags in its level of control over market processes and of public intervention. Even so, the modest attempts of the Budapest municipality to foster public involvement are criticized by other stakeholders, namely the major developers, who complain that the public sector constrains development with unnecessary regulations. Meanwhile, the environmentalists complain that the public sector is too weak and corrupt to regulate private development.

Thus, in the adjustment stage of the transition substantial barriers still hamper the much needed increase in public control over market processes. With no easy solutions in sight, conflicts continue between the municipality and the districts over green areas and building rights, between the municipality and the surrounding settlements over spillover effects of development, between the public actors and the private developers over shopping centers, and between public/private actors and the local residents. However, compared to those in western European counterparts, the territorial conflicts are still relatively peaceful. This could be attributed to the still relatively small proportion of the marginalized strata of society, Roma and immigrant groups, within the urban population. Another factor may be the limited opportunities for the affluent strata of society to move to segregated, high-prestige housing areas. That situation, however, is changing fast as the supply of high-quality new housing increases both within and outside the city.

Accession to the European Union (EU) could help the Budapest municipality regain some control over market-driven urban development, as well as increasing its financial means and political power. But that beneficial outcome would require more comprehensive and better formulated urban policies at the EU level, concentrating not only on environmental issues and physical infrastructure, but also on the development of integrated public policies similar to the EU's Community Initiative URBAN, already extended to its second seven-year 2000-2006 term. A strong incentive from the EU is needed to prompt Budapest to develop integrated public policies and prepare for the increasing global urban competition.

7.4 Conclusion – Budapest 15 years after

The aim of this chapter was to show, analyse and explain the spatial restructuring of Budapest in the post-socialist period. The 15 years of transition were divided into three time periods to clarify the significant differences in political and administrative factors of development. Within these periods, the spatial development processes were described in the framework of the four territorial zones of the larger Budapest area. Economic forces, illustrated by commercial investments, were shown to play a significant role, favouring the inner parts of the city as opposed to suburban areas. The spatial re-allocation of population, however, showed a strong tendency towards suburbanization, driven mainly by the suburban land supply that was created by re-zoning decisions of the suburban settlements.

Privatization of assets and decentralization of decision making authority contributed to the weakness of the public sector in controlling market processes. The strengthening of public control could be observed only at the end of the transition period. In the absence of that control, territorial conflicts emerged in both the dynamic and the deteriorating urban areas. It remains to be seen how strong the newly developed strategic powers of the public administration (development concept and programme) prove to be in orienting further developments and handling territorial conflicts. For the more efficient functioning of the public sector, changes are needed as well in the administrative system and power allocation, to give more weight to the regional level over individual settlements and to the municipal level over the Budapest districts.

On the basis of our analysis the following answers can be given to the questions raised at the beginning of the chapter: With regard to the main driving forces of post-socialist urban development in the transition period, different patterns might be conceptualized. There are examples, e.g., in German cities, of the leading role of suburban economic and commercial investments, which preceded and partly caused suburbanization of the population. Budapest however shows the opposite picture, with outward mobility much more characteristic of the population than of the developers.

Regarding the question, of the extent to which Budapest is moving towards the model of a market-oriented city, losing its characteristics from the socialist period, our analysis has shown the following:

- The CBD is losing residential density, as the first two stages of transition, especially, led reduced residential function.
- The outer parts of the inner city are becoming more dense, as in the third stage of transition the smaller brownfield areas and single family areas are being rebuilt with higher density (see the Zugló case).
- The inner periphery with the large housing estates (which earlier constituted the "back" of the density camel) is slowly losing population.
- The quick densification of the suburban areas is starting to slow down at the end of the transition.

Thus, at least in its residential density structure, Budapest seems to be losing its camel-back anomaly and heading towards the "normal" density pattern of market-oriented cities. Just as in Hungary the post-socialist transition was relatively fast, with short vacuum and adaptation periods, the development of the city points more directly in the direction of market-driven development.

The market orientation of city development does not mean that within 15 years Budapest became a mainstream capitalist city. Some aspects of the socialist development period remain important, for example, the leading role of public transport and the high proportion of the population living on large housing estates. Indeed, the legacy of a dominant public transport system is one aspect that should be preserved from the socialist period. To keep the primary role and the high density network of public transport is however a difficult task, especially given the explosion in the number of private cars. Although the new developments of the last years, especially the densification of the outer parts of the inner city, raise new arguments for improving public transport, it is difficult for the public sector to finance the very costly investments needed to keep public transport competitive with private car use.

The 'heritage' of the large housing estates is an even more difficult question. This housing form has substantial advantages in terms of sustainable urban development, being a dense urban residential form with good public transport links and an environment-friendly heating system (Tosics 2004). The popular opinion of large housing estates is, however, low. Most residents would move to other housing forms. Substantial public investments would be needed to modernize large housing estates, preserving them as a competitive form of residence as opposed to the suburban forms, however less sustainable these are from a public perspective.

From our overview it can be seen that the emerging public sector, urban planning and policy making, played different roles in the successive stages of transition in terms of 'management' of the changes and control over the market processes. The 1990s, with the vacuum and adaptation periods, can be characterized as spontaneous development in Hungary and in Budapest, dominated by the privatization of the economy and liberal policy, with no or minimal public interventions and no coordination on the regional level. The results of this development track were mixed: Budapest absorbed a very significant amount of FDI, and the market-led processes resulted in quick development of economic poles within and around the city. However, the sustainability aspect of the development was weak: massive suburbanization, the dominance of green-field development over brown-field redevelopment, growing traffic problems. Furthermore, social inequalities increased. In the new Millennium, gradual changes towards more comprehensive public policies and strategic planning are observable. As with this adjustment period the transition comes to an end, the question is still open: how much will the newly emerging public policies be able to influence the functioning of the strong market forces?

The transition period of development was more or less oriented toward the free-market in other post-socialist cities as well. At the end of the transition from socialism into capitalism, however, there is intensified need for a new version of public control over market development processes, in order to avoid these serious problems of purely market-dominated urban development: spreading out of cities, growing differentiation between the dynamic and the stagnating/deteriorating areas, sharpening social conflicts with increasing socio-spatial segregation, etc. The new orientation calls for more pro-active public leadership and a new type of urban governance, which – in intense cooperation with the private actors – should lead to a more balanced, controlled market development of the post-socialist cities.

References

Bennett RJ (1998) Local government in postsocialist cities. In: Enyedi G (ed) Social change and urban restructuring in Central Europe. Akadémia Kiadó, Budapest, pp 35–54

Bertaud A, Malpezzi S (2003) The spatial distribution of population in 48 world cities: implications for economies in transition. Http://www.alain-bertaud.com [Accessed December 2005]

Bertaud A, Buckley R (1997) Cracow in the twenty first century: Prince of merchants? A City's structure under the conflicting influences of land markets, zoning regulations and a socialist past. Mimeo, Budapest

Bird RM, Ebel RD, Wallich CI (eds) (1995) Decentralization of the socialist state -- Intergovernmental finance in transition economies. World Bank Regional and Sectoral Studies. World Bank, Washington, DC

Central Statistical Office of Hungary - CSO (2005) Demographic trends in east-central European capitals. CSO, Budapest

Central Statistical Office of Hungary - CSO (1991-2005) Statistical Yearbook of Budapest, CSO, Budapest

Enyedi G (1996) Urbanisation under socialism. In: Andrusz G, Harloe M, Szelényi I (eds.) Cities after socialism: Urban and regional change and conflict in post-socialist societies. Blackwell Publishers, Oxford, pp 100–118

Grime K, Kovács Z (2001) Changing urban landscapes in East Central Europe. In: Turnock D (ed) East Central Europe and the Former Soviet Union -- Environment and society.: Arnold, London, pp 130-139

Hegedüs J, Tosics I (1996) Disintegration of East-European housing model. In Clapham D, Hegedüs J, Kintrea K, Tosics I (eds) with Kay H, Housing privatisation in Eastern Europe. Greenwood Press, Westport, pp 15–40

Herfert G (1997) Suburbanisierung in Ostdeutschland. In: Kovács Z, Wiessner R (eds) Prozesse und Perspektiven der Stadtentwicklung in Ostmitteleuropa. Münchener Geographische Hefte 76, L.I.S. Verlag, Passau, pp 269-287

Iceg–Corvinus (2005) SEE (South East European) Monitor 19:5

Kovács Z (2002a) Az urbanizáció jellemzői kelet-közép Európában a poszt-szocialista átmenet idején (In Hungarian) [The characteristics of urbanization in east-central Europe during the post-socialist transition]. In: Földrajzi Közelmények CXXVI. Kötet. 1-4 szám, pp 57-78

Kovács Z (2002b) Budapest und Umgebung. In: Hitz H, Sitte W, Forster F (eds) Das östliche Österreich und benachbarte Regionen. Verlag Ed. Hölzel, Wien, pp 419-448

Michalski A, Saraceno E (2000) Regions in the enlarged European Union. Background Note prepared for the 18th European Carrefour on Science and Culture, Forward Studies Unit, Budapest, 20–21 March

National Bank of Hungary (2005) Data quoted with reference to the NBH in The Hungarian Economy, II/2005, ITDH The Hungarian Investment and Trade Development Agency

Pallai K (2003) The Budapest model, a liberal urban policy experiment. OSI/LGI, Budapest

Sármány-Parsons I (1998) Aesthetic aspects of change in urban space in Prague and Budapest during the transition. In: Enyedi G (ed) Social change and urban restructuring in Central Europe. Akadémiai Kiadó, Budapest, pp 209-232

Szelényi I (1996) Cities under socialism – and after. In: Andrusz G, Harloe M, Szelényi I, (eds) Cities after socialism: Urban and regional change and conflict in post-socialist societies. Blackwell Publishers, Oxford, pp 286–317

Tosics I (2005a) City Development in Central and Eastern Europe since 1990: The Impact of internal forces. In: Hamilton FEI, Dimitrowska-Andrews K, Pichler-Milanovic N (eds) Transformation of cities in Central and Eastern Europe -- Towards globalization. United Nations University Press, Tokyo, pp 44-78

Tosics I (2005b) The post-socialist Budapest: the invasion of market forces and the attempts of public leadership. In: Hamilton FEI, Dimitrowska-Andrews K, Pichler-Milanovic N (eds) Transformation of cities in Central and Eastern Europe. Towards globalization. United Nations University Press, Tokyo, pp 248-280

Tosics I (2004) European urban development: Sustainability and the role of housing. *Journal of Housing and the Built Environment* 19:67-90

Tosics I, Szemző H, Kőszeghy L, Erdősi S (2003) National city contexts, urban development programmes and neighborhood selection. The Hungarian background report. Urban development programmes, urban governance, social inclusion and sustainability, Urban Governance, Social Inclusion and Sustainability (UGIS) Working Papers. OASES-GARANT, Antwerpen-Apeldoom

8 Poverty and inequality in Greater Tirana: The reality of peri-urban areas

Luan Deda and Sasha Tsenkova

Introduction

Albania is one of the poorest countries not only in Europe but among the former socialist block. The country's poverty, together with uncontrolled development during the transition period and its general political, social, and economic instability, has created the context for rapid and explosive growth of poverty in the peri-urban areas of Tirana. Since the end of the dictatorial regime in 1991 the country has been establishing a new regime based on the market economy and pluralist democracy. The structural change from a centrally planned to a market economy has been accompanied by rapid urbanization, particularly to the Greater Tirana Region. The consequent pressure on urban services, land and housing has intensified at a time when public authorities are unable to respond effectively. During the last decade, Tirana's population, density and area have expanded beyond its administrative boundaries. The new peri-urban areas, though outside the city limits, are now integrated with the city's economy, society and property markets.

This chapter takes a close look at a new phenomenon in post-socialist cities— the growth of urban poverty and its spatial manifestation. Evidence from several analytical studies and representative surveys profiling the nature of poverty in Greater Tirana's peri-urban areas can illuminate the multifaceted problem of urban poverty and inequality in post-socialist Albania. The problem clearly is significant. The country has prepared a long-term *Growth and Poverty Reduction Strategy* (KMRSH 2001), which however lacks a clear picture of poverty at the city level. Similar policies in other countries in South East Europe also aim to address growing unemployment and poverty, and the proliferation of illegal settlements. In all these national strategies the lack of explicit urban focus is surprisingly similar, as is also the lack of methodologies and of baseline data on poverty and its spatial manifestations in the region's large, post-socialist cities (Atal 1999; World Bank 2000).

Research has shown that worldwide, poverty's characteristics differ among countries and regions and also among the regions within a country (Atkinson 1998; Gordon and Townsend 2000; World Bank 2000). Thus broad national policies on poverty reduction may fail unless they are translated to local strategies that respond to local problems. This chapter therefore seeks new insights on poverty in Albania from examining the new urban reality of Greater Tirana and its poorest peri-urban neighbourhoods. The analysis should aid government initiatives for poverty reduction and guide the formulation of contextually appropriate local programs.

The main objectives of this analysis are: (1) to provide data on the incidence of poverty in Tirana's peri-urban areas and to compare those data with the national average, (2) to profile the peri-urban poor and their specific needs, (3) to analyse the main causes of poverty in that specific group, and (4) to propose concrete steps to be considered in policy's for reducing poverty in Albania's peri-urban areas and other informal settlements. The main hypothesis is that at the household level, poverty in peri-urban Greater Tirana is not due entirely to insufficient income for maintaining optimal consumption, but rather to the higher costs of housing and basic services. The available data will show that the priority of housing and access to basic services means that people have no choice but to spend less on food and non-food items, substantially reducing their standard of living. That being the case, measures to combat poverty should focus on the supply side, i.e., affordable provision of urban basic services, rather than raising household incomes.

Although the empirical work here focuses on Greater Tirana, other large cities across South East Europe may face very similar challenges. Hence our analysis and policy recommendations may be of interest to a wider audience of researchers and policy makers (Council of Europe Bank 2004; Tsenkova 2005).

8.1 Defining and measuring poverty

In the last decade, the problem of poverty has drawn increasing research attention. Recognition of the multidimensional nature of poverty has broadened its definition as well as suggesting possibilities for crosscutting to other sectors of development. In post-socialist Europe poverty has risen since the demise of the 'iron curtain,' along with an increase in social differentiation (World Bank 2000; UNDP 2002); at the same time, the alternative proffered by the area's previous regimes, of socially just societies without poverty and inequality, has been revealed as largely only a facade.[1] In each case, the importance is clear of international agreement on how to define poverty as well as on yardsticks for measuring it. Both are essential for valid poverty analysis.

> One definition that is universally accepted, formulated at the Copenhagen World Summit in 1995, distinguishes absolute and relative poverty. Absolute poverty is "a condition characterised by severe deprivation of basic human needs, including food, safe drinking water, sanitation facilities, health, shelter, education and information. It depends not only on inadequate income, but

---

[1] The period after WWII to the early 90's was a fierce race of the two ideologies. In one camp, the capitalist system claiming the reduction poverty by the "trickling down" of the benefits of economic growth, while in the other camp the socialist system claiming total equality and a just distribution of benefits to society's members and therefore the non-existence of poverty.

also incorporates lack of access to social services" (Social Summit 1995, Chapter 2 para 19).

Relative poverty, according to the document, has:

various manifestations, including lack of income and productive resources sufficient to ensure sustainable livelihoods; hunger and malnutrition; ill health; limited or lack of access to education and other basic services; increased morbidity and mortality from illness; homelessness and inadequate housing; unsafe environments; and social discrimination and exclusion. It is also characterized by a lack of participation in decision-making and in civil, social and cultural life (para 19).

The *Pyramid of Poverty* in Fig. 8.1. is a simple illustration of the wide range of concepts involved in discussing poverty (see White and Killick, 2001 for an in-depth account). The important point of departure is the level of private consumption, often termed income-based poverty: the ability to acquire food, shelter and access to basic services. Absolute poverty, as defined above, is measured partly in terms of access to social services and other support provided by the state, which can grow incrementally to include personal assets, security and dignity. The *Pyramid* can be enriched with other dimensions that may widen the base, such as autonomy and participation in civic and social life, the lack of which is noted in the Social Summit definition of relative poverty. The *Pyramid of Poverty* is particularly helpful in positioning our case study research in a wider framework of poverty analysis and we will use it in the evaluations of survey data in the four neighbourhoods of Greater Tirana.

To measure absolute poverty, attempts have been made to develop internationally applicable indicators using a "non-welfareist" approach (Atkinson 1998). The result marks absolute poverty by a consumption-based poverty line comprising expenditures for a minimum standard of nutrition and other basic needs according to each country's context (Atkinson and Micklewright 1992). That notion is embodied in the World Bank's definition of the absolute poverty line as per capita income (in purchasing power parity, PPP, terms) of $1 a day in Asia and Africa, and $2 a day in Latin America and Eastern Europe (World Bank 2003). That method has been criticised as applicable only to less developed countries and thus resulting in different standards applied around the world, instead of a unique international standard (Gordon and Townsend 2000). Milanović (1998), for example, has proposed absolute poverty line set at US$4 per person per day for the Central and East European (CEE) countries. In short, the absolute poverty line is highly dependent not only on the living standard of the country, but on the perception of poverty in the country context, as well.

The other approach for measuring poverty is the concept of relative poverty developed by the European Commission. That concept defines poverty as the percentage of population with income or expenditures under 50 percent (or other thresholds 40% or 60%) of the national income average (Gordon and Townsend

2000). The relative measurement of poverty aims to show the level of inequality, but it is highly dependent on the availability of adequate institutions for collecting the accurate information. It is difficult to apply this method in developing countries or transition economies, where the reliability of such information is poor and the share of the informal economy is high.

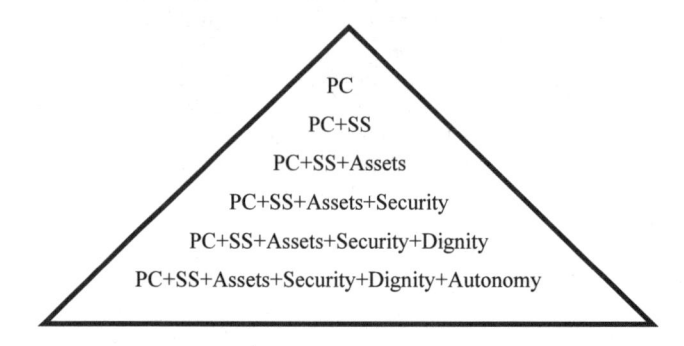

```
                    PC
                  PC+SS
               PC+SS+Assets
            PC+SS+Assets+Security
         PC+SS+Assets+Security+Dignity
      PC+SS+Assets+Security+Dignity+Autonomy
```

Fig. 8.1. Pyramid of poverty concepts

Source: Adapted from White and Killick 2001
Note:
PC - Private Consumption
SS - State Services

The search for suitable methods of poverty measurement in the context of Albania can be informed by the experience of other CEE countries. In Poland, Hungary, the former Soviet Union republics and the Czech Republic, the absolute poverty line is independent of public welfare systems. It refers to a particular "basket of goods" to maintain a minimum standard of living (for a discussion on these methods see Deda 2003). Different approaches to poverty measurement can be very important in the analysis. In CEE countries the measurement method raises questions not only of the reliability of information collection, but also of the possible reluctance of people to provide personal information on income and expenditure. In particular, people may have low incomes but be able to maintain a certain level of consumption due to borrowings or savings (Atkinson and Micklewright 1992).

Albanian institutions have experimented with different definitions and measurements of poverty. The most recent ones refer to a nationally defined poverty line (INSTAT 2002). Extreme poverty—food poverty line—is measured in terms of monthly income per capita where the national benchmark specifies the minimum amount necessary to ensure the purchase/consumption of food. Absolute poverty lines are anchored to a nutritional basket and/or to specific welfare levels, allowing for easy comparison across time and groups. Relative poverty lines, instead, reflect the degree of destitution of a household or individual in relation to the income of the rest of the population. Another important operational definition—full poverty line—entails the acceptance of a national poverty line based on monthly income per capita to ensure purchase of essential food and non-food items (INSTAT & World Bank 2003: 13).

8.2 Poverty in Albania

As in other former socialist countries, poverty was never publicly discussed during the socialist regime in Albania. There is no research on poverty for the period before 1990. During the transition, the official political and economic difficulties crowded out concerns about the incidence of poverty, food shortages and deprivation. The problem was not really addressed in any systematic manner until the end of the 1990s, when the World Bank stressed its importance for the country's economic growth in the Bank's preparatory process for the third *Country Assistance Strategy* (World Bank 2002). In response, the Government of Albania prepared a national *Growth and Poverty Reduction Strategy* (KMRSH 2001). Both policy documents required extensive investigation of poverty at the national level, identification of its causes and indicators for measurement.

In 1998, a survey mapped out a depressing picture of poverty in the country. About 1 in 6 households lived on less than 1US$ per day per person (extreme poverty according to the World Bank definition), and almost 1 in 2 households lived on less than 2US$ per day per person (absolute poverty). Apart from income, poverty studies considered other dimensions arising from people's inability to fulfil basic needs because of lack of income or very low income or assets. Therefore, poverty in the Albanian context is defined as exposure to a high risk of ill health and lack of access to adequate health service; illiteracy or low educational level; high exposure to risks; lack of voice in decision-making institutions (KMRSH 2001).

A qualitative assessment of poverty in Albania lists these main causes of poverty: "unemployment; insufficient and poor quality land; a lack of formal institutions, including marketing mechanisms, to support the industrial and agriculture sectors; the government's inability to respond to their increasingly fragile situations with adequate infrastructure, public security, healthcare, education services, and social security programs; and the inability of informal coping mechanism to continue to support the minimum needs of households under duress" (De Soto et al. 2002: 7).

However, a recent survey of living standards in Albania shows a slightly different picture of poverty (INSTAT 2002). The changes reflect the differences in methodology of data collection and the adjustment of the statistical system to the standard international approach for data collection in poverty measurement recommended by Statistical Institute of the European Union. According to this study, only about 4.7 percent of households live in extreme poverty with income per capita below the food poverty line and a quarter of the country's population lives below the nationally defined full poverty line (income to secure minimum food and non-food consumption) (Table 8.1.).

Table 8.1. Comparison of poverty definitions in the context of Albania, 2002

Poverty Line	Value ALL*	Headcount (%)
Food poverty	3,047	4.7
50% median per capita consumption	3,349	7.0
US$ 2 PPP	3,775	10.8
60% median per capita consumption	4,019	13.5
Full poverty Line	4,891	25.4
US$ 4 PPP	7,550	59.3
Source (INSTAT & WB, 2003)		

Source: Adapted from INSTAT and World Bank 2003
Note:
*ALL is an abbreviation for Albanian Lek; 1 Lek=US$0.007, exchange rate effective April 30, 2002.
**The data refer to measurement of relative poverty developed by the European Commission; definitions of poverty reflect the percentage of the population with income under 50% or 60% of the median per capita.

The share of people living in absolute poverty in Albania in 2002, measured by US$2 per person is 10.8 percent, which is comparable to the share in other transition countries—Bulgaria (7.9%), Romania (6.8%), Former Yugoslav Republic of Macedonia (6.7%). The absolute poverty rates are twice as high in countries such as Georgia (18.9%), and Azerbaijan (23.5%) (World Bank 2003).

Correspondingly, using the European Commission concept of relative poverty, defined as the percentage of population with income per capita under 50 or 60 percent of the national income average, the level of poverty in Albania is 7 and 13.5 percent (see Table 8.1.). The data demonstrate that different approaches to poverty measurement elicit different results; consequently this leads to inconsistency in the design of public policy measures addressing poverty and inequality in society. The search for suitable methods in Albania and other transition economies is constrained by the lack of institutional capacity and access to reliable database on household income and expenditure.

The data in Table 8.2. present key aspects of the spatial distribution of poverty. Households in rural areas are more disadvantaged, than those in urban areas. In Tirana the level and depth of poverty appear to be the lowest in the country. In the city only 2.3 percent of the population is in extreme poverty and about 18 percent in full poverty. Increasing inequality is indicated by the Gini coefficient results, which are higher in Tirana than in urban and rural areas. The mean monthly consumption per capita in Tirana is Albanian Lek (ALL) 9,043 compared to ALL 7,801 at national level (INSTAT & World Bank 2003).

The official statistics have two major weaknesses as far as information on the incidence of poverty in Greater Tirana is concerned: they do not represent the informal areas within the city, nor do they consider poverty in the newly urbanised areas outside the city boundaries. The sample for the living standards survey represents Tirana with 600 households in the official urban area of Tirana Municipality (INSTAT 2002).

Table 8.2. Poverty and inequality in Albania

Survey Year	Albania 2002	Bulgaria 2001	Romania 1998	Macedonia 1996	Georgia 1999	Azerbaijan 1999
US$ 2 PPP	10.8	7.9	6.8	6.7	18.9	23.5
US$ 4 PPP	59.3	31.9	44.5	43.9	54.2	64.2

Source: Adapted from INSTAT and World Bank 2003
Note:
*In the category 'poor', the data refer to share of households experiencing full poverty defined in accordance with nationally accepted poverty line of ALL 4,891 per capita/month in 2002/2003. 'Extreme poverty' means 'food poverty' or income per capita lower than ALL 3,047.
**The Gini coefficient is a number between 0 and 1, where 0 corresponds with perfect equality (where everyone has the same income) and 1 corresponds with perfect inequality (where one person has all the income, and everyone else has zero income).

8.3 Economic growth and poverty in Greater Tirana

During the transition period, Tirana has grown rapidly in both population and area. The city population rose by close to 100,000 from 1989 to 2001, while the peri-urban areas doubled their population (Table 8.3.). Studies on urban land management in Tirana during the mid-1990s have reported dramatic figures of population growth, up to 7 percent a year (PADCO 1996), which has slowed down since then to an overall annual average of 2.5 percent. Similarly, despite the fact that the administrative boundaries of the city have not changed, the total urban area almost *de facto* doubled during the same period (Fig. 8.2.). In its expansion the city has integrated surrounding areas so that the total area is commonly referred to as Greater Tirana.

The growth of the city, spurred by rapid urbanization, increased the pressure for urban services in Tirana. Suddenly there was excess demand for land, housing, and other public services in a situation of almost non-existent government institutions to respond to that demand. As a result, most of the urban development activity during the 1990s took place outside the formal system. Despite its chaotic development, however, Greater Tirana is the main concentration not only of population, but of the social and economic potential of the country. The city possesses 35 to 50 percent of the new start-up businesses officially accounted for in Albania since 1990 (PADCO 2002). The construction sector is booming, as new offices, retail and housing projects change the city's landscape. The 2001 census data show that the number of buildings within Greater Tirana doubled in the 1989-2001 period. The construction boom has given a boost to the building materials industry there, as some of the large producers and traders are located within the region.

Table 8.3. Population in Greater Tirana

	Tirana		Other urban		Rural		Total	
	Poor	Extr poor	Poor	Extr poor	Poor	Extr poor	Poor	Extr poor
Headcount	17.8	2.3	20.1	4.8	29.6	5.2	25.4	4.7
Poverty Gap	3.8	0.6	4.7	0.9	6.6	0.7	5.7	0.8
Poverty Gap squared	3.8	0.6	4.7	0.9	6.6	0.7	5.7	0.8
Mean per capita consumption ALL	9,043		8,468		7,212		7,801	
Gini	0.30		0.28		0.27		0.28	

Source: PADCO 2002. Strategic Plan for Greater Tirana

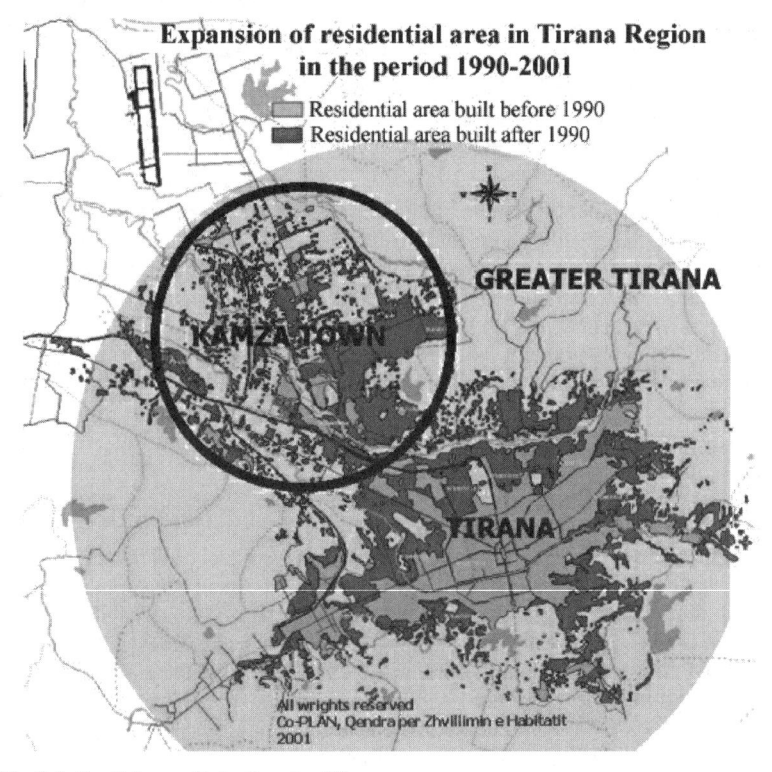

Fig. 8.2. Spatial growth in Greater Tirana

In general, there are insufficient data on the economic indicators for Greater Tirana. However, the available estimates show that the major part of labour force work in the service industry whereas on the national level the agriculture sector still dominates the total employment. About one-third of workers in Tirana are in trade and financial services, 25 percent in construction, 20 percent in industry and the remainder in the public sector or agriculture (INSTAT 2001; Deda 2002). Yet, the official statistics on unemployment show that about 25 percent of the labour force does not have regular jobs in Tirana (Deda 2003). Thus the data are questionable in a situation where an estimated 40 percent of the work force operates in the informal sector. That sector includes day labourers in construction and other fields, street vendors, moneychangers, as well as skilled workers in manufacturing, metalworking, and automotive repair. The informal sector is the main entry point into the urban economy for low-income migrants in Tirana (PADCO 2002).

Despite the overall pattern of economic growth and relative prosperity, poverty and social problems do exist in Tirana. Table 8.4. uses some Unmet Basic Needs (UBN) indicators to compare the city with other urban as well as rural areas. These indicators define relative poverty (non-income-based) in terms of access to basic services, education and adequate housing. The survey results show that 8.5 percent of Tirana's residents lack adequate housing, and only 2 percent lack access to basic services (water, sewer, energy supply). Those shares are relatively low compared to the national levels of 12.5 percent and 17.5 percent respectively, and are even lower than the percentages for rural areas (16.5% and 28.6%). The study shows that the incidence of poverty as measured by unmet basic needs is lower in Tirana (11.5%) than in the other urban and the rural areas, where the poverty levels are 16.6 percent and 47.2 percent respectively (INSTAT & World Bank 2003).

Table 8.4. Comparative indicators of unmet basic needs in Albania

	Tirana	Albania Urban	Albania Rural	Albania Total
1. Inadequate water and sanitation	0.5	2.6	28.6	17.5
2. Inadequate housing	8.5	6.3	16.5	12.5
3. Inadequate energy supply	1.7	9.0	18.1	13.5
4. Crowding (more than 3 persons/room)	10.3	15.6	18.6	16.7
5. Education (Households head with primary or less education)	34.7	47.0	74.8	61.2
Poor (two or more UBN)	11.5	16.6	47.2	33.8
Extreme poor (Three or more UBN)	2.3	3.2	18.3	11.9
Non poor (one or no UBN)	88.5	83.4	52.9	66.2

Source: INSTAT and World Bank 2003

In summary, in terms of non-income poverty the contrast between the figures for Tirana and those for other urban areas and for the rural population is high. The data are supported by data from other policy documents such as the *Strategic Plan for Greater Tirana* (PADCO 2002). The implication is that the concentration of economic activity in Tirana during the transition period has in one way or another improved living standards in the city in comparison to those in other urban and in rural regions of Albania.

8.4 Poverty in urban and peri-urban Greater Tirana

According to approximate estimates, more than 60 percent of Greater Tirana developed informally during the transition period, (Deda 2002) and most of the urban structure is stretches on agricultural land outside the city borders. The recent *Strategic Plan of Greater Tirana* shows that the number of households living in informal settlements within Tirana city boundaries accounts for about 25 percent of the total population, and that about 30 percent of the total Greater Tirana population lives outside the formal city borders (PADCO 2002, Table 8-3-2). Thus, approximately 55 percent of the population live in informal conditions, i.e., illegal status of land ownership, lack of conformity to building regulations and/or illegal connection to infrastructure (when available). Consequently, the real figures for poverty in Greater Tirana will be different if the data are collected in the area outside the municipal boundaries. In this regard, two aspects of poverty in Greater Tirana are particularly worth looking into: first, the nature of poverty in peri-urban Tirana, and second, in what ways policy instruments can reduce the level of poverty there.

The poverty analysis will use the data from four neighbourhood surveys in the informal settlements of urban and peri-urban Greater Tirana.[2] The neighbourhoods—Selita, Mihal Grameno, Bathore, and Frutikultura—were developed during the transition period without conformity to land and building regulations. Two of the areas are at the edge of the official city boundaries (Selita and Mihal Grameno); the two others are part of the new peri-urban, highly urbanized land indicated as Kamza in Fig. 8.2. (Co-Plan 1999, 2000). Following the approach presented in the *Pyramid of Poverty*, this analysis will consider household consumption, access to state services and, to a certain extent, household assets as the main factors in measuring and comparing poverty levels (refer to Fig. 8.1.). That is not to ignore the importance of other indicators of poverty at the household level that are related to social status, dignity and involvement in civic politics and social life; but those lie beyond the scope of our analysis.

On a quick city tour of Tirana, one would easily observe that in terms of living standards, the informal developments of the last decade bear the signs of extreme urban poverty. Although in close proximity to the city centre, these neighbourhoods have conditions comparable to those in poor rural areas. Residents lack infrastructure and other public services: schools, health care, and police control. The

---

[2] Data were collected by Co-Plan through face-to-face interviews with randomly selected households in the four areas. For specific information on sample size, please refer to Table 8.5.

services they do have access to are often secured by means of illegal connections to existing infrastructure (UNECE 2002).

Table 8.5. profiles the four neighbourhoods schematically, presenting the key characteristics of size and location of the area, demographics, economic status, housing and level of servicing. With respect to poverty (income-based), Bathore and Frutikultura are the poorest neighbourhoods, with 25 percent and 35 percent of households in extreme poverty and 50 percent and 65 percent of the residents experiencing full poverty with income below the national poverty line in Albania. The other area (Selita) has about 20 percent of households in extreme poverty and 40 percent living in full poverty. All three neighbourhoods concentrate a disproportionately high number of poor people compared to the average for Tirana.[3] On the other hand, the Mihal Grameno area, although an informal settlement, is distinctively better off than the Tirana average, with almost no extreme poverty and only 17 percent of the residents with income below the national poverty line.

For other, non-income indicators of poverty, a comparison of Tirana and the peri-urban areas further demonstrates the spatial concentration of poverty. The data on economic status, for instance, are astonishing: in the four neighbourhoods the level of unemployment exceeds 23 percent and in Frutikultura is as high as 82 percent. Gender-segregated analysis of the data shows that 88 to 94 percent of women are unemployed, while among males 40 to 70 percent report being unemployed or having no regular job (Co-PLAN 2000; Deda 2003). The neighbourhoods have a relatively young, family-centred demographic structure. Given the high unemployment rate, it is not surprising that most households have a member working abroad (13-20%). Most people own their houses (average size around 100 m^2), so they have acquired some assets; and the rate of illiteracy is relatively low, from 1 to 5.5 percent. However, the figures on literacy and school attendance in themselves provide no substantial information on the quality of education. The conditions at the school, the professional level of teachers, distance from home and number of children per classroom are significant indicators of quality. Those indicators show the quality of schooling to be appalling particularly in the two peri-urban areas, Bathore and Frutikultura. Children have to walk for more than 30 minutes to get to the school, classes operate in shortened periods because the school is operating three shifts a day to serve the high number of children. In the Bathore area there is only one primary school for 25,000 inhabitants, with about 2,500 children attending it though the school capacity is for only 1,200 children (Co-PLAN 2000, 2002; Co-Plan and IHS 2002).

The poorest neighbourhoods in the survey, Bathore and Frutikultura, have almost no connections to piped water. In Bathore, 79 percent of households have no water connection and have to transport drinking water from nearby areas or public taps. About 60 percent of households have wells that provide only unpotable water. In Frutikultura 75 percent of households have no connection to a water system. Similarly, piped sewage systems are non-existent in both neighbourhoods,

---

[3] The comparable figures for Tirana from Table 8.2 are 2.3% of residents live in absolute poverty and 17.8% in full poverty.

Table 8.5. Profile of four neighbourhoods in peri-urban Tirana

Topic	Key Indicators	Selita	Mihal Grameno	Bathore2	Frutikultura
Number of households interviewed (population sample)		90 (444)	150 (656)	50 (308)	67 (67)
Physical characteristics	Distance from city centre	3 km	Less than 1 Km	6 Km	7 Km
	Pre estimated size of the area	30 Ha	25 Ha	25 Ha + (11 Ha pilot site)	30 Ha
Demographic characteristics	Total estimated population	2741 inhabitants	3652 inhabitants	2196 inhabitants	2269 inhabitants
	Average age	31.5 years old	33.1 years old	23 years old	26.5 years old
	Size of family	4.94 members per family	4.4 Persons per family	6.1 Persons per family	6.2 persons/family
Housing characteristics	Total house number	555	430 apartments + 400 individual houses = 830	360	366
	Average dwelling area	104 m2	110 m2	100 m2	108 m2
Roads	Quality	91% unpaved, 7% asphalt	38% unpaved, 36% asphalt, 24% gravel	38% unpaved, the rest is gravel	54% unpaved; 46% covered with gravel
Water	Main source of supply	Tap inside the house 79%; tap outside 19%	Tap water inside 98%	60% well, 19% from the public tap	Well 75% Tap 23%
Sewage	Main type of discharge	Sewage system 66% Spill over in drainage system 31%	90% to the city main 8% spill over to drainage system	67% cesspit and the rest in the drainage or irrigation system	Cesspit 89.4%
Waste disposal	Way of disposal	Assigned place 92%	88.7% to the assigned place, 10% wherever they can	56% wherever, 42% burning	Throw all over 52% Burn 40%
Electricity	Type of connection	96.7% formally with meter	90% formally with meter, 8% informally	84.8% informally	57% informally, 25% formally without meter, 8% formally with meter
Labour Force	Unemployment rate	51% of labour force	23% of labour force	58% of labour force	82% of labour force
	Households with at least one person abroad (%)	20%	12.7% of households	18% of households	13.4%
Poverty (%)	Extreme poverty	20%	0.5%	25%	35%
	Full poverty	40%	17%	50%	65%

and 10-30 percent of households discharge sewage into the open irrigation channels. In addition, the connections to the power supply are poor and often illegal. About 84 percent of households in Bathore and 57 percent of those in Frutikultura have illegal connections to the power supply system. Not surprisingly, interviews indicated that in the peri-urban areas people feel abandoned by the state and ignored by society, and that they have very little hope for a good life.

The main conclusion drawn from the above evidence is that poverty within Greater Tirana is highly concentrated. Moreover, the official statistics on poverty in the city have so far ignored a significant part of the metropolitan area. Within the new urban reality, the surveys present a different profile, one of neighbourhood-based concentration of poverty, with higher incidences in the peri-urban areas with respect to both extreme and full poverty, than the city average and/or that in the rural areas.

8.5 Why are people poor in peri-urban Greater Tirana?

The evidence from the survey in the illegal settlements of Tirana, carried out by Co-Plan, demonstrates higher incidence of poverty in these areas and its spatial concentration in particular neighbourhoods such as Selita, Bathore, and Frutikultura. Some of the highlights from the survey in the previous sections profile patterns of extreme economic and spatial inequality and deprivation. The survey data also shows, we argue, that people's need to invest in the construction of their homes, basic shelter and access to basic public services, is crowding out their ability to consume food and other non-food items. Therefore people in the informal settlements, although having total expenditure per capita comparable to that in the formal part of the city, bear the extra costs for settling, i.e., provision of housing and services.

The survey considers the total cost of housing and investment in infrastructure for a period of 7 years (1993-2000) and estimates the average per month within this period. Table 8.6. compares the composition of household expenditures at neighbourhood level with data for Tirana and Albania. The data indicate that the mean expenditure per capita in peri-urban Greater Tirana is similar to that in the formal part of the city (within the formal city boundaries), in the range of ALL 9,000. However, monthly expenditures (food and non-food) in the neighbourhoods under study are on average 40 percent lower than those in the formal part of the city, with Mihal Grameno being the obvious exception. People in the poorest informal neighbourhoods have spent 35 to 45 percent of their total household budget on housing and access to infrastructure. This figure is lower for Tirana municipality (about 15%) and much lower for the national level (about 12%). In particular, households need to invest in some access to infrastructure, which officially is a responsibility of state and local governments. These costs, in addition to capital intensive work on their homes, are at the expense of household budgets allocated to food and other consumer items. The lack of piped water, sewer, roads, electrical supply and other essential urban services in peri-urban areas additionally

Table 8.6. Comparison of household expenditures at the neighbourhood, city and national level

Household expenditures in Leks	Selita	Mihal Grameno	Bathore	Fruti-kultura	Tirana***	Albania***
1 Total neighbourhood expenditures in Infrastructure* (1993 to 2000, ALL, 000)	1,685	5,580	4,152	4,920		
2 Housing construction and improvements (1993 to 2000, ALL Million)	130.2	254.3	69.9	121.6		
3 Total expenditures for housing and infrastructure for the period 1993 to 2000 ALL, Million (3 = 1 + 2)	131.9	259,9	74,1	126.5		
4 No of HH interviewed for each area.	90	150	50	67		
5 Total expenditure in housing and public services per HH for the period after 90's in ALL, 000** (5 = 3 / 4)	1,466	1,733	1,482	1,888		
6 Total expenditure per HH distributed per month in ALL (6 = 5/ {7 years * 12 months}).	17,450	20,630	17,640	22,480		
7 Monthly expenditure in housing and public services per HH per capita (7 = 6 / the household size for each area)	3,532	4,688	2,891	3,625	1,320	
8 Monthly expenditures per capita (declared food and non-food expenditures)	5,716	7,411	5,320	4,390	7,533	
9 Mean of total expenditures per capita (9 = 7 + 8)	9,248	12,099	8,211	8,015	9,043	7,801
Proportion of household expenditures in housing and access to services.						12.3%
10 (10 = 7 / 9 in percentage)	38%	39%	35%	45%	14.6%	
11 Estimated future utility charges for low income	2950	2950	2950	2950	2950	2950

Source: Combined data from Co-Plan, 2000, INSTAT & World Bank, 2003 and authors' estimates.
Note:
*Investment in infrastructure include (i) the cost of constructing the pit latrine, (ii) cost of constructing a well for water or provision of pipes for either legal or illegal connections to the city mains, (iii) cost of power transformers (household share among a group of households) as well as poles and wires, (iv) improvements in pathways for access to main roads etc.
**Proportion of households that have invested in infrastructure is lower for Selita and Mihal Grameno areas while it is almost 100% in the two other neighbourhoods.
***Source from LSMS, INSTAT 2002.

aggravates the living conditions of the poor in peri-urban Greater Tirana.

Furthermore, the fact that people in informal housing have invested in illegal connections to infrastructure networks provides only a temporary solution to their problem. Their investment in wells, pit latrines, and illegal connections to the power supply provide only inadequate and substandard access. People continue to either buy or transport water and/or to use well water unsuitable for drinking and cooking. Additional public health concerns are significant given the lack of piped sewer and waste collection systems (Co-Plan 2001; Deda 2003).

8.6 Policy measures to alleviate poverty in peri-urban Greater Tirana

The evidence presented here shows that extreme poverty, affecting 20-35 percent of the residents, is prevalent in peri-urban Tirana, and that these households are forced to spend three times more on housing and basic services than do the residents of the formal city. This spatial concentration of poverty and marginalization in the post-socialist city affects close to 100,000 inhabitants in Greater Tirana. It should not be ignored (PADCO 2002).

Fig. 8.3. The infrastructure in Bathore, one of the poorest neighbourhoods in peri-urban Tirana, is upgraded through community-based partnerships

Although households have acquired assets in the process, those assets may well be dead capital (De Soto 2000), which would require a substantial investment in infrastructure and other basic services such as health care, education, and public order to be integrated into the housing market. The provision of infrastructure and basic public services should be integrated in the upgrading schemes that give people legal titles to land and housing, thus converting dead capital into one that generates wealth (see Figure 8.3). Without such policy intervention to bridge these serious gaps, economic growth will have little impact on the poverty in the informal areas.

The provision of basic infrastructure and public services in peri-urban Greater Tirana could both directly and indirectly improve the living standards in these areas. A direct social effect would be visible in the immediate improvement of public health through preventing the epidemic diseases caused by the lack of sewer and waste collection systems as well as through improvement of the local health care systems. Improving access to education will similarly have a direct social effect, not simply on the literacy level, but by enabling more women to join the labour force. The survey of the four neighbourhoods showed that women could not enter the labour market mainly because of their total preoccupation with children and household activities. In addition, adequate infrastructure is directly related to substantial improvement of the immediate and city-wide environment. Availability of running water, adequate electricity, a proper sewerage network and waste collection system will reduce the population's exposure to health hazards and the contamination of underground water. The underground water pollution in Bathore, Frutikultura and the wider Kamza area could well have catastrophic consequences for the city.

The present situation of unauthorized interventions in existing infrastructure due to the pressing demand for services of course represents a severe loss for public utility companies. Part of their cost recovery for production and maintenance of services is problematic; non-payment is massive. For instance, the water company of Tirana receives payments from only 34 percent of the households using the water, and collection toward the cost overall of production of water is 56 percent. Similarly, the electricity company claims to lose about 55 to 60 percent of its potential revenue as a result of illegal connections to the system (PADCO 2002). There is evidence that the existing infrastructure networks have reached their capacity and are already overloaded by the excess construction of the last decade, as shown by the frequent interruption of services—water, electricity, heating—even for households in the formal part of Tirana.[4] So improving access to basic services in the peri-urban areas will have direct and indirect economic effects on the quality of life in peri-urban areas and will improve the efficiency of the public utility companies, as well.

---

[4] For instance, almost every household in Tirana has invested in a water reservoir and water pumps because of the low water pressure. Similarly, many households have invested in alternative supply of electricity (generators when they can afford it) or alternative heating systems (electric, gas heating as well as wood) (Deda 2003).

Conclusions

The new urban reality in peri-urban Greater Tirana displays the most challenging aspects of the transition process, bringing together the problems of extreme poverty, unemployment, and inadequate access to basic public services. This intermediate phase of poverty with its own specifics is found also in other cities in Albania (KMRSH 2001), but also in some of the large metropolitan areas in South East Europe (Council of Europe Bank 2004; Tsenkova 2005). Peri-urban poverty has been largely ignored in national poverty strategies and in other city development documents in Albania, yet it requires particular attention because:

- It represents a considerable number of inhabitants and households with particular needs;
- It is mostly part of the informal housing and labour market and therefore unknown, ignored, and difficult to consider in the policy making process;
- It is the main cause of the deterioration of infrastructure in the urban areas of the new metropolis.

Fig. 8.4. Mihal Grameno neighbourhood in peri-urban Tirana has the lowest concentration of poor households but still lacks basic infrastructure

Failure to address the problems of peri-urban areas is likely to impose significant economic, social and environmental costs on society in general and on the city of Tirana in particular. While the issues are no doubt complex and require solutions contextually appropriate to each neighbourhood, it seems that government investment in the provision of public services and infrastructure would surely make a difference (see Fig. 8.4.).

The people living in peri-urban areas of Greater Tirana have proven their capacity to generate sufficient income to improve their living conditions through investment in housing and some level of service provision (Co-Plan 2001).[5] That capacity can be used to design mechanisms for financial and/or in-kind collaboration among residents, community groups and levels of government to leverage resources for the provision of infrastructure. Sustainable solutions are essential, since at the moment the poorest households pay three times more than others for housing and basic services, driving them deeper into poverty and social deprivation. Correspondingly, better-balanced household budgets could 'free' some income for better nutrition, education for the children and other activities for social integration (Deda 2004). In short, investing in infrastructure in the peri-urban areas of Greater Tirana is the starting point toward concrete and sustainable results to alleviate poverty.

Such a response can be considered the optimal scenario for government intervention in the context of Albanian transition. The actual development process in Greater Tirana is now operating independently of government policies and planning documents. The economy, whether formal or informal, has created its network of institutions and markets and is slowly reaching the required maturity to respond to demand and supply. A workable strategy would be to focus on enabling those markets to perform more efficiently by providing infrastructure, which is still a public responsibility, thus improving living standards in poor neighbourhoods. The main government concern so far has been the lack of money to invest in infrastructure, but political will may also be lacking.[6]

Finally, we cannot ignore the fact that in general, poverty results from the lack of enough income to cover household's needs. Nonetheless, we are trying to show that households in peri-urban Greater Tirana could be better off even with the same level of income if allowed access to basic public services. Focusing on public services can have the impact needed to reduce poverty and create conditions in which households can improve their living situation.

Yet, that focus alone is not the ultimate solution to poverty. As we mentioned initially, poverty is multidimensional; its dimensions intersect with many development issues and tend to be especially complex in the context of transition, given the institutional and economic transformation in society. However, we believe one point is clear: it is important to focus on implementing the right policies with the highest impact for the most disadvantaged groups, such as the urban poor in the peri-urban areas.

---

[5] For example, even in the poorest neighbourhood of Bathore, people have invested US$ 7,000 per household in housing for the period 1992-1999, which is exceeds the requirements for infrastructure investment (Co-Plan 1999).

[6] The World Bank portfolio of assistance to the Government of Albania includes a loan for upgrading several illegal settlements in peri-urban areas. The project aiming at the provision of infrastructure in Bathore neighbourhood is facing serious difficulties due to the lack of political will (Deda 2003).

References

Atal Y (1999) Poverty in transition and transition in poverty. Recent development in Hungary, Bulgaria, Romania, Georgia, Russia, Mongolia. Berhahn Books, UNESCO.
Atkinson AB (1998) Poverty in Europe. Blackwell, Oxford
Atkinson AB, Micklewright J (1992) Economic transformation in Eastern Europe and the distribution of income. Cambridge University Press, Cambridge
Co-PLAN (1999) Social economic survey for urban Bathore. Study for the appraisal of the project "Roads to Stronger Civil Society" in Bathore area. Co-PLAN, Tirana
Co-PLAN (2000) Household survey for Mihal Grameno, Selita, Bathore, and Frutikultura. Study for the social assessment of the urban land management project of the Ministry of Public Works and Tourism. Co-PLAN, Tirana
Co-PLAN (2001) The Lana survey. A survey of illegal economic activities along Lana River in Tirana city centre. Co-PLAN, Tirana
Co-PLAN, Institute of Housing and Urban Development Studies (HIS) (2002) Strategic urban development plan for Kamza municipality. Report on Strengthening Local Authority and Community-based Initiatives in Tirana Programme. Centre for Habitat Development Tirana and HIS, Rotterdam/Tirana
Council of Europe Bank (2004) Housing in South Eastern Europe. Solving a puzzle of challenges. Council of Europe Bank, Paris
Deda L (2002) City made by people II. New roles of community in new urban reality. Co-PLAN, Tirana
Deda L (2003) Economic growth and poverty in Greater Tirana. MSc thesis. Development Planning Unit, University College London, London
De Soto H (2000) The mystery of capital. Why capitalism triumphs in the West and fails everywhere else. Basic Books, NY and Bantam Press/Random House, London
De Soto H, Gordon P, Gedeshi I, Sinomeri Z (2002) Poverty in Albania: A qualitative assessment. World Bank Technical Paper No. 520. World Bank, Washington DC
Gordon D, Townsend P (ed) (2000) Breadline Europe: the measurement of poverty. The Policy Press, Bristol
INSTAT (Albanian Institute of Statistics) (2001) Population of Albania in 2001. Main results from the registration of population and housing. Albanian Institute of Statistics, Tirana
INSTAT (2002) Living standards measurement survey in Albania. Albanian Institute of Statistics, Tirana
INSTAT, World Bank (2003) Albania: Poverty during growth. Input to the 2003 Albanian Poverty Assessment and the National Strategy for Socio-Economic Development (draft). Word Bank Country Office, Tirana
Keshilli i Ministrave te Republikes se Shqiperise (KMRSH) (2001) Strategjia per rritjen ekonomike dhe reduktimin e varferise (Growth and Poverty Reduction Strategy Second Draft). Keshilli i Ministrave te Republikes se Shqiperise, Tirana
Milanović B (1998) Income, inequality, and poverty during the transition to a market economy. World Bank, Washington DC
Planning and Development Collaborative International (PADCO) (1996) Tirana structure plan. Report for the Urban Land Management Program of the Ministry of Construction and Transport. PADCO, Washington DC
Planning and Development Collaborative International (PADCO) (2002) Strategic plan for Greater Tirana. Volume 1: Main report (Draft). Urban Land Management Project. PADCO, Inc. Value Add Management Services, Mix Tecnic, Washington DC

Social Summit (1995) Report of the World Summit for Social Development World Conference for Social Development Copenhagen, 6-12. Document A/CONF.166/9. http://www.un.org/esa/socdev/wssd/agreements/poach2.htm (accessed September 205)

Tsenkova S (2005) Trends and progress in housing reforms in South East Europe. Council of Europe Bank. Paris

United Nations Economic Commission for Europe (UNECE) (2002) Country profiles on the housing sector: Albania. United Nations Economic Commission for Europe, Geneva

United Nations Development Programme (UNDP) (2002) Human development report 2003. Human development indicators. http://www.undp.org/hdr2003/ (accessed June 24, 2003).

White H, Killick T (2001) African poverty at the millennium: Causes, complexities, and challenges. World Bank, Washington DC

World Bank (2000) Making transition work for everyone. Poverty and inequality in Europe and Central Asia. World Bank, Washington DC

World Bank (2002) Albania country assistance strategy. World Bank, Washington DC

World Bank (2003) 2003 World development indicators. World Bank, Washington DC

PART III

URBAN FUNCTIONS: HOUSING AND RETAIL

9 Urban housing markets in transition: New instruments to assist the poor

Robert M. Buckley and Sasha Tsenkova

Introduction

It is now 15 years since events fundamentally changed the political, economic and social systems of the former socialist economies of Europe and Central Asia. For many countries, the transition has been difficult. Some have suffered civil unrest and wars that inflicted destruction and displacement. All experienced economic shocks, which in many cases were very severe. For example, during the 1990s average growth for the 26 transition countries in the region was negative 4 percent. Such long-term national economic distress is highly unusual and is reflected by the fact that of the 27 countries throughout the world which had negative growth for the entire decade, these countries accounted for 21. Not surprisingly, during the 1990s poverty and deprivation increased significantly in this part of the world, particularly outside the capital cities (EBRD 2004; World Bank 2002).

Nevertheless, remarkable progress has also occurred. Civil liberties and democracy have taken root, and new opportunities are being exploited as the region is opening up to the world economy. Some of the region's nations have joined the European Union. In the past few years, the basis for sustainable growth appears to have been established in most of these countries. Nevertheless, for some of the countries, particularly those from the former Soviet Union (FSU), the transition process remains fragile. The initial economic, social and institutional conditions in Central and Eastern Europe (CEE) as well as FSU countries affected the performance of transition economies and the operation of their urban housing markets (Renaud 1995; Struyk 2000; Lowe and Tsenkova 2003). While this is not surprising, what is noteworthy is that those initial conditions continue to affect the options available to housing policy-makers, often undermining the efficacy of the fiscal instruments thought to be optimal for providing housing assistance. We argue that the usual subsidy instrument of choice to assist the poor in market economies—demand-based subsidies passively distributed according to a set of rules—will often be ineffective in the urban markets of transition countries. Rather, until clearer property rights systems are established, other instruments will be needed. In many cases there is a strong rationale for adopting more proactive supply-side subsidies.

9.1 Objective and approach

The objective of this chapter is to consider an aspect of the transition that has received limited attention: the design of market-based subsidies in a sector— housing— that under socialism was one of those most isolated from market pressures. The chapter addresses three questions:

- What was different about the initial housing circumstances in the transition economies?
- How did the transition process interact with those initial conditions?
- What are some implications of those differences for new housing policy instruments intended to assist the poor?

These questions guide our comparative analysis of the main challenges in the urban housing markets of CEE and FSU countries in the context of transition. Despite the risk of oversimplification, these broadly defined clusters provide an opportunity to highlight some of the most salient features of post-socialist urban housing markets. More generally, we argue that given the market uncertainty and the lack of efficient market responses in the case of housing policy assistance, the usual approaches are reversed. That is, in contrast to the situation with many other policies, where uncertainty about the effects of instruments on policy targets makes rule-based, passive policy attractive, in the urban housing sector of many transition countries these same conditions lead to the opposite conclusion. Uncertainty about impact in those markets makes discretionary interventions more likely to be effective.

The chapter is organized in the following sections. In section two we briefly present a framework clarifying the relationship between policy instruments and the goals of housing policy. In the next section, data on housing conditions and prices are examined with an emphasis on the differences between the transition countries and market economies as well as on those within transition countries. The fourth section reflects on socialist urbanization policy and the differences in the location and spatial organization of housing. The fifth section reviews the impact of economic performance on housing demand and the establishment of well-functioning housing markets. Finally, some suggestions are made for new housing policy instruments to assist the poor and the need to align housing policy instruments with their targets is emphasized.

9.2 Framework for analysis

Our basic framework is an adaptation of Brainard (1968) on the need to have at least as many policy instruments as there are policy targets to achieve policy effectiveness. Our use of this perspective is a naïve one that abstracts from concerns about econometric identification and the reaction of policy-makers to the effects of policy.[1] The perspective nevertheless suggests ways to think about housing policy objectives and the impact of the transition process on policy formulation. For example, a major implication of Brainard's (1968) work is that if there is uncertainty about the effects of a policy instrument on a policy target, policy-makers should be both more cautious as well as more passive about interventions. In other words, under such uncertainty, following a set of rules rather than undertaking discretionary interventions is likely to be appropriate policy stance. Following Brainard's work, rule-based policy rather than "fine tuning" interventions became a standard practice of monetary authorities around the world (see Soderstrom 1999).[2]

For fiscal policy in the housing sector, a similar, though largely unremarked policy perspective has emerged. Analyses of how to deliver housing subsidies to the poor most effectively have thus lead to prescriptions for the use of rule-based schemes that passively supply vouchers to those eligible (see Friedman and Weinstein 1981 or Boelhouwer 1997). Such policy framework leaves little room for the public sector to encourage building or housing rehabilitation directly. Policy-makers simply define the rules and passively respond to demand. Like their counterparts at central banks, they do not attempt to fine tune the working of the market. The idea is that well-functioning housing markets should be best able to respond to subsidy-enhanced demand. Armed with housing vouchers to augment their purchasing power, the poor can search for the best deal. They can select new or existing units of a minimum standard in the locations they chose—subject, of course, to the resource costs of providing the minimum standard unit. If a poor household wants a better location, or higher level of housing-related amenities, it can purchase or rent it in the market. However, rather than using public assistance to augment their demand, they have to use their own resources.

This rule-based and passive approach to augmenting housing market outcomes stands in sharp contrast to the approaches used, for instance, at the end of World War II. At that time most developed market economies, particularly in Europe, adopted fairly strict rent control regimes that constrained housing supply while simultaneously undertaking active housing production programs. Much more than fine tuning was involved because the draconian rent controls often suppressed market incentives with the result that public sector production effectively replaced private producers. Even in the U.S., where public production has never reached very high levels, the public sector intervened extensively in the housing market through rent control and a variety of selective credit policies that were fine-tuned to help smooth the business cycles.

Today, in contrast to Europe's early post-war housing policy, even those countries where public housing continues to be widespread, provide most low

---

[1] The basic notion of the targets and instruments literature is that if, for example, the monetary authority has one monetary policy instrument, say the short-term interest rate, then policy can meet only one target–say the exchange rate or the inflation rate–but not both.
[2] In addition to the targets and instruments literature, this shift in policy orientation was also the result of the policy inconsistency work of Kydland and Prescott (1977).

income housing assistance through vouchers given to lower-income families (see Priemus and Kemp 2004 for a discussion of how demand side subsidies have replaced supply side subsidies in most Western European countries). Such programs have different terms and conditions across countries, but generally use demand-based, portable vouchers referred to as housing allowances. This approach has been accepted as the most effective instrument for assisting the poor because it gives them the ability to rely on competitive markets and seek the greatest range of affordable choices at the lowest cost to the government (see Struyk and Bendick 1981, and Bradbury and Downs 1981). At the same time, vouchers also contribute to diffuse the spatial concentration of the poor so that they can move away from run-down neighbourhoods.

Such market-based schemes, now almost universal in developed economies, have been widely recommended for adoption and have been adopted in many transition countries, for example Latvia, Poland, the Czech and Slovak Republics and, on a limited scale, Hungary.[3] However, the transition countries' circumstances differ from those of North America and Western Europe in a number of important ways. Most importantly, the conditions under which the subsidy instrument works best—i.e., a competitive supply of housing services, either does not exist there, or exists only on a very limited scale (Tsenkova 2003a). Accordingly, the increased purchasing power generated by vouchers generates little or no supply response. As a consequence, while the vouchers can provide a safety net protection for the poor, they do not necessarily ensure an increase in the housing supply. Second, as shown by Lovei et al (2000) and Lux (2003), housing vouchers are not the most effective means of providing protection to lower income households against housing cost increases caused by increases in utility prices. When utility costs rather than housing costs cause rent increases, those studies show that other instruments—such as utility service lifelines—are more cost-effective ways to protect the poor.

In some respects, the lack of housing supply response to demand-based subsidies is somewhat surprising, since almost all transition countries have created private housing markets by quickly privatizing the housing stock (see Struyk 2000 and de Melo and Gur 1999). It would seem that private owners of property should, in contrast to the state, be more motivated by market opportunities. Consequently, it is reasonable to suppose that the basic conditions of a market would have been established by privatization. Unfortunately, the wholesale transfer of property succeeded only partially in creating housing markets (Tsenkova 2003a). The kinds of housing markets established in the transition countries lacked one of the important providers of housing services in market economies: private landlords who own and operate entire multi-apartment

---

[3] See Hegedus, Struyk and Tosics (1992) for an earlier treatment of the use of housing allowances in Hungary; and Struyk, Puzanov and Lee (1997) for an analysis of Russia. The articles in Lowe and Tsenkova (2003) describe housing policy reforms in a number of other transition countries. World Bank studies in Hungary, Russia and Poland have recommended the use of housing vouchers.

buildings.[4] We now turn to explaining how their absence interacted with the configuration and location of the existing stock of housing to make housing vouchers less effective than they are in other market economies.

9.3 The supply of housing in transition economies

Housing policy in the FSU was largely determined by its role in the socialist state—one which designated housing as an un-priced social sector. Despite that designation, housing had a significant claim on resources because it was a right to which all citizens were entitled (Kornai 2000; de Melo et al. 1997). In its extreme form, housing policy abolished private property rights, and the state controlled the production, distribution, operation, and pricing of housing. For example, Buckley and Gurenko (1996) show that in Russia in the early years of reform in the 1990s, the income elasticity of housing demand was zero, implying that increases in income did not allow households to bid more for housing. In such an environment the increased purchasing power provided by housing allowances would obviously have no supply effect. In addition, the characteristics of dwellings were limited to a few types by the large-scale panel construction techniques. Perhaps most importantly, as shown by Bertaud and Renaud (1996), the location of housing estates was determined without reference to the scarcity value of land. Finally, rents were adjusted infrequently and were unrelated to costs of either maintenance or operations; subsidies were determined with little reference to either 'need' or ability to pay.

In other words, in all socialist countries a rationing mechanism, rather than a subsidized market, determined the allocation and structure of most housing. But the breadth of this mechanism was by no means uniform. For instance, housing delivery systems in some CEE countries, such as Hungary and Poland, embodied only some of the rationing features noted above, and in varying degrees markets were allowed to operate.[5] Indeed, one of the earliest empirical analyses of housing conditions in socialist economies, by Szelenyi (1983), showed that the Hungarian system, like housing subsidy systems in most market economies, was similarly regressive rather than distributionally progressive as in Russia (Buckley and

---

[4] Housing privatization did of course create private landlords, as many owners rented their units. The distinction we are making, which is discussed below in the text, is between landlords for entire buildings (institutional landlords) and those who rent out a limited number of units in one or more buildings.

[5] Under socialist rules, employers, usually state-owned or "socially owned" (as in the former Yugoslavia) institutions were responsible for providing a large range of social services to their employees, ranging from vacation facilities to health services and housing. Private ownership of housing was 'business as usual' in most rural areas, but was also encouraged in cities. For example, homeownership in Bulgaria and Hungary was over 80 percent under the socialist regime (Tsenkova 2000). In the FSU the exchange of housing was permitted, but the state controlled almost every other feature of housing market operation.

Gurenko 1997). The CEE systems frequently had high ownership rates as well as active and widely used housing co-operatives; the FSU systems did not. Nor was there nearly as much flexibility in the FSU in exchanging and subletting apartments. To mention just one of these restrictions, internal passports still controlled intra-city migration in Russia until the late 1990s, even after the broader reforms. These differences contributed to a more entrenched and pervasive public role for housing in the FSU than was the case in the CEE, particularly since the system had been in place for 30 years longer. In sum, to varying degrees the socialist system had implications for:

- Housing conditions
- Price of housing services
- Location and spatial organization of housing.

We consider each of these features in turn and then discuss how the varying transition processes affected the development of housing markets and access to housing by the urban poor.

9.3.1 Housing conditions

Two sets of indicators are commonly used to contrast and compare housing conditions—housing consumption (quantity of housing) and amenities (housing quality) (Buckley and Tsenkova 2001). With respect to housing consumption, many observers of the Eastern European housing model have characterized its operation as a paradox—a sector of both subsidy and scarcity (Hegedüs and Tosics 1982). Subsidies to the housing sector in many CEE countries were often on the order of three to five percent of GNP during the 1970s and 1980s (World Bank 1989). At the same time, however, there was evidence of housing shortages—long waiting lists, pervasive disproportion of households in relation to the stock of dwellings, and high black market prices for rental and owner-occupied housing (Dübel and Tsenkova 1997).

The diagnosis in a study by Hegedüs, Mayo and Tosics (1996) provided the first comparable quantitative evidence on housing market performance in the region. Surprisingly to many, the data showed that housing conditions of CEE cities were strikingly good as compared to those elsewhere in countries with similar incomes, and were indeed—on the basis of square meters consumed and amenities—often relatively close to those of Western European cities even though per capita incomes were much lower than those in Western Europe (a 1990's mean of US$2,552 for CEE countries, compared to US$19,792 in Western European countries). Every key indicator of crowding suggested that relative to income levels, CEE cities had less crowding than did countries with similar income levels—with 40 percent more floor area per person and 77 percent more dwellings per 1000 people. Similarly, the quality of the CEE urban housing stock appears to have been much better on average than that in countries with similar incomes. The only major exceptions were Albania, Bulgaria, Romania and

Lithuania, which, with the low percentages of units serviced with piped water and bathrooms, were well below the average level for the region.

While the quantity of housing and associated amenities in transition countries was relatively high on an income-adjusted basis, the energy efficiency of housing was extremely low (Guzanova 1997), and inputs declined in quality, particularly in the FSU from Stalin's time and the expansive housing investment program of Khrushchev. The lack of variety and further standardization of housing production in urban areas (prefabricated apartment buildings) effectively limited housing choices. The result, as shown by hedonic price models, such as that of Romanik and Struyk (1996), is that all other factors held constant, newer prefabricated stock now continues to be worth considerably less than older buildings.

These comparisons suggest that in many countries (e.g., Hungary, Bulgaria and Slovenia) housing shortages that were frequently alleged, were the result of a rationing system that distributed supply with little regard to demand, rather than physical shortages. For example, there is ample evidence that even those countries with high overall levels of housing quality and quantity had significant problems in the distribution of housing. In particular, many more large households occupied small dwellings, and small families large dwellings than is the case in market economies (Tsenkova and Turner 2004).

Many more families, particularly in urban areas, resided in multi-apartment dwellings as compared to market economies. For example, in a review of the data for seven transition countries, Vecvagare (2004) shows that the percentage of multi-apartment stock ranged from 46 to over 90 percent, figures three to six times higher than the 15 percent of multi-apartment stock of the U.S. (Goodman 2003), but more similar to the levels that Gilbert (2003) showed characterize many Western European cities. As is shown below, this characteristic of the transition countries' housing stock is important, because if it was built by private investors, as is largely the case in market economies, the density and location would reflect market incentives. Under such circumstances, it does not matter whether a landlord owns the entire building or just a limited number of units. Rents reflect the response of suppliers of housing services minimizing cost. In contrast, when such multi-apartment buildings are built in locations decided upon by the public sector, the rents reflect the locational/density choices of planners, with—as we show in the next section—important implications.

9.3.2 The price of housing services

The central way of maintaining what from a cost-of-resources basis was clearly a "perverse" rationing system was through an extensive and overlapping system of subsidized prices. Table 9.1. compares the percentage of household budgets allocated to housing, utilities, transport, and local public expenditures in transition and market economies. These figures are based on data from several different sources. The first column shows that in market economies, a household spends on average between 45 and 65 percent of its budget on these four major urban expenditure items: 20 to 25 percent on housing, 15 to 20 percent on related urban government services, about 5 percent on utilities, and about 11 percent on urban transport (user fees for public transportation, car expenditures including leasing, vehicle financing, gas, repair and maintenance).[6]

Table 9.1. Household expenditures on urban services in market and in transition economies

Services	OECD* countries 2000	Pre-Reform Transition Economies 1989	Transition Economies 2000
Housing	20 to 25	3	3 to 9
Utilities	3 to 6	3	5 to 9
Transportation	10 to 12	2	7
Taxes Financing Local Expenditure	15 to 20	3	8
Total	48 to 63	11	23 to 30

Sources: Latest data possible; see Quigley and Raphael (2004) and various econsumer expenditure surveys as indicated in the citation sheet in Buckley and Mini (2001).
Note:
* Organization for Economic Cooperation and Development (OECD)

In the transition economies (both pre-reform and more recent experiences) the expenditure was much lower than those in OECD countries. On average, in transition economies, total household expenditures on urban services at the beginning of the transition period were only around 11 percent of income, less than one-fourth that of OECD economies. Overall, this figure has more than doubled to an average of about 26 percent by 2000. In the case of housing, household expenditures are still significantly below those of the typical 'effort ratio' in market economies, and are particularly low relative to such expenditures in the U.S (Quigley and Raphael 2004). To some extent the lower housing costs/rents in transition countries are offset by higher costs of utility payments, which absorb a larger portion of the household budget.

Cumulatively, in market economies housing, commuting and utility costs account for a major share of households' expenditures of households, particularly of poorer households. Indeed, it is the aggregation and weighing of these costs that

---

[6] These comparisons illustrate relative expenditure patterns and do not represent expenditures on a similar bundle of services. The composition of the "bundles" of services was clearly very different both within and across types of economies. The use of averages, for instance, can aggregate very different tenure forms, financing patterns and even tax incentives. Nevertheless, the patterns observed in each type of economy appear to be quite similar and robust.

make spatial economics so important in housing markets. When commuting expenses or utility costs account for significant shares of income, families change their locations and unit sizes to economize on those costs. Obviously, however, the opposite also applies. That is, when such costs do not vary, neither does the locational choice or unit size matter much. Thus, perhaps the central post-privatization change required for housing policy in transition economies to become more market oriented is a significant increase in the relative price of housing services. Notwithstanding the motivation to bring that about, however, such price increases are difficult to implement in a recessionary environment and rapidly increasing poverty (Milanovic 1992; Tsenkova 2003b; World Bank 2001, 2004).

9.4 Location of housing

9.4.1 Intracity locational differences

In market economies, where land and housing markets perform their allocation function, residential densities tend to follow what Mills and Tan (1980) describe as one of the strongest empirical regularities in economics: the predictions implied by the monocentric model of urban location. That is, as long as there is flexibility in substitutions between factor inputs, and under some general price and income elasticity, land will be cheaper further away from the city centre, and housing services will be provided using more land and fewer non-land inputs, e.g. there will be detached houses instead of high-rise apartment buildings.

In contrast, in the cities of the FSU for which there are data, the density pattern is opposite to the typical market economy city: rather than declining, density increases with distance from the city centre (Bertaud and Renaud 1997). As shown in the case of Moscow (Fig. 9.1.a), much of the centrally located land was allocated to industrial plants, reflecting the industrial priority and the ambitious aspirations of the "catch-up" industrialization plan and the restrictions on land use (Andrusz 1979). Public housing was developed by adding "rings" around the city centre. As the older stock deteriorated and more people needed housing in the city, it was cheaper to add a new outer ring than to renovate the existing one, which also allowed city officials to enjoy the political success of new socialist accomplishment.

Transition cities in CEE have much more of a market-economy pattern (Fig. 9.1.b). In particular, while the density initially decreases moving away from the city centre, it rises again, creating "anomalous bumps" at distances where the public housing sector dominates. This feature can be explained by the timing of construction. Since the city centres in most CEE countries were built at the beginning of the 20th century, socialist plans affected mostly the development of the suburbs (see Bertaud in this volume for an in-depth discussion). The socialist

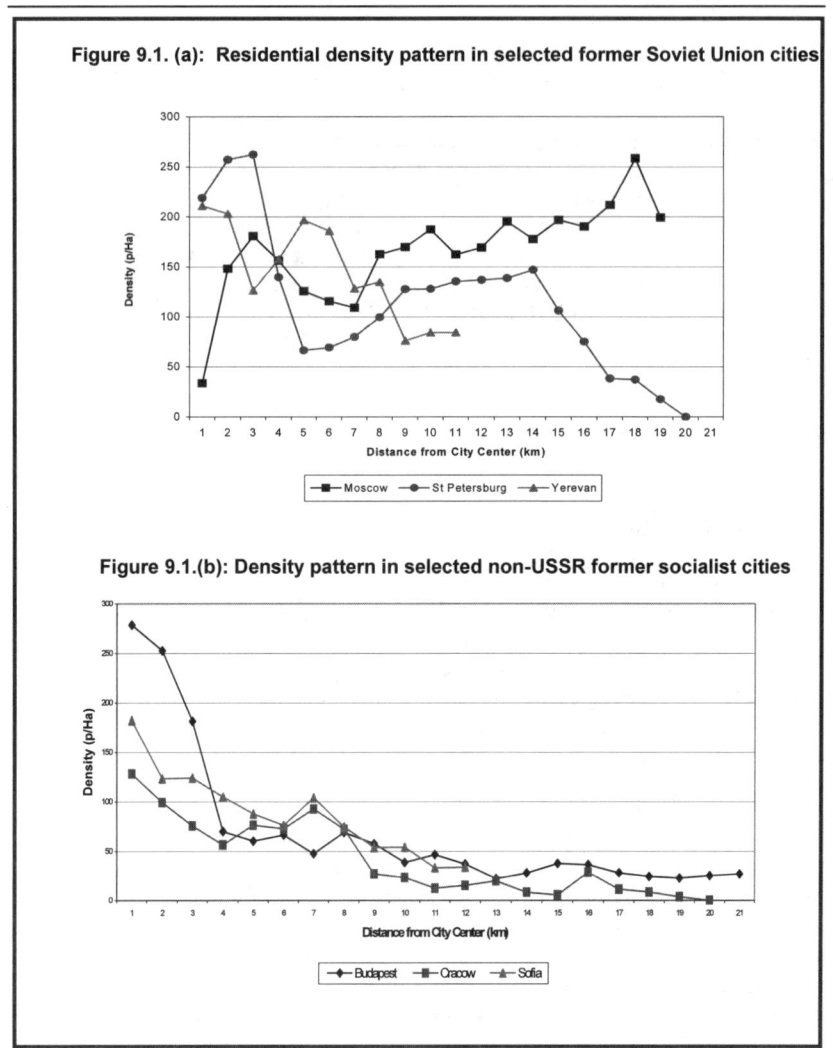

Figure 9.1. (a): Residential density pattern in selected former Soviet Union cities

Figure 9.1.(b): Density pattern in selected non-USSR former socialist cities

Fig. 9.1. Density patterns in selected cities
Source: Adapted from Bertaud 2004

pattern was characterized by a mix of large industrial estates, high density public housing and low density residual private housing, which existed given the less stringent planning control in CEE countries.

9.4.2 Intercity locational differences

Similar in concept to the Muth-Mills model of intra-city location choice is the literature examining profit maximization across locations that results in a system of cities (Henderson 1985). Like the models of monocentric cities, these models are highly abstract mathematical simplifications, and are based largely on key assumptions about the role of profit maximizing land developers. Nevertheless, like the intra-city models, models of systems of cities have yielded predictions about industrial location that have received considerable empirical support (see Henderson 1985).

Perhaps the best known, empirical observation on the sort of population distribution that a market-based system of cities would create is the well-known rank-size rule about city size. The rank of city in terms of its size follows a special case of the Pareto distribution where the largest city, the second largest, to the nth largest, serves as a strong predictor of city population size, with the second largest city having half the population of the largest and so on. When such kind of distribution of city population rank is plotted logarithmically, it results in a slope of rank and city population size equal to one. Rosen and Resnick (1980) show that this description characterizes the population distribution of market economies, with the coefficient for 44 countries satisfying the prediction of a coefficient of one for "a" in equation (1)

(1) $N(S) = AS^{-a}$,

where

N is the number of cities with population of S or more,

A is a constant, and

'a' is a Pareto exponent.

In contrast, Buckley and Gurenko (1997) estimate that in Russia 'a'= 1.37, a figure higher than those for 41 out of 44 countries studied by Rosen and Resnick (1980). The figure for Russia also suggests, as does the literature on Soviet urbanization (see inter alia, Harris 1970, Morton 1984), that population mobility across cities in the FSU was constrained, but not proscribed. Cumulatively, whether from rank-size evidence or other econometric evidence about inter-city mobility, it appears that there was limited ability to move between cities in FSU countries.

Fig. 9.2. provides some sense of how rapidly the CEE and FSU planned cities grew after World War II relative to those in both Western Europe. In the figure the size of a city's population is indicated by the size of the dot, as identified in the legend. The shaded ring around the dark image represents the growth in population size between 1950 and 1990. The figure shows that with the exception of a few cities in Portugal, Italy and Turkey, the rapid population growth in the post war period occurred in the socialist countries prior to the change in regimes at the beginning of the 1990s. While growth certainly occurred in all CEE capitals, more than two thirds of the rapidly growing socialist cities were in the FSU.

In sum, the intra-city and inter-city location of some of the longest-living fixed capital investments were not determined according to resource costs. Thus, these

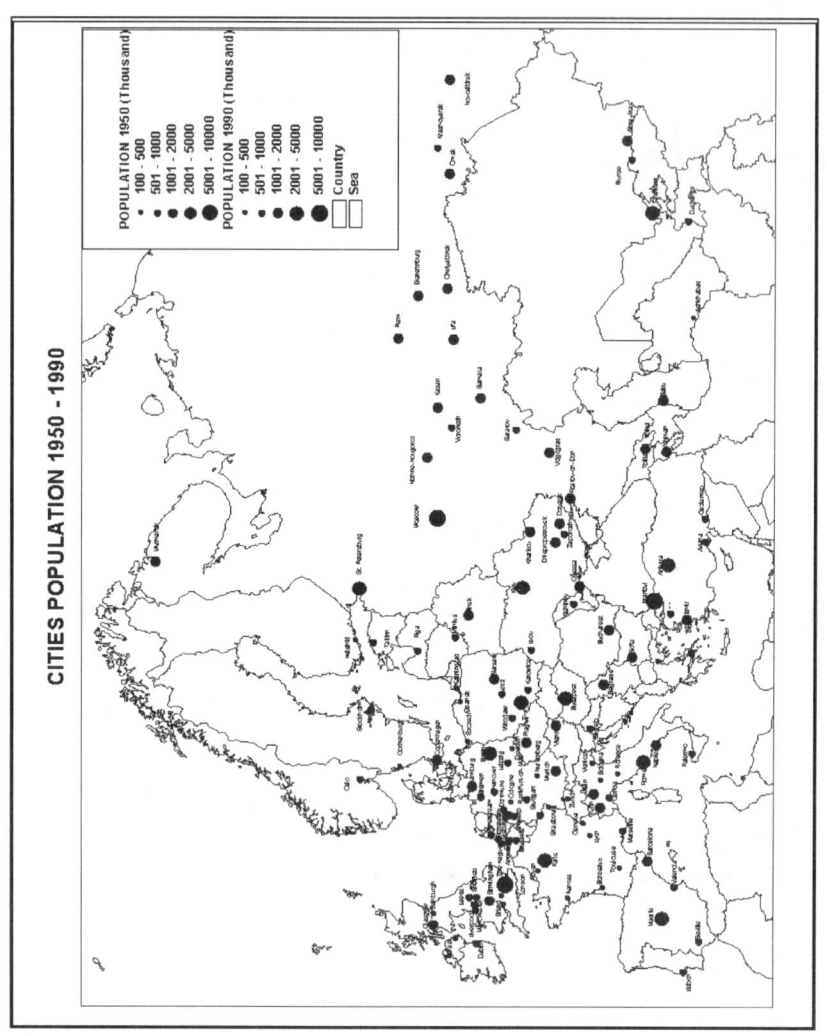

Fig. 9.2. Population growth in European and Central Asian cities

Source: Data derived from United Nations Center for Human Settlements 2001

spatial patterns have left a strong legacy for the value of the capital so located. A shift to market-based economy will accordingly require relocations both between and within cities to fully exploit the economic values ignored under socialism. These shifts will be more pronounced in the FSU than in CEE because the socialist system operated longer there and the rationing system that controlled investment decisions was more rigid and extensive.

It should be recognized that for these shifts to take place, a change in the type of building will be required so that the underlying value of land can be better realized. Low rise inner city buildings, for instance, will often have to be replaced by high rise buildings to bring higher rents and/or resale prices adjusted to market levels. Such a change in land use, however, will require ownership structures to allow property redevelopment (see Golubchikov and Baldina in this volume). Unfortunately, such ownership structures were not created, both in CEE and FSU countries, because only individual units rather than entire buildings were privatized and required ownership control over entire buildings is non-existent (Tsenkova 2005; Vecvagare 2004). Under the privatization that took place, the providers of rental housing were limited to small scale landlords. As a result, the service levels which they provide are those dictated by the non-market determined location and configuration of the housing stock.

9.5 Housing demand during the transition

As shown by Mayo (1981). housing demand is affected by price, income, demographics and the need for mobility. Various studies have shown that housing demand, at least the portion dictated by income, has varied enormously across countries in the region (World Bank 2000, 2001). For example, the effects of the transition recessions can be seen in the growth records for 1990-1999 of two different groups of countries: two of the best performers in the region—Poland and Slovenia—and three of the worst-performing economies—Moldova, Georgia, and Tajikistan. In Poland and Slovenia the contraction in income during the transition, measured by annual GDP growth, was roughly comparable to that in the U.S. from 1973-1982 in reaction to the oil-price shock. By contrast, the worst performing transition economies had a more severe recession than did the U.S. in the ten years following the Great Depression (1929-38) or the Soviet Union in the years after the October Revolution (1917-26) (see Buckley and Mini 2001 for further discussion). Moreover, ten years after the Great Depression or the October Revolution, the U.S. and the Soviet Union had fully recovered, while Moldova, Georgia, and Tajikistan have only recently begun to show signs of sustained growth. Thus, for some countries, the transition has been far worse than either of these two extreme historical periods, while for others it has been similar to a severe economic business cycle in market economies. Thus the impact of transition recessions on the demand for housing has varied across of the region— reducing it sharply in some countries (FSU) but increasing in others (mostly CEE). The data on 1999 GDP per capita in these two clusters of countries confirms that pattern (see Table 9.2.).

Not surprisingly, given the reductions in income, housing production for the past 15 years has been extremely low across the region, as shown in Table 9.2. In most of the FSU countries housing production in 1999 was less than one third of the pre-transition levels. The average housing production for Uzbekistan was 79

Table 9.2. The changes in the housing stock, income and population in selected countries, 1990 – 1999

	1999 stock as % of 1990 stock (depreciated at 1% annually)	1999 GDP per capita as % of 1990 GDP per capita	1999 population as % of 1990 population	1999 housing production as a % of 1990 housing production
Azerbaijan *	102	41	111	15
Armenia*	99	60	107	14
Belarus	108	84	99	56
Georgia	94	33	100	17
Kazakhstan	101	65	94	14
Kyrgyzstan*	101	57	108	26
Russia	105	60	99	52
Tajikistan *	98	48	117	13
Uzbekistan*	115	77	120	79
Ukraine	100	42	96	35
Latvia	97	64	91	25
Estonia	95	88	92	19
Lithuania	100	66	99	35
Hungary	100	106	97	50
Bulgaria	95	82	94	45
Poland*	102	136	102	66
Slovenia	102	115	99	96
Romania	100	83	97	141

Source: Authors' estimates based on data in country specific statistical publications
Note:
*Transition countries experiencing population growth in the 1990s.

percent of the 1990 output, while in Russia and Belarus, it hovered around 50 percent. In these three countries, public/state housing programs were still operational, but in the others private investors had to shoulder the economic difficulties of the transition. The housing stock contracted in 6 of the 18 countries for which we have data, if we conservatively assume a market economy's depreciation rate of one percent. At this conservative level of depreciation, estimated for market economies by Abadir and Talmain (2001), 14 of the 18 countries experienced a reduction in the size of the housing stock of housing in the 1990s. When supply shocks of this magnitude are combined with the break-up of the housing combinants, which had produced housing under the socialist system, the result is a sharply reduced ability to respond to changes in housing demand.

As also shown in Table 9.2., the region generally is characterized by slow population growth (see Tsenkova in this volume on changing population growth patterns in post-socialist cities). With the six notable exceptions, marked by asterisks in Table 9.2., the demographic demand for housing has been low. Hence, while the demographic demand due to household formation will be relatively mild in 10 of the FSU countries, the transition has undoubtedly created pressures and demand to reshuffle the existing stock. Of course the demand to trade up or trade down housing will be intensified by the economic adjustment process forcing people to move. That process, however, requires a tradable, flexible housing stock to facilitate market mobility.

It is clear, however, that mobility can be limited by housing market conditions if those who would like to move to a new location are unable to do so. It is much less clear what will be the mobility patterns in the cities of transition economies where people after many years are just beginning to exploit the gains from spatial economics. While we do not have evidence from different urban markets, we note that a long literature emphasizes the importance of available rental housing to most effectively accommodate growing demand for mobility (Goodman 2003; Gilbert 2004).

9.6 Targets and instruments for housing policy: present and future

Housing reforms in transition economies have proceeded through 'trial and error', focusing on privatisation and the establishment of market-based institutional, legal and financial frameworks for the housing sector. Most post-socialist countries today have a myriad of housing-related initiatives 'enabling' housing markets to work. Despite some diversity of housing policy experiences, the housing reform path emphasizes less prominent controlling and subsidizing role of the state and a stronger reliance on market forces. Generic subsidies have been cut back and responsibilities for social housing devolved to local governments. However, new transfers have emerged, such as deductibility of mortgage interest in Poland, Hungary and Russia, and contract savings in Croatia, the Czech Republic and Romania (Dübel 2003; Struyk 2000; Tsenkova 2005). New programs to provide public/social housing for low-income households have been introduced in Romania and the Former Yugoslav Republic of Macedonia. Recently housing reforms have marked a shift to mixed instruments such as demand-based subsidies to support homeownership or post-war reconstruction, as well as efforts to build market-based institutions of housing finance and other market intermediaries.[7] In the realm of 'compulsory instruments', housing policy activity has focused on harmonization of the legal framework for housing management, property registration, mortgage and construction. Provision of public housing has remained limited. A harsher public expenditure regime has led to less investment in social housing, although in some countries income-based support for low income and

---

[7] Refer to Hegedüs et al. (2004) for a discussion on the impact of mortgage interest rate write-downs and income-targeted down-payment subsidies on the housing purchase capacity in Budapest and Moscow.

socially disadvantaged groups has been launched (e.g., housing vouchers, allowances, utility subsidies, etc.).

The direction of change is no doubt much the same across the region, and the underlying elements are similar. Nonetheless, some countries have been more successful than others in designing and implementing housing reforms. In fact, notions of convergence do not really match the reality of widening differences in the structure and operation of housing markets: between Albania and Croatia for example, or between Bosnia and Herzegovina and some of the countries in Central Asia.

Most of the new forms of support are directed to homeownership, including a combination of public housing provision for sale and demand-based assistance (grants, interest subsidies and tax incentives). Although there has been an attempt to reduce the commitment of governments through state provision of housing, an overwhelming majority of the countries in the region still maintain such programs even under economic difficulties,. In Albania the target group is limited to households affected by restitution. In Romania and Moldova public housing agencies continue to use state subsidies, in the form of frozen assets in unfinished housing construction, completing the projects with additional funding from potential homeowners. In Romania, the national housing agency is also building subsidized housing for young households. Serbia and Montenegro until recently maintained a socialist type of housing provision through a Solidarity Fund. Similarly, a several countries have grants and subsidies for homeowners with a mix of programs assisting war reconstruction (e.g., Bosnia-Herzegovina, Croatia and Kosovo).

Support for the public rental sector is limited to a handful of countries in the region (see Lux 2003; Tsenkova and Turner 2004; Tsenkova 2005). Romania, and more recently the Former Yugoslav Republic of Macedonia have initiated programs for new construction of social rental housing. Similar pilot projects using credits from the Council of Europe Development Bank are under preparation in Bosnia-Herzegovina and Serbia. To summarize: most countries in the region have fiscal policies that support homeownership through a combination of public housing provision (supply side subsidies) and demand-based assistance (grants, interest subsidies and tax incentives). Targeting of beneficiaries, however, is generally ineffective, because in most cases programs facilitate access to newly built housing, currently the most expensive form of housing provision and purchasers are expected to match the subsidy with their own savings or mortgages (Dübel 2003; Struyk 2000; Tsenkova 2005). Such beneficiaries obviously tend to have incomes well above the national average. While these types of programs leverage investment in new construction, it is questionable if scarce public funds should be used to support upper middle-income households. Meanwhile little government funding is directed to public rental housing or to help low-income households experiencing affordability problems.

The urban housing stock in much of the region consists of multi-apartment buildings. In the FSU countries those were mostly publicly owned and constructed without reference to either underlying land values or economically-viable employment (see Figure 9.3). Moreover, since the privatization of public housing, ownership rights to the buildings are less consolidated and land titles are unclear (see Council of Europe Development Bank 2004; Tsenkova 2005). Another difficulty is that important ingredients of housing markets—institutional entities capable of managing and maintaining the stock—have not been established (Vecvagare 2004; Lux 2003). Such large-scale suppliers of rental housing will become even more important in post-socialist cities, given the high rates of homeownership. Until those develop, most of the housing stock will remain outside the ambit of market forces, and subsidies designed for markets will accordingly be less effective.

Fig. 9.3. Housing estate on the outskirts of Riga, Latvia[8]

In such environments, it is perhaps obvious to say that providing more affordable housing for low-income households through an instrument which requires a market to be in place is a policy target that cannot be hit with any consistency. Housing vouchers can provide safety net protection, but without achieving legal ownership of multi-apartment buildings and an effective framework for landlord operations, the vouchers will not lead to the sorts of improvements that a well functioning housing market can provide. Such

---

[8] Photo by Sasha Tsenkova.

expenditures will only improve the managerial, but not the economic efficiency of the socialist regime's non-market delivery of housing.[9]

In these places two different policy targets should be pursued. First, the prerequisites of an efficient housing market should be established. Pursuing this objective will require an active policy stance which places considerable emphasis on changing the sets of rules and regulations for real estate transactions and consolidation of ownership in multi-apartment buildings. Such policies will be quite distinct from the passive, rule-based fiscal housing policies pursued in market economies.

But besides more emphasis on extending the breadth of markets, more discretionary and activist fiscal policies will be required in countries with rapidly growing and/or shifting populations, affecting many of the cities of the FSU. Instruments to achieve this end, are primarily those allowing the prices of land to reflect its underlying scarcity value. Housing production programs, and particularly those which have the potential to have spill over effects on neighbouring units, such as Ellen et al. (2003) demonstrate occurred in New York City with supply-side subsidies, may be effective ways to establish the incentives needed to create housing supply response. Such programs could, for example, be used to increase the density of relatively low-density inner city neighbourhoods.

Besides housing production programs designed to better exploit underlying land values, there is also a rationale for other sorts of supply-side programs to build new social housing for the urban poor. In cities suffering the dislocations associated with civil war, such as in Serbia, Bosnia-Herzegovina, Azerbaijan and Georgia, there is immediate need for new housing. Public production may be needed until a competitive private housing industry develops—a process that will often not be rapid in countries that have experienced severe transition recessions with considerable levels of income reductions as well as war-related economic distress.

Finally, in many cities in the region new forms of social exclusion have emerged, such as the development of Roma communities in run-down areas. As suggested by a number of studies in the Policy Journal for the Local Governance Reform Initiative (2004), housing and social conditions in some of these slums are often worse than in those developing countries. Such circumstances also require very different subsidy instruments.

---

[9] In conjunction with the poor quality of materials used in housing production during the socialist regime, these units have not been maintained since the regime change. In many places under-funded maintenance companies target their limited resources on addressing only emerging situations rather than performing on-going maintenance. The result is that crises have been avoided by effectively eating the capital of the stock.

Conclusion

To sum up, the post-socialist countries began the transition with housing market conditions, legal infrastructures, and traditions very different from those of market economies. They have also experienced extreme dislocations and rapidly increasing poverty (EBRD 2004; Jones and Revenga 2000). In such environments the uncertainty about the effects of policy is undoubtedly great (de Melo et al 1997). The differences in the initial housing conditions, combined with the impact of transition recessions on emerging housing markets, continue to affect the options available to housing policy-makers and undermine the efficacy of what are assumed to be the optimal fiscal instruments for providing housing assistance.

In particular, the subsidy instrument of choice in market economies—demand-based subsidies passively distributed according to a set of rules—has had limited impact in only a few transition economies (e.g. Russia, Poland, Latvia and Hungary). That instrument will be even less effective in most transition countries, and particularly those of the FSU. We argue that in places where effective housing markets have still not been established almost fifteen years after the housing reforms began, particularly in cities with growing urban poverty, there is a need for policy instruments other than the simple rule-based housing vouchers to more effectively address housing needs. Until markets are more fully established, uncertainty about the impact of such instruments will not reduce the need for proactive, supply-side interventions. Indeed, uncertainty about policy impact makes discretionary interventions more likely to be effective.

Acknowledgement

Comments on earlier versions of the paper by participants in seminars at the University of Illinois Centre for Russian and East European Studies, and the European Network for Housing Research in Cambridge, and particularly those of Alain Bertaud, Raymond Struyk and Peter Marcuse were very helpful. The authors acknowledge the financial support of the Social Sciences and Humanities Research Council of Canada.

References

Abadir K, Talmain G (2001) Depreciation rates and Capital Stocks. The Manchester School 69(1)

Andrusz G (1979) Some key issues in Soviet urban development. International J of Urban and Regional
  Research 3(2): 21-30

Bertaud A, Bernard R (1997) Socialist Cities Without Land Markets. J of Urban Economics, 41: 137-151

Bertaud A (2004) Population densities in different cities, database. http://alain-bertaud.com/, accessed on 21 January 2006

Boelhouwer P (ed) (1997) Financing the Social Rental Housing Sector in Western Europe. Housing and Urban Policy Studies. 13: Delft University Press, Delft

Brainard, W (1967) Uncertainty and the Effectiveness of Policy. American Economic Review, 57(2): 411-425

Bradbury K, Downs A(eds) (1981) Do Housing Allowances Work. Brookings Institute, Washington DC

Buckley R, Gurenko E (1997) Zhivago's Legacy. World Bank Research Observer (9):2-14. The World Bank: Washington DC

Buckley R, Gurenko E (1998) Housing Demand in Russia: Rationing and Reform. Economics of Transition Vol. 6(1):197-209

Buckley R, Mini F (2000) From Commisars to Mayors: Cities in the Transition Economies. The World Bank, Washington, DC

Buckley R, Tsenkova S (2001) Housing Market Systems in Reforming Socialist Economies: Comparative Indicators of Performance and Policy. European Housing Policy 1(2):257-289

Council of Europe Development Bank (2004) Housing in South Eastern Europe. Solving a Puzzle of Challenges. Council of Europe Development Bank, Paris.

De Melo M, Denizer C, Gelb A,Tenev S (1997) Circumstance and Choice: The Role of Initial Conditions and Policies in Transition Economies. Policy Research Working Paper No.1866, The World Bank

De Melo M, Gur O (1999) The Russian City in Transition: The First Six Years in 10 Volga Capitals. Policy Research Working Paper No.2165, The World Bank

Dübel, HJ (2003) Housing Policy in Central European Countries in Transition: Czech Republic, Hungary, Poland, and Slovakia. Centre for Legal Competency, Vienna.

Dübel A, Tsenkova S (1997) Human Settlement Developments in the Transition Economies of Central and Eastern Europe. United Nations-ECE, Geneva

Ellen M, Schill A, Schwartz, Voicu I (2003) Housing Production Subsidies and Neighborhood Revitalization: New York City's Ten-year Capital Plan for Housing. In New York Federal Reserve Bank's Economic Policy Review

European Bank for Reconstruction and Development (2004) Transition Report 2004. EBRD, London

Friedman J, Weinstein, D (1981) The Demand for Rental Housing: Evidence from the Housing Allowance Experiment. J of Urban Economics, No 9(3): 311-323

Gilbert A (2003) Rental Housing: An Essential Option for the Poor in Developing Countries. United Nations Center for Human Settlements –HABITAT, Nairobi

Goodman, J (1999) The Changing Demography of Multi Family Rental Housing. National Coalition of Multi Family Housing, Washington DC

Harris C (1996)Cities of the Soviet Union, Studies in Their Functions, Size, Density and Growth. Rand-McNalley and Co. Chicago

Hegedüs J, Mayo S, Tosics I (1996) Transition of the Housing Sector in the East Central European Countries. Review of Urban and Regional Development Studies. 8:101-136

Hegedüs J, Rogozhina N, Somogyi E, Struyk R, Tumanov, A (2004) Potential Effects on Subsidy Programmes on Housing Affordability: The Cases of Budapest and Moscow. European Journal of Housing Policy 4(2): 151–184

Henderson V (1985) Economic Theory and Cities Academic Press, Chicago

Jones C, Revenga A (2000) Making Transition Work for Everyone: Poverty and Inequality in Europe and Central Asia, World Bank

Kdyland F, Prescott, E (1977) Rules Rather than Discretion: The Inconsistency of Optimal Plans. Journal of Political Economy, No 85: 473-491

Kornai J (2000) What the change of system from socialism to capitalism does and does not mean. J of Economic Perspectives 14: 27-42

Lovei L, Gurenko E, Haney M, O'Keefe P, Shkaraian M (2000) Maintaining Utility Services for the Poor: Policies and Practices in Central and Eastern Europe and the Former Soviet Union. The World Bank, Washington, DC

Lowe S, Tsenkova S (eds) (2003) Housing change in Central and Eastern Europe. Ashgate Publishing Limited, Aldershot

Lux, M. (ed). (2003). Housing Policy: An End or a New Beginning. Local Government Initiative, Open Society Institute, Budapest

Mayo S (1981) Theory and Estimation in the Economics of Housing Demand. J of Urban Economics No10: 95-116.

Milanovic B(1992) Income distribution in late socialism: Poland, Hungary, Czechoslovakia, Yugoslavia and Bulgaria compared. World Bank Research Project "Income Distribution during the Transition", working paper no. 1.

Mills ES, Tan JP (1980) A comparison of urban population density functions in developed and developing countries. Urban Studies 17(3):313-321

Morton H (1980) Who Gets What When and How? Housing in the Soviet Union. Soviet Studies, v. 32(2):235-59

Open Society Local Government Brief (2004) Policy Journal for the Local Governance Reform Initiative, Budapest Summer 2004

Priemus, Kemp P (2004) The Present and Future of Income-Related Housing Support: Debates in Britain and The Netherlands. Housing Studies 19:653-668

Quigley J, Raphael S(2004) Is housing unaffordable? Why isn't it more Affordable? Journal of Economic Perspectives, vol. 18(10): 191-214

Renaud B (1995) The Real Estate Economy and the Design of Russian Housing Reforms. Urban Studies
32(9)1437-51(November) and 32(8)1247-64 (October)

Rosen K, Resnick S (1980) The Size Distribution of Cities: An Examination of the Pareto Law and Primacy. J of Urban Economics, 8(2):156-86

Soderstrom U (1999) Monetary Policy with Uncertain Parameters. Working Paper No.308, Stockholm School of Economics.

Struyk RJ (ed) (2000) Homeownership and Housing Finance Policy in the Former Soviet Bloc: Costly Populism. Urban Institute Press ,Washington, DC

Struyk R, Puzanov A, Lee L (1997) Monitoring Russia's Experience with Housing Allowances. Urban Studies 34(11): 1789-1818

Struyk R, Bendick M (1981) Housing Vouchers for the Poor: Lessons from the Housing Experiment. Urban Institute Press, Washington DC

Szelenyi I (1983) Urban Inequalities Under State Socialism. Oxford University Press, London

Tsenkova S (2000) Housing in Transition and the Transition in Housing: Experiences of Central and eastern Europe. Kapital Reclama, Sofia

Tsenkova S (2003a) Housing Policy Matters: The Reform Path in Central and Eastern Europe: Policy Convergence? In Tsenkova S, Lowe S (eds) Housing Change in Central and Eastern Europe. Ashgate Publishing Limited, Aldershot, pp 193-205

Tsenkova S (2003b) Post-socialist Cities in a Globalizing World. PLANUM, pp 1-20 http://www.planum.net/topics/east-tsenkova.html

Tsenkova S (2005) Trends and Progress in Housing Reforms in South East Europe. Council of Europe Development Bank, Paris

Tsenkova, S,Turner B (2004) The Future of Social Housing in Eastern Europe: Reforms in Latvia and Ukraine. European Journal of Housing Policy, 4 (2): 133-149.

United Nations Centre for Human Settlements - HABITAT (2001) Cities in a Globalising World. Global Report on Human Settlements 2001. Earthscan Publications Ltd., London

UNHCR (2004) *Closing the Circle: From Emergency Humanitarian Relief to Sustainable Returns in South Eastern Europe.* Sarajevo: UNHCR.

Vecvagare, L (2004) Community Driven Development Approaches in Housing Sector Projects in Transition Economies. Social Development Notes No. 71, Aug. 2004, World Bank.

World Bank (1987) Poland: Reform, Adjustment and Growth. The World Bank, Washington D.C.

World Bank(2000) World Development Report 1999/2000: Entering the 21st Century. The World Bank, Washington, DC

World Bank (2001) World Bank Development Indicators Database. The World Bank, Washington, DC

World Bank (2002) Transition – the First Ten Years: Analysis and Lessons for Eastern Europe and the Former Soviet Union, Europe and Central Asia Regional Department (ECA). The World Bank. Washington, D.C.

World Bank (2004) Committee on Development Effectiveness. An Evaluation of World Bank Assistance to the Transition Economies. The World Bank, Washington, DC

10 Conquering the inner-city: Urban redevelopment and gentrification in Moscow

Oleg Golubchikov and Anna Badyina

Introduction

Urban regeneration campaigns are pursued in cities all over the globe, leading to dramatic changes of their physical and social landscapes. Public-private partnerships are the driving force, the real estate market is the fuel, and the political rhetoric of rejuvenating otherwise declining inner city neighborhoods encourages active governmental interventions and support. This phenomenon is often associated with the rise of the service-based economy, which imposes new functions and status on post-industrial inner cities. The political foundation of the phenomenon is attributed to neoliberal ideology, which has been prominent in political-economic views since the 1970s and saw its triumph in the fall of state socialisms in Eastern and Central Europe. Neoliberal urbanism – i.e., an urban dimension of neoliberalism – privileges private interests in the competition for urban space. Their incorporation into the new forms of urban governance is enabling for market force, but repressive to other interests, including those of the local population (Brenner and Theodore 2003; Moulaert et al. 2001). Such circumstances place urban regeneration squarely in the discourse of social exclusion and inequalities, and bring the theory of *gentrification* to bear on its interpretation.

Gentrification is generally understood as a complex socio-spatial phenomenon, in which the physical upgrading of low-status residential neighborhoods in inner cities is accomplished through large-scale displacement and replacement of the neighborhoods' residents by wealthier newcomers, who then bring their own lifestyle into the upgraded neighborhoods (Clark 1995, 2005; Hamnett 1991; Smith 1987; Warde 1991). As Smith (2003) argues, gentrification, an initially marginal process in a few major capitalist cities in the 1960s, has evolved into a global urban strategy deliberately pursued in various parts of the world. It's features, globally, include the systematized, large-scale rebuilding of inner-city dwellings, corporate-government partnerships, and a repressive attitude towards native people. Gentrification thus suggests particular power relationships and a struggle for urban space that are in many respects similar to those of colonialism (Atkinson and Bridge 2005). However, thought observable globally, the gentrification process arises nonetheless in diverse, even contrasting urban experiences. That manifests neoliberalism's contextual mutations (Peck and Tickell 2003). Gentrification now takes diverse forms: for example, alongside 'classical' gentrification, which is the piecemeal individually-driven rehabilitation of disinvested neighborhoods, there may also be extensive rebuilding of residential and non-residential areas by corporate developers - gentrification with newly build structures (Davidson and Lees 2005). That contextuality and diversity calls for examining the 'geography of gentrification' in more detail (Ley 1996; Lees 2000).

This chapter explores the gentrification phenomenon by considering experiences from post-socialist Moscow. When the largest city in Europe became the financial centre of a major emerging market economy, that economic success not only fueled a building boom in Moscow, but also set off a wave of human migration within the city, with people moving through the new residential markets. As housing became a marketable commodity, the living space in prestigious locations became contested and increasingly acquired by the new economic elites, squeezing out the poorer population. The Moscow government's entrepreneurial strategy has facilitated that process by encouraging renovation of the inner city's housing and has privileged market forces vis-à-vis the inner city's original residents and even vis-à-vis the interests of this city's historic conservation institutions. The physical improvement of central Moscow is a departure from the Soviet legacy of underinvestment in inner city housing, but a socio-spatial polarization has resulted that undermines equalities achieved by the Soviet system and denotes the triumph of a neoliberal regime.

This chapter presents a case study of Ostozhenka, one of the most expensive districts in Moscow. The case is emblematic of neighborhood-based transformations: a once neglected residential area is remade as exclusive and affluent quarters. During the Soviet period the district was zoned for rebuilding into administrative use, but the plans were never implemented. Thus the residential buildings remained were left without proper maintenance and deteriorated. From the late 1990s, however, the district has undergone major rebuilding that substantially changed its appearance. The original residents have been displaced. Wealthy newcomers have moved into rebuilt or rehabilitated properties. The area is now an entirely new neighborhood that celebrates its privilege and satisfies the tastes of the new upper classes.

10.1 Capitalist Moscow: Unlocking the market genie

As other contributions to this book show, unlocking the mismatch between the functions and morphology of the socialist cities, and the logic of the new market economy has triggered new urban processes and markedly changed both the functions and the physical appearance of post-socialist cities. The social topography of urban space has also been altered. While housing privatization has created the supply for the residential markets, socio-economic stratification has created differential demand and varying ability to maintain the residential units. The result has been the accentuated socio-spatial fragmentation of post-socialist cities (Lowe and Tsenkova 2003).

The post-socialist transformations are especially visible in cities high in the urban hierarchy, such as Moscow with its population of over 10 million.[1] The concentration of Russia's financial wealth has meant a rapid deployment of the post-industrial economy in Moscow. Mushrooming financial and business services have driven renovation of the built environment to suit those new socio-economic conditions. In Moscow's rapid restructuring and reconstruction, city policies and business interests have been inextricably interwoven in this process, held by some as the reestablishment of Moscow as a world/global city (Brade and Rudolf 2004; Gritsai 2004; Kolossov et al. 2002).

The changes have been particularly intensive in Central Moscow, which traditionally had been both the administrative and business centre and a prestigious place of residence. For example, in 2003, Moscow's Central Administrative District accounted for only 6.1% of the city's area and 6.7% of its population, but captured 69% of the capital investment and 31% of the construction work in the entire city.[2] Not only new retail and office developments, but also large-scale rebuilding of the housing stock have transformed the District.

With the Russian financial sector and major headquarters becoming concentrated in Moscow, the city has acquired a considerable segment of affluent population. By the early 1990s well-off individuals were buying privatized apartments near the center and renovating them to the highest standards. However, gaining a central location and spending large sums to renovating an apartment became insufficient achievements for the new elite's aspirations, tastes and financial capacities. Soon, a newly constructed, luxurious house and entry to the 'appropriate' social milieu became increasingly important for the so-called 'elite housing' -- i.e., deluxe accommodations for the rich. Since land in central Moscow is limited, certain old residential quarters were torn down to make room for exclusive condominiums. That evolution from apartment-by-apartment to house-by-house and then block-by-block (re)construction of elite housing constituted the systematic gentrification of inner Moscow. Thus, the limited residential segregation of Soviet-period Moscow that had been based on non-economic factors (Andrusz 1984; Bater 1989; Morton 1980) yielded to a pronounced, socio-economic residential polarization.

10.2 Moscow's 'Golden Mile'

Although gentrification pervaded all of central Moscow, the process was particularly intensive in certain locations, among them the Ostozhenka neighborhood, of

---

[1] The official estimates for January 2005 put the population of Moscow at 10.4 million; in addition 6.6 million live in Moscow Province (administratively separated from Moscow). The Census of 2002 showed that the population of Moscow was almost 2 million more than had previously been estimated. The actual population of Moscow may therefore be even greater.

[2] Calculated from the data of Rosstat (2004) as the percentage of the total of Moscow's ten districts.

about 0.5 km², which lies one kilometer south-west of the Kremlin (Fig. 10.1.). Today it is one of the most expensive districts in Moscow, named 'the Golden Mile' by the estate agents.[3] Depending on micro-location, project and construction stage, in early 2005 the prices for new condominiums varied between $4,000 and $12,000 per m², with some penthouses exceeding $20,000 per m². Those prices were well above the average residential property price, of approximately $2,800 per m² in the Central Administrative District and $1,800 per m² for all Moscow. Although the credit market is expanding in Moscow, the buyers of Ostozhenka projects are usually people who can pay cash, between one and over eight million US dollars, for an apartment. The high prices in Ostozhenka are explained not only by its proximity to the Kremlin, to the beautiful Cathedral of Christ the Savior, and to the picturesque embankment of Moskva River, but also by a unique attraction:

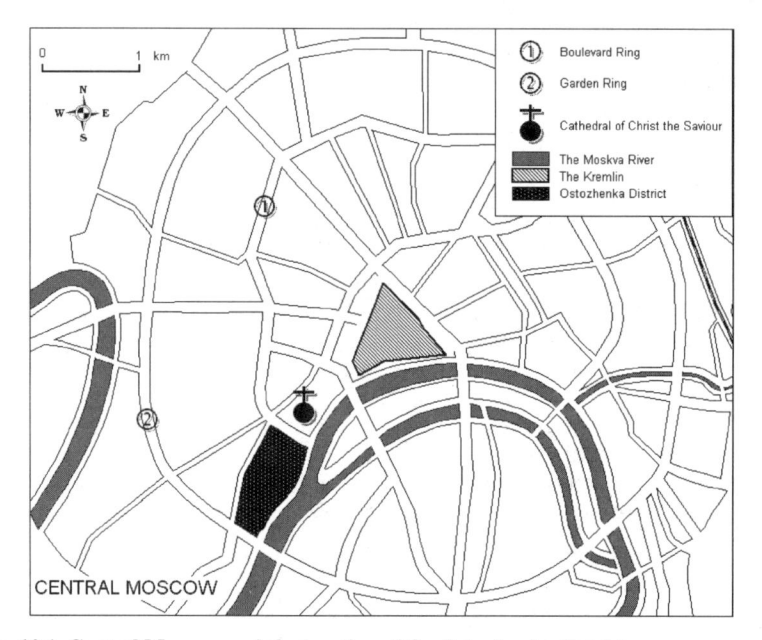

Fig. 10.1. Central Moscow and the location of the Ostozhenka district

Ostozhenka is becoming the first neighborhood in the heart of Moscow to be totally rebuilt as an agglomeration of upscale properties. Houses there built in the nineteenth and early twentieth century are giving way to exclusive condominiums, offices and restaurants. A major factor driving Ostozhenka's comprehensive reconstruction was the fact that it was the only area close to the Kremlin with a large

---

[3] The word 'mile' is used metaphorically. It sounds 'posh' as it is not used in the official metric system of Russia.

stock of pre-revolutionary properties in poor condition. In contrast to similar central locations, the district had neither been rebuilt nor even considerably renovated during the Soviet era, among other reasons because it bordered on the ill-fated Palace of the Soviets. The Palace had been intended to be the tallest building in the world, built on the site of the Christ the Savior Cathedral, a monument to the Russian victory over Napoleon that had been dynamited in 1931. Soviet planners left Ostozhenka untouched in order to redevelop it along with the Palace. However, first a structural problem with the foundation for the Palace and then the Second World War delayed implementation of the plan. In the 1950s, the project was abandoned and the area of the former Cathedral was made into an open-air swimming pool. But even after giving up their ambition for the Palace, the government continued to limit investments in new construction and the maintenance of existing housing stock in Ostozhenka, making new plans to redevelop the neighborhood as an administrative quarter. Lack of funding delayed that project, but the government never abandoned it and thus left the neighborhood in limbo for years.

In the 1980s the deteriorating neighborhood attracted the attention of conservationists. They realized that Ostozhenka had preserved much of the pre-revolutionary appearance of Moscow. In 1989 city planners designed a program for neighborhood regeneration, which was approved by the new Moscow Administration in 1992. In contrast to previous plans, the new Program sanctioned continued residential use of Ostozhenka. It also sought to establish a coherent urban environment through a contextual approach and a comprehensive rehabilitation of the structural, historic and aesthetic values of the district as a whole. The Program's implementation was to be through: a) comprehensive repair of the existing residential and historic buildings, including the former convent and churches; b) restoration of lost buildings; and c) the removal of 'inappropriate land users,' mostly industrial and administrative premises established during the Soviet era or that otherwise did not blend into the district's historical ambience. The Program's social aspect stressed that the current residents would remain, but had to improve their housing (Fig. 10.2.).

However, once again none of the activities planned for Ostozhenka were pursued, this time because the economic crisis of the early 1990s diverted budget allocations from heritage restorations. Consequently, private capital was allowed to pursue somewhat different interests in the area. The plan for conservation and restoration of Ostozhenka was not legally binding, and had no oversight through participatory or other external processes. The destiny of the district therefore became the subject of closed negotiations between property developers and city administrators. The resulting *ad hoc* and flexible implementation of the Program departed from its intentions. The Program was first 'adjusted' after each new project and was abandoned by the late 1990s.

Fig. 10.2. A restored historic building in the Ostozhenka district

10.3 From proletarization to privatization

In the late imperial period, Ostozhenka was a mostly residential area, home to the bourgeoisie and the aristocracy. The 1917 Revolution quickly changed the district's profile. Properties were nationalized and converted into housing for families of the proletariat, who moved into the spacious apartments and split them into 'communal apartments' (*kommunalki*) where several families shared a bathroom and a kitchen.

As the new Soviet social stratification developed in accordance with the new political ideology and communist (non-market) economy, Ostozhenka became socially mixed. Although the residential areas near the center were favored by Soviet political and professional elites, segregation based on social status was very inconsistent. Typically, people from different social strata lived next-door to each other in central Moscow. The social profile in Ostozhenka was even more diversified than that in many other districts because of its general deterioration. The state was providing better living conditions in newly built housing, so Muscovites lost interest in this district. The in-migrants from the provinces replaced them in shared *kommunalki*.

In 1989, city planners conducted a survey of the district's social makeup. The registered population of the neighborhood was then 3,800. People born outside Moscow accounted for almost half of Ostozhenka's working-age population and for 60% of pensioners. Less educated population dominated the neighborhood; almost 70% of the adult respondents did not have a higher degree. However, the occupational structure was mixed (Table 10.1.). Although in the Soviet 'classless' society the interrelationship between occupation, wealth and social status was much more complex and indirect than in a capitalist society, the data show that people classified as *intelligentsia*, administration and professionals were approximately equal in number to those employed in occupations such as sales, social services, security personnel, laborers and related occupations. The latter cohort was more frequent, however, among incomers to Moscow than among Muscovites – roughly 60% versus 40%. That distribution is due to the restricted in-migration to Moscow during the Soviet period, when it was easier to obtain a Moscow resident permit by taking less prestigious jobs which allowed employment of non-Muscovites according to special quotas (*limit*). Even if similar in their ethnicity, education or skills, to Muscovites, work migrants (*limitchiki*) were considered to be of lower status by Muscovites. That Ostozhenka sheltered many such people indicated its unfavorable conditions.

Table 10.1. Occupational profile of the working-age respondents, 1989 (percentage)

Occupations	Muscovites	In-migrants to Moscow	Average for Total Sample
Intelligentsia and administration	40	22	32
Professionals without higher education	20	19	19
Sale and social service personnel	18	26	21
Plant operators and laborers	10	8	9
Transport laborers	8	10	9
Construction laborers	4	7	5
Police and security personnel	0	8	4

Source: adopted from unpublished materials of the Architectural Bureau 'Ostozhenka'

The largest proportion of the Ostozhenka population lived in *kommunalki*. According to the archive data obtained from the Ostozhenka General Directorate, an *ad hoc* local administration, in 1992 as many as 70% of the total number of Ostozhenka apartments were 'communal'. That was well above the average of 45% for central Moscow. The *kommunalki* gave shelter to 80% of Ostozhenka's population and 86% of Ostozhenka households.

The major form of housing tenure in Ostozhenka was 'long-term use' of municipal/state housing, the widespread arrangement for apartment buildings in Moscow, as opposed to the less common, tenant-owned 'cooperative housing'. Since the start of housing privatization in 1991, Moscow's residents have been granted the right to privatize, free of charge, the dwellings where they live permanently. That ownership opportunity opened the way to great residential changes. Wealthy individuals and real estate agencies started to buy the privatized rooms in shared *kommunalki* and to amalgamate them into spacious apartments and offices. The process in central Moscow has been documented by Vendina (1997, pp. 358-359):

> Mediating firms would select the options of resettling a communal flat and would find a buyer for it, paying for the operation. Separate apartments on the city periphery would be purchased for all the families leaving the centrally located communal flats. The profit was as high as 150-200%. The fact that within 2 years [1992-1993] the ratio of communal flats in the centre fell from 45% to 22% is a good illustration of the process intensity.

In Ostozhenka, such conversions occurred in the most prestigious areas, around the neighborhood's northeastern edges – along Ostozhenka Street and closer to the Kremlin. In combination with the city programs for rehousing the *kommunalki* dwellers, the ownership shifts affected the social structure of the neighborhood: its total population decreased while the share of high-income people there began to rise.

This 'unmediated' process of 'buying into' Ostozhenka was the first wave of gentrification in the neighborhood. It was, in fact, less contentious than the process that ensued, because it was both piecemeal and welcomed by many *kommunalki* dwellers, who were glad to negotiate for an unshared flat. It was not until 1998 that more intensive redevelopment of the neighborhood by corporate capital arrived. In the early 1990s, however, corporate developers had little interest in the run-down Ostozhenka. The city administration even provided incentives for investors, but with only partial success. Until 1998, building activity in Ostozhenka was sluggish; about three or four residential or commercial projects were being carried out concurrently. Nonetheless, those first projects created an adverse precedent for Ostozhenka. At that time Gdaniec (1997) noted that in setting up the new projects the preservationist rhetoric of the Ostozhenka regeneration program had been forgotten.

10.4 Systematic rebuilding: Market/government interplay

By 1997 the economic potential of the district had begun to attract more attention, coinciding with the Russian financial crisis in 1998 and the rapid pace of Russian economic growth afterwards.[4] If previously Moscow had been an island of prosperity in a sea of decline, since the late 1990s Moscow has been at the forefront of the nation's economic growth. The building boom in Moscow has even accelerated.

---

[4] Between 1999 and 2004 average annual GDP growth in Russia was 6.8% (7.2% in 2004 and predictably near 6% in 2005). This has been the inverse of a very poor performance of the economy from 1991 to 1998, when GDP was falling by the average of 6.6%.

With land in central locations in Moscow increasingly scarce and the growing prestige of Ostozhenka, more developers found it profitable to work in that neighborhood, where entire blocks could be rebuilt under relatively relaxed city regulations. That regulatory tendency is inherent in the entrepreneurial strategy of the present Moscow administration (Kolossov et al. 2002; Pagonis and Thornley 2000). Since decentralization, the city administration has been responsible for generating its own revenues, and has found a major source in the property sector. Most land in Moscow has stayed in the city's ownership. Its land ownership places the city in an advantageous position and able to capture a monopolistic rent. To build residential units in Moscow, developers have to conclude an 'investment contract' with the city administration. The contract is a form of public-private partnership agreement by which developers take on financial responsibilities in exchange for their land leasehold, building rights, and access to the city's infrastructure. In central Moscow the investment contracts for housing projects have normally required the investors to transfer as much as 50% of the building volume to the city. Previously the city had accepted 'in kind' compensations if developers who were able to provide the city with equivalent building space or social infrastructure elsewhere in Moscow. Recently, however, with the prohibition of such in kind transactions, the city has demanded cash for the market value of its share. More constructions and more expensive projects mean more revenues for the city.

Under those circumstances, more and more large-scale building projects – mostly homes but also offices – were pursued in Ostozhenka because only major developers could afford to enter into the contracts with the city. In aggressive marketing campaigns, the developers and real estate agents promoted the ultimately elitist environment of Ostozhenka. The public-led rebuilding of the Cathedral of Christ the Savior, the biggest Orthodox cathedral in the world, which took place from 1994 to 2000 was also an attraction. The cumulative effect of all the projects and circumstances was that the more rich people moved to Ostozhenka, the more prestigious it became.

This second wave of gentrification in Ostozhenka beginning in the late 1990s is distinguishable from the first in many respects, but most clearly in the scale of construction. Fig. 10.3. shows the 'net increase in floorspace each year and the consequent increase in the 'cumulative residential floorspace' and 'non-residential floorspace' (the latter including underground car parking, offices, restaurants and shops). In 2004, the volume of building space in Ostozhenka was about twice as high as in the early 1990s; in 2006 it will be three times as high. Then the rate of new construction is likely to drop because of limited availability of land and also the likely opposition to change from the already established, affluent residents of the neighborhood.

The new projects in Ostozhenka have recycled the land where non-residential properties such as small industrial facilities, administrative buildings and warehouses stood and have occupied the previously public spaces (parks, yards). By and large, however, most of the new construction has been conducted at the expense of existing residential buildings. We estimate that of the 51 houses, in the neighborhood at the beginning of the 1990s, by 2006 only 17 remain standing. The 1989 Program had envisaged saving 44 houses. Even when officially described as 'reconstruction,' most new projects in Ostozhenka demolished old buildings and replaced them with new ones, often of a contemporary design. In some cases the original facades of demolished buildings were saved (or rebuilt), but professional restoration became very limited after 1998. The cost of restoration is estimated to be three times that of new construction. Further, the extremely profitable and popular underground car parking cannot be constructed without demolition.

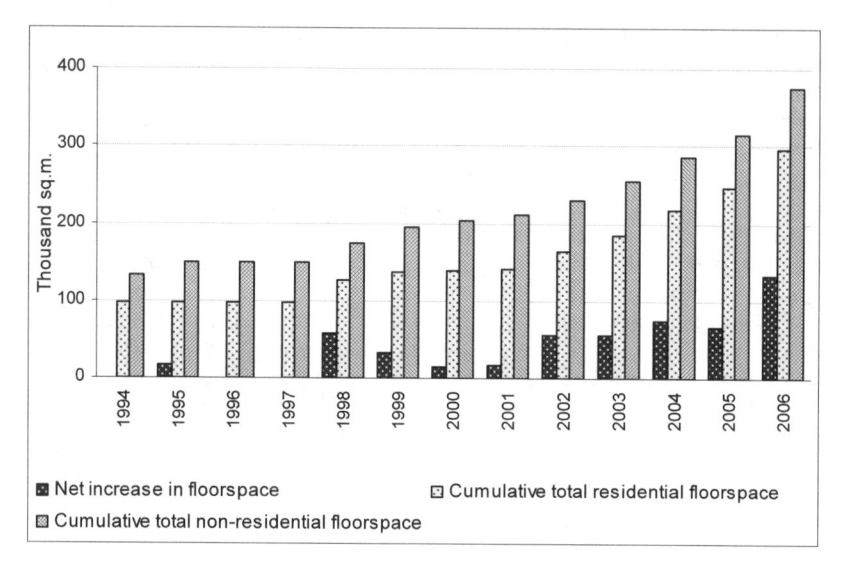

Fig. 10.3. Building activity in Ostozhenka between 1994 and 2006

Source: authors' estimation based on unpublished materials of the Ostozhenka General Directorate and field surveys

The neighborhood redevelopment process can be understood as an interaction between the market actors (owners of capital) and the government (owners of power). The government's proactive attitude and entrepreneurial strategy facilitated the developers' acquiring a site and permits for redevelopment. The city's financial participation and financial interest in the new developments ensured that the developers would enjoy relaxed preservation rules and even circumvent the city's own planning. During Ostozhenka's transformation, then, the city government was neither strict enough to protect the historic heritage, nor prepared to subsidize the developers undertaking its preservation. On the contrary, the government itself enabled the downgrading 'by reason of a state of disrepair' of buildings that had been listed for conservation, and recommended their 'reconstruction via demolition' -- although not always legitimately. The responsible architectural organizations would find 'evidence' of their physical obsolescence. If necessary, the Moscow Administration for the Preservation of Monuments would validate their exclusion from the heritage protection list (Vesti Moskva 2004). Economic, ecological and social justifications for rebuilding would be put forward by other agencies. In the end, the share of residential buildings dating from the Tsarist period has fallen from more than 80% in 1992 to less than 20% in 2006 (Fig. 10.4.). Moreover, the share in terms of space is even smaller, because the new houses are much larger than their predecessors (Fig. 10.5.).

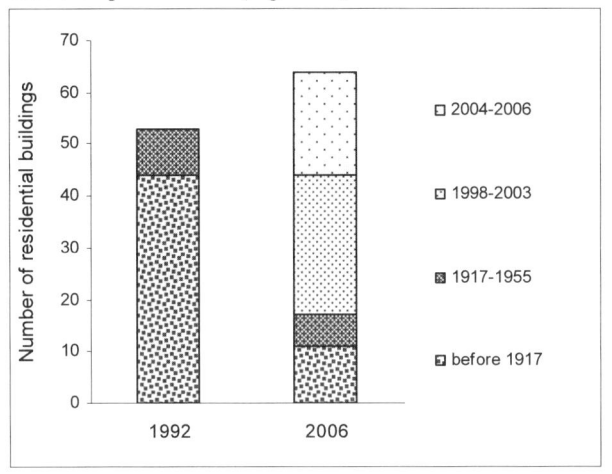

Fig. 10.4. The estimated number of residential houses (units) by construction period in 1992 and 2006

Source: authors' estimation based on unpublished materials of the Ostozhenka General Directorate and field surveys

The process of development negotiations and approvals was never free from benefits to privileged developers. And as soon as the district gained in prestige, it became difficult to penetrate the pool of Ostozhenka's developers. The relationships between the authorities and the investors took on an intimate character, sometimes involving a complex web of personal relationships. Although the investment contracts to access land are supposed to be concluded through competition, non-transparent 'closed competitions' have often been used. Through the pro-development 'closed schemes', builders avoided both the barriers as presented by potential conflicts between public and private interests in the built environment and the necessity of abiding democratic planning procedures.

The open strategies, on the other hand, have been complicated by the complex system of public sanctions and regulations. It is true that it is difficult to find a place in the world where once the most desired urban sites are at stake, the relationship between developers and public officials would be transparent. Nonetheless, through somewhat underdeveloped participatory mechanisms for urban planning and control of development (Golubchikov 2004), the construction businesses' reliance on the discretion of the city leaders and the personal/informal nature of their interactions seems to have been fostered to a marked degree in the case of Moscow.

Fig. 10.5. The same view photographed in June 2003 (left) and September 2005 (right). The historic buildings wait for a new wave of investment.

10.5 Social change and conflict

One negative consequence of gentrification is social displacement. The social structure of Ostozhenka has changed considerably after the physical renovations in the area. Replacement of Ostozhenka's native residents happens either through purchase/exchange of their rooms by developers and estate agents or through the government's 'resettlement schemes.'

The government-based schemes have been less beneficial for the residents, but cheaper for developers because they are arranged outside of the market and allow the developers to economize on time and money. Each year the city designates residential buildings for demolition due to their 'state of disrepair' and resettles the affected households. By law, the dwellers of such buildings are required to move at the city's expense. The city either rehouse the tenants from non-privatized, municipal rooms into other apartments in accordance with the established norm of space per inhabitant or, in the case of privatized dwellings, compensates the owners in kind or in cash. This resettlement mechanism has turned out to be an effective tool for authorizing the immediate displacement of a large number of residents.

When the old housing stock in Ostozhenka remained highly deteriorated, it was easy to recognize which buildings were in need of reconstruction (in effect, demolition and rebuilding) and whose inhabitants consequently would have to be resettled. With rehousing, generally speaking, the resettled tenants are likely to improve their living conditions, though the location, the quality, and consequently the value of their new dwelling depend greatly on their bargaining position and ability. The bargaining position of the residents depends on their ownership status.

If resettled, the owners of privatized dwellings can claim more compensation for their expropriated property than the 'municipal tenants' for their rented space. While in-cash compensation for owners is usually offered at below market value, in-kind compensation in the form of new apartments is negotiable. The residents are not allowed, however, to privatize dwellings if the building has been already slated for reconstruction. If resettled, the municipal tenants are usually moved to properties on the outskirts of Moscow, where massive housing construction is rising.

The compulsory resettlement schemes were especially popular in the late 1990s, when they were underpinned by private capital. As soon as corporate interests established themselves in the Ostozhenka neighborhood, developers started to participate in the public compulsory rehousing through public-private partnerships in which they paid the cost of resettlement in exchange for the right to access the sites.

According to the Ostozhenka General Directorate, in 1992 there were 3,725 residents/1,620 families permanently registered as tenants in the district. Between 1992 and 2004, in partnerships with developers, the government carried out compulsory resettlement of 1,263 residents/627 families (with over 70% of them rehoused after 1998). Yet others (1,584 residents /891 families) were rehoused through the quasi-voluntary 'secondary market,' by swapping their rooms for apartments in other places through privately arranged negotiations with developers or estate agencies. If we add to those numbers the Ostozhenk native residents who rented out or sold their (privatized) rooms and moved out of the neighborhood without being formally counted as 'rehoused', and the individuals who died during the period, we may conclude that very few of the former residents and their families have remained in Ostozhenka. Of those, many still live in kommunalki: by early 2004 there were 77 kommunalki with 440 residents/199 families scheduled for resettlement.

As might be expected, the resettlement was not always smooth. The violence that occurred reveals the forced nature of displacement and reminds one of Smith's (1996) 'revanchist city'. Most of the resettled residents were attached to Ostozhenka and wanted to stay. To attract attention to their distress, the Ostozhenka native residents organized protest rallies and sent petitions to both the Moscow and Federal authorities. Many brought their cases to court. But their protests were fragmented and weak vis-à-vis the more powerful development interests. A strategy used against stubborn residents, has been to deliberately house 'problem' individuals (e.g. street people or ex-prisoners) in vacated rooms in kommunalki in order to induce the remaining neighbors to stop bargaining and to accept the city's or developers' conditions. Some of the most resistant individuals have even experienced reprisals such as the cut-off of public utilities. Ultimately, in one way or another, these residents were persuaded to move.

The Federal authorities have criticized Moscow for its development policy. The new 2005 Federal Housing Code has secured the right of associations of owners to the land on which multi-dwelling houses stand. The law guarantees the members of owner associations the right to remain in the same area if the city does designate their houses for reconstruction. This mechanisms, however, protects only the property owners; the same Housing Code actually limits the rights of the tenants of 'social rental housing' – a newly-defined category for formerly non-privatized dwellings.

Until recently, the ability to remain in Ostozhenka has depended simply on residents' financial power. Poorer households, even those in privatized apartments, cannot afford to maintain the physical condition of their properties and especially, their shared spaces to a safely high standard. In contrast, wealthier residents can easily pool their resources and employ private services to maintain the highest standard in their buildings. The fact that houses in which most of the apartments were already restored during the first phase of gentrification do not attract the developers shows the difficulties they face in reaching agreements with established and generally affluent owners. Furthermore, the city does not dare classify such properties as needing reconstruction; instead, the authorities consider buildings that house poorer residents as 'good prospects.'

The wealthy residents benefit from further gentrification. That was particularly so during the second phase of gentrification in Ostozhenka, when property prices skyrocketed in this 'Golden Mile'. Interestingly, the wealthy residents who first came to Ostozhenka in the 1990s -- these pioneers of the new wealthy urban frontier (Smith 1996) -- now feel impelled by the market to sell their apartments to even wealthier people.

A further noteworthy aspect of social change is expressed through the architecture of the newly constructed buildings and the lifestyle of newcomers in Ostozhenka. This compounded effect is a qualitatively different urban environment with a new social value and meaning. The promoters of Ostozhenka like to speak about 'Europeanization' of the neighborhood. By 'Europeanization' they imagine an ultimate manifestation of prosperity that implies a sort of disparagement of the rest of Russian society. A well-known architect expresses this in the following way (Revzin 2003, translated from Russian):

> [New buildings] seem to be located not here, but sometimes in France, sometimes in Switzerland, more often in Finland. They have the elements unimaginable for Russian homes - well-groomed yards, elegant lawns, carefully paved paths, underground parking, impossible for Russia, luxurious terraces and lobbies. It is not the Moscow quality of life, it is rather a very prestigious, very bourgeois neighborhood of top-managers in an old European capital city.

The bearers of this 'Europeanized' – and ultimately 'globalized' – lifestyle of the second gentrification phase in Ostozhenka are those whom Lees (2000) calls 'financifiers'. They are the owners and CEOs of large and medium-sized Russian businesses in a variety of industries and financial groups, joined by well off art and media elites. Many of the properties in Ostozhenka are purchased as capital investments and rented out by their owners, often executives in extractive industries who do not live permanently in Moscow. Their tenants are affluent families who prefer renting to buying an apartment. Other members of this cohort are foreign businesspeople and diplomats working in Moscow, and top managers of the

Russian branches of international companies. In many respects, the Ostozhenka elite share an identity with the new upper classes colonizing the 'elite' districts in other major world cities (Atkinson and Bridge 2005).

The residents who settled during the second wave of gentrification in Ostozhenka conflict in their philosophy with both the original population and the gentrifiers of the first wave. The cultural clash between these groups is complicated by the re-establishment of the Zachat'evsky Convent, an autonomous community, in the central part of the neighborhood. Socio-culturally, therefore, Ostozhenka is a mosaic micro-space. The outer parts of the district containing the restored properties of the first wave used to be the most prestigious. They are now less expensive than some quieter inner areas of the district that have undergone a full-scale rebuilding; these are vigilantly controlled by hundreds of closed-circuit television (CCTV) units and scores of armed guards. Such a heavy presence of security undermines the remaining public space, since as the casual passers-by feel unwelcome in proximity to the wealthy homes. And even if some areas are still mixed, with islands of kommunalki and construction sites, those are continuously transforming into the space of prosperity.

Conclusions

Moscow has been one of the winners among the cities in the post-socialist countries. The politico-economic transformation since the collapse of the state socialism has brought Moscow wealth and prosperity. On the other hand, it also has introduced soaring inequalities inherent to the capitalist system. A predictable consequence has been the growing spatial-economic polarization.

Meanwhile, the continuing legacy of the spatial equality of Soviet Moscow is Moscow's uniform and extensive high-rise suburban townscape: the standardized, subsidized and centralized maintenance of residential property, which as yet does not present the negative characteristics of the so-called 'social housing' in many Western countries. As well, the ethno-spatial segregation has remained almost absent, despite increased ethnic immigration to Moscow since the establishment of freedom of residence and a liberalized international migration regimen in the 1990s (Vendina 2005). Those factors have so far helped Moscow avoid the emergence of stigmatized and 'outcast' neighborhoods such as are met in London, New York and almost all the other large cities of the world.

However, that positive aspect is being slowly eroded by the growing disproportion between the residents of the central and the peripheral locations in Moscow. Introducing a housing market has set in motion demographic filtering by price, to which has begun to distribute people in space according to their economic wealth. The central places are being colonized by the new upper classes, while the less wealthy are being continuously forced toward the city's periphery.

Moreover, Moscow now has acquired 'elitist' enclaves, exclusive residential zones for the upper classes. With land in the center of Moscow limited, such targeted developments can take place there only by large-scale rebuilding of existing properties. Moscow government encourages that process because eradication of urban decay and stimulation of urban regeneration is among its major priorities. Gentrification, the twin of regeneration, is assumed to be an inevitable by-product of the penetration of the market economy that has little to do with government. In fact, however, as demonstrated in the preceding discussion, the Moscow administration has been the enabler of such developments. Although market forces drive the process, the Moscow government has been a major player in Moscow's gentrification.

The answer to the question of whether the changes in Central Moscow have on the whole been 'wrong' or 'right' inevitably would be ideologically biased (Atkinson 2003). For example, the proponents may argue that the winners in the Ostozhenka gentrification are not only the new residents enjoying their luxurious life in the heart of the Russian capital and the developers counting their profits, but also the original residents of *kommunalki* who, although displaced, have improved their standard of living; the city economy which has greatly benefited from a financial injection from the high-profile property market; and the city as a whole which has received a renovated piece of the built environment.

However, those benefits have a down side: the loss of historic value and architectural integrity, the privatization of public space, growing social polarization, and the undermining of the social mix and equality achieved under Soviet socialism. The last, particularly, presents a danger for the long-term sustainability of a society known for its egalitarian ideals and strong belief in social justice. In addition, the lack of democratic procedures in the redevelopment of Ostozhenka undermines of '*urban democratic memory*', which is as important as capital for a city to accumulate.

It is, however, possible to notice that as Russia's social and political context is changing, the Moscow government's authoritative, opportunistic and pro-private-sector *modus operandi* is increasingly challenged. Recently, heritage legislation has been toughened, and the Federal authorities have taken historic preservation under stricter control. Some developers were surprised recently when they found themselves under criminal charges for unlawful demolition of historic landmarks. That way of handling urban change, conventional during the past ten years is no longer without risk. It is not yet clear whether this flurry of responsibility by the higher administrative bodies is a genuine effort to reinforce the rule of law protecting historical heritage, or a political challenge to Moscow's leadership and its position in the development business. Either situation may, in effect, mean the beginning of the end of the 'authoritative neoliberalism' of Moscow government. With the contours of the coming order not clearly identifiable, it remains to be seen whether it will offer a more emancipatory alternative.

Overall, the case of gentrification in Moscow is not philosophically different from what has been observed in many Western contexts (Brenner and Theodore 2003). The processes in Moscow are characteristic of the neoliberal phase of urbanism. Political regimes liberalize urban space and grant private interests a privileged position in their contest with the public interests. As in other cases, we see the unwillingness of the Moscow government to tackle growing socio-spatial polarization. On the contrary, the city itself is pro-active in pushing forward with a strategy similar to what Harvey (1989) termed 'urban entrepreneurialism'. We have distinguished two phases of gentrification in Ostozhenka – the spontaneous, individually-driven process of housing rehabilitation before 1998, and the systematic gentrification led by large-scale developers and investors thereafter. Both types of gentrification have counterparts in other major world cities. Similarities in forms but differences in functions, processes and styles compose an exciting illustration of the global / local dualism of gentrification, the main rationale for attention to the 'geography of gentrification' (Lees, 2000).

Acknowledgement

This chapter draws on material published in Geografiska Annaler, Series B (Badyina and Golubchikov 2005). The authors are extremely grateful for help from Judith Pallot of Oxford University.

References

Andrusz G (1984) Housing and urban development in the USSR. MacMillan, London
Atkinson R (2003) Introduction: Misunderstood saviour or vengeful wrecker? The many meanings and problems of gentrification. Urban Studies 40:2343-2350
Atkinson R, Bridge G (eds) (2005) Gentrification in a global context: the new urban colonialism. Routledge, London
Badyina A, Golubchikov O (2005) Gentrification in central Moscow – a market process or a deliberate policy? Money, power and people in housing regeneration in Ostozhenka. Geografiska Annaler 87B:113-129
Bater JH (1989) The Soviet scene – A Geographical perspective. Edward Arnold, London
Brade I, Rudolph R (2004) Moscow, the global city? The position of the Russian capital within the European system of metropolitan areas. Area 36:69-80
Brenner N, Theodore N (eds) (2003) Spaces of neoliberalism: Urban restructuring in North America and Western Europe. Blackwell, Oxford
Clark E (1995) The rent gap re-examined. Urban Studies 32:1489–1503
Clark E (2005) The order and simplicity of gentrification - a political challenge. In: Atkinson R, Bridge G (eds) Gentrification in a global context: the new urban colonialism. Routledge, London, pp 256-264
Davidson M, Lees L (2005) New-build 'gentrification' and London's riverside renaissance. Environment and Planning A 37:1165-1190
Gdaniec C (1997) Reconstruction in Moscow's historic center: conservation, planning and finance strategies – the example of the Ostozhenka district. GeoJournal 42:377–384
Golubchikov O (2004) Urban planning in Russia: towards the market. European Planning Studies 12:229-247
Gritsai O (2004) Global business services in Moscow: patterns of involvement. Urban Geography 41:2001-2024
Hamnett C (1991) The blind men and the elephant: the explanation of gentrification. Transactions of the Institute of British Geographers 16:259-279

Harvey D (1989) From managerialism to entrepreneurialism: the transformation in urban governance in late capitalism. Geografiska Annaler, Series B 71:3-17

Kolossov V, Vendina O, O'Loughlin J (2002) Moscow as an emergent world city: international links, business developments, and the entrepreneurial city. Eurasian Geography and Economics 43:170-196

Lees L (2000) A Re-appraisal of gentrification: Towards a geography of gentrification. Progress in Human Geography 24:389-408

Ley D (1996) The new middle class and the remaking of the central city. Oxford University Press, Oxford

Lowe S, Tsenkova S (eds) (2003) Housing change in Central and Eastern Europe: Integration or fragmentation. Ashgate, Aldershot, UK

Morton H (1980) Who gets what, when and how? Housing in the Soviet Union. Soviet Studies XXXII:235-259

Moulaert F, Swyngedouw E, Rodriguez A (2001) Social polarization in metropolitan areas: the role of new urban policy. European Urban and Regional Studies 8:99-102

Pagonis T, Thornley A (2000) Urban redevelopment projects in Moscow: market/state relations in the new Russia. European Planning Studies 8:751-766

Peck J, Tickell A (2003) Neoliberalizing space. In: Brenner N, Theodore N (eds) Spaces of neoliberalism: Urban restructuring in North America and Western Europe. Blackwell, Oxford

Revzin G (2003) Ostozhenka v russkoi arkhitekture (Ostozhenka in Russian architecture), Proyekt Klassika VI-MMIII, available online:
<http://projectclassica.ru/m_classik/06_2003/06_classik_01b.htm> (accessed in December 2005)

Rosstat (2004) Regiony Rossii: Osnovnyye sotsial'no-ekonomicheskiye pokazateli gorodov (Russia's regions: The main socio-economic indicators of cities). Federal Service for State Statistics (Rosstat), Moscow

Smith N (1987) Gentrification and the rent gap. Annals of the Association of American Geographers 77:462-465

Smith N (1996) The new urban frontier: gentrification and the revanchist city. Routledge, London

Smith N (2002) New globalism, new urbanism: gentrification as global urban strategy. In: Brenner N, Theodore N (eds), Spaces of neoliberalism: Urban restructuring in North America and Western Europe. Blackwell, Oxford, pp 80-103

Vendina O (1997) Transformation processes in Moscow and intra-urban stratification of population. GeoJournal 42:216-243

Vendina O (2005) Migranty v Moskve: grozit li rossiyskoy stolitse etnicheskaya segregatsiya? (Migrants in Moscow: is Moscow heading towards ethnic segregation?) Center for Migration Research, Moscow

Vesti-Moskva (2004) Moscow Regional TV news, RTR TV Channel. August 6

Warde A (1991) Gentrification as consumption: issues of class and gender. Environment and Planning D 9:223-232

11 The role of property rights reforms in Warsaw's housing market

Annette M. Kim

Introduction

Of the many changes that have occurred in transition economies, one of the most fundamental and significant has been the (re)introduction of private property rights. Private claims to property have provoked a wholesale transformation of economic systems, decentralized control over resources, and redistributed wealth. It is no wonder that property rights have consistently been central to transition policy discussions since their inception. However, these policy discussions have been largely limited in scope. Relying on natural law theories of law and economics, many observers assumed that efficient markets would spontaneously arise if new game rules were set up to unleash optimizing behaviour in place of the behaviours constrained by the command economy (Pipes 1996). Not surprisingly, though, the empirical evidence shows that although their reforms have been similar, there has been considerable diversity among countries' propensity to shift to property markets, as well as among the shapes their transitions have taken (Tsenkova 2000).

Beyond those variations, there is conflicting evidence about the relationship between property rights laws and the formation of markets. While the three strongest European transition economies (Hungary, Poland, and the Czech Republic) have been identified as exemplars of property rights reforms, some Asian transition economies with the most incomplete property rights and institutional reforms have been among the fastest growing economies in the world (IMF 2000; Heritage Foundation 2005). Some scholars argue that it is not a rigid and formalized legal system, but rather other institutions that account for why the more successful transition economies have been able to grow so rapidly (Fforde and de Vylder 1996; Gillespie 1999; Gainsborough 2002; Kim 2004).[1] Just as one can have the same property rights reforms with different results, it is possible to have similar economic results but for different reasons.

Research into a variety of institutional factors beyond law and economics has proliferated, with "new institutionalist" literature in many disciplines. An example of such factors, is the way in which political interests may capture a new rule-making process meant for group benefit or may limit the meaningful implementation of changes (Hall and Taylor 1996; Hall and Soskice 2001). Social networks, culture, and historical path dependence can also help to explain diverse

---

[1] Others balk at this interpretation and warn that in actuality this transition path sets up a flawed institutional framework that will eventually reach its limits (Lo and Tian 2002).

responses to similar formal policy reforms (Granovetter 1985; Collier and Collier 1991). Micro-scale institutions may develop between agents in order to lower the risks and other transaction costs of actually engaging the market (Williamson 1996). What remains poorly understood is how such institutional factors interact and their relative importance (Granovetter 2002). That is where examining specific cases can help to disentangle the confluence of factors. This chapter I examine how much of the success of an exemplar transition case can be attributed to the introduction of legal property rights and how much to such other factors. In what ways do they work together? I explore this question by examining the case of the newly emerging urban housing market in Warsaw, Poland, and the roles that the law and legal institutions have or have not played in its development.

Poland's is an apt transition to investigate not only because its economy has grown, but because its property rights reforms have been lauded as exemplary. The International Monetary Fund (2000) assessed Poland as having one of the best sets of pro-market institutions among 31 transition countries, particularly for its conduct of small-scale privatization.[2] In fact, when in 2003 the Central European Land Knowledge (CELK) Centre established the Regional Centre of Excellence for Real Property Rights and Land Market Development, to promote adequate legislation on real property rights and their monitoring as emphasized by the European Commission and its Enlargement and External Relations Directorate, CELK's mission statement cited the property rights reforms of the Czech Republic, Poland, and Hungary as role models for other Eastern European transitions. But how much of Poland's land market development can be attributed to its property rights?

The conventional theory is that legal property rights are necessary to raise property values and to promote market exchanges and investment, by reducing sellers' and buyers' risks and the costs of protecting their property from an expropriating state or unscrupulous parties (Demsetz 1967; Hart 1995). However, much of the world buys and sells property outside formal legal institutions. Nonetheless, informal property rights not only make taxation for public services difficult but also are not recognized by formal banks which could finance improvements to the property. Furthermore, lack of clarity in ownership title does dampen property values and slow down transactions (de Soto 2000). For all these reasons, the early transition policies heavily emphasized legal restoration of property rights (World Bank 1996). In the area of developing real estate markets, these reforms typically emphasized three components: legal amendments, property title registration in modernized cadastral systems, and court resolution of disputes (UNECE 1997).

This exploratory study of the relationship between property rights reforms and Warsaw's housing market employs key-informant interviewing as the primary research method. The interviews were conducted with private homebuilding entrepreneurs and associated legal professionals to learn how the transitional

---

[2] The Heritage Foundation also praised Poland's economy as "one of the most successful and open in Central Europe" and ranked it 31 out 155 countries around the world in terms of its promotion of free markets.

reforms of property rights have affected their investment decisions. This agent-based approach not only helps to test economic behavioural assumptions, but also characterizes amorphous entities such as "the state" and "the private sector" in specific and contextually situated terms. I hypothesize that if property rights are functioning in Warsaw's housing market as theorized, we should see increased development and sales transactions and should confirm the key role of the legal amendments and of cadastral and court systems in the firms' investment activities: their ability to secure a site, obtain financing, and sell developed units.

Therefore this chapter asks: how instrumental have Poland's property rights institutions been in the emergence and operations of Warsaw's private housing market as compared to other institutional factors? Specifically, the following questions are explored:

1. **Social norms and path dependency**: Is legality in Warsaw's housing market a result of appropriate policy reforms or of path dependency and culture? To what extent are the operations of private development firms bound by historical social norms as compared to formal legal ones?
2. **Property rights and institutional arrangements:** How helpful in practice are the formal legal institutions (laws, cadastres, courts) in lowering the risks and costs in development firms' operations? What formal and/or informal institutions do firms engage to lower their transaction costs and make their projects feasible?
3. **Social networks and privilege:** How critical are social networks and the privilege of firms' members, to its operations and investment opportunities? Are firms in the industry characterized more by adversarial competition mediated through legal relations or by cooperation to surmount market risks?

11.1 Literature review and methods

In the limited literature on post-socialist Poland and Warsaw's urban transition (Youngblood 1995; Dowall et al. 1996; Struyk 2000), only a few works examine the operations of the market. However, industry experts have been tracking the trends in the housing market (REAS 2002; Szafarz 2003; PMR Ltd. 2004). The industry's reports suggest that cooperatives played an important part during the early transition period, until the private sector started to grow significantly in 1998 and by 2003 dominated the annual production of housing (Fig. 11.1.). What accounts for the emergence of the private housing industry? Could it be the more detailed version of the *Law on Property Ownership* passed in 1997, which defined the procedures for selling, buying, managing, and compensating for land and housing in Poland? As noted in the introduction, the common assumption is that such legal reforms were instrumental in the transition to a private housing market. However, the conflicting evidence from other transition cases and the debates in the literature prompt a closer look at that relationship and consideration of other possible causal factors.

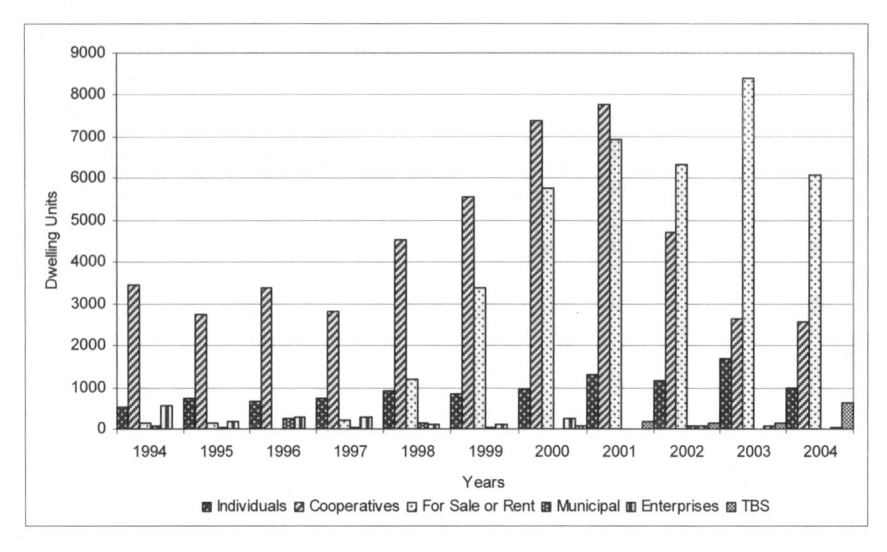

Fig. 11.1. Housing completions in Warsaw, 1994 - 2003

Using a combination of secondary data and interviews with key informants, this chapter focuses on three areas. First, it examines how much of the current system of property rights can be attributed to the legacy of Poland's historical property regimes. Market-oriented systems of property rights require major governmental reforms that many transition countries have not been able to realize. One problem is how to create the elusive "rule of law" so that official reforms transfer into new attitudes and actions by agents (Gillespie 1999). Perhaps it was Poland's pre-transition and pre-communist conditions rather than new laws and policies that predisposed it to the current set of institutions and market outcomes. Second, the chapter investigates how the agents in the housing development industry actually engage the legal system and institutions. Poland may have an impressive institutional framework on paper, but, as in many developing countries, alternative institutions may be more widely used (Doebele 1983; Payne 2001). We check for a disconnection between law and practice. Finally, this chapter explores the importance of the law relative to that of social networks. The literature in law and economics and in economic sociology emphasizes that social networks are important to economic transactions and sometimes substitute for the law (Ellickson 1991). However, such substitutions are usually not sustainable in large urban communities, where social ties reform and social sanctions are not binding (Ellickson 1993).

The research questions addressed in this chapter require a careful examination of the key agents -- their actions, the conceptions behind their actions, and their place in history and social norms. Qualitative research methods are preferred for this type of inquiry because they can analyze processes, the interaction of many factors, organizational issues, and agents' motives and perceptions.. Qualitative methods have another advantage: they offer possibilities for detect important issues that may not have been theorized a priori (Yin 1984).

Firms are the key unit of observation and analysis in this study. Firms have been missing from previous broad-brush comparative studies (Hall and Soskice 2001; Johnson et al. 2002). They have also been overlooked in previous research about for post-socialist transition, tends to focus on reform of the state and state-owned enterprises and how transition policies affect households. Studying firms is particularly apt in the context of transition economies, where the development of a private sector is essential for achieving a market economy.

Table 11.1. Description of firms studied

Firm	Firm type	Housing type	Market segment	# of units built by 2004	Key informant	Years of experience in Polish real estate
1	Foreign investor	Mid and high-rise apartment buildings	Upper income	489	General director, founder	3
2	Polish, private	Mid and high-rise apartment buildings	Upper income	266+	General director	12
3	Polish, private	Rowhouses, mid and high-rise apartment buildings	Middle income	15,120	President, founder	10
4	Polish, former state enterprise	Mid-rise apartment buildings	Mid-upper income	1,260	President	7
5	Polish, private	Single family, custom homes	Middle and upper income	200+	President, founder	14
6	Foreign investor	Single family homes	Upper income	100	Project manager	14

With help from a local real estate consultancy firm (REAS) that has been tracking the industry in annual reports since 1999 and is familiar with the context and players of Warsaw's housing industry, six residential development firms were chosen for the case study. The firms varied in their size, development types, and ownership (Table 11.1.). The types of urban residential development firms are comparable to the types found in other transition economies (Kim 2002). Five additional key informants were interviewed: two property lawyers, a representative from a title insurance company, and two Polish academics. Two commercial real estate consultants with experience in residential development helped to verify the findings.

In developing the case study of each firm, several lines of questioning were pursued with each firm's key investment decision-maker (Appendix A). The interviewees were asked about their background, social group membership, and interactions with other firms and their answers were triangulated with REAS and other key informants in order to explore questions about social networks and privilege. I asked a series of questions about their experience in developing each phase of their projects to identify their greatest challenges and how they overcame them. The objective was to discover whether property rights were an issue to their operations and if so whether the legal institutions were instrumental in their remedy. In addition to the interviews, I visited the firms' offices, reviewed their project designs and documents, and walked their project sites. The fieldwork for this study was conducted in April 2004.

11.2 Findings

11.2.1 Social norms and path dependency

In all the interviews, a great emphasis was placed on creating documents that conveyed the legal nature of transactions. Notarization of documents was repeatedly mentioned as an important part of all real estate transactions.[3] "This is a country obsessed with stamps – it's traditional," explained a Polish ex-patriot real estate consultant who had returned to Poland from the United Kingdom in 1991. However, though documents may be notarized, an Office of Consumer Protection survey of the contracts made by housing developers found that many contracts lack the necessary legal form (Lopinski 2005). Nevertheless, the evidence suggests that a strong norm about the legitimacy of legal institutions – rather than knowledge of the actual law – pervades Warsaw's housing market. In interviews exploring why people focus so much on detailed, notarized contracts, several reasons were cited. During the socialist period people were accustomed to following regulations and producing the necessary paperwork. Even now,

---

[3] Every voivodship (province) in Poland has its own association of legal counsellors, and notaries. Private notaries play a particularly important role in checking whether the contract is legal and bearing witness to it. In order to become a notary, one must attain a master of law degree and pass a credentialing exam. The institution of notaries was a part of public administration both before and during the communist years. In the early 1990s notaries became private entities, but their fees are regulated by the government.

photocopies have to be notarized to have legitimacy. People also want an independent witness to economic transactions.

This norm is not surprising in light of Poland's long legal history of private property rights in the Civil Code tradition, rooted in Roman Law and the Napoleonic Code. The institution of mortgaging property in its modern form was actually invented in the 19th century in Silesia, which is now in Poland. Since 1918, there has been a system of title registration called "mortgage books" that integrates three historical systems – Russian, German and Austrian. At that time banks started to use properties as loan collateral and mortgage bonds as a means to securitize bank portfolios. During the communist regime in Poland, private property conventions were not completely eradicated. Even though after World War II many properties were nationalized and communalized, the majority of small farmers, individual homeowners, and owners of units in multifamily buildings retained their titles. However, properties owned or abandoned by Germans or the German state were nationalized, but the old property registers were preserved. That situation has fuelled restitution disputes, especially in the city centre. Poland, like some other post-socialist countries, also had allowed entrepreneurial activities throughout the communist regime (Serageldin and Nielson 1994). Transactions of farmland and houses in the provinces were performed as before, with proper registration in the "mortgage books" in special courts. With the beginning of the political and economic transition in 1989, many elements of the pre-socialist institutions of property rights could be resumed.

However, Poland did not simply revert to its pre-socialist legal institutions. Multi-lateral development organizations such as the U.S. Agency for International Development (USAID) and the World Bank co-financed foreign advisors to help draft new laws and ordinances such as the Condominium Law and Mortgage Fund Regulations, for more effective connection to modern capital markets. The external intervention in reconstituting of property rights was also prompted by the perceived weaknesses of the Polish judicial system, for example in this Heritage Foundation note about corruption scandals: "The transformation from communism to democracy, reports the Financial Times, did not guarantee that democratic institutions would function properly. Institutions were imported from the west without making sure they could function. According to the U.S. Department of State [m]any investors – foreign and domestic – complain about the slowness of the judicial system...Investors often voice concern about frequent or unexpected issuance of or changes in laws and regulations' " (2005: p.320).

In light of the importance that participants in Warsaw's housing market place on notaries and contracts, but their disconnection with the post-communist versions of property law, certainly social norms and path dependency are significant factors that help to explain Poland's propensity in transition to adopt legal reforms.

11.2.2 Property rights and institutional arrangements

11.2.2.1 Site acquisition

The interviewees unanimously pointed to securing project sites (site acquisition and development approval) as the main risk and difficulty in developing housing projects in Warsaw. Interestingly, those are the same constraints reported in other transitional real estate markets that lacked Poland's substantial legal reforms (Kim 2002). In Warsaw, the problem with site acquisition arose from the inefficient resolution of disputes.

In the early 1990s, developers usually bought land from agricultural owners. The difficulty with agricultural land was its fragmentation by inheritance subdivisions. To assemble a project site, the developers would often have to negotiate with 50-70 landowners. In order to avoid higher prices, firms would usually hire someone locally to buy parcels on their behalf. For the holdouts, they would either pay a lot more or exclude the last parcel, whose owner would end up capitulating in order to sell at all. More recently, some of the developers have bought land from non-agricultural investors who had already assembled parcels over the years. In either case, the land sellers sign preliminary notarized contracts that firms use to secure the first development option and to transfer the property right to the firm. Sellers willing to accept a lower price can receive a lump sum payment; otherwise, contracts specify instalment payments based on the project's completion stages, after an initial 10% down payment.

The down payment functions as a development option pending development approval from local government. The price that a firm is willing to pay is based on estimates of the number of units it will be allowed to build and be able to sell. While awaiting development approval, financing and economic conditions may change so that the firm or buyer will want to re-negotiate the contract. The interviewees stated that they have been writing increasingly complex contracts. For example, in the contracts they stipulate that the amounts of future instalment payments are subject to changes in the number of units approved by authorities, the size of units, and infrastructure costs. Meanwhile, the developers collect their project development capital through pre-sales of units.

As discussed earlier, parties involved in land transactions rely heavily on notarized contracts that have a legal appearance. Yet, in practice many contracts lack specificity, fostering the conditions for disputes that are not easily enforced or resolved by courts. Thought the terms of contracts and prices should be negotiable, firms often use generic "boilerplate" contracts whose vagueness favours the developer. For example, the price of the unit in the contract may be expressed as a price per square meter without specifying the total size of the unit; or may use price indexing for increases in building materials costs, but without details about which indices would be used. Such vagueness allows the developers to later change the prices for buying land or selling the developed units. Not surprisingly, non-professional parties tend to be at a disadvantage in negotiating and implementing contracts.

Those uncertainties lead to many disputes and delays in securing project sites. Given that property rights exist only if they are enforced (Cole and Grossman 2002), the Heritage Foundation (2005) lowered Poland's institutional ranking because of the courts' unpredictable and slow enforcement of property rights. The low rates of decisions and executions of residential disputes display the courts' weaknesses (Table 11.2.). In a sign of that judicial inadequacy, contracts have started identifying arbitration institutions as a substitute for the judicial process. However, the lawyers who were interviewed did not turn to the Warsaw Court of Arbitration in the National Chamber of Commerce because in their experience, decisions were based not on the wording of contracts but on social equity. In commercial real estate projects involving foreign investors and developers, the parties are increasingly choosing foreign arbitration courts. Polish parties who cannot use that option sometimes write clauses to arbitrate, according to international rules of arbitration where each party chooses one arbitrator and they jointly choose a third. Arbitration is not cheaper than going through the courts, but it usually resolves disputes faster. Nonetheless, both courts and arbitration are last resorts; most firms prefer to re-negotiate the contract.

Table 11.2. Residential eviction proceedings in the Mazowieckie Voivodship

Year	Number of proceedings	Number of court decisions	Number of evictions executed
1998	4,122	1,369	392
1999	4,310	1,501	592
2000	4,493	1,398	678

Source: Warsaw Statistical Office, 2001

In summary, the legal institutions have not helped to solve the problem of incomplete contracts for site acquisition. In practice, contracts are enforced not so much by the courts as by re-negotiation and the norms for legality. Altogether, the expensive delays and uncertain costs of this property rights risk have become one of the largest impediments to property development in Warsaw – a finding strikingly similar to those for other transition countries with less developed legal institutions (Woodruff 1999; Kim 2004). However, in Warsaw's case, the combination of apparent formalism and the lack of clarity can serve a useful purpose for the developers. With payment contingent on development approval, the contracts provide a mechanism by which development firms can try to lower their costs by re-negotiation.

11.2.2.2 Development approval

Housing development firms have a stronger negotiating position than the land sellers and customers have, but they have a weaker position in dealing with local governments, which approve projects, and with the environmental and neighbourhood interest groups that can contest their plans. The firm's ability to exercise the right to develop its property has depended on the level of centralization of local government. Over the transition years, the administration of land development approvals has been first decentralized and then recentralized (REAS 2002).

In 1990, constitutional revisions fundamentally re-organized the state. The administrative structure of Poland was realigned from 49 to 16 provinces or voivodships. These were further subdivided into self-governing gminas or boroughs as the important local government unit (Regulski 2003). Warsaw's central gmina was further subdivided into seven districts. As part of the decentralization, in the mid 1990s all development authority was transferred to the gminas, which had their own councils, while some aspects of building permits and planning approvals were still controlled by other local government agencies. The administrative reform helped to cut the transaction costs for firms by reducing the number of special units involved in development projects. Firms could attain approval for land development projects with a preliminary opinion from the gmina and start the project within a couple of months of submitting the application. The interviews suggest that the decentralization of development approval authority contributed significantly to the rapid take-off of the housing market in Warsaw in the late 1990s. In addition to land costs, the firms interviewed related their project location decisions to whether a gmina had a pro-development attitude and expeditious handing of applications. That is shown by the variation in the number of building permits issued by the various gmina (Fig. 11.2.).

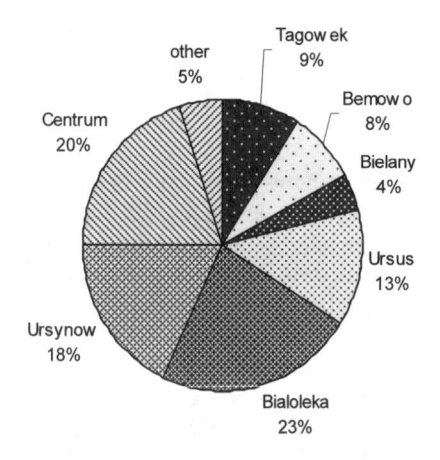

Fig. 11.2. Warsaw building permits by gmina, 2002

Interestingly, the independence exercised by the gminas was the main reason that the procedure was recentralized. The autonomous gminas were allowing development even if it violated the city's master plan, also making it difficult to coordinate larger-scale transportation and infrastructure projects. With their greater fiscal autonomy, some gminas diverted the funding for public services to projects such as new council offices. Gminas also sold public land for development through public auctions. Most of the firms interviewed avoided buying land at public auctions because the considerable investment needed to prepare a bid was likely to be subject to a corrupt process with predetermined winners. In addition, the government agencies would often have an unwritten agenda of public works that they wanted to exact from the developers. Only firms with established relationships with a government agency or borough could bid successfully. For example, one firm entered an auction because its staff had relatives and friends who worked at the gmina and told them what was needed for a competitive bid. Another firm used its status as the private arm of a state agency to receive state-owned land.

By a law enacted in 2002, Warsaw's eleven gminas were dissolved. Warsaw became a city with powiat or county rights like other major Polish cities and was sub-divided into 18 dzielnice or districts (REAS 2002). From December 2003, development authority was recentralized to Warsaw city, which adopted a new process: when a development firm's proposal complies with the master plan, it should receive prompt approval and building permits. However, only about 14% of the greater Warsaw area had master plans at that time. For the remaining 86% without plans, the developers have to apply in a two-step procedure. First they provide a detailed description of the proposed project, including a preliminary architectural concept. To be approved, the proposed sites must have access to existing public roads and be adjacent to developed parcels. A Decision on Development Conditions or "Decyzya o warunkach zabudowy" is made case by case, by Warsaw's Chief City Architect. The mayor re-created this position in 2003 as part of his anti-corruption effort.

The recentralization of development authority has slowed down development approval and made it less predictable. Projects have ground to a halt because recentralization complicated the pre-sale contracting method of investment financing and discouraged landowners from sales of property depending on the city's approval and permit. To deal with the problem, Deputy Prime Minister Jerzy Hausner appointed a working group of developers to recommend desired policy changes that would help the industry.

The period that is most informative for this study is the second half of the 1990s, when the private supply of housing increased substantially. Before the recent change in procedures, having a good working relationship with the local gmina was crucial for development approval. It was the local authority who could make or break a project, through bureaucratic processing and by mediating contests from other interest groups. The local authority set the conditions and required changes for project approval. Once a gmina supported a project, it would also help protect the project from rivals. It is not surprising, then, that firms' decisions on project location were influenced by both the market and the orientation and efficacy of the gminas. Property rights risks were reduced not so much through the law as through cooperation with bureaucrats, and were enforced by their planning authority.

11.2.2.3 The importance of the title registry in Warsaw's housing market

Unlike the courts and legal contracts, the property cadastre institution, which records ownership, has significantly influenced both the growth of the industry and the day-to-day operations of firms. Perhaps the greatest impact that property titling has had on Warsaw's housing market has been through the mortgage market. Table 11.3. shows the rapid expansion of the banks' residential mortgage portfolio since the mid-1990s. The banks require registered titles in order to make loans, and bank mortgages are efficiently registered in district courts. Most of the customers of the firms interviewed in this study use bank mortgages. In fact, the sales offices of the more successful developers provide information about mortgage financing products along with the information on their housing units for sale.

Table 11.3. The Polish residential mortgage portfolio, 1995-2001

Year	Annual increase (PLN millions)	Annual Change percentage	Cumulative portfolio (PLN millions)
1995	244.4	-	244.4
1996	492.4	101	736.8
1997	777.6	58	1514.4
1998	1395.1	79	2909.5
1999	2104.8	51	5013.8
2000	4500.0	114	9513.8
2001	4600.0	48	13800.0

Source: Dr. Jacek Laszek, NBP in REAS 2002

Once again, however, for mortgages the major risks are borne by the consumers. Borrowers obtain mortgages for un-built units that the developers have pre-sold to them in order to finance the housing project. Yet, the title can be obtained only for a completed unit, which on average takes about two years. If for some reason the developers do not deliver the unit, the buyer still owes the mortgage but cannot deliver the collateral. The banks can then go after the borrower's personal assets. In theory the buyer could take the developers to court but a buyer's position is often weak compared to the creditor's.[4]

Partly that is so because, although banks and firms understand the importance of legal title, it is not always true of their customers. Firms reported in the

---

[4] To deal with this risk, two institutions are emerging: gap insurance during the construction period and escrow accounts to protect the funds.

interviews that during pre-sales most of their customers do not want notarized contracts even if they have the option, because they do not want to pay the fees; instead, they rely on the firm's reputation. In fact, developers sometimes have difficulty in getting clients to pay the last $US 1,000 for the final transfer of their title. According to one lawyer, "They don't want to pay and don't seem to understand that they legally don't own it otherwise." In his opinion, this anomaly also serves the developers' interests since buyers end up in a weaker bargaining position if the sales price is re-negotiated.

Other potential site acquisition risks such as restitution claims and multiple sales of the same plot are also helped by Poland's title registry system. Restitution claims have frozen some development projects in Warsaw as in many transition countries.[5] But, those were not cited as a major risk for residential development firms. The firms can make calculated risks by researching the old mortgage books, even though they had not been maintained perfectly during the socialist regime. This, in fact, is what Warsaw's only title insurance company does. The company's founder interviewed lawyers for months and found that the title risks were manageable. He also learned that some commercial firms, especially foreign firms and those seeking development financing from banks, would be willing to pay for insurance against the risk. Such supplementary insurance policies are provided only for commercial projects, because the transaction costs of the due diligence for residential projects are not worth it. In addition, commercial real estate projects have larger budgets and greater scale, and attract more attention; consequently, they face more restitution claims than residential projects do. The title insurance company found that residential developers are willing to carry the risk themselves, which also shows that it is not debilitating.

In Warsaw in particular, the problem of missing cadastral records is not as large as in the rest of Poland, according to one interviewed lawyer. One can look at the pre-World-War II records and check for gaps in ownership. In some cases firms have cleared up titles by brokering negotiations between the parties from previous transactions in order to formally discharge their property rights in the cadastres. In general, though, the main strategy for coping with the risks of restitution and other title disputes has been to avoid sites that have exchanged hands several times. One implication of that strategy is for residential projects to locate more in Warsaw's outer areas where one can obtain private land held by the primary owners. That trend, in addition to the lower costs of land and easier changes in zoning in the outer urban areas, has contributed to the sprawling land use patterns in the periphery of Warsaw.

A final small but manageable risk is delay in processing of titles. Once a sales contract for land is signed, it normally takes about two months for the new owner to be recorded. During the interim an unscrupulous owner could sell to another

---

[5] Large landholdings within the 1945 boundary of Warsaw that were nationalized and given to public entities are more susceptible to restitution claims. In 2004, there were approximately 1700 restitution claims in Warsaw, constituting about one-third of its total land area.

buyer. Reforms continue to try to shorten the interim and the title insurance company and some banks offer temporary insurance for that specific period. For most buyers, however, the norms about notarization, the regulations, and Warsaw's functional bureaucracy are generally sufficient to manage this property rights risk.

According to regulations, the priority of recording is based on the time of application, down to the minute. A key task, then, is to file the application for the transfer of title to a new owner before any other such applications can be made. A good lawyer will not tarry in filing the papers after a sale. One lawyer recounted that he has a junior colleague on the phone in the registry's office at the time the sales contract is signed in order to make sure that no other applications have been filed in the meantime. An interviewee from a development firm recalled an instance of stopping the sales contract at the last minute because the staff had discovered that another application had been filed a few days earlier. Nevertheless, such situations are perceived as unusual and manageable. In conclusion, although the current efforts to expedite title registration will be helpful, more efficient processing will not significantly change the rate of investment and transactions. Firms are already able to use Warsaw's fairly well developed and functioning title registries to manage some property rights risks and have benefited from their role in increasing housing demand through mortgage lending.

11.2.3 Social networks and privilege

The interviewees were unanimous in their view that little social networking goes on amongst real estate developers in Warsaw. Apparently they neither contact each other for formal business purposes nor socialize informally. The main reason suggested is the fierce competition among them. No one could recall an example of cooperating for mutual gain. An expatriate real estate consultant who has been working in Poland since 1991 reflected that Poland's business culture is different from those he has worked with in the U.S., U.K. or Germany. There, even competing parties can see how a deal might offer gains to both sides, but Poles tend to think only in terms of losers and winners. "They are happy to start negotiating, but it is hard to come to a decision because there is a sense that you might be one-upped." He attributes the lack of trust to the environment fostered during the socialist regime.

Another possible reason for this lack of networking is the diverse backgrounds of the firms established at different points in the industry's evolution. During the early 1990s, real estate developers were mostly foreigners providing housing for their corporate clients. The foreign firms hired local staff who could better navigate the Polish bureaucracy, and trained them in the business. As transition progressed, the local staff branched out and started their own firms. Later on, returning Polish expatriates who had gained experience overseas in the real estate business became a major presence in the new domestic firms.

In summary, the lack of social networking and trust among the development firms discourage the use of alternatives to legal business relations. The Polish Homebuilders Association is an organization with a mission to enable social networking, influence public administration, and provide information and education. It has 700-1,000 members (individuals and firms), with about 150 in Warsaw. So far, however, the influence of this association on the industry and on the broader business environment is unclear.

Conclusion

Warsaw's housing market has grown explosively in the last seven years. The private sector now produces the majority of new housing. This study finds that the reforms of legal property rights played an important but limited role in the establishment of private real estate firms and in their investment levels. Warsaw had the advantages of a historical title registry system that survived the communist regime, and a high level of private homeownership in the urban periphery throughout the socialist period that allowed land to come quickly to market. The reliability of the registry and its long history of mortgage financing facilitated the rapid development of the housing mortgage industry, which fuelled housing demand and the supply response to it by new development firms. Therefore, the reform of legal property rights reforms allowed Poland to propel its particular pre-transition condition into a modern housing market.

Poland's long legal tradition also helps to account for the contemporary social norms about the legitimacy and importance of legal institutions. Those norms have a significant function in Warsaw's housing market. In many instances, the housing development firms and customers use the vestiges of legal paperwork, but without the correct form and also aware of the practical unavailability of enforcement institutions. Yet, they continue such practices because the norms give them some confidence about the bounds set around the economic actions that could be taken by other parties. The firms have been able to reduce their investment risks and to profit from the perceived legitimacy of legal formalism – sometimes to the peril of consumer protections.

Despite the property rights reforms and strong social norms, the development firms stated unequivocally that securing sites for development is their greatest challenge. Because of the institutional weaknesses in enforcing contracts, they rely on the support and authority of sub-city government bodies to surmount the risks. Until the recent re-centralization of development authority, nurturing cooperative working relationships with the gminas had been key to the firms' success. Interestingly, this same strategy is used by firms in other countries with weak legal institutions (Kim 2004) However, unlike those in other transition countries, the firms in Warsaw have not developed collaborative relationships or informal social networks with other firms in order to share information or risks for mutual gain.

The findings of this study suggest that a shift in the focus of property rights reform might more effectively address the barriers in evolving housing markets. The predominant focus is on legal institutions, but an alternative would be to consider the context of administrative planning and urban development procedures. The key bottleneck for housing developers lies in their relationship with local governments for site acquisition and development approval. Making those processes more predictable and efficient would help the developers. However, the local governments also should structure efficient processes that will protect consumers and enable future public goods projects. The importance of this challenge has been clearly demonstrated in the case of Warsaw, where administrative decentralization is being pursued concurrently with market-oriented reforms.

References

Cole DH, Grossman PZ (2002) The meaning of property rights: law versus economics? Land Economics 78:317-330

Collier D, Collier R (1991) Shaping the political arena. Princeton University Press, Princeton, NJ

de Soto H (2000) The mystery of capital. Basic Books, New York, NY

Demsetz H (1967) Toward a theory of property rights. American Economic Review 57:347-359

Doebele WA (1983) Concepts of urban land tenure. In: Dunkerley HB (ed) Urban land policy: Issues and opportunities. World Bank, Washington DC, pp 63-107

Dowall D, Sadowy M, Zalewski A (1996) The Warsaw economy in transition. Avebury, Brookfield, VT

Ellickson R (1991) Order without law: How neighbors settle disputes. Harvard University Press, Cambridge, MA

Ellickson R (1993) Property in land. Yale Law Journal 102:1315-1400

Fforde A, de Vylder S (1996) From plan to market: The economic transition in Vietnam. Westview Press, Boulder, CO

Gainsborough M (2002) Understanding communist transition: Property rights in Ho Chi Minh City in the late 1990s. Post-Communist Economies 14:227-243

Gillespie J (1999) Law and development in the market place: An east asian perspective. In: Jayasuriya K (ed) Law, capitalism, and power in Asia. Routledge, New York, pp 118-150

Granovetter M (1985) Economic action and social structure: The problem of embeddedness. The American Journal of Sociology 91:481-510

Granovetter M (2002) A theoretical agenda for economic sociology. In: Guillen MF, Randall C, England P, and Meyer M (eds) The new economic sociology: Developments in an emerging field. Russell Sage Foundation, New York, pp 35-60

Hall PA, Soskice D (2001) Varieties of capitalism. Oxford University Press, New York

Hall PA, Taylor RCR (1996) Political science and the three new institutionalisms. Max-Planck-Institut fur Gesellschaftsforschung, Scientific Advisory Board Discussion Paper 96/6, Cologne, Germany

Hart O (1995) Firms, contracts, and financial structure. Oxford University Press, Oxford

Heritage Foundation (2005) Index of economic freedom. Heritage Foundation and the Wall Street Journal, Washington, DC

International Monetary Fund (IMF) (2000) IMF world economic outlook: Focus on transition economies. International Monetary Fund, Washington DC

Johnson S, McMillan J, Woodruff C (2002) Property rights and finance. American Economic Review 92:1335-1356

Kim AM (2002) Making a market: the institutions supporting Ho Chi Minh City's urban land development market. Ph.D. dissertation, University of California Berkeley, Berkeley

Kim AM (2004) A market without the 'right' property rights: Ho Chi Minh City, Vietnam's newly-emerged private real estate market. Economics of Transition 12:275-305

Lopinski R (2005) The Legal protection of dwellings under construction: Purchasers in Poland and in the chosen EU countries. Zeszyt Hipoteczny 19: 48-62

Payne G (2001) Urban land tenure policy options: Titles of rights? Habitat International 25:415-429

Pipes R (1996) Human nature and the fall of communism. Academy of Arts and Sciences Bulletin 54:38-52

PMR Ltd. (2004) Residential construction in January 2004. Polish Construction Review 36:5

REAS Sp. z o.o. (2002) Warsaw residential market report 2002/2003. REAS, Warsaw

Regulski J (2003) Local government reform in Poland: An insider's story. Open Society Institute, Budapest

Serageldin M, Nielson D (1994) Urban regeneration and housing in a transitional economy: Lublin, Poland. Monograph, Graduate School of Design, Harvard University, Cambridge

Struyk R (2000) Homeownership and housing finance policy in the former Soviet Bloc: costly populism. Urban Institute, Washington DC

Szafarz P (2003) Draft of the new zoning law: act for equals and more equals. Eurobuild Poland 58:34-35

Tsenkova S (2000) Housing in transition and transition in housing: The experience of Central and Eastern Europe. Kapital Reclama, Sofia

United Nations Economic Commission for Europe (UNECE) (1997) Human settlements trends in Central and Eastern Europe. United Nations: United Nations Economic Commission for Europe, Geneva

Williamson O (1996) Mechanisms of governance. Oxford University Press, Oxford

Woodruff C (1999) Dispute prevention without courts in Vietnam. Journal of Law, Economics, and Organization 15:637-658

World Bank (1996) Legal institutions and the role of law. In: World development report. Oxford University Press, Oxford, pp 87-97

Yin RK (1984) Case study research: Design and methods. Sage Publications, Beverly Hills, CA

Youngblood WR (1995). Poland's struggle for a restitution policy in the 1990s. Emory International Law Review 9(2)

Appendix A: Interview protocol

Field procedures: Selection of firms for case study
1) Interviews and meetings with REAS to select firms to be interviewed and identifying key decision-maker in the firm to interview.
2) Triangulation of group selection through other key informant interviews.

Case study questions
Background and social position of interviewee:
How long have you been working in real estate? With this firm? What did you do before this? How did you get involved in real estate?
Where in Poland are you from? Where were you educated?
Triangulate responses with information from key informants.

Factual information about the firm
How long has this firm been in existence? Explain its history of key players in forming the firm? What is the organizational structure of the firm?

Project information
How many projects has your firm completed? How many units? Size of land parcel? Location? Housing type and target market?
What in your experience is the most challenging aspect of developing residential projects?

Property Rights issues: If they bring up property rights issues, I follow up with the following questions:
How do you identify the current landowner of a potential site?
How do you negotiate the price and conduct the transfer?
Any strategies to minimize these risks?
Do you use lawyers or other professionals?
How do you find out which parcels will be approved?
Why do you choose one location in a city over others?
Are there certain boroughs you like to work with more than others? If so, why?
How has the gmina impacted a project?
Who in the firm has contact with the local government?
How long does the development approval process take?
What are the risks or problems you have experienced?
What are strategies you pursue to lower this risk? Can anyone help them?

Social networking
Has your firm engaged in a joint project with another development firm?
Do you meet or socialize with people from other firms?
Do you participate in the homebuilder's association and other professional groups?
Do you know people from firm X?

12 The retail revolution in post-socialist Central Europe and its lessons

Yaakov Garb with Tomasz Dybicz

Introduction

Decentralization of retail activities and facilities has been a major trend in developed countries for the past several decades. Now that trend is occurring, often in accelerated form, in transitional and developing countries. The rapid spread of new, large and typically peripheral shopping centres in post-socialist Central and Eastern Europe (CEE) is a striking example of this "retail revolution." Though "big box" retailing was entirely absent before the political transition of the early 1990s, Warsaw, Prague, and Budapest are now close to saturated with such commercial development. It is spreading as well into smaller towns (fewer than 100,000 or even 50,000 inhabitants) in those countries, and into the large cities of the countries, among them Bulgaria, Croatia, Russia and Lithuania. For urban life in those places, the spatial, economic, and behavioural consequences of the retail revolution have been profound. This essay surveys the retail decentralization and the reasons for its rapid establishment in Central Europe, its effects (especially on travel patterns), and the lessons that can be drawn for improving retail policies in post-socialist cities and internationally.

The essay has several overlapping purposes. One is to provide an empirically informed sketch of the effects, often noted, of retail deconcentration on travel behaviour. Although it is a common assumption that the consequences of peripheral retail are longer trips and more car-borne shopping, systematic evidence for that is lacking. The speed and recent date of Central European retail decentralization offer a rare opportunity to make before-and-after comparisons that can illuminate those consequences.

Another goal is to show the ways in which central themes of this volume—transition, diversity, and competition—characterize the retail sphere. We describe a remarkably rapid shift, in which hypermarkets have approached half of the retail market share within one decade. This trend is complemented, however, by the ongoing establishment of new retail centres still occurring in city centres and around smaller towns, which has drawn back some customers who had travelled to the peripheries of their own cities, or even for hundreds of kilometres to hypermarkets at the periphery of capital cities, during the first wave of retail deconcentration when these were the only form of modern retail available. We note tremendous diversity among cities, among the patronage patterns at individual shopping centres, and among the retail habits of geographically and socio-economically distinct populations. Underlying the post-socialist retail revolution is a set of far-reaching, competitive dynamics. Large western European retail chains, for example, having reached growth limits and encountered regulation barriers in their home countries, have surged into Central and Eastern Europe to maintain growth, fighting one another for key sites and market share in this newly opened terrain. Peripheral facilities around the major cities have started to compete not only with retail in the traditional city centres but with facilities in a large radius of surrounding towns and villages, as well.

Next, moving beyond description, we present some of the lessons that planners and decision-makers in CEE and other countries can learn from the dynamism and diversity of Central European retail. Other transitional economies, for example, can take note of the major structural impact that the wave of largely unregulated retail development has had on Central European post-socialist cities. Developed countries can draw lessons from the fact that significant and unique niches of sustainable retail patterns remain in CEE cities even after this major transformation.

12.1 The flash malling of post-socialist Central Europe

After the Second World War, the retail sectors in countries under Soviet influence were systematically dismantled and reconstructed according to Marxist-Leninist ideologies and economic priorities (Michalak 2001; Smith 2003). Like other aspects of the economy, the retail sector became state-owned and controlled in most aspects: location, price, purchasing and stock, staffing (Kulke 1997; Michalak 2001). By the end of the 1980s, for example, 80% of stores, accounting for over 95% of turnover, were state owned (Michalak 2001). Almost all higher-order retail was located in the centres of the main CEE cities, which were compact and well served by public transport —subway, tram, and bus.[1] Other places—smaller towns, villages, and even the massive housing estates established in peripheral ("suburban") locations around the main cities—had only very basic shops. The provision of goods and food articles at factories, through "grey" retailing, and through self-help production supplemented the formal retail market, which was notorious for its limited quality and range.

The rapid changes in the retail sector in post-socialist Central and Eastern Europe are well recognized and can arguably be considered a symbolic hallmark of the transition. After a few transitional years of privatization, deconcentration of retail ownership, and some domestic-capital initiatives, from the late 1990s onward there was rapid consolidation and the establishment of multinational, large-format, modern retail facilities.[2] These were usually occupied peripheral locations on major highways—radials and/or ring roads. Within a decade, retail in modern

---

[1] For an overview of the impact of socialism on urban spatial structures, see Bertaud in this volume.

[2] The authors are not aware of any good overview of the spatial organization of retail in Central and Central Europe during the socialist period, except for Kulke's (1997) excellent presentation of the East German situation.

formats, foreign ownership, and ex-urban locations jumped from being negligible to being the majority.[3]

While the growth of large-format, peripheral retail was similarly rapid in many countries, several factors made for an exceptionally rapid malling of post-socialist Central and Eastern Europe:

- The planning system after the departure from socialism was allergic to central planning in any form, including the regulation of retail location. In addition, changes in territorial government and administration removed the regional level of governance that had existed between the municipal and the national levels, and that might have been the natural locus of such planning and regulation.[4]
- Various aspects of post-socialist, urban real estate as well as planning procedures made it nearly impossible to site large modern retail facilities in town centres or sub-centres. For example, the ownership of re-privatized properties was unclear; the use of large, vacant or underused land was blocked for various reasons; and the approval of changes in zoning status to allow retail was lengthy and uncertain (Jackson and Garb 2002; Garb and Jackson forthcoming). In contrast to those ordeals, large retail facilities were welcome on greenfield sites in many small communities around large cities, which competed for the anticipated jobs, and where the lure of profitable land sales could sway local councils and mayors.
- The massive capitalization of international retailers in contrast to the incomes of government and municipal officials meant that bribery was frequent and could override residual attempts to regulate land use.
- Modern retail facilities were symbolic of the new freedoms, since a key characteristic of socialist economies had been the limited range and amount of commodities and the great difficulties in obtaining even those.[5] Retail freedoms were thus unstoppable, symbolically and politically.
- The transitions in Central and Eastern Europe in the early 1990s coincided with difficulties for large Western European retailers, in their home markets, where they were feeling the pinch of increased retail competition, saturation, and zoning regulation that hindered the establishment of new hypermarket facilities.
- The geographic proximity of Western European retailers to Central and Eastern Europe made for logistic convenience in supplying the stores, while cultural similarities with Western Europe made for a more fluent working relationship between the stores and Western European headquarters. At the same time, the prospect of the CEE countries joining NATO and then the European Union

---

[3] These dynamics have been described in Dries et al. (2004), local and business periodicals, and real estate and development trade literature in these countries. They are also reflected in the data available from various consultancies, such as Cushman & Wakefield Healy & Baker, INCOMA, CEERetail, PMR, Colliers International, and A. C. Nielson.

[4] For a discussion on some of these features in the Czech Republic's case see Maier (1998).

[5] For an ethnographic account of the condition of shopping under socialism in Hungary and reflections on the transition see Smith (2003). See also Stenning's (2005) account of Nova Huta, Poland.

guaranteed the rise in purchasing power and political stability required by Western investors.

Retail deconcentration in Central and Eastern Europe differs from the familiar trend in developed countries, especially in Western Europe and North America, in several ways:

- Decentralization occurred massively and rapidly over a single decade. In 1995, there were literally a handful of hypermarkets in CEE countries; today there are over 500.
- Decentralization occurred in towns and cities that were traditionally compact and well served by public transport.
- Retail usually led urban decentralization, proceeding rather than following residential and job sprawl. Thus, in the early years of decentralization, out-of-town hypermarkets did not serve shoppers from adjacent suburbs (which barely existed), but rather urban shoppers travelling outward and long-distance shoppers from surrounding villages and cities.
- While the format and offerings of the new retail facilities were virtually identical to those of their Western European counterparts, the purchasing power of their customers was only a fraction of that of Western Europeans. During the first decade of CEE retail decentralization, companies were willing to operate in the red and absorb losses in the scramble for initial market share and key retail locations.
- CEE retail is overwhelmingly foreign-owned. A list of the top ten retailers in most CEE countries will not show any domestically owned shops. In the Czech Republic, for example, the top ten companies, which in 2004 accounted for aggregate sales revenue of over 7 billion Euro,[6] are all Western European retail chains. The global annual revenues of several of these chains approach or exceed the GDPs of their host countries.[7]

12.2 The travel consequences of the 'big box' retail revolution

In Western Europe, the reworking of urban geographies by the movement from smaller retail outlets within cities to large, car-accessible sites on cheaper land at city margins occurred several decades earlier than it did in Central and Eastern Europe, and at a slower pace. In the UK, for example, it began in the 1970s and continued in new forms (such as the grouping into retail parks of several large

---

[6] INCOMA Research, as reported in the CEERetail news alert on January 25, 2005.

[7] The annual revenues of Carrefour of $52 billion during the formative years of Central European retail were less than Poland's GDP ($154.1 billion), but almost equal to the Czech Republic's GDP ($56.4 billion), and higher than Hungary's (48.4 billion), Romania's ($33.7 billion), and the Slovak Republic's GDP ($19.3 billion). Figures are for 2000, extracted from Chung et al. (2001), pp. 68-71.

stores offering both food and non-food items) through the 1980s and onwards. Experience with those changes began to concern planning authorities in the mid-1980s and more so through the mid-1990s, and consequently gave rise to various kinds of retail regulation (Garb and Lichfield 2005). Planning concerns cantered on the threat of reduced economic (and thus cultural and social) activity in the urban core, the conversion of greenfield (usually agricultural) land at the city edge, the discrimination against less mobile populations unable to easily reach the new facilities, and the rise in travel as people made longer and more car-borne trips for retail purposes. This section examines the latter effects in some detail, as a window into the suite of behavioural changes entailed by the retail revolution in post-socialist Central Europe, and also as an empirical contribution to the study of retail travel.

This section presents selected findings from three sources of evidence:

- A national-level household survey in the Czech Republic
- A questionnaire survey of 4 hypermarkets in Prague
- Traffic counts and questionnaire surveys at 5 Warsaw hypermarkets.

The research findings illustrate the characteristics of shopping trips (especially in terms of frequency, travel distance, and travel mode); the complex interrelationships between those characteristics and socioeconomic and other factors; the nature of the transition from a pre-hypermarket to a hypermarket retail landscape; and the diversity of shopping patterns in different cities, different malls, and among subpopulations. Overall, the findings show that while Central European retail travel is rapidly coming to approximate the expected features of retail travel in the U.S. and Western Europe, the compact post-socialist cities still maintain important opportunities for transit- and pedestrian-based shopping.

12.2.1 National-level household survey in the Czech Republic

The graphs in Fig. 12.1. show the use of cars for grocery shopping and its distribution by gender, age, education, income, size of a town, and store type. The data were derived from a household survey conducted throughout the Czech Republic by INCOMA Research in November 2001.[8] Approximately 2000 people (1669, or 83.5%, of them women) were surveyed, in households in five municipal-size classes representative of the Czech population, and with four main shopping formats well represented (at least 350 people designated each one as their "main shopping facility").

As expected, the results point to more car dependence among those who shop at hypermarkets, working-age people, those with higher income and education, and – somewhat surprisingly – of those living in small or very small towns. At the same time, those who use smaller shops do so using relatively little car travel. Strikingly, the number of people reporting that they do not need a car to shop rises with

---

[8] INCOMA Research is a commercial retail consultancy in Prague, which conducts shopper and household surveys.

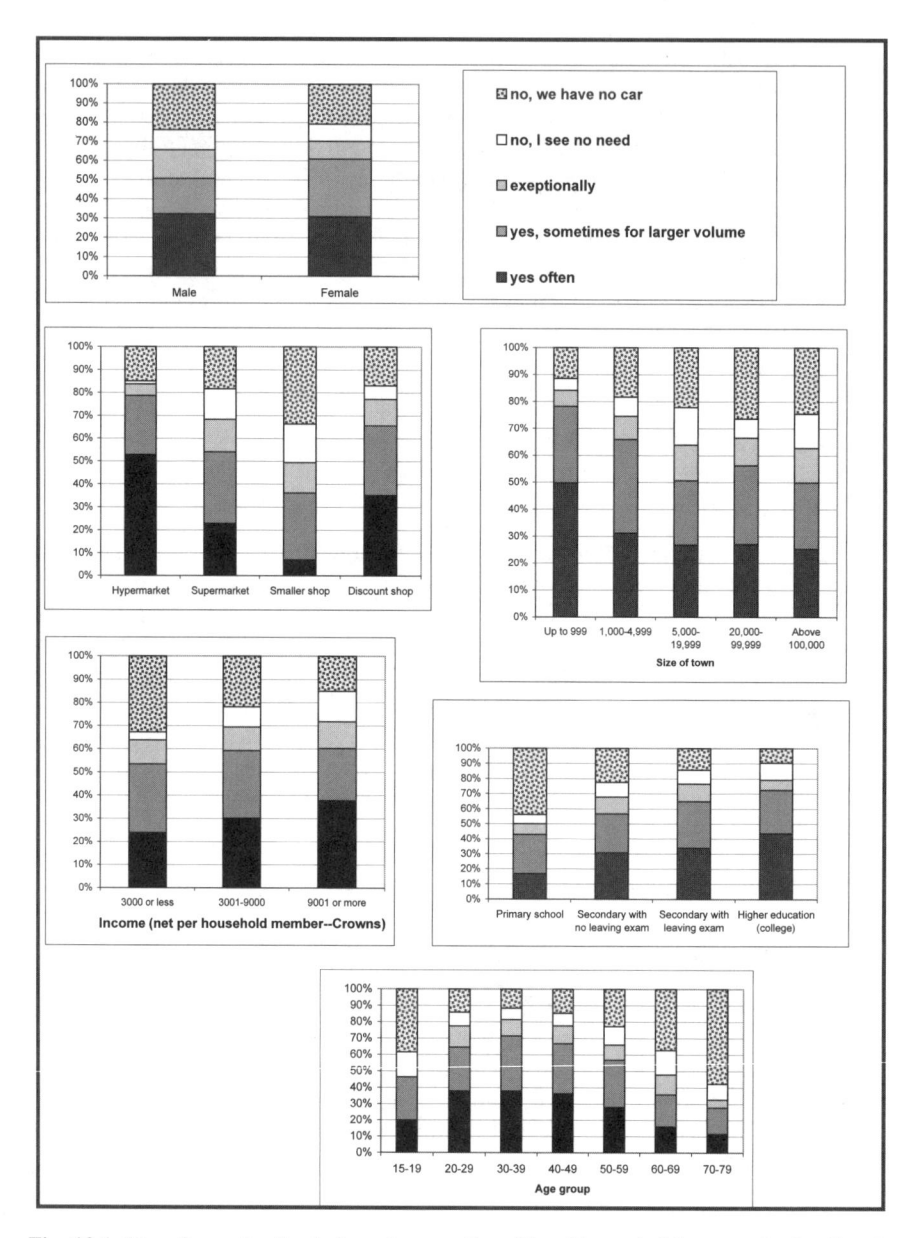

Fig. 12.1. Use of cars for food shopping - national level household survey in the Czech Republic
Source: Derived from data gathered by INCOMA Research, 2001
Note:
Responses to the survey question: "Do you use a car to shop for food?"

income. Towns above 5,000 inhabitants are less car-dependent, and the responses to other questions, not presented in Figure 12.1, show that people in these towns, and especially in towns above 100,000 inhabitants, place more importance on and are more satisfied with transit access to their shopping outlet. Those who shop in small shops care less about the quality of transit access to their shop than do those in other shopping formats, probably because they reach their shops on foot. Thus at the national level, on aggregate we see both the car dependence of hypermarkets, and the survival of non-car-dependent shopping at small retail outlets and in the larger cities. These national findings become clearer when examined through the perspective of the surveys of mall shoppers conducted in Prague and Warsaw, which are described below.

12.2.2 Survey of four hypermarkets in Prague

This survey was conducted by The Institute for Transportation and Development Policy (ITDP) in the fall of 2001. Questionnaires were administered at 4 different mall locations in and around Prague (Fig. 12.2.) and had a total of 1649 respondents. The malls surveyed included two typical peripheral malls, one (Zlicin) just inside and the other (Prohinice) just outside the city limits; and two "infill" malls located closer to the city centre and surrounded by areas with higher residential densities. It is important to note that even the "decentralized," peripheral malls in Prague and Warsaw (discussed below) are quite close to those cities in North American terms: the farthest is 14 km (under 9 miles) from the town centre.

These questionnaires gathered information about respondent's demographics, his or her shopping trip (e.g., pre- and post-mall activity and location, travel time, and purpose), their shopping behaviour at the mall (e.g., frequency, duration, and expenditure), and, most importantly, the characteristics of the shopping trips they had made for the same purpose prior to the existence of the mall where the survey was conducted. An extensive analysis of these findings is provided in Garb (forthcoming). Fig. 12.3. summarizes the factors (e.g., travel mode, distance and duration, mall location, shopping duration and expenditure, current and prior shopping frequency, income, age, gender, car availability, number of people in the car) that were found to influence key trip parameters – distance of travel, modal distribution and frequency. The relevance of each factor is indicated by the extent to which selected subpopulations of shoppers differed on the given trip parameter. The directions of most of the listed effects, if not their magnitudes, could be anticipated as typical of retail travel in Western Europe and the U.S., albeit with average distances and modal splits that would be the envy of U.S. planners in particular. For example, the average round-trip length for all surveyed mall trips originating or ending within the Prague agglomeration was 21 kilometres, with 68% of arrivals by private vehicle, 28% by transit, and 4% pedestrian. This modal split is almost identical to the modal split reported from a 2003 national household survey of shopping centre travel by INCOMA. Further analysis showed, for example, that trips were longer for the car and subway trips and shorter for the other modes, and that longer trips were made by people of working age, were less

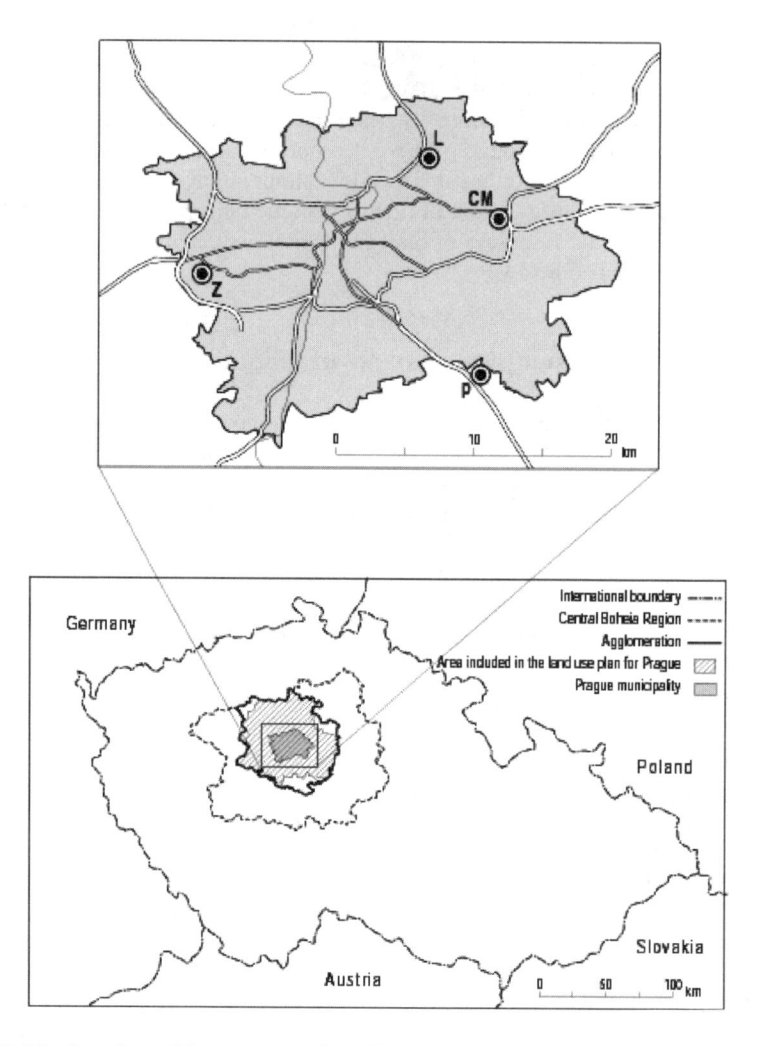

Fig. 12.2. The location of four surveyed malls within the Prague municipal boundaries.
Note: Z=Zlicin; P=Prohinice; CM= Cerny Most, L=Letnany

12 The retail revolution in post-socialist Central Europe and its lessons   239

Trip parameter	Influencing factors and indicative examples (all significant at the 0.0001 level)
Distance (average round trip: **21.4 km**)	• **Travel mode** (car trips average **20** km longer than pedestrian ones) • **Current shopping frequency** (trips done biweekly or less average **12** km more than trips done weekly or more) • **Duration** of mall visit (stays of over 2 hours average **10** km longer than stays under one hour) • **Location** of the mall (Zlicin trips average **9** km longer than Letnany ones) • **Prior frequency** of shopping (trips done biweekly or less average **7** km more than trips done weekly or more) • **Grocery** vs. other trip purpose (non-grocery trips average **6** km longer than grocery trips) • **Purchase amount** (visits with expenditure over 1000 crowns average **5** km longer than those of under 1000 crowns) • **Day of week** (weekend or weekday) (Weekend trips average **4** km longer than weekday ones)
Modal distribution (overall percent coming by car: **68%**)	• **Availability of car** (**17%** of those in carless households come by car versus **75%** of those having one car in household) • **Mall expenditure** (**39%** of the group spending under 500 crown, come by car versus **88%** of the group spending over 1000 crowns) • **Reported income** (**89%** of those reporting above average income come by car, versus **65%** of the others) • **Distance** of trip (**39%** of those traveling under 6.5 kilometers round trip come by car, versus **72%** of those traveling over 6.5 km) • **Mall location** (**57%** of shoppers at Letnany come by car versus **90%** of those at Prohinice) • **Age** (**46-49%** of those over 62 or under 21 come by car versus **83%** of those in the 29-42 age bracket) • **Prior shopping mode** (**32%** of those who used to shop by public transport prior to the mall's existence now shop by car versus **92%** of those who used to shop by car) • **Gender** (**60%** of women versus **77%** of men come by car)
Frequency (average monthly frequency: **3.6**)	• **Number of passengers** in the car (those without a passenger come **3.1** times more a month than those with one or more passengers) • **Distance** (those traveling under 11 km come **2.0** times a month more than those traveling over 11 km) • **Prior frequency** of shopping (those who used to shop weekly or more now average **1.8** times more a month than those that used to shop biweekly or less) • **Travel time** to mall (those traveling 15 minutes or under come **1.6** times a month more than those traveling 30-45 minutes) • **Mall location** (Shoppers at Cerny Most come **1.1** times a month more than those at Zlicin) • **Is public transport available** (those who declare that public transport is available for their trip come an additional **1.0** time a month more than those who don't) • **Duration** of mall stay (those who spend under an hour come an additional **0.8** times a month compared to those spending between one and two hours) • **Used to shop locally** (those who used to shop locally now shop an additional **0.6** times a month compared to non-local shoppers)

Fig. 12.3. Factors influencing key trip parameters (after Garb, 2004)
Note: Income, mall expenditure, shopping frequencies, age, trip purpose and travel time were all reported by respondent. Distance is distance on the road network based on reported origins and destinations.

frequent, involved a longer stay and larger expenditure at the mall, and were less likely to be for grocery shopping.

Rather than dwell on these and various other effects modelled for trip frequency, mode share, distance, and other variables (summarized in Figure 12.3 and detailed in Garb, forthcoming), we will focus here on findings that are relevant for retail policies internationally. The following analyses illustrate the changes in retail travel that have occurred with the emergence of hypermarkets, the persistence of non-car travel to hypermarkets being the most interesting result. They also show that although car travel to hypermarkets by car is quite extensive in absolute terms, in a motorized society the policies for reducing it are not at all clear-cut.

12.2.2.1 The effects of transition to hypermarkets on modal choice

Because the malls surveyed in Prague had opened only 2-4 years before the survey, shoppers could reliably be asked about their prior (pre-hypermarket) shopping patterns. Fig. 12.4. highlights the changes in mode, frequency and duration of shopping since the transition to hypermarket shopping. Table 12.1. shows where people used to shop before they began shopping at the surveyed hypermarket and how they used to get there. We can see that local retail (local supermarkets or shops) was reached mostly by walking or biking (69%), while the more distant retail outlets (hypermarkets, supermarkets, company price clubs, or other centres) were reached mostly by car (72%).

Figure 12.5 summarizes the shifts in travel mode by comparing the modal choices that current hypermarket shoppers made before and after they started to use this particular facility. The horizontal axis in the mosaic is partitioned according to the prior mode share, and the vertical axis shows the conversion of each mode once the respondents started to use the new hypermarket. While the car users hardly changed modes, transit users shifted considerably to car use, and pedestrian shoppers overwhelmingly abandoned that mode, for cars and to a lesser degree to transit. Thus, 25% of all shopping trips had switched to cars from modes considered more environmentally friendly. Four percent regained by car users who moved to more environmentally friendly modes should be deducted from this figure. The total number of trips made by surveyed shoppers was 60% more in prior (pre-hypermarket) shopping patterns than currently.[9]

---

[9] The total reported frequencies multiplied by the number of people who reported the frequencies was 7,614 for the prior shopping pattern, versus 4,663 for the surveyed trips.

12 The retail revolution in post-socialist Central Europe and its lessons   241

Growth in car shopping and elimination of pedestrian shopping

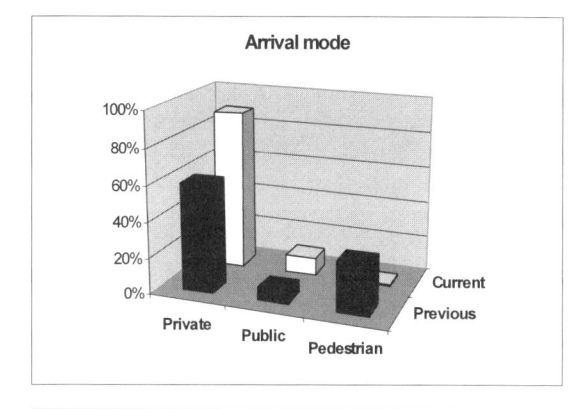

Arrival mode

Trip frequency drops sharply

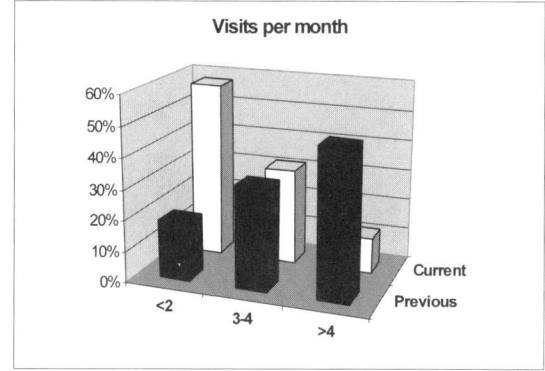

Visits per month

Predominantly short visits replaced by long and very long visits

Duration of visit (hours)

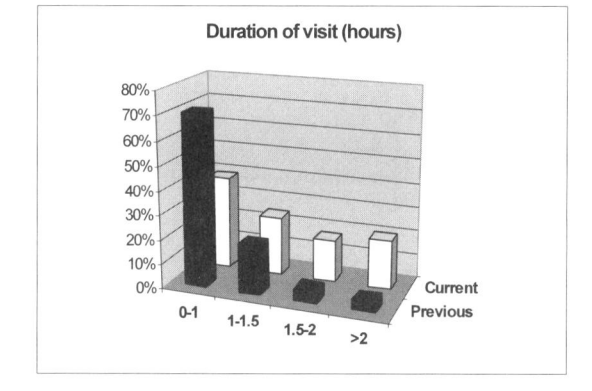

Fig. 12.4. Summary of changes in travel patterns in the transition to hypermarket shopping: arrival mode, monthly frequency and duration of visits

Note:
The data is for Pruhonice, Prague; the n for each of two groups in the three graphs range from 335 to 357).

Table 12.1. Travel mode prior to the use of the surveyed facility by type of shopping—shoppers at 4 malls (n=1542)

Column % / Row %	Local shops	Local supermarket	Another supermarket	Another centre	Company shopping club	Another hypermarket	Other
Private car	24 / 9	24 / 9	57 / 35	70 / 8	50 / 5	78 / 23	41 / 11
Public transport	11 / 10	5 / 4	26 / 39	22 / 6	19 / 5	14 / 10	41 / 26
Walk or bike	65 / 34	71 / 35	18 / 15	9 / 1	31 / 5	8 / 3	18 / 7

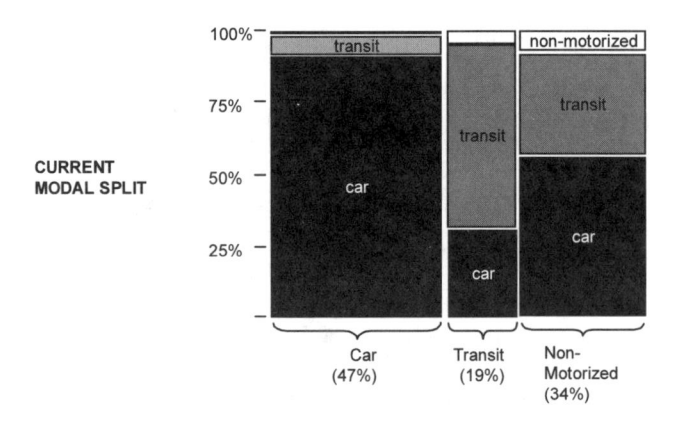

Fig. 12.5. Conversion of trip modes with the emergence of hypermarkets

12.2.2.2 The accessibility of hypermarkets by transit and walking

Car ownership strongly determines the modal choice for shopping. With no car in the household, the chance of coming to a hypermarket by car (predominantly as a passenger) is 16%; it rises to 79% when one car is owned by the household, and to 87% with two cars. At the same time, as Figure 12.6 shows, a sizeable percentage of hypermarket shoppers still arrive by means other than the car, and many do so despite having a car available. For example, 57% of those arriving at the mall by public transport have at least one car in the household, as do an even higher percent of those arriving by foot.

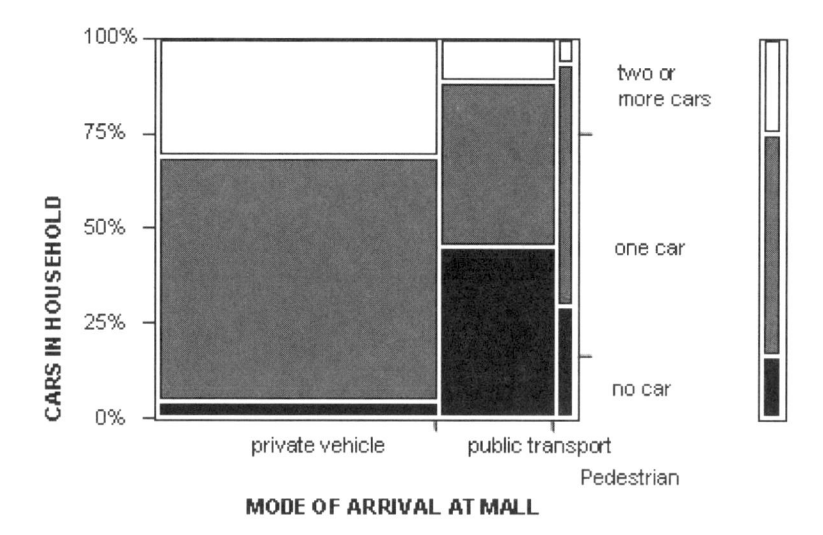

Fig. 12.6. Breakdown of household car availability by travel mode of arrival at the surveyed Prague malls.
Note:
The left vertical scale indicates the portion of respondents belonging to each car ownership category, and the horizontal scale the portion arriving by each mode. The separate scale on the right indicates the overall breakdown of car ownership with aggregated arrival mode.

However, these modal splits vary by mall. For instance, 90% of trips to the peripheral mall Prohinice are by car. This is much higher than 52% of trips to the more central mall Letnany. There are also large shopping centres in Prague, such as the National Theatre Tesco, where almost no shoppers arrive by car. In other words, public transport is still a viable mode for hypermarket-related travel of those that have cars, not just the only alternative available to carless "captive" transit riders.

12.2.2.3 Travel generation – overall and outside Prague

In order to estimate absolute amount of travel, the length of trips within the Prague's agglomeration as derived from the survey was compared with a commercial count of traffic to one of the surveyed malls. The commercial traffic count included all public and private vehicle entries over 24 hours, on both a weekday and a weekend day. The overall travel generated by this large mall is on the order of 170 million kilometres annually. A rough conservative estimate of the overall annual travel to Czech malls nationally is in the order of tens of billions of kilometres, producing over a million tons of carbon dioxide (CO_2) from the car trips alone (that is, over 3.5% of total CO_2 emission from all fossil fuels in the Czech

Republic).[10] Some portion of that travel would have occurred prior to retail deconcentration, but the survey shows that a substantial portion of the shopping travel would not have been car-borne before the existence of hypermarkets (as described above). Thus, varied retail configurations seem to significantly influence travel patterns and consequently environmental quality.

The above estimate of total mall-related travel is based on surveyed trips originating and ending within the Prague agglomeration—Prague's sphere of influence for traffic modelling, which is an extensive area approximating the area in land-use plans of Prague (see Figure 12.2). However, a significant number of trips (16%) to the four surveyed malls originate outside the Prague agglomeration. Almost all (91%) of those long distance trips are made by car; 84% are primary trips (i.e., home-mall-home); they are sporadic (half are monthly or less); and their predominant (65%) purpose is other than grocery shopping. Although the outside-Prague trips are a minor component in terms of their number, they average 200 kilometres per round trip and are an important component of the overall traffic. These trips are responsible for 50% more person-kilometres than are the majority (84%) of trips that originate within the Prague agglomeration. In other words, the above estimate of tens of billions of kilometres annually of the national traffic generated by hypermarkets represents only 40% of the full amount of such travel that would be estimated if we included the long distance trips. The long distance trips however have started to diminish, however, as more local, modern retail stores became available in smaller towns.

Interestingly, even though the shoppers who travel to Prague's hypermarkets from other cities and villages report that they are on a home-mall-home trip, it is not simply the ex-urban malls at the points of entry into the city that are picking up the long distance trips, but central ones as well. For example, Prohonice ("P" in Figure 12.2), which is one of the four surveyed malls most distant from Prague's centre, has the smallest portion of these long-distance trips. In complex ways, the peripheral malls draw both outward trips from the city and trips from long distances. Figure 12.7 illustrates the incoming trips to Zlicin mall at Prague's edge. The majority of the trips come from within Prague; a significant portion come from places outside the boundary of the agglomeration (the traffic model assigns these trips to the point where they enter the agglomeration); and a negligible proportion come from Prague's urban agglomeration.

We can understand these travel dynamics in light of the national pattern, which shows that people in smaller municipalities do much more of their shopping by car. As there are no hypermarkets in the smaller towns, it is likely that the inhabitants do their occasional bulk or comparison shopping at the nearest major city. It is important to see whether a similar long-distance component prevails in developed countries, or whether the long-distance trips are part of a transitional phase

---

[10] There were about 80 hypermarkets in the Czech Republic at the time of the survey, but only some were as large or peripheral as the reference mall—Centrum Praha, which is part of the Zlicin complex. At the same time, this figure does not include the extensive amount of travel from outside of Prague's agglomeration.

12 The retail revolution in post-socialist Central Europe and its lessons   245

Fig. 12.7. Trips from Zlicin mall, Prague; line width denotes volume of trips to each destination zone.

that will cease once hypermarkets penetrate the smaller municipalities and remove these trips from the regional grid. The component of analogous long-distance trips to Warsaw's malls, described below, is smaller (5%), perhaps because distances are shorter and orientation toward urban centres is greater in the Czech Republic.

Time will tell the extent to which the marked long distance travel component observed in this 2001 Prague survey was a transient feature of retail travel. If it continues to hold true, that will have important implications for the debate on the most sustainable locations for hypermarkets. With 60% of Prague's mall travel (in terms of VKT—vehicle kilometres travelled) on any given day actually unrelated to the urban form or the city's travel patterns, but generated instead by longer trips from remote smaller places, travel generation becomes a question of regional and national rather than municipal retail structure.

12.2.3 Traffic counts and survey at five hypermarkets in Warsaw

Surveys of 4254 shoppers and traffic counts were conducted in 5 malls in and around Warsaw in 1999. Traffic counts focused on flows and car occupancy levels over time. The surveys focused on pre- and post-mall locations and activities, trip purposes, mode and frequency, and the perceived next-best shopping mall. To illustrate the variety of travel patterns, Figure 12.8 compares Centrum Janki, a peripheral mall, with HIT Kabaty, a mall at a subway station in a fairly dense residential area. The diagram displays striking differences between these malls in the number of originating trips in each traffic analysis zone (for weekday entry trips), the modal split, and distribution of trip lengths.

The Warsaw data set also demonstrates why trip chaining must be an important consideration in understanding and optimizing retail travel. The differences in chaining patterns can be observed between various malls within a city and between cities in their aggregate patterns. For example, the overwhelming majority of trips in both Prague and Warsaw are unchained (primary) home-mall-home trips: 85-95% in Warsaw's malls and 74-86% in Prague's malls, even on weekdays during the hours when people are returning from their workday.[11] The high proportion of primary trips indicates the importance of malls in generating rather than simply redirecting travel. In Prague, the largest component of the chained trips were the mall stops on the way home from work in the afternoon. However, on weekdays such trips represented only about 10% of all trips, an anomalously low figure in comparison to other international data (Garb, forthcoming). Warsaw shows a more common pattern, with 27% of weekday mall trips being a stop on the way home from work. In Prague, trip chaining is less likely among transit users than among car users, but the reverse is the case in Warsaw.

If we compare trip chaining patterns with respect to the different malls in each city, we again detect a considerable variety. There are small but statistically significant differences among the malls in Prague, with the peripheral malls Pruhonice and Zlicin, for example, having somewhat larger portions of (12% and 15% respectively)chained trips than the central malls have (7-8%). The differences between malls are much more notable in Warsaw. For example, 41% of the trips to Reduta and only 15% of those to HIT Kabaty are stops on the way home from work, with the differences resulting from factors such as the proximity of the malls to work and home and the routes between them. While Reduta is surrounded by extensive office space and may be attracting a high proportion of visitors who are on their way home from work, HIT Kabaty, at a subway station in a dense residential area, has visitors who are likely to have already stopped at home before visiting Kabaty.

---

[11] Surveys in both Prague and Warsaw did not include the home-to-work commute hours.

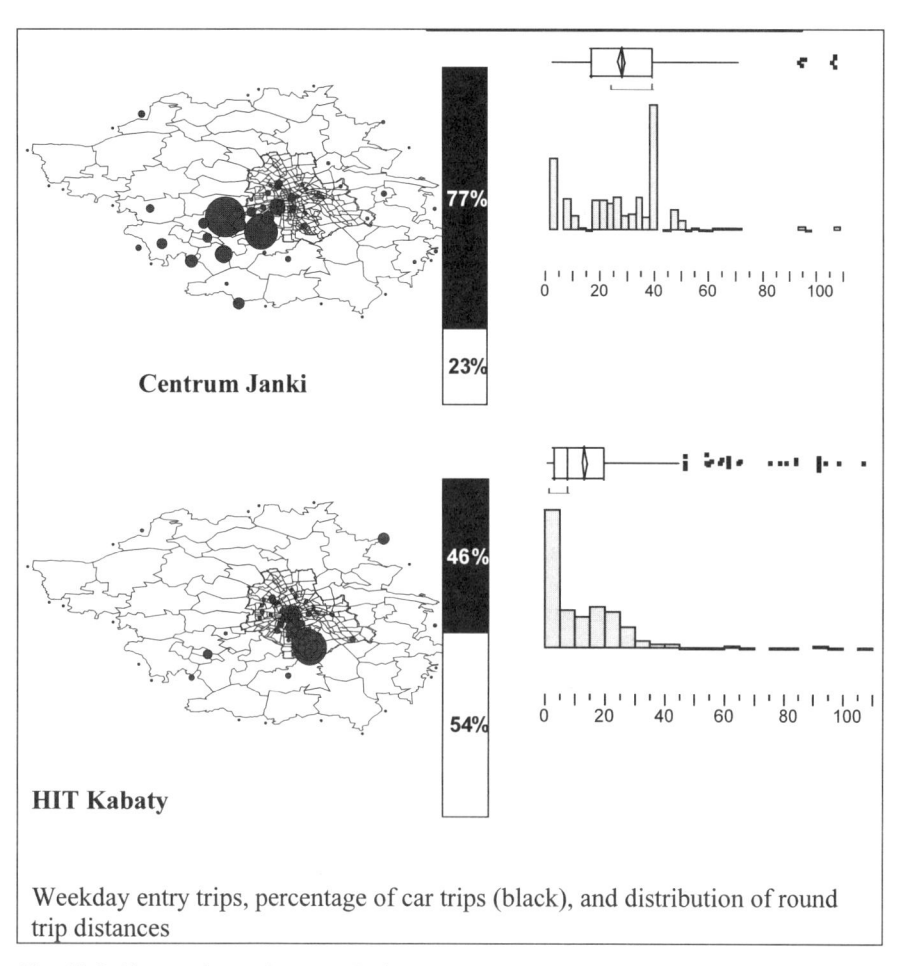

12 The retail revolution in post-socialist Central Europe and its lessons   247

Weekday entry trips, percentage of car trips (black), and distribution of round trip distances

Fig. 12.8. Comparison of two malls in Warsaw: Centrum Janki, an out-of-town mall, versus HIT Kabaty, a mall on a subway stop station in a fairly dense residential area.

Conclusions and policy implications

In Central and Eastern Europe the retail revolution was intensive, and in contrast to its course in most other countries, it preceded rather than trailed residential sprawl and suburban lifestyles. Moreover, it occurred in the absence of regulatory or other restraints. For these reasons, it offers unusual insights into the effects of retail deconcentration on travel. These insights are internationally relevant as the multinational retail chains increasingly turn their attention to the transitional countries. A recent survey by PriceWaterhouseCoopers (2004/5) of the patterns of growth in retail and consumption in transitional economies provides the following summary:

> As the transitional economies develop, the lives of their populations will open up to discover a whole new range of consumer goods. Shopping centres with their malls, and the creation of adjacent leisure activities will become one of the important poles of future consumption patterns. Emerging regional players, as well as the multinationals already present in these countries, will be seizing the significant potential for expansion from the increasingly saturated major cities into smaller, regional urban centres (p. 17 of the Executive Summary).

There are pressures on the expanding retail sector to locate in ex-urban areas: that was the case in the first phase of retail growth in major cities of Central and Eastern Europe, and is likely to be the case in the smaller urban centres as well. We expect that the drive for retail development in Central and Eastern Europe, tied to images of Western lifestyles, and the power wielded by international retailers as compared to that of local authorities will frequently overcome the planning restraints that are in place in transitional economies.

While large retail chains have traditionally relied on the hypermarket model in their overseas expansion, they are not necessarily wedded to it, and are likely to experiment with other formats, locations and business models as they try to tap new and lucrative markets. These markets lie not only in the well-off populations that use smaller urban supermarkets (e.g., Tesco's "Tesco Metro" or Ahold's "Albert Heijn" models), but in the extensive poor and even subsistence-level populations in transitional countries who now are loyal to small family stores, which offer a remarkably sophisticated response to their needs.[12] In post-socialist economies, sub-optimal peripheral locations have sometimes been chosen by retailers blocked from their preferred central locations. As the CEE urban retail market eases up with brownfield reuse, clearer ownership, and faster rezoning procedures, retailers may be able to move closer to their still predominantly urban customers.

As the retail revolution goes global, the role of planners is not simply to warn about potential adverse consequences of the new developments. They can also underscore good practices for the nature, location and accessibility of retail, and translate those principles into regulatory tools and requirements. The brief sampling of empirical findings presented here shows the importance and complexity of their task.

During its first decade of expansion, Central and Eastern European retail in post-socialist cities approximated the North American model – unregulated and

---

[12] Booz-Allen-Hamilton conducted a fascinating study of traditional and small retail in Argentina, Brazil, Chile, Colombia, Costa Rica, and Mexico in 2003 for the Coca-Cola Retailing Research Council—Latin America, a group of major retail leaders in the region.

market-driven.[13] In the U.S., however, due to its large size, lack of land-use powers at the federal level, and strong emphasis on local policy determination, there are no national policies and very few state-level initiatives governing the location of retail. There it is only local ordinances that can temper the encroachment of new 'big box' stores, and the circumstances and actions taken vary from community to community. Planners in the U.S. are more often reactive in the face of proposed development, rather than establishing retail strategies and policies such as are seen at a national level in other countries.[14]

Western Europe, on the other hand, has evolved a fairly diverse and sophisticated toolkit of measures for regulating retail (Garb and Lichfield, forthcoming). Zoning has been used to restrict retail development to town centres, or to urban areas with good access by all forms of transport. Countries have set thresholds for the maximum size of new retail projects, the kinds of goods sold, and even their open hours, in order to reduce competition with small retailers. In the Dutch case, the impact on existing small retail is avoided by specifying a limited number of the national "large scale concentrated retail establishments," which have a minimum size threshold (Garb and Lichfield, forthcoming). Yet another set of tools regulates retail by manipulating of incentive structures and stakeholder relations rather than by zoning, by redistributing business taxes paid by large retailers to retailers in traditional locations, or by allowing a regional planning authority to veto the proposals of another adjacent authority on the basis that they will have an adverse regional effect. At various in times, some countries have mandated obligatory retail research that would map out the needs for and impact of retail development.

From the empirical findings in this paper one may see how subtly these and other tools must be formulated and applied, and their complex linkages with policies on motorization and other forms of deconcentration (e.g., of jobs and housing). Our findings show that hypermarkets significantly reduce the number of trips made, but convert them into motorized and longer distance trips. In the extreme case, in a motorized country, larger and thus more appealing retail will draw significant numbers of people from smaller towns on occasional trips that are hundreds of kilometres in length. In such a context, finding the optimal location for a large mall would not always be simple. An in-town location will increase the distance travelled for many shoppers coming from out of town, and will put their car traffic onto urban roads rather than inter-urban highways.[15] At the same time, the

---

[13] See, for example, Walter's (2003) detailed study of retail regulation in the Polish context, which shows that while existing legal tools were adequate, the lack of enforcement made for more or less free-market development. The drive toward retail modernization overrode any concerns about spatial consequences. Impact analysis of new retail facilities was required; but they were prepared by the developer, and there were no guidelines as to what to measure or what the goals or benchmarks were. As might be expected, such reports focused on (unsubstantiated) claims about increased employment opportunities and highly local (parking-lot level!) assessment of impacts on air quality.

[14] This summary and the following summary of Western European retail draws from a comprehensive survey by Garb and Lichfield, forthcoming from ITDP.

[15] Similar findings from simulations are provided by Hay (2005).

construction of more malls in smaller cities can reduce some long distance travel. An examination of trip origins of existing malls, case by case, can inform policies for such difficult balancing of local and regional travel.

The findings on CEE countries also show the variety of ways in which retail can interact with different travel modes, trip chaining patterns, and locational settings, including some important sustainable retail niches, past and current. For example, our Warsaw survey shows a "stop-on-the-way-from work" mall with over 40% of its visits being part of such trip chains, and a "transit mall" where more than half the customers come by non-car transportation. Indeed, in general, retail in Central and Eastern European cities remains very transit-based. More than half of the people surveyed in large (>100,000) cities report that transit is "very important" for them in their shopping for food and basic foodstuff, and almost everyone (nearly 90%) is either very satisfied (50%) or satisfied (40%) with the level of transit access they have. On the other hand, a niche that has been most severely hurt by the growth of hypermarkets comprises the local shops and local supermarkets that were formerly reached on foot by 65%-71% of people surveyed, and by transit by another 5-11%.

The analysis we began here should be extended. It hints at exciting directions for furthering existing retail policies and impact assessment approaches for promoting more sustainable retail. An alternative to prohibitory regulation may be to support retail actively at locations that have been demonstrated to facilitate desirable travel characteristics; in a highly competitive market, this may have some of the same effects as outright restrictions. Or, more drastically, using the characteristics of such "better practice" facilities as benchmarks for permitting proposed developments would provide legitimacy and validity to *ex ante* retail impact assessments. Stipulating a minimal non-car modal share or maximum average travel distance for retail (enforceable through free shuttle services, for example) would introduce new locational criteria to developers searching for suitable sites and would encourage more accuracy in the impact assessment reports they commission.[16] Also, in an era of increased sensitivity to greenhouse emissions, the considerable, measurable, and perhaps tradable reduction of emissions due to improved access to a shopping facility could spur better policies on retail location.

These kinds of policies and tools are urgently needed in Central and Eastern European countries as "big box" retail deconcentration now spreads from the large cities to towns with population of 50,000 people and less. They may also be useful to planners in other transitional economies and in developing countries worldwide, as similar pressures are likely to be felt from the rise in purchasing power and motorization rates. In developed countries, where retail deconcentration occurred few decades ago and more gradually, planners can sharpen their understanding of that process and of retail alternatives. The different outcomes and "irregular" patterns shown where hypermarkets are located in and around cities that are still relatively compact and well served by transit can point to the potential for

---

[16] On the example of the "Centro" peripheral shopping and leisure centre in Oberhausen (Germany), and the achievement of the mandated 35% public transport mode share despite 10,500 free parking spaces, see International Association of Public Transport (2002).

more sustainable land use patterns. (From the U.S. perspective, the land-use/transport conditions in CEE are still enviable, even after the decade of "degradation" described here.)

Finally, the CEE case raises a question for transnational civil society groups.[17] Should large transnational retail chains, which increasingly operate abroad, be immune from regulation as they "export" sprawling land-use practices? This question is especially applicable to Western European corporations, which were extremely aggressive in exporting their operations and formats to post-socialist Central and Eastern Europe with a lack of spatial oversight they would never have been allowed in their home countries. The question is even more pointed in the case of international financial institutions such as the European Bank for Reconstruction and Development , which is a large and active lender for private exurban retail facilities in Central, Eastern, and Southeastern Europe.

Acknowledgements

This research was supported by the Institute for Transportation and Development Policy (New York), and the Rockefeller Brothers Fund initiative on smart growth in Central Europe. The authors are grateful to Jirina Jackson, Karel Maier, Karel Stransky, Andrzej Kassenberg, Nadace Via, and others who a generous introduction to Central European urban processes. We also thank Jirina Jackson and Greg Newmark for assistance in designing and administering the Prague questionnaire, to UDI Prague for data entry and use of their Prague traffic model, and to Jonathan Levine, Walter Hook, and Eran Razin for providing valuable feedback on drafts of this chapter.

References

Booz-Allen Hamilton (2003) Creating value for emerging consumers in retailing. A study conducted for the Coca-Cola Retailing Research Council—Latin America. Summary available at http://www.coke.net/app/home/portal/_pagr/109/_pa.109/135 (accessed in 2005).

Chung CJ, Jeffrey I, Koolhaas R, Leong ST (eds) (2001) The Harvard Design School guide to shopping. Koln, Taschen.

Dries L, Reardon T, Swinnen J (2004) The rapid rise of supermarkets in Central and Eastern Europe: Implications for the agrifood sector and rural development. Development Policy Review 22(5):525 – 556.

Florini AM (ed) (2000) The third force: The rise of transnational civil society. Carnegie Endowment for International Peace and Japan Centre for International Exchange, Washington DC.

Garb Y (forthcoming) Retail deconcentration and its impacts on travel patterns: Findings from the Czech Republic. In: Eran R, Vazquez C, Djist M (eds) Deconcentration in

---

[17] On transnational civil society, see Keck (1998) and Florini (2000).

European metropolitan areas: Market forces vs. planning regulations. Kluwer, Dortrecht.

Garb Y, Lichfield S (forthcoming) A survey of measures for retail regulation in Western Europe and their evolution. Institute for Transportation and Development Policy (ITDP), New York.

Garb Y, Jackson J (forthcoming) Brownfields in Central Europe: A unique urban planning challenge, and a NGO advocacy response. In: Altrock UG, Güntner S, Huning S, Peters D (eds) Berlin spatial planning and urban development in the new EU member states. Ashgate, Altershot.

Hay A (2005) The transport implications of planning policy guidance on the location of superstores in England and Wales: simulations and case study. Journal of Transport Geography 13:13-22.

INCOMA (2001) Sheet # 5 in *SHOPPING MONITOR 2001*. http://www.incoma.cz/en/.

International Association of Public Transport (2002) Public transport connections to out-of-town shopping and leisure facilities. International Association of Public Transport (UITP), Brussels, http://www.uitp.com.

Jackson J, Garb Y (2002) The search for brownfield leadership in Central European cities: Overview and case study of the Czech Republic. Policy report, Institute for Transportation and Development Policy, New York/Prague.

Keck ME, Sikkink K (1998) Activists beyond borders. Cornell University Press, Ithaca, NY.

Kulke E (1997) Effects of the economic transformation process on the structure and locations of retailing in East Germany. Journal of Retailing and Consumer Services 4:49-55.

Maier K (1998) Czech planning in transition: Assets and deficiencies. International Planning Studies 3:351-365.

Michalak WZ (2001) Retail in Poland: An assessment of changing market and foreign investment conditions. Canadian Journal of Regional Science 243:485-504.

PriceWaterhouseCoopers (2004/5) From Beijing to Budapest: New retail and consumer growth patterns in transitional economies. Executive Summary, 3rd edition. www.pwc.com (accessed in 2005).

Smith J (2003) From hazi to hyper market: Discourses on time, money, and food in Hungary. Anthropology of East Europe Review 21 (electronic).

Stenning A (2005) Post-socialism and the changing geographies of the everyday in Poland. Transactions of the Institute of British Geographers 30:113-127.

Walter M (2003) Einzelhandelsentwicklung in Polen: Probleme der planerischen Steuerung des Einzelhandels in Warschau. MA thesis. Institute for Town and Regional Planning, Technical University, Berlin.

13 Spatial imprints of urban consumption: large-scale retail development in Warsaw

Karina Kreja

Introduction

Since 1989, when major political change occurred in Central and Eastern Europe (CEE), the most significant factor influencing the functioning and organization of cities has probably been the trends in urban consumption. Their changing patterns have had their strongest spatial expression in the new retail developments. Hypermarkets and shopping centers, which in the last ten years have been built in most Polish cities, both generate and benefit from the ongoing urban transformation. The in-depth case studies presented in this chapter aim to identify the urban changes that find spatial articulation in the large-scale retail developments in a post-socialist city.

This study of Warsaw's large-scale retail developments provides insights into the emergence of a simultaneously post-socialist and post-industrial city. The process is driven by the political and economic shifts occurring from 1989 in all CEE countries, previously known as the Soviet block. Cities of Hungary, Poland, former Czechoslovakia, East Germany, former Yugoslavia and the former Soviet Republics undoubtedly have spatial similarities due to their common socialist past and its policy, planning and building strategies. Moreover, in some CEE countries the economic pressures and challenges of accession to the European Union may even have intensified those similarities.

People in CEE countries are rapidly entering the 'mass consumer society', which differs radically from the 'mass society' during socialism. In the West a 'consumer society,' has been longstanding, but in the CEE region to the adjustment to such a society means new cultural phenomena with various manifestations in the regions' cities. Like local interpretations of the common ideology of the past, however, the seemingly unifying processes of transformation in fact happen in socially and culturally diverse settings. The contextualized nature and outcomes of those processes are thus fairly distinctive.

This chapter focuses on the physical aspects of the spatial change that arrived with the construction of large-scale retail development in Warszawa (Warsaw), the capital of Poland. Its main trends are traced through a two-step case study of the developments grouped along one of Warsaw's radial roads. The study first considers all nineteen large-scale developments along the corridor; the second step focuses on three western-style shopping centers. Three aspects are observed: 1) the location of large-scale retail developments in the city structure; 2) their location in the immediate context; and 3) the types of development. The discussion first notes the function and typology of the retail establishments build before the 1990s. The more recent, western-style developments present new typologies of large-scale retail, which are key to describing the characteristics of the spatial changes they have introduced, and to understanding their implications.

13.1 Urban consumption

The increased urban consumption in CEE has prompted interest in understanding its effects there on contemporary lifestyles and the standard of living. Such research on consumption should focus not only on the individualized pleasures of (private) consumption, but also on how the practices of (public) consumption influence the formation of contemporary societies (Clarke and Bradford 1998). Consumption, 'the selection, purchase, use, maintenance, repair and disposal of any product or service' (Campbell 1995), also is a means of reproducing culturally specific ways of life. Applying a consumption paradigm to cities implies that they can be viewed no only as landscapes of production but also as landscapes of consumption (Zukin 1991). In that context, consumption functions as a bridge between the individual and her/his experience of the urban environment (Miles and Paddison 1998).

13.1.1 The rising consumerism in post-socialist cities

The rapid shift from a socialist to a market economy and the associated growth in consumption initiated a set of abrupt spatial changes in Central Eastern European cities. The changes are transformative, with the unprecedented expansion in retail establishments as both the physical manifestation of consumption and a highly visible signpost of the ongoing urban spatial changes.

Nonetheless, the assumption that consumerism is a completely new phenomenon in post-socialist societies is largely misleading. Undeniably, the communist ideology that dominated CEE countries for over forty years did overemphasize production. That ethos of the working class with its focus on production stood in opposition to a bourgeois lifestyle with consumption as its hallmark. Socialist regimes saw people as workers first and as consumers at a very distant second (Bauman 1997). Whatever the official slogans, however, consumption has always been important in people's lives (Crowley 2003). Even the most regime-dependent structures, for example, the system of gratification for work performance, distributed those commodities that were in demand as prime rewards (e.g., private cars and household appliances). Moreover, under the conditions of politicized personal life, consumption was a means of self-identification, self-positioning and resistance. As Miller (1995) puts it, "[t]he arousal and frustration of consumer desire and East Europeans' consequent resistance to their regimes led them to build their social identities specifically *through consuming*. Acquiring consumer goods and objects conferred an identity that set one off from socialism. To acquire objects became a way of constituting your selfhood against the regime you despised." (p.56)

Prevalent throughout the Soviet block, that attitude toward consumption became especially prominent in the 1980s in Poland. After the repression of the Solidarity trade union in the early 1980s, control over the flow of goods was widely understood as oscillating between displays of relative largesse and punishment by ordeal (Crowley 2003). At the same time, the images of western lifestyle reproduced by popular culture and recalled from travels abroad constantly underlines the growing disparity between the Western and CEE countries in access to commodities. The increasing gap between expectations and the availability of goods generated 'consumer hunger.' Unsatisfied consumer desires certainly were one of the hidden currents in the 1989 political shift. After the political change, recognizing consumer wants became a symbol of social transformation.

The residents of CEE, then, entered the brave new capitalist world with certain expectations about the availability of consumer goods. The unprecedented retail expansion in CEE firmly presupposes the ability and willingness of the postsocialist societies to accommodate western patterns of consumption. In Poland, as in other countries in the region, a dramatic change occurred in the philosophy and practice of retailing. The previously nationalized and centralized system of the distribution of goods was replaced by a market system. Queue-based shopping, in which shop assistants hand the goods to customers, was replaced by a self-service model (Crowley 2003). In response to the new demands and consumption models, many new retail developments emerged. The growing number of developments and size of retail space built are presented in Fig. 13.1.

The unprecedented dynamism of these developments has obscured some aspects of the large-scale retail establishments in Poland. One area of confusion is the classification of the new establishments, as various types of large-scale retail units have been introduced simultaneously. The new diversity of retail options somewhat disorients customers unaccustomed to so many. They lack retail-related vocabulary or a system of shopping behaviors. For example, the consumer language does not differentiate between hypermarkets and shopping centers. In public policy debate on new forms of retail, the relatively limited understanding of large-scale retail forms[1] is obvious.

A clear, common terminology is important for understanding one's environment and its issues. The only definition of large-scale retail in Poland is that used by Main Statistic Bureau (GUS), which denotes the large-scale retail developments as having 400 sq. m or more of retail space. In the planning regulations, the threshold for large-scale retail is set at 2,000 sq. m of Gross Leasable Area (GLA). Those definitions fit the Polish retail reality but fail to capture basic differences in the ways of retailing, which relate to the spatial location of a unit. Based only on the size of retail space, they also fail to consider such other modes of consumption as entertainment, recreation or food courts, which are often incorporated in a single commercial development. In fact, most businesses included in a retail group

---

[1] See, for example, Komunikat po Radzie Ministrów (Ministers Council Announcement) from 12.03.2002 (www.kprm.gov.pl), or CBOS 1999.

succeed because retail is combined with services and leisure. Last but not least among the elements that contribute to successful retailing is publicly accessible internal space, a forum for social interaction.

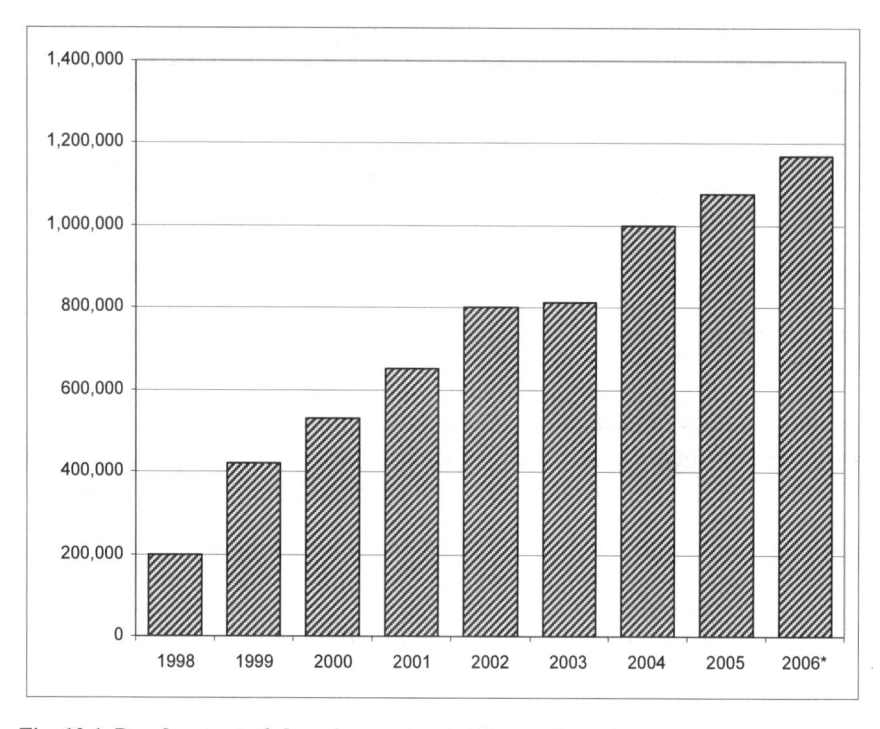

Fig. 13.1. Development of shopping centres in Warsaw in sq m.

Source: Jones Lang LaSalle forecast 2005

13.1.2 Impact of urban consumption on the townscape of Warsaw

Several phenomena in post-socialist cities may be usefully examined in the context of the growing urban consumption. From a spatial perspective, consumption may be seen to drive urban change, but also to actively shape the construction of space and place. Indeed, the strongest spatial articulation of the current changes comes from the retail sector. The new, large-scale retail developments are among the most visible evidence of Warsaw's post-socialist metamorphosis.

For many reasons, Warsaw offers a conceptually appropriate case study. After about eighty-five percent of the city was destroyed in the Second World War (WWII), it was rebuilt according to socialist objectives.[2] The city has often since

---

[2] Only some key areas, like the Old Town and Royal Tract, were deliberately rebuilt in historic style. Old Town is listed on UNESCO World Heritage list.

been invoked as epitomizing the brutal environment built by Soviet aesthetics and planning principles (Crowley 2003). It has been a point of reference for urban planning in the country and the proving ground for various social trends. It became a city of extremes: the combination of the socialist character of Warsaw's rebuilt urban structure and the concentration of wealth there helped to establish the city's unique image.

However, the city's image has changed considerably since 1989, Contemporary Warsaw is a prime example of the on-going transformation that Andrusz creatively labels "From Wall to Mall" in the following chapter. The rise in urban consumption and its physical expression in contemporary retail are the challenges now being handled in Warsaw's traditionally over-reactive way. The extreme marginalization of retail and marketing under the socialist authorities was replaced during the 1990s by extreme praise of their value and importance (Crowley 2003). In that respects, the scale and intensity of the changes observed in Warsaw do not necessarily reflect the trends in other CEE cities.

13.1.3 Stages of retail transformation in Warsaw

Three stages of transformation in the retail structure can be identified in Warsaw over the last fifteen years: 1) spontaneous trading; 2) explosion of small shops and bazaars; and 3) expansion of western-style retail units. Although all stages are still present in the city's townscape, their intensities and proportions have changed significantly over time.

The first stage arose with the political shift in the late 1980s, when response to the hitherto underestimated and neglected consumer demands found a new and *ad hoc* spatial expression, daily and in numerous locations. Previously strictly controlled, retail blossomed in its most basic form - small traders' temporary kiosks and stands filled the main city streets. That so-called 'small initiative' quickly became a symbol of irreversible change. The term 'selling from the bed,' coined at that time, accurately described the trade's physical form. The streets were lines with folding beds that served as stands for the numerous beginners in private retail. At first the new sellers enjoyed a period of almost unrestricted, rising prosperity, unhampered by the newly established local authorities. The people's private initiative was then ahead of the upcoming structural changes (Staniszkis 2004).

The second stage of Warsaw's retail transformation began in the early 1990s, when street retail was taken under administrative control. Street marketing was first restricted by licensing and was banned soon thereafter. The two subsequent presidents of Warsaw placed the 'fight against illegal street marketing' high on their political agenda. Most of the small retailers then established small shops,[3] and others moved to areas designated as *targowisko* or *bazar*.

Bazaars, or markets consisting of rows of shops or stalls selling miscellaneous goods, were not new in Warsaw's townscape. Even before the 1990s transforma-

---

[3] The overall number of shops has grown from 152 thousand in 1989 to about 451 thousand in 1998, when the proliferation of retail reached its peak (KRM 1995, 2000).

tion there had been 13 permanent and over 25 seasonal marketplaces all over the city. But the infusion of new spaces was unprecedented, with over 25 new bazaars and about 315,000m² added to the existing 75,000m² of permanent market places—a fourfold increase since 1989 (The City of Warsaw Council 1995). In the 1990s, bazaars were popular places for everyday shopping, especially in the big Polish cities. According to the Public Opinion Research Center (CBOS 1996), in 1996 the bazaars were the place of convenience shopping for over one-third of the city residents.

The third stage of retail structure development began with the opening of the chains of western hypermarkets, mostly French and German. From 1997 on, large-scale retail units were constructed on a massive scale. Comparative studies of the shopping habits of Poles showed the growing popularity of shopping centers and hypermarkets. In 1999 they were the preferred choice for thirty-nine percent of respondents, compared to seventeen percent of respondents in 1997 (CBOS 1999).[4] Bazaars were still preferred by over thirty-three percent of the city's consumers.

The current and perhaps almost completed phase of retail developments, the massive construction of super- and hypermarkets and the ongoing construction of new shopping centers, is leaving an irreversible imprint on Warsaw's townscape. The coexistence of diverse, large-scale retail structures and their ever stronger competition may be explored through several perspectives -- old versus new, or small and local versus big and foreign. The perspective of this chapter, however, highlights the spatial change inflicted by the construction of large-scale retail units.

13.2 The case studies

This case study research was conducted to evaluate the scale and nature of large-scale retail development in Warsaw and to show its impact on the townscape. The research examines Puławska and Marszałkowska streets – which together constitute one of Warsaw's main radial roads -- from the city center to the border with the satellite city of Piaseczno (Fig. 13.2.). The choice was based on both historical and current urban processes, including the diversity of retail forms in this corridor.

Historically, the route represents a cross-section through several functional clusters in the city structure (from the center of Warsaw to a local center), as well as through all the significant stages of socialist city development: pre-WWII neighborhoods, post-WWII reconstruction and the housing estates of 1960–1980s. The corridor was selected also for the extensive reshaping that it has sustained

---

[4] The surveys are related to Christmas shopping. In the questionnaire repeated in 1999, a new category of 'hypermarkets, or shopping centers consisting of multiple retail and non-retail units' was added. Having such a choice of categories, 29% respondents planned to do Christmas shopping in supermarkets and 10% in hypermarkets and shopping centers. Multiple answers were possible.

13 Spatial imprints of urban consumption: large-scale retail development in Warsaw 259

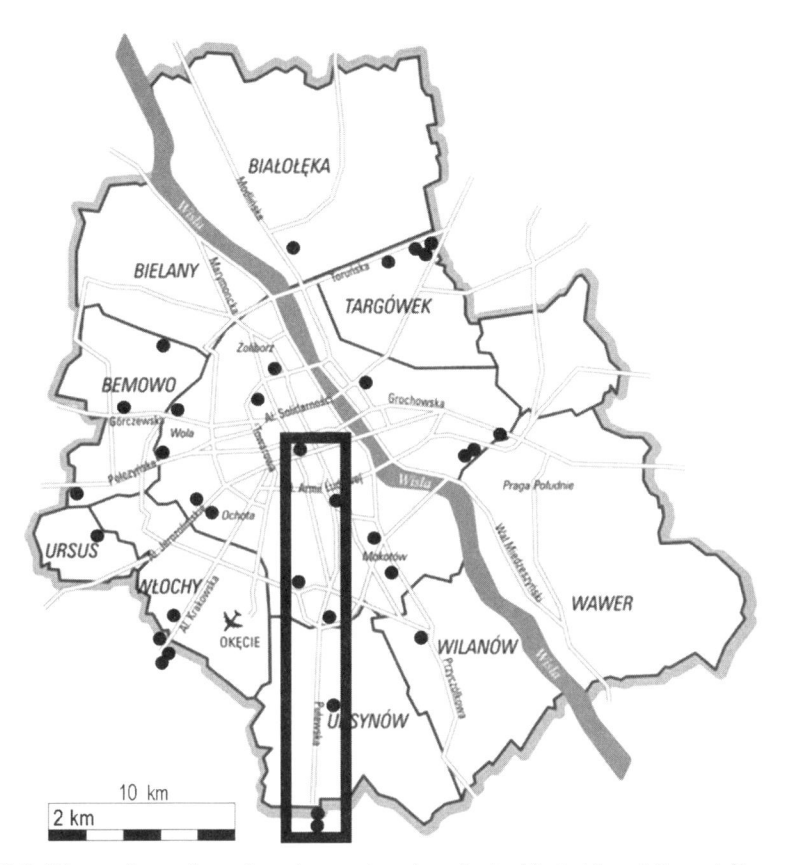

Fig. 13.2. Warsaw's modern shopping centres (marked with dots) and the retail corridor

from the existing retail developments and the planned location of several other centers.

The case studies consist of two parts: 1) a study of a linear retail node (corridor) that explores qualitative and quantitative changes in the retail structure and forms; 2) a study of how a retail cluster--three western-style shopping centers--has affected the immediate urban structure. Finally, the case study results are combined to highlight the character of the ongoing changes in urban structure.

Our examination of the Puławska/Marszałkowska strip begins at the foot of the Palace of Culture and Science, opened in 1955 to honor Joseph Stalin. The 30-story skyscraper soon became a landmark of Polish social-realist architecture and the focal point of Warsaw. Located in front of the palace, Plac Defilad (Parade Square) was intended to serve for 'civil' parades. The entire district between Plac Defilad and Plac Konstytucji (Constitution Square) is the finest example of socialist planning of the 1950s. Plac Konstytucji and Marszałkowska Dzielnica Mieszkaniowa (Marszałkowska Living District), with their monumental scale and form, are materialized objectives of the early socialist planning. The district is the showcase of Warsaw's townscape as remodeled after the Second World War.

Further south is The Old Mokotów district, where pre-WWII tenement houses and urban villas mix with the urban infill from the 1960s and 1970s. Since the 1960s, the area around Wilanowska subway station (7 km south of the city center) had been developed as a new district center that would connect Old Mokotów with the housing estate projects to the south. The intensive growth of this once rural area from the late 1960s and through the 1970s included several large complexes of housing estates, the largest being Ursynów, with almost 100,000 inhabitants. That high pace of urban change was wittily summed up in a cartoon showing a block of flats growing directly out of a cabbage field. Further south is an area of mixed rural and urban use. The development along the remaining part of Puławska Street to the nearest satellite town, Piaseczno, exemplifies recent urban sprawl.

13.2.1 The retail corridor

As in many European cities, the majority of shops along Marszałkowska and Puławska streets are of small or medium size and are located in the street sections that cross the central areas of the city and the local districts. In addition to the individual shops, along the route there are 19 large-scale (over 400m^2 of GLA) retail developments of various types. Those 19 centers can be grouped according to their place in the hierarchical and functional structure of the socialist city, in three clusters: central, Upper Mokotów district center and local/neighborhood center in Służew housing. Already established as important urban nodes, those three centers have been structurally and functionally influenced by the addition of modern retail facilities.

Identifiable processes are transforming the retail landscape of the corridor: the emergence of new developments and the forms and modification of the retail clusters. The retail, or generally commercial, establishments now range from small and simple to large and complex, from fully assisted to self-service, and from mono- to multifunctional a the typical axis of modern retail transformation (Cheuk 2003). However, this expansion of the range of retail in the post-socialist conditions has specific characteristics different from those of their western counterparts.

Most of the retail developments examined in the case study (Fig. 13.3.), i.e. bazaar, department store, superstore, supermarket, hypermarket, shopping center and retail park, have been extensively studied (ICSC 2001). Others, like the hybrid of shopping center and department store or the metro station shopping center, are well-known variants. Some of the less well-known and possibly unique forms in post-socialist cities, like topical arcades and topical shopping centers, are outlined below.

The high number of new retail developments is the measure of the scale of transformation in the corridor, with only five out of 19 operating prior to 1989 (three department stores and two supermarkets). A closer look at the five older, large-scale retail units (Table 13.1., numbers 4, 5, 9, 11 and 17) reveals the changing attitude toward consumption after the transformation from a socialist to a market economy. Located in the Mokotów district center, supermarket Supersam (number 9) was the first self-service shop in Poland, built in 1959. Built in the middle of 1970, Domy Towarowe 'Centrum' department stores (Wars and Sawa - number 4, and Junior – number 5 in Table 13.1.) mark a further shift towards consumerism. Nonetheless, both in scale and in form these flagship shopping facilities from the Polish socialist period were far behind western ones.

All the pre-1989 retail developments in the studied corridor have recently undergone considerable modifications. First, they were privatized in the early to mid 1990s. Then, in order to be more competitive, their owners upgraded them with modern commercial formats to accommodate western chain stores; for example, one part of Supersam, previously a milk bar (a socialist-type workers' canteen), became a McDonald's restaurant. However, that change turned to be only short-term. A recently revealed rebuilding plan for Supersam proposes a 50,000 sq. m mega-structure to be completed by 2008. The 'Centrum' department stores Wars, Sawa and Junior have been fully renovated and reopened as Galeria Centrum (number 4, primary fashion destination) and Empik (number 5, books and media superstore). The further evolution of Domy Towarowe Centrum, with several shops of large international brands on the ground floor, makes them the closest equivalent of High Street that Warsaw has.

The more recent expansion in retail is remarkable in both quantity and quality. Since 1994, fourteen existing large-scale retail developments along Marszałkowska and Puławska streets have been, introducing new types of retail such as western-style shopping center, topical shopping center, and retail park.

The bazaar has experienced a renaissance in Poland since 1989. For example, three new bazaars have been located at the Wałbrzyska and Puławska intersection (number 13 and 14), which is an important public transport node. As noted above, however, bazaars were already an established element in the Warsaw townscape. Some of them, like the well-known *Bazar Różyckiego* or *Bazar Polna*, even drew consumers from beyond Warsaw. Their layout has often been used as a model for new developments consisting of numerous kiosks or stands owned by private small traders organized along internal pedestrian malls. Evenly distributed throughout the city, bazaars are located within walking distance of local neighborhoods and serve their populations (Sulima 2000). Each bazaar has its own management and a unified, written code of rules imposed by Warsaw's authorities (The City of Warsaw Council 1995).

Following the initial *ad hoc* phase of small-scale trading, temporary bazaars were the second, more controlled phase in the post-socialist retail establishments in Warsaw. Because the authorities viewed bazaars as an unwanted child of market transformation - temporary solutions to last no more than five to seven years (The City of Warsaw Council 1995), only provisional constructions like kiosks or stalls were allowed. As a consequence, today bazaar traders struggle not only with the administrative constraints, but also with the outflow of customers who prefer modern retail developments (Piskiewicz 2000). The prosperity of many bazaars is

262 Karina Kreja

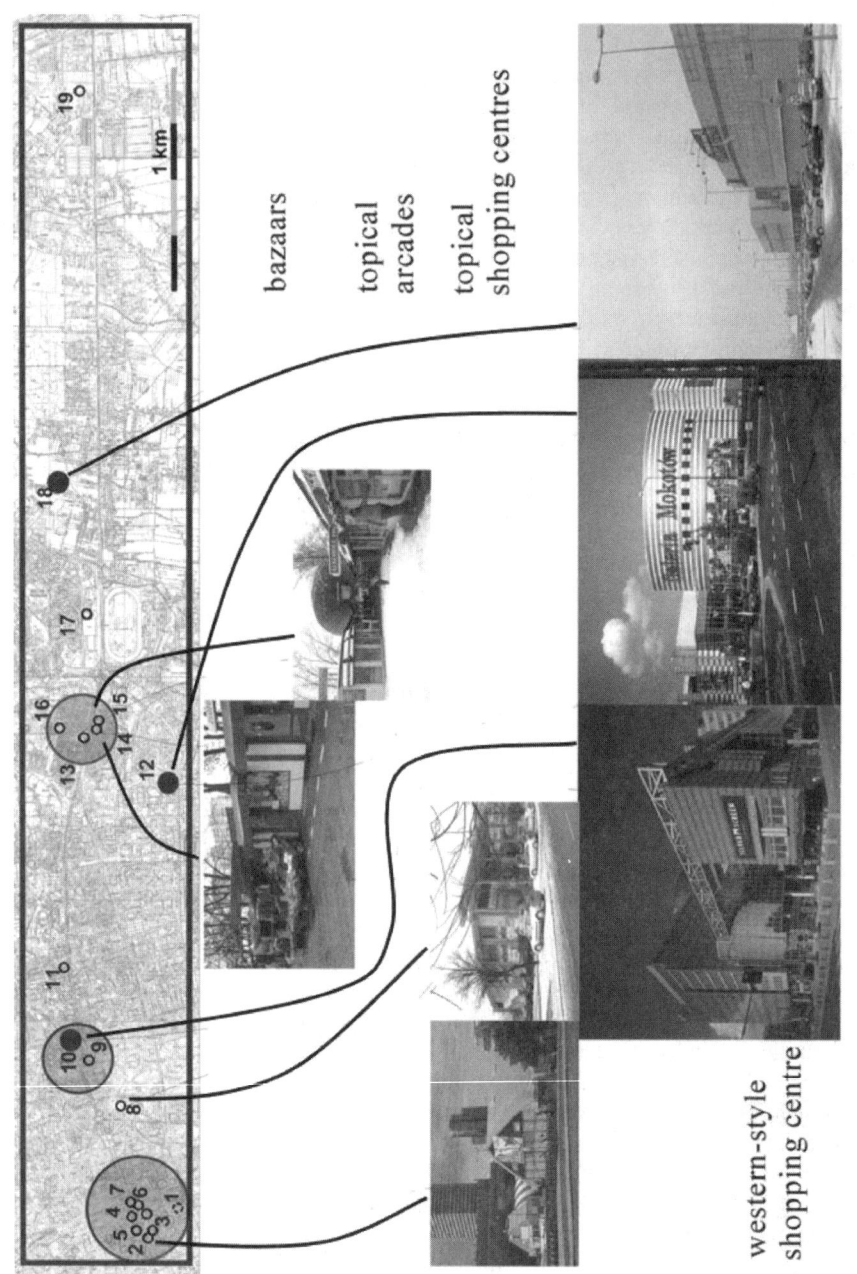

Fig. 13.3. Typologies along corridor : 19 retail developments along the Marszałkowska / Puławska corridor and three identified clusters.

Note: Legend used in this and following figures: large-scale retail ○ existing; ◌ under construction; ● selected case studies; ● clusters.

Table 13.1. Nineteen large-scale retail developments along Pulawska / Marszakowska corridor

	Name	Type	Built	GLA [1000m^2]	No of tenants	Anchor
1	Złote Tarasy	Multifunctional development (office/retail)	2005	60	Not yet fixed	multiple
2	Kupieckie Domy Towarowe	Topical shopping centre	2001	10,5	700	None
3	Hale Marcpol	Topical shopping centre	2001	2 x 2,2	2 x 60	supermarket
4	Wars and Sawa / Galeria Centrum	Hybrid of shopping centre and department store	1975/ 1998	22	App. 10	fashion superstore
5	Junior / Empik	Superstore	1975/ 1997	11,5	3	None
6	Pasaż Centrum	Metro station shopping centre	1998	1	n/a	metro station
7	Upominki	Underground passage	1996	0,5	40	None
8	Bazar Polna	Topical shopping centre	1998	1,5	50	None
9	Supersam	Supermarket	1959	2	3	McDonald's
10	**Europlex**	Office building + shopping centre	1999	7,5	20	cinema
11	DT	Department store	1970	1,5	n/a	RTV superstore
12	**Galeria Mokotów**	Regional shopping centre	2000	59	250	multiple
13	Bazar Wałbrzyska	Bazaar	1995	1,65	40	None
14	Bazar Al Lotników	Bazaar	1995	n/a	170	None
15	Pasaż Smyczkowa	Topical shopping arcades	1995	8,4	45	None
16	Land	Topical shopping centre	1999	47	100+ 200	post office
17	Megasam	Supermarket	1980	0,5	1	None

Table 13.1. (cont.)

	Name	Type	Built	GLA [1000m^2]	No of tenants	Anchor
18	**King Cross**	Retail park (hypermarket anchored)	1997	33	26	hypermarket, fitness club
19	Centrum Handlowe Piaseczno	Retail park (hypermarket anchored)	1996	13+4	50	hypermarket, superstores

Note:
The three developments presented in detailed case studies are in bold.

threatened by the new retail establishments, which take a bigger share of the market each year. For two bazaars located near the crossroads of Al. Lotników , Wałbrzyska and Puławska Streets (number 13 and 14),their approaching demise is plain. As their tenants relocate to new retail projects, these bazaars have gradually shrunk, with numerous kiosks already vacant. The inevitable extinction of the majority of the bazaars is foreseeable.

However, many of the bazaar traders have already found two distinctive ways to avoid liquidation: absorption into topical shopping arcades and construction of topical shopping centers. Unlike the more traditional large scale retail types - hypermarkets, shopping centers and retail parks, these two types of retail are specific to Warsaw's ongoing market transformation. Topical shopping arcades, as in Pasaż Smyczkowa, have two advantages over bazaars: spatial order and considerable weather protection with the light roof stretched over the kiosks. The topical shopping arcade as a form of 'civilized bazaar' is apparently preferred by both consumers and the local authorities.

By far the more desirable solution among the traders is the construction of a topical shopping center, that is, a shopping center that involves local interest and action. In the researched area, these had already been established in four cases (examples 2, 3, 8 and 16). A topical shopping center constitutes cross fertilization between shopping center and bazaar characteristics, in both management and layout. Unlike a western-style shopping center, where tenants lease retail space, the tenants of a topical center are members of the retailers' federation that manages it. The modern designs of many new topical shopping centers (Bazar Polna, Land – examples 8 and 16) seem no worse than those of western-style shopping centers. However, the lack of a main anchor tenant and the 'dead end' alleys created to house more small retailers create a layout that no western developer would accept. The comparative analysis of solid and void (Fig. 13.4.) among the different types of retail along the corridor reveals their diverse layouts, which influences their internal functioning, and also their urban imprint.

The transformation of Warsaw's townscape by the creation of new retail facilities is far from over. Presumably the construction of Złote Tarasy (1), a mixed-use development in the heart of the city center, will change the pedestrian flows in the area adjacent to the main railway station. With its underground connection to the central train station, the key transportation node of Warsaw, and its connections to streetscapes from its upper levels, the project is intended to reconnect the surrounding public spaces. In fact, the pedestrian system of the key area of the city will become highly integrated into the private development.

13.2.2 Western-style shopping centers

The study next focuses on a subset of three western-style shopping centers selected from the 19 large-scale retail developments along the Marszałkowska/Puławska corridor. There are several reasons for examining this specific form of retail closely. As signposts of the third phase of large-scale retail establishments, the three shopping centers already greatly influence both the city's economy and its structure. They have also triggered new urban phenomena such as modifications urban travel patterns and the emergence of privately managed but publicly accessible spaces, entirely new to Polish townscapes. Furthermore, by integrating many other attractions and functions with retail, such shopping centers effectively compete with or prompt changes in other types of retail centers near by. Built in various locations, the large-scale shopping centers tend to undermine each one's existing urban hierarchical structure of clearly defined functional centers on all levels (city, district and local community), previously planned and implemented in Warsaw; their character and function are altered.

Urban and architectural analysis to detect the scale and range of the ongoing spatial changes compares the lot before and after the shopping center's development. Quantitative data were acquired from several sources, including the management of the three developments. The comparison of land uses (Fig. 13.5.) is based on sketches of urban layouts that register solid to void relationships. This technique exposes the spatial effects both of the development as an entity and of its internal public space.

13.2.3 Europlex

Built in 1999, the multi-use buildings of Puławska Financial Center and Europlex (number 10) occupy a prime lot in the centre of Mokotów district. Previously used as an urban park with freestanding Moskwa cinema built in the 1950s, this area was the centre-point of the district. In the 1990s, the growing market pressure on the city centre has meant the demise of such low-intensity (and non-profit) uses.

The new developments have accommodated modern architectural design and multi-functional properties. The general principle applied by the architect of Europlex, Tadeusz Spychała, was to place two blocks of varied heights (towers), across each other on a 5-story stylobate . The architect grouped all publicly accessible functions on the ground and mezzanine floors and designated the remaining

266   Karina Kreja

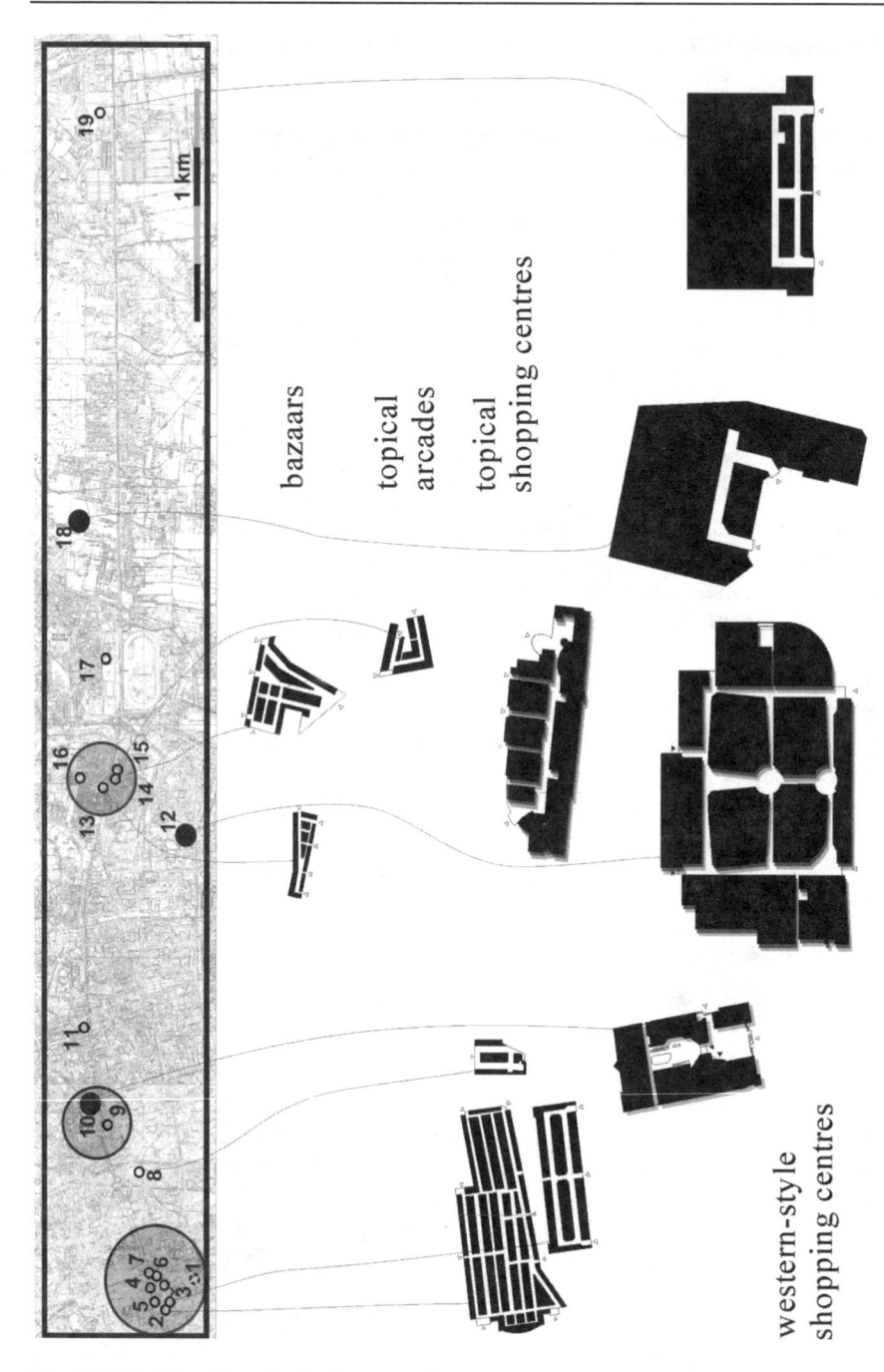

Fig. 13.4. Solid-void analysis of case studies

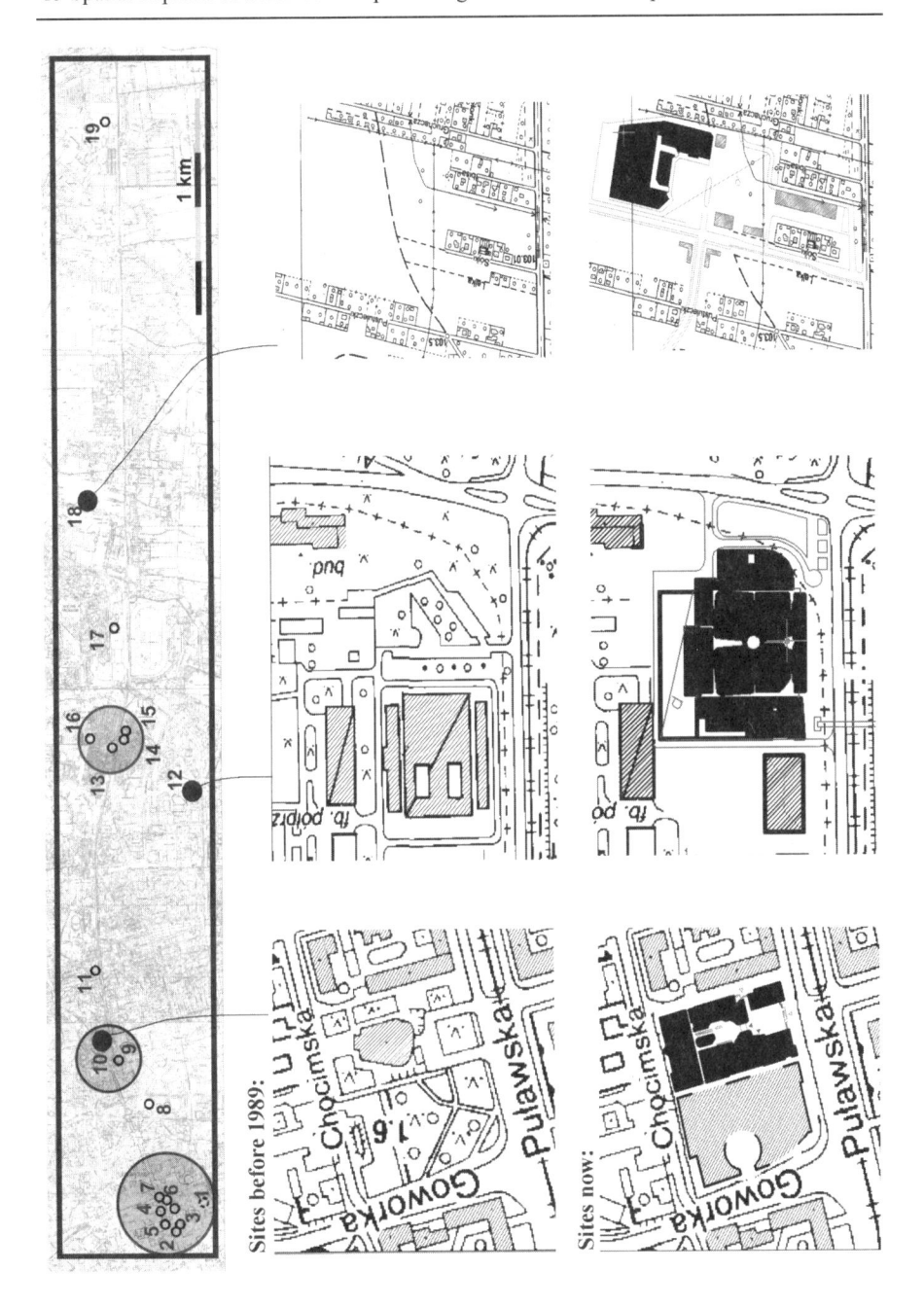

13 Spatial imprints of urban consumption: large-scale retail development in Warsaw 267

Fig. 13.5. Land use comparison: before and after transformation

space for offices. The entrance to the cinema theatre and the stairs to the mezzanine level were located next to the main shopping mall entrance from Puławska.[5]

With the erection of the Financial Center and Europlex, the central space of the district received a new articulation. The main new feature is a sunken square with entrances to all the publicly accessible functions, creating one of the first examples of privately managed public space in Warsaw. This design was intended to enhance the attractiveness of the shopping center and draw more pedestrians to the property. It exemplifies, however, a new category, 'ambiguous urban space', within the post-socialist townscape (Madanipour 2003).

The new building arrangement dominates the existing urban structure. Although contained within the premises of the lot, the changes drastically increased the area's density and reversed the solid/void relationship. The metamorphosis of the center of Mokotów district manifests a shift from non-profit, public, open spaces to enclosed, privately-owned, mercantile spaces. That transformation of a central space from a socialist to a market-driven format exemplifies an overall societal and political change.

13.2.4 Galeria Mokotów

With its 60,000 sq. m of retail space, Galeria Mokotów (number 12) is one of the largest shopping centers in Poland. It is located in the middle of Służewiec Przemysłowy – a central zone that has been transformed from industrial to business, services and leisure functions. Opened in 1998, the shopping center's identity was forcefully established by the contrast between its colorful interior the dull industrial surroundings.

Galeria Mokotów is a pole of mercantile attraction independent of the centers in the neighboring districts. It is 2 km from the planned Wilanowska district center and subway station, but close to a major traffic junction. A shuttle bus connects the shopping center with the subway station. The center generates most of the area's pedestrian flow and vehicle traffic.

Windowless and huge, the development is a rare example of a freestanding regional mall in the middle of an urban area. However, a remodeling of the shopping center, finished in 2002, aimed to minimize its original out-of-town character. A new, well-lit façade, additional architectural detail and a square at the main entrance were introduced. A new passageway over Wołoska Street now connects Galeria Mokotów with Mokotów Business Park, creating a physical link between the supposedly synergistic modern office and retail functions. In addition, public transport stops were redesigned to facilitate access to the mall. As efforts to harmonize the center with its surroundings, however, they turned to be inadequate. Despite its more urban image and the new activities introduced in the square, such as an open-air bar, the center has not been able to create a vigorous and rich environment in the middle of the post-industrial area.

---

[5] Information in this paragraph comes from the developer's press note. Source: www.europlex.pl

The case of Galeria Mokotów highlights one of the most important urban processes ongoing in post-socialist cities: The metamorphosis of a medium-density lot in the industrial zone into one of the largest shopping centers in Poland marks the shift from an industrial to a post-industrial city.

13.2.5 King Cross

Built in 1997, the King Cross (number 18) Geant hypermarket with shopping gallery and retail park was one of the first developments in Warsaw on such a large scale. This type of suburban shopping center, anchored by a hypermarket, has now spread all over Poland, built mainly by French and German developers like Apsys or Metro.

The King Cross hypermarket-based development is strategically located on the outskirts of the city between the Ursynów housing estate and Puławska Street. Since the mid-1990s, this area's green fields have been rapidly filled-up with commercial, residential and office buildings. The center is laid out on a typically narrow and long agricultural lot, which has determined both the road system and the position and form of the center's structures. Indeed, in order to cope with the elongated site, several separate buildings were necessary.

Those shoppers who depend on public transport are a considerable group of clients in this suburban retail park. Yet, the center with its huge parking area is mostly oriented toward car-owners. At the same time, access to it is facilitated by one public and one private shuttle bus line. That accommodation of mass transit is not complemented, however, by any effort to make the shopping center pedestrian-friendly. The 100m-long route between the bus stops and the center inconveniently traverses the parking lot. Thus, overall the customers without cars are effectively downgraded.

Gymnasion Fitness Center was opened in 2000 as a part of this retail park. It signifies a growing trend towards new, non-retail forms of urban consumption. Such forms of consumption, e.g., fitness and leisure, are considered to carry the most potential for commercial expansion.

The King Cross suburban shopping center illustrates the overlapping of different modes of consumption in a post-socialist city, as its introduced activities range from the sale of traditional convenience goods in a hypermarket setting to modern leisure-oriented fitness units. Even more significant is the extent to which such large-scale retail developments partake in suburbanization, urban sprawl, and especially the creation of environments where the only public space is inside the commercial developments. The earlier era's centrally planned and ordered, and well-preserved dichotomy between the urban and rural areas around major urban centers is quickly disappearing. Several Polish architects and urban planners express their surprise at the effects of neo-commercialism on the city, describing the emerging suburban landscape as follows: "Despite having filled the landscape with buildings, the reality represents only absurd urbanization. Neither an empty field nor a town, but a frightening townscape of the future consisting of incompatible buildings, located either too far from or too close to one another"

(Stiasny 2001). The suburban developments laid out in the traditional agricultural land divisions are considered by Polish urban planners to be 'a rural urbanization.'

Conclusions

The success of the new retail developments in Warsaw reveals the consumer values firmly founded rooted in both the socialist and then the post-socialist Polish society. Although already articulated in the city structure, the phenomenon of post-socialist consumption has not been seriously studied. There is no doubt that the observed, unprecedented expansion of retail is the spatial and economic manifestation of previously hidden social currents. Therefore, it is not the direction but the scale and the dynamism of changes that have been unpredictable. For example, in the case study here of the Marszałkowska/ Puławska corridor in Warsaw, only five out of 19 large-scale retail units were built before 1989. Moreover, all of them have already undergone refurbishment.

The observed spatial phenomena display an interesting diversity. In the investigated area, various forms of retail coexist and characterize different phases of social, retail and consumer development. Thus, the observed types cover a wide spectrum of retail--from the street marketing, bazaars, and small shops to the hypermarkets and shopping centers. Each type of retail is set up to satisfy unique consumer groups and desires. Indeed, the recently introduced large-scale retail centers along with the well-established bazaars and topical shopping centers create a more diverse shopping environment than is found in countries with a longer tradition of modern shopping facilities.

The simultaneous appearance of the spatial forms typical to neo-consumerism is illustrated by the bazaar-versus-shopping center dichotomy. The two types originate from different 'consumer eras' and accommodate different customer desires. In a sense, topical shopping centers or arcades are interesting phenomena they bridge the gap between two mutually exclusive retail forms. The future of topical shopping centers is difficult to predict at this stage. Still, the outflow of customers from bazaars and the growing popularity of hypermarkets and shopping centers outline the most probable scenario for the near future. Currently planned along with several other similar developments, the project Złote Tarasy (number 1) is a multi-use development with numerous retail facilities and an internal plaza, designed by the world's best known architect of shopping centers -- Jon Adams Jerde (the Mall of America and Canal City Hakata in Fukuoka). That development is bound to dramatically change the center of Warsaw. The existing and the planned retail developments and shopping centers together will reshape the character of the chosen radial route by reinforcing its high-street character in the center of Warsaw and simultaneously weakening the local centers.

The case studies portray the changes in a post-socialist city mainly in the following terms: from the socialist public space to the privately owned space of a mall; from an industrial to a post-industrial city; and the Polish version of urban sprawl.

The relationship between the underlying problems that drive the changes in urban structure and the identification of retail developments as the spatial articulations of those changes offered a viable research target. The closer look at the three western-style shopping centers reveals their impact on the design of urban public space and on the changing perceptions of place in post-socialist cities. is the case studies highlight how the introduction of shopping centers marks the appearance of an entirely new type of public space, one shaped by mercantile powers. Given the key role of public space in social life, its changing nature calls for further investigation.

The currently observed extent of recent structural changes and the ongoing transformations are the greatest Warsaw has experienced since its rebuilding after WWII. However, the scale and range of the phenomena observed in Warsaw are not directly similar to the processes going on in other cities in Poland or in Central and Eastern Europe. Rather, they highlight the growing importance of neo-consumerism in the development of a post-socialist city.

References

Campbell C (1995) The sociology of consumption. In: Miller D (ed) Acknowledging consumption: A review of new studies. Routlege, London, pp 96-126
Centrum Badań Opinii Społecznej (CBOS) (1996) Supermarkets and the consumer behaviour of Poles. Research report [in Polish]. Warszawa, source: www.cbos.pl
Centrum Badań Opinii Społecznej (CBOS) (1999) Saving and shopping. Research report [in Polish], Warszawa, source: www.cbos.pl
Cheuk FN (2003) Satisfying shoppers' psychological needs: From public market to cybermall. Journal of Environmental Psychology 23:439-455
Clarke DB, Bradford MG (1998) Public and private consumption and the city. Urban Studies 35:865-888
Crowley D (2003) Warsaw. Reaktion Books Ltd, London International Council of Shopping Centers (ICSC) (2001) ICSC's dictionary of shopping center terms. ICSC, New York
Jones Lang LaSalle (2005) Warsaw city profile. Jones Lang LaSalle, Warsaw, September, www.joneslanglasalle.pl
Kancelaria Prezesa Rady Ministrów (KRM) (1995) The announcement after the Council meeting [in Polish] 30.05.1995, www.kprm.gov.pl
Kancelaria Prezesa Rady Ministrów (KRM) (2000) Domestic trade development program [in Polish]. In: Komunikat po Radzie Ministrów 06.06.2000, www.kprm.gov.pl
Madanipour A (2003) Public and private spaces of the city. Routledge, London
Miles S, Paddison R (1998) Urban consumption: An historiographical note. Urban Studies 35:815-823
Miller D (1995) Worlds apart: Modernity through the prism of the local. Routledge, London
Piskiewicz L (2000) Large-scale shopping units in the view of consumers [in Polish]. Institute of Domestic Market and Consumption, Warszawa
Staniszkis J (2004) Farewell to Poland [in Polish]. Przekrój 5:12-13
Stiasny G (2001) Center along the street [in Polish]. Architektura-Murator 5:42-48

Sulima R (2000) Anthropology of everyday life [in Polish]. Wydawnictwo Uniwersytetu Jagiellońskiego, Kraków

The City of Warsaw Council (1995) The Resolution No 193/XXII/95 from the 7th September 1995 [in Polish]

Zukin S (1991) Landscapes of power: From Detroit to Disney World. University of California Press, Berkeley and Los Angeles

PART IV

URBAN PLANNING AND POLICY RESPONSES

14 Planning and societal context – The case of Belgrade, Serbia

Miodrag Vujošević and Zorica Nedović-Budić

Introduction

Urban planning takes place in and is adapted to a rapidly changing and increasingly turbulent world. Despite the claims made for the shift from state socialism in Central and Eastern Europe (CEE) as being a gradual process, the actual dismantling of the communist system in the late 1980s constituted a substantial change in all aspects of societal organization. The extent of the CEE socio-economic and political changes of the late 1980s and early 1990s prompted, among other shocks, "a new notion of planning" (Maier 1994, p. 263) there. The changes that most directly influenced urban development and planning were the privatization of urban land and structures, the decentralization of government, and the relinquishing of the land development process to market forces and a multiplicity of investors and other participants. That societal transformation created turmoil and controversy in the planning profession. Although the formal legal power of planning survived and in fact new laws were enacted, from the viewpoint of citizens, planning's legitimacy was challenged, and was a non-priority for the politicians (Sýkora 1995, 1999); planning was deemed ineffective in managing local urban issues (Maier 1998).

Appreciation for the context in which planning is practiced in Central and Eastern European cities is essential for its effective adjustment to the new conditions and for development of new planning systems (Nedović-Budić 2001). However, there is a notable scarcity of research on the effects of the societal transformation on urban planning practice and theory, and also of methodical attempts to conceptualize the processes and factors characterizing the contextual nature of planning. For example, in the case of Serbia, academics in the field of urban planning mostly replicate the approaches of neo-liberal or institutional economics (Begović 1995); only rudimentary steps are taken toward more ambitious alternatives in theoretical approaches to planning in the transition (Vujošević 1996, 2002a, 2003, 2004; Vujošević and Spasić 1996).

This chapter uses the example of Serbia to illustrate the dynamics among the political and socio-economic context, governance, and the emerging planning system. The chapter proceeds from an overview of the post-WWII and pre-1989 planning system and its collapse, to a discussion of the new institutional arrangements and recent legislation. The chapter considers two recent planning documents: the Regional Spatial Plan of the Belgrade Administrative Area and the Master Plan of Belgrade. This case study illuminates the interplay between urban planning and changing political, governance, and socio-economic circumstances. The study is most relevant to the Central and Eastern European region, but also to other countries worldwide that are undergoing a similar transition from state socialism to democratic and market-based regimes.

14.1 Conceptualization of the context

Planning is a future-oriented activity for managing urban development and change. As such it is inseparable from the societal context and the circumstances in which it is practiced. Wu (2003) suggests that "urban process" is fundamentally a political-economic process. Friedmann (1987) defines modern planning practice as "a social and political process in which many actors, representing many different interests, participate in a refined division of labour" (p. 25). It is a process that takes place in the public domain: the territorially based system of social relations that subsumes politics, bureaucracy, and planning under its political order. Here we complement Friedmann's framework with economic relations and governance, which arise from social relations and from the bureaucracy, respectively. We also add market as an institutionalized socio-economic relation with direct impact on planning (Fig. 14.1.).

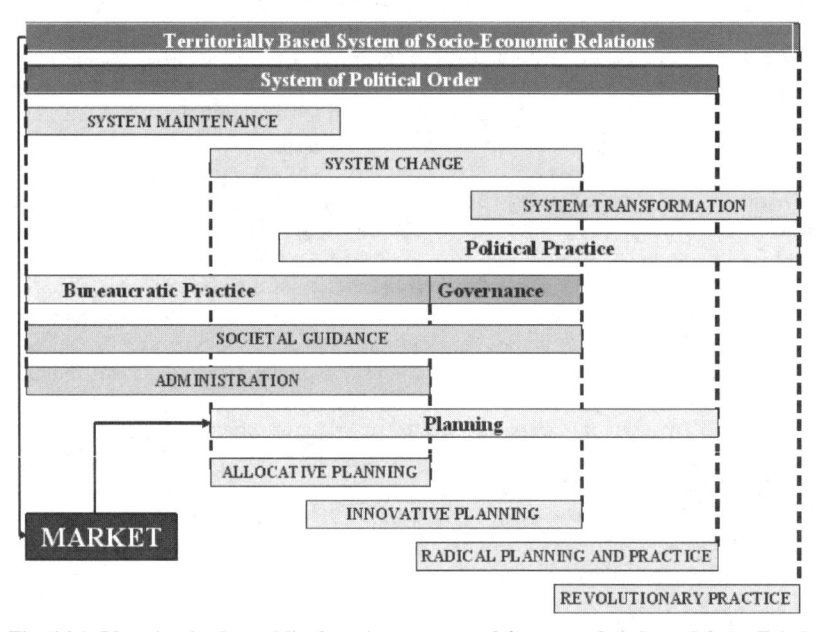

Fig. 14.1. Planning in the public domain: conceptual framework (adapted from Friedmann, 1987)

Territorially based, social systems are typically organized as political systems having institutions of government (legislative, executive, and judiciary branches), legal and constitutional frameworks, and political cultures, as well as such other agents of governance as political parties, interest groups, and citizens. As a component of the political system, planning is conducted through both bureaucratic and political practices. Both practices -- the former "articulated through the institutional structures of the state," and the latter having "its origin in the politically active community" – are necessary, although often in conflict (Friedmann 1987, p. 35). Despite the inevitable conflicts, Johnson (1989) holds that the purposes and dynamics of politics and planning are more complementary than contradictory.

Whatever the variations in the style of planning from a fully administrative to a participatory and inclusive process, it remains strongly government-centred. The continuum between technocratic and participatory planning parallels the government-governance continuum, in which governance relies more on non-government partners and less on authority and control (Kettl 2002). Among the planning process's many components, the levels at which governing is carried out bear a particular importance, since planning takes place at the relevant level of a territorial organization and sometimes cuts across multiple levels – national, state, and local. Of the three levels, the state government tends to be the main actor in the public domain (Friedmann 1987) and the main locus particularly of planning conducted in the mode of social engineering (Scott 1998). It has been through the power of state, particularly under the communist regimes, that bureaucracy, modernist ideology, the use of authority and coercion, and incapacitated civil society have appeared in their extremes. It is also state government that has displayed the most rigidity and resistance toward any political conflict and toward innovative ideas in various realms, including planning.

The private sector, representing market forces, also significantly affects planning process and outcomes. In market societies, central coordination of planning is not possible. Rather, the public interest is deliberated at the interface between market rationality and social rationality (Friedmann 1987). Given the inherent tension between those two rationalities, planning as their product either facilitates or restrains market forces as the balance between them shifts. Therefore, underlying any planning system is the balance established between the role of government and the role of the market in urban development.

Urban planning evolves in response to and by adjusting to the specific contexts and circumstances – political, socio-economic, and governing. It is also affected by history, or what Thomas (1998) and Stark (1992) refer to as the "pre-transitional situation" or as "path-dependency." Planning context-specific practices constitute a planning doctrine (model). Faludi (1999) defines planning doctrine as "a conceptual scheme giving coherence to planning by means of conceptualizing an area's shape, development challenges, and ways of handling them" (p. 333). Once formalized and translated into laws and institutions, a planning doctrine constitutes a planning system unique to a specific configuration of circumstances. Planning systems can be differentiated by "variations in national legal and constitutional structures and administrative and professional cultures;" they include plan-making, urban development and regulatory functions (Healey and Williams 1993, p. 701). Booth (1996) categorizes development control practices as discretionary or regulatory, the former entailing maximum flexibility, and the latter providing certainty in development process and outcomes. The types of practices on that continuum are determined by governmental structure, the role of law, culture, and history. There seem to be more hybrids and variations than prototypical cases.

The case of the former Yugoslav republic of Serbia (now in Serbia and Montenegro) illustrates well how a planning system changes in response to changing political and socio-economic circumstances. The post-WWII dynamics there differed from those in most other communist countries. The more extreme variations in planning practice and the response to the societal circumstances since 1989, offer rich opportunities for observing the relationships between planning and its broader context. The lingering transition (or what Thomas (1998) terms "the moment of discontinuity") in that former Yugoslav republic, which was more complex and less predictable than in other post-socialist countries in Europe, also presents an extended time period for studying the processes and issues in adapting and formulating of a planning system.

14.2 The collapse of socialist planning

Serbia is one of the six republics of the former Yugoslavia, which from the early 1990s disintegrated into five states: Slovenia, Croatia, Bosnia and Herzegovina, Macedonia, and Serbia and Montenegro (Fig. 14.2.). The planning systems that had emerged in this region over the past 60 years can be placed in three time frames: (a) central-command planning, from 1947 to 1965; (b) political decentralization and societal self-management planning, from 1965 to 1989; and (c) 'democratized' planning, from 1989 to the present.

Beginning in the mid-1940s, urban planning in Yugoslavia reflected the communist institutional and ideological framework, although with an early departure from Stalinism in 1948: state ownership and distribution of the nationalized means of production and property; and rejection of market principles and mechanisms except in the case of agricultural land ownership and market. Under this framework the underlying public interest justified government intervention the existing urban structure, with the state acting as the main urban land developer and having a particularly strong role in providing housing (Fisher 1962; French and Hamilton 1979; Pioro 1965). The planning model was locally adapted, Soviet-based, centralized administrative planning, with hierarchical control mechanisms and substantial legal power exercised through 5-year plans. Spatial planning and controlled urbanization were used to pursue economic growth objectives and to ensure rational use of resources through "top-down" allocation (Dawson 1987; Papić 1988). In the late 1950s and early 1960s, more attention was given to the physical aspects of urban growth. Regional and comprehensive plans were introduced as the key instruments of industrial decentralization (Enyedi 1996) and to address persisting regional inequalities (Plesković and Dolenc 1982).

Fig. 14.2. Location of former Yugoslavia and Serbia and Montenegro in the context of the Balkan Peninsula

Starting in 1965, the political and administrative system of Yugoslavia was politically decentralized and economically liberalized. Economic restructuring introduced self-management of enterprises by their employees, a fundamental change in economic management (Dawson 1987). Yugoslavia was known for having one of the most decentralized systems of decision-making, applied equally to social, economic, environmental, and spatial (urban) planning and policy, and shared by the central, republic, and communal branches of government as well as by individual enterprises (Vujošević 2003; Simmie 1989). Planning legislation designated local communities (or communes) as the main planning and implementation authorities and was updated in 1984 to improve the coordination and integration of plans and policies. The federal level dealt with socioeconomic development and environmental policy, but no spatial planning. Republics and provinces made their own long-term plans (Vujošević 1996). The essential characteristic of the system, at least nominally, was a "bottom-up" participatory approach, with the principle of "cross-acceptance" practiced more than a decade before it was contemplated or practiced in certain developed Western countries (Cullingworth 1997). Ironically, eventually the preparation, discussion, and implementation of planning decisions became over-loaded by the various types of individual, group, and general public participation.

By the end of the 1980s, both the system and the practice of socio-economic and spatial planning in Yugoslavia was dysfunctional despite its innovative features; spatial disparities had increased or merely been shifted from one territorial level to another (Očić 1998). The crisis was not ascribed to planning per se, but rather to the hypertrophied and bureaucratized system of "societal self-management" and the associated system of participative planning. After the break-up of Yugoslavia a new system was sought by the new governmental and other relevant institutions, to manage the impact of new factors and to be ultimately based on market approaches and institutions. The aim also was to balance the vision and the implementation of sustainable development policies.

14.3 New institutions and legislation

As in other post-socialist regions of Central and Eastern Europe, in Serbia the 1990s began with attempts toward political pluralism, democratization, and establishment of a civil society, as well as market reforms. However, the autocratic regime of Slobodan Milošević and the ensuing civil war, political and economic isolation and crisis halted the transitional reforms; there was almost no sign of transformative processes. Societal retrogression was pervasive in Serbia. Societal integration was driven by negative nationalistic forces, in contrast to the integration in other countries that drew on cultural identities, political regimes, and modes of production (Offe 1996). In Serbia, more progress toward democracy did occur after fall 2000, when the dictatorship was replaced by a freely elected president and government.

The main characteristic of the 1990s was the re-centralization of government and the weakening of the constitutional role and planning authority of the local communes. Attempts to strengthen market institutions and promote privatization were unsuccessful (Lazić 1994). Cosmetic legal changes simply substituted "state/collective land ownership" for the former "societal land ownership" and improved slightly the terms of compensation for compulsory sale of private agricultural land. An upsurge of new, legitimate private interests paralleled the collapse of many previous, unequivocally public interests. At the same time, however, the institutional and procedural arrangements were lacking that could make partnerships between the two domains workable. Both domestic and foreign investments were only sporadic, while the informal sector of the economy expanded under the circumstances of the countries international isolation. Not until the late 1990s did the first true signs of post-socialist proto-capitalist laissez-faire, privatization and marketization appear.

On the planning front, a number of new "ideologies of planning" surfaced, rendering planning practice a peculiar mix of various "quasi/pseudo planning" exercises, imbued with new biases; partisanships dominating the public scene; the notion of public interest almost lost, and non-transparent priorities and interests behind the planning. Initially, the fairly negative experience with the former planning system fuelled a wide-spread rejection of planning, particularly among the engineers of the transition reforms, most of whom were economists with neo-liberal ideological inclinations. They discarded any relatively ambitious notion of planning, reducing its role to so-called "project-led cum market-based" planning and concomitant methodologies. The new planning practice was steered by a mixture of old habits, few institutional innovations and the social, economic and political turbulence of the transition period. Indeed, the process was not too much different from planning in other post-socialist countries in the Balkans (Vujošević 2001). However, due to re-centralization and the loss of local planning function and authority, the former Yugoslav republics assumed the key role in socio-economic, spatial/urban and environmental planning. In accordance with the 1995 planning legislation, the republics of Serbia and Montenegro prepared a number of spatial plans and also approved the general / master urban plans prepared by local authorities. These plans fulfilled symbolic and mostly political purposes rather than those conventionally attached to the formal planning documents (Sillince 1986).

The context and issues of planning practice in the 1990s in post-socialist Serbia can be summarized by the following points (Vujošević 2003; Vujošević et al. 2000): 1) the lost legitimacy of planning; 2) a nonexistent or vague notion of public interest; 3) centralization of government and planning institutions; 4) lack of planning expertise, support, and administrative capacity at the local communal level; 5) lack of regional governance and planning (Stojkov et al. 1998); 6) lack of strategic planning; 7) inadequate or ineffective implementation mechanisms; 8) prevailing "physicalism" in planning; 9) lack of participation, openness and transparency in the planning process; 10) confusion regarding local ownership patterns and revenues, which hindered foreign direct investment (FDI) Đorđević (2005); 11) persisting distortions in land markets; 12) undeveloped national land-use policy; and 13) political instability, manipulations, corruption and clientism. Thus by the new century, planning in Serbia laboured under a range of contextual difficulties.

The political changes in the early 2000's have brought about legal and institutional adjustments with regard to spatial and urban planning. *The Act on Self-governance/Закон о локалној самоуправи* (2002) outlines the framework for planning, giving legal powers to local authorities and giving them an increased role in development programs and strategies, urban plans, and budgeting. However, then *The Planning and Construction Act/Закон о планирању и изграњи* (2003), which substantially narrows planning practice, passed in 2003 despite opposition from the professional planners. They view the Act as driven by political motifs and regressing from the standards of planning practice established throughout the post-WWII period (Vujošević 2002b). This Act indeed defines the spatial and urban planning system as limited mainly to traditional physical planning, construction and building control. It is modelled after the 1931 *Building Law*, which has a strong focus on of engineering and shows the influence of the French planning system. The 2003 Act is quite radical in its return to private ownership of denationalized urban land, its very few restrictions on development rights, and procedures that make possible the quick legalization of illegally constructed buildings. It encourages market rationality as a guidance mechanism, but ineffectively, since it relies more on rules than on establishing procedures. The planning and decision-making are envisioned as linear procedures, in the hands of politicians and planners, with little attention to other participants' views.

The Planning and Construction Act defines two categories of plans: spatial plans and urban plans. Spatial plans include: 1) the Spatial Development Strategy of the Republic of Serbia; 2) spatial development schemes; 3) spatial plans for special-purpose areas; 4) regional spatial plans; and 5) municipal development plans. Urban plans include: 1) master (general) plans; and 2) regulation plans.

That system of plans is hierarchial, with *The Spatial Development Strategy of the Republic of Serbia/Strategija prostornog razvoja Republike* at the top. Planning at the republic and regional levels (including the so-called *spatial development schemes/šeme prostornog razvoja*) is the prerogative of the representative/legislative and executive branch of the government – the National Parliament of the Republic of Serbia and the Government of Serbia. The plans from the upper levels of government are binding for the lower levels, following a "top-down" pattern. Communal spatial plans, urban plans and regulation plans are under the auspices of local authorities. The Act stipulates preparation and enactment of long-term spatial plans covering at least 10 years and comprising the key strategic development elements.

Implementation of the plans involves the so-called "implementation contracts," also derived from French planning practice. Harmonization with contemporary European development planning practice ("standards and normatives") and transboundary and international cooperation is taken into account by the recent legislation. The republic's strategy and the schemes of spatial development correspond to the European Union's nomenclature of statistical territorial units (NUTS) at level NUTS1. *Regional spatial plans/regionalni prostorni planovi* are being prepared for the autonomous provinces — territorial entities at the NUTS2 and NUTS3 levels, as well as for Belgrade's administrative area. Municipal spatial plans are at the NUTS 4 level.

The Self-governance Act establishes the role of the Chief Architect (*glavni arhitekt*), who has responsibility for plan monitoring, implementation and modification. This introduction of the Chief Architect position at the communal/municipal level, along with the establishment of the Communal Manager (*opštinski menadžer*) with responsibility for general governance and administrative duties, testifies to at least two aspects of the most recent legal reforms: the supremacy of physicalism in spatial and urban planning, and the strong neo-liberal inclination of the political and ideological "engineers" of the transition. The system of spatial, urban and environmental planning was "touched-up" in the 1990s, and additional legal changes were introduced in 2002-2003. However, those adjustments were not suited to the societal factors described above. Planning continues to be practiced as crisis-management, focusing on projects that are rarely coordinated and harmonized, given the inappropriate institutional setting and lack of an overall strategic development framework. On this point, Krešić (2004), although generally supportive of the new legislation, questions the readiness of Serbian society and institutions for its radically different approach to urban planning and management. He recognizes that many of the premises of the 2003 planning law are built on unrealistic expectations and inaccurate assessments of the local circumstances and context.

14.4 Plan-making under the new system

The propositions of *The Planning and Construction Act* in terms of approach, methodology and contents were applied in the preparation of The Regional Spatial Plan of the Belgrade Administrative Area: RSPBAA (*Regionalni prostorni plan Administrativnog Područja Beograda, RPPAPB*, 2004) and in The Master Plan of Belgrade: MPB (*Generalni Plan Beograda 2021*, 2003). The role of a regional plan is defined by *The Planning and Construction Act* as "working out of the spatial organisation principles, and defining the objectives of spatial development, organisation, protection and utilisation of space, as well as of other relevant elements."[1] The content is stipulated in very broad terms (article no. 22): a plan is to comprise text and graphical interpretation.

The work on the RSPBAA started in 2001 and the plan was adopted in 2004. The Plan covers the territory of the 16 municipal communes (*gradske opštine*) of Belgrade, of which 11 are its urban core, totalling 3,224 km^2 with 1,572,000 inhabitants (of whom about 1,280 000 are urban, and about 292 000 suburban). As estimated in 2005, the average Gross Domestic Product (GDP) per capita for this region is still below 2000 US$. The RSPBAA sets the goal of supporting implementation of the principles of sustainable development set forth in Agenda 21, Habitat II and other relevant declarations. It sets four main dimensions: natural, social, economic and institutional; and three time horizons: 2006, 2011, and post 2011. The graphical interpretation of its land use and infrastructural elements is presented in Fig. 14.3. The following are the strategic tasks suggested in the Plan:

1. Redefining and positioning metropolitan Belgrade with regard to its European surroundings and definition of its place and role in the European context;
2. Establishment of effective and sustainable transportation infrastructure and relevant connections to the European network (TENs and TINA);
3. "Dispersed concentration" – restructuring and improving economic structures to increase the competitiveness of the metropolitan area;
4. Enhancement of spatial cohesion through the development and improvement of the network of infrastructure and its better accessibility for the residents of urban and rural settlements;
5. Defining new land and housing policies in accordance with the goals of economic and social development;
6. Protection and betterment of the city's natural and cultural heritage to strengthen the city's identity;
7. Protection, revitalization and enhancement of the environment that has been degraded by human activities; and
8. Profiling the metropolitan area through specialization of economic activities, and services in particular.

---

[1] With the exception of Strategy of spatial development of the Republic of Serbia, this applies to all spatial plans, including the spatial development schemes.

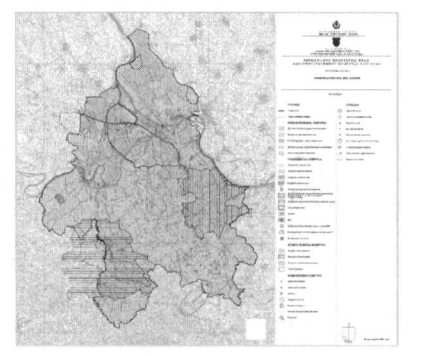

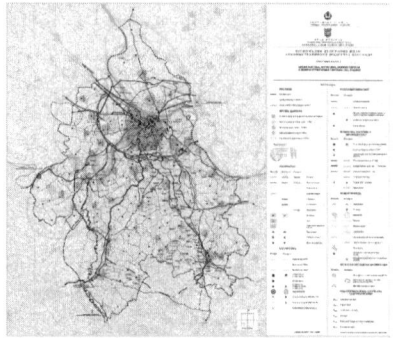

Fig. 14.3. The Regional Spatial Plan for the Administrative Area of Belgrade: land use and infrastructural elements

Source: http://www.beograd.org.yu/cms/view.php?id=203587

The preparation of The Master Plan of Belgrade was also launched in 2001[2], and the plan was enacted in 2003. The planned area covers about 7700 ha, out of which 3600 ha is built area (Fig. 14.4), with about 1,320 000 inhabitants and 420 000 employed in 2001. GDP per capita is estimated at 2,500 US $ in 2005. *The Planning and Construction Act* determines the role of a master plan as "defining a long term perspective of settlement development and spatial organisation" (article no. 36). The content of the *Act* addresses the following main themes: designating building areas and dominant planned destinations therein; defining the key spatial parameters for various types of technical infrastructure (i.e., transportation, energy, water supply, and other utilities); and zoning for specific urban plans. Within the legal framework, the MPB effectively represents a strategic physical plan, and also comprises a number of elements of socio-economic development and environmental policy.

Like the RSPBAA, the MPB has as its priorities to promote integration into Europe and to capitalize on the city's location on the corridors VII and X. The goal is to recover the comparative advantages lost during the isolation of the 1990s. Continued political and economic reform, revived social and housing policies, prevention of illegal construction, promotion of the city's cultural and natural values, sustainable and balanced development, and enhanced urban management are additional elements contributing to this overall objective. Orientation toward the Danube River as a resource and transit node is also emphasized. The other functional areas covered in the plan are:

- nature (morphology, hydrology, geology, seismology, climate, and pedology)
- society (demographics, social phenomena and processes, economics, law)

---

[2] The first urban development scheme for Belgrade was worked out in 1842, followed by another plan in 1868. There were three plans after World War II -- in 1950, 1972, and 1981 (modified in 1985 and 1999).

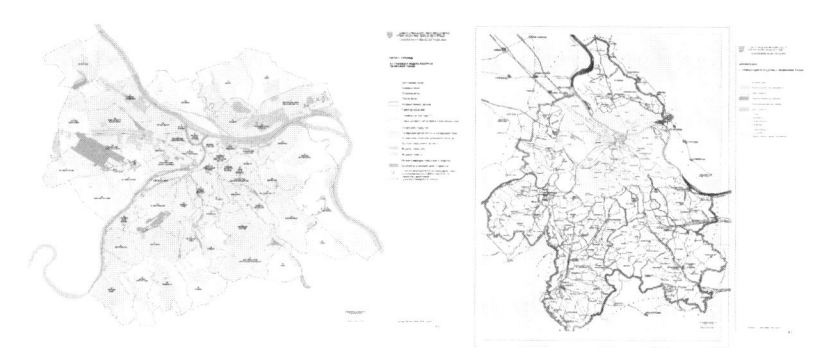

Fig. 14.4. The Master Plan of Belgrade: urban boundary and the metropolitan region

Source: http://www.beograd.org.yu/cms/view.php?id=201126

- urban land (areas, cadastre, ownership, land use, market, land policy)
- urban activity areas (housing, centres, commercial activities, public services, economic zones, public space)
- city parks and landscape (natural elements, green space)
- transportation (public, individual, rail, air, river, pedestrian, bicycle, transportation networks, streets)
- infrastructure (energy, telecommunications, water, sewage)

The graphical representation of several of the plan's elements -- land use, green space and implementation priorities – is shown in Fig. 14.5.

The conceptualization of the future development of Belgrade is based on the following key ideas:

1. Internal urban transformation with new locations for economic functions, open and recreational space and ecological infrastructure, and needed additions in housing stock
2. Support for large scale development projects, without neglecting small investors
3. Adequate supply of communal and transportation infrastructure
4. Better connection with and respect for the natural environment
5. Future reserves of corridors and developable land.

The two plans fomulated general and specific aims, goals and targets to address the pressing problems of the planned area(s), on the one hand, and to make the best of the development potentials of the broader Belgrade area, on the other. The problems, which present significant challenges for planning, are as follows:

- inadequate implementation of urban plans; anarchic and illegal building practices

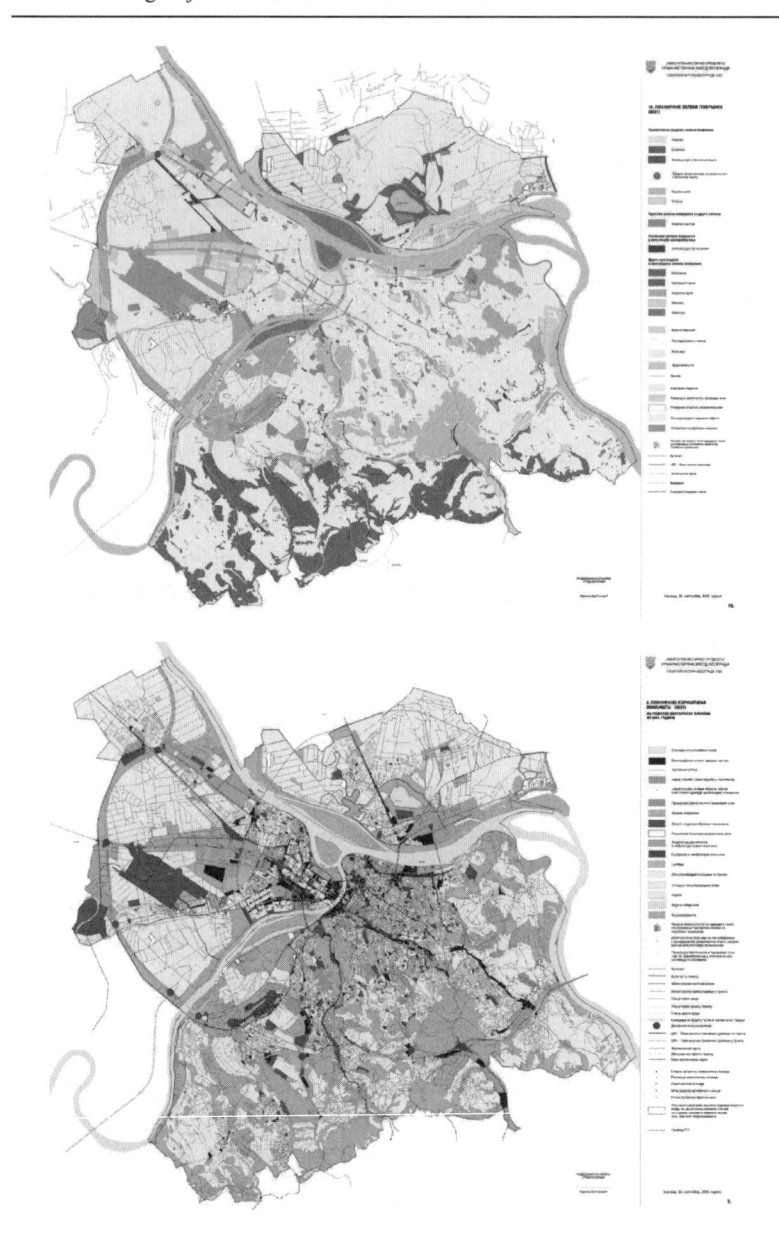

Fig. 14.5. A sample of functional elements of The Master Plan of Belgrade: land use, green space and implementation priorities

Source: http://www.beograd.org.yu/cms/view.php?id=201126

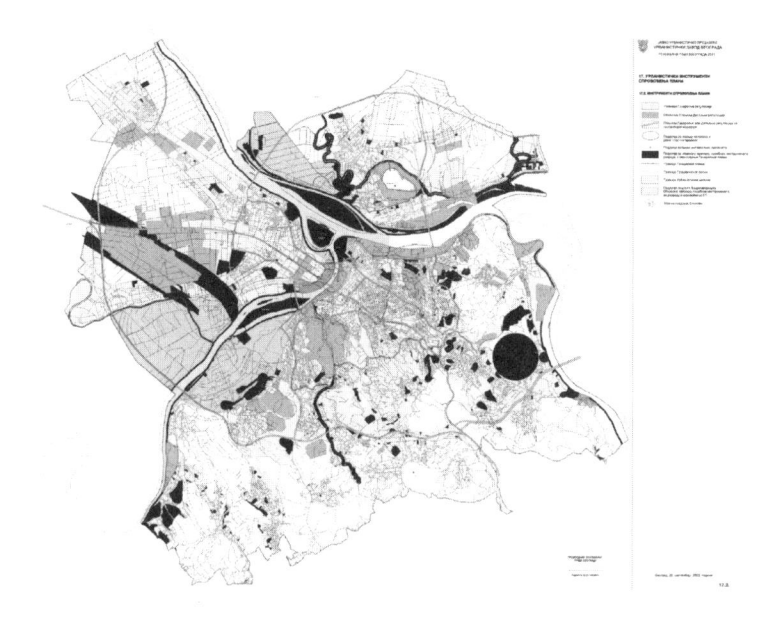

Fig. 14.5. (cont.)

- distributed but undeveloped urban land; the emergence of poor sections and slums
- the inactivation of existing industrial zones
- the widespread presence of the "kiosk economy"
- a devastated transportation system
- unregulated urban agriculture
- the increasing presence of unregulated landfill sites
- illegal use of communal services
- and deteriorating urban aesthetics

Further societal and urban issues join this already challenging list:

- a major demographic change and a shift in the city's urban image caused by the emigration of thousands of its most vital and educated young people and the immigration of population groups from war-torn areas
- the degraded environmental conditions and endangered eco-systems that have resulted from the generally poor ecological culture, inefficient and disregarded environmental legislation and widespread illegal construction; intensive urban sprawl
- undeveloped urban and regional governance and administrations
- collapsing, technologically out of date, and unmaintained public utilities

- burning traffic problems due to undeveloped infrastructure, the disconnects between transport sectors, and poor integration into regional, national and international networks
- abandoned state-owned enterprises, brownfield properties, and other planned but underdeveloped or unused spaces

Finally, massive illegal construction as a long-lasting tendency is perhaps the most complex and serious obstacle to introducing a more organized spatial pattern (Žegarac 2000).

Given the context of formidable problems outlines above, the RSPBAA and MPB are commendable and timely efforts with comprehensive appeal and good intentions. Nevertheless, in some respects the two planning documents fall short of the new expectations for methodological effectiveness or planning innovation. The following are brief points of assessment:

- The roles of the documents are poorly defined, roaming between their attempt to respect the 'insuperable role of the market' and to fulfil a genuine social and political mission.
- Physicalism is the key feature. Although they are not entirely devoid of the environmental and socio-economic development elements of policy and planning, as the only source for promotion of such elements strategic planning documents should feature them more prominently.
- The concept of sustainable development has only been flirted with; what is missing is a sound doctrine upon which to direct and articulate development — one relevant for a territorial entity with a GDP of no more than US $ 2,500 per capita. For that context, no analytical concept or system of operational and sustainable development indicators applicable to an actual city/area has been worked out.
- The two plans are deprived of systematic evaluation. The fact that rigorous ex post evaluation of past decisions has not been performed strongly implies that future steps will be based on no more than anecdotal insights in the existing power structure, institutional and organizational arrangements and the communication and interaction modes currently dominant in planning.[3] Although the intention of the planning exercises is to work out a "hard product," i.e. an urban development plan, no ex ante evaluation scheme and criteria have been produced, leaving the professional audience and the public at large without the sound answers on key questions: What are the criteria upon which the evaluation has been undertaken? Whose criteria are they? What interests stand behind them? Who decides on the criteria? Apart from softening the rigour of the ex-

---

[3] For example, Gilg and Kelly (1996) suggest four assessment levels: (1) Statistical and cartographic analysis; (2) Technical analysis of the decision-making process as a source of information, or as a way of testing hypotheses about the effectiveness of planning policies ("logical positivism"); (3) Examining the decision-making process as a power struggle; (4) Examining the planning process in a 'post-modern' way, i.e. as a sequence of events.

pertise, this flaw also allows too ample manoeuvring space for subsequent arbitrating by politicians.
- The plans' key prognostic technique is trend-based extrapolation; that is inadequate given its poor predictive power, the unstable institutional arrangements, and the skewed nature of data for the 1980s and 1990s.[4] What is required is rather a number of realistic and plausible alternative scenarios of possible/desirable future development elaborated and presented for deliberation and decision-making both in expert arenas and in public forums.
- Perhaps the weakest parts of these planning documents concern the implementation of planning decisions. They give way to "visioning" instead of dealing directly with the pressing realities of development.[5] Moreover, even the more elaborated steps for implementing the key development objectives are shadowed by the lack of political will for undertaking them. Consequently, the documents examined exhibit a sharp discrepancy between "should" and "is."[6] For example, no corroboration is offered in terms of available resources and implementation instruments, for how to bridge the gap between the current grave situation and poor development prospects, on the one hand, and on the other, the extremely optimistic and enthusiastic growth path that is projected.[7]
- Finally, an open, transparent and publicly verified "offer to strategic partners" will be needed, because Belgrade (like other cities and regions in Serbia) does not have enough indigenous resources to cope alone with its economic, social, physical and environmental renewal. In this respect, Europe (Stojkov and Subotić 2004) and the Balkan region (Vujošević 2001) are the most relevant contexts for realizing the strategic goals for Belgrade's metropolitan area.

The major effort put into the preparation of the RSPBAA and MPB is well respected. However, if they are to be effective instruments for guidance and implementation, both the planning approach and the methodology should be improved. These plans are likely to have considerable demonstrational effects throughout the planning scene in Serbia, so their highly professional execution is essential. As most of the plans' flaws relate to their contextual settings, the focus should be on improving of those highly influential elements: better articulation of public institu-

---

[4] The 1980s were a decade of economic stagnation; then in the 1990s the country (then Yugoslavia) experienced the almost complete collapse of all key social, economic, health and cultural parameters for development.

[5] Vujošević and Filipović (2002) report on more than 15 key problems of development in Yugoslavia (Serbia and Montenegro), including a deep crisis in the economy (foreign debt, public finances, no growth, unemployment of over 30%), social polarization, health, refugees, 'brain drain,' environmental pollution, housing deficit.

[6] This most notably applies to 1996 *Spatial Plan of the Republic of Serbia*.

[7] In the Master Plan of Belgrade 2021, the GDP per capita is predicted to grow at an annual growth rate of 5.3% over the period of 18 years. In the same period the total number of employed is predicted to increase from 430,000 (in 2003) to 545,000 (in 2021). According to the same forecast, the gross capital investment would reach 21 billion Euros in total.

tions and interests, reliance on and trust in democratic decision-making, and thorough understanding of private sector activities and land markets.

Conclusion

The premise of this paper is that planning activities are embedded in a particular societal context or territorially based system of socio-economic relations: the political system and practices, the bureaucracy and governance, and the economic system (in this case, the market). The characteristics of both the existing planning system and its transformation are closely tied to those other societal dynamics. During major change of a societal context, as has been the case since 1989 in the Central and Eastern European countries, the mutual adjustment between planning and the other systems has been dramatic and therefore challenging. This paper has reviewed concepts that clarify how context affects planning in the public domain, and illustrated those concepts with information about the planning system, legislature and plan-making in Serbia and its capital city of Belgrade. The case study points to how planning relates to the shifts in the economic, political, and institutional settings in which it takes place.

Almost 15 years after the fall of the Berlin Wall, Serbia still finds itself in a post-socialist proto-democracy ("post-socialist proto-capitalist *laissez-faire*"),[8] yet without developed institutions of representative democracy, civil society and a market economy. On the one hand, the better parts of the former self-management system of the ideological and political monopoly have been abandoned and almost forgotten; on the other, that system's shortcomings have been kept and transferred through the 1990s reigned over by paternalism, manipulation and clientism. "Wild capitalism" and concomitant privatization have taken place without authentic social and political dialogue or consensus on the strategic issues of the transition.

The problems of planning system and practice in Serbia have been concomitant with the overall institutional changes (Nedović-Budić and Vujošević 2004). Namely, although the previous period's comfortable institutional and other certainties for planning simply evaporated in the 1990s, most planners seem to have then avoided any fundamental debate about the theoretical and institutional underpinnings of the existing planning system. Key issues of its legitimacy, role, mission, political background, contents, and procedures were ignored. Rather, planners inclined to discuss safer issues of development policy/planning as narrowed down to technical problems. Particularly, little theoretical or general methodological research has examined alternative planning modes in the transition. In that respect, the situation in Serbia sharply contrasts with that in the West. For example, Allmendinger and Tewdrw-Jones (2002) write on an "explosion of new texts in planning theory" over the period of the recent decade. In Serbia, there has been neither

---

[8] This broadly corresponds to the hybrid system in the contemporary China (of course, at completely different physical scale). Friedmann (2005) points to dual nature of municipal government – part state bureaucracy, part – what he terms "buccaneering capitalism."

systematic study of the "dark side of planning – the domain of power" (Yiftachel 1998), nor of the transferred and newly generated distortions in the triangle power – knowledge – action (Friedmann 1987), although those aspects are acutely relevant to changes in planning during the post-socialist transition.

Although the situation of planning in Serbia clearly leaves much to be desired, avenues to its recovery come readily to mind. Serbia should seek a new planning and policy model that is (a) is compatible with and supportive of the development of a civic society, and (b) harmonizes with the European Union rules. New planning should be grounded in the authority of law and traditional social rules. Planning and policy process ought to be: open, transparent, fair, participative /inclusive, and accountable. General principles of planning would include the following qualifiers: pro-active, flexible, indicative, adaptive, inclusive, monitored, evaluation-and-feedback-based. So-called "technocratic" planning would give way to "sociocratic" planning (Faludi and van der Valk 1994). Expanding on Begović's (1998) suggestions, we propose the following contextual components to be closely considered in conjunction with the needed changes: (a) selective privatization and establishment of a new balance between private and public ownership; (b) efficient functioning of urban land markets and the associated legal and financial mechanisms and institutions; (c) evaluation and redefinition of the role of local authorities; (d) achievement of a new balance between the roles of planning and the market in land allocation, management, and control. Changes in these components would have strong implications for both the role and the format of planning and policy.

References

Allmendinger P, Tewdwr-Jones M (eds) (2002) Planning Futures - New Directions for Planning Theory. Routledge, London New York

Begović B (1998) Gradsko zemljiste: zaboravljeni resurs? *Ekonomika* XXXIV, 9-10: 212-214 (in Serbian)

Begović B (1995) *Ekonomika urbanistickog planiranja* / Urban Planning Economics. CES MECON, Belgrade (in Serbian)

Booth P (1996) Controlling development: certainty and discretion in Europe, the U.S. and Hong Kong. UCL Press, London

Cullingworth B (1997) Planning in the USA – Policies, Issues, and Processes. Routledge, New York

Dawson AH (1987) Yugoslavia. In: Dawson A (ed) Planning in Eastern Europe. St. Martin's Press, New York, pp. 275-291

Đorđević S (2005) Opštine bez imovine / Communes without Property. *Danas,* 8. decembra. (in Serbian)

Enyedi G (1996) Urbanization under socialism. In: Andrusz G, Harloe M, Szelenyi I (eds) Cities after socialism – Urban and regional change and conflict in post-socialist societies. Blackwell Publishers, Oxford, pp. 100-118

Faludi A (1999) Patterns of Doctrinal Development. *Journal of Planning Education and Research* 18: 333-344

Faludi A, van den Valk A (1994) Rule and order -- Dutch planning doctrine in the twentieth century. Kluwer Academic Publishers, Dordrecht

Fisher JC (1962) Planning the city of socialist man. *Journal of the American Institute of Planners* 28: 251-265.

French RA, Hamilton IFE (1979) The socialist city: Spatial structure and urban policy. John Wiley & Sons, New York

Friedmann J (2005) China's Urban Transition. University of Minnesota Press, St. Paul, MN

Friedmann J (1987) Planning in the public domain: From knowledge to action. Princeton University Press, Princeton, NJ

Генерални урбанистички план Београда 2021/*Master Plan of Belgrade 2021* (2003), Службени лист града Београда, XLVII, 27. (in Serbian)

Gilg A, Kelly M (1996) The analysis of development control decisions. A position statement and some new insights form recent research in south-west England. *Town Planning Review* 67: 203-228

Healey P, Williams R (1993) European urban planning systems: Diversity and convergence. *Urban Studies* 30: 701-720

Johnson WC (1989) The politics of urban planning. Paragon House, New York

Kettl DF (2002) The transformation of governance – Public administration for twenty-first century America. The Johns Hopkins University Press, Baltimore, MD

Krešić M (2004) Serbian Planning and Constructing Law approach to city politics and urban management. Were we ready? In: Nedović-Budić Z, Tsenkova S (eds) Winds of societal change: Remaking post-communist cities. Russian, East European and Eurasian Center, University of Illinois, Urbana-Champaign, pp. 171-180

Lazić M (ed) (1994) Razaranje drustva - Jugoslovensko drustvo u krizi 90-tih. Filip Višnjić, Beograd (in Serbian)

Maier K (1994) Planning and education in planning in the Czech Republic. *Journal of Planning Education and Research* 13:263-269

Maier K (1998) Czech planning in transition: Assets and deficiencies. *International Planning Studies* 3:351-365

Nedović-Budić Z (2001) Adjustment of planning practice to the new Eastern and Central European context. *Journal of the American Planning Association* 67:38-52

Nedović-Budić Z, Vujošević M (2004) Interplay between political, governance, socio-economic and planning systems: Case study of former Yugoslavia and present Serbia and Montenegro. In: Nedović-Budić Z, Tsenkova S (eds) Winds of societal change: Remaking post-communist cities. Russian, East European and Eurasian Center, University of Illinois, Urbana-Champaign, pp. 111-132

Očić (1998) Ekonomika regionalnog razvoja Jugoslavije. Ekonomika, Beograd (in Serbian)

Offe C (1996) Varieties of transition – The East European and East German experience. The MIT Press, Cambridge, MA

Papić Z (1988) Stanje i perspektive razvoja planiranja u nas. *Ekonomist* 41:210-214 (in Serbo-Croatian)

Pioro Z (1965) Socialist city planning: A re-examination. *Journal of the American Institute of Planners* 31: pp. 31-42

Plesković B, Dolenc M (1982) Regional development in a socialist, developing, and multi-national country, The case of Yugoslavia. *International Regional Science Review* 7:1-24

Регионални просторни план административног подручја града Београда/Regional Spatial Plan of the Belgrade Administrative Area (2004) Службени лист града Београда, XLVIII, 10 (in Serbian)

Scott JC (1998) Seeing like a state – How certain schemes to improve the human condition have failed. Yale University Press, New Haven, CT

Sillince J (1986) A Theory of Planning. Aldershot, Gower

Simmie J (1989) Self-management and town planning in Yugoslavia. *Town Planning Review* 60:271-286

Stark D (1992) The great transformation? Social change in Eastern Europe. *Contemporary Sociology* 21:299-304

Stojkov B, Subotić S (2004) Strateški cilji razvoja Beograjske metropolitanske regije v okviru evropskega prostorskega razvoja / Strategic Development Objectives for the Belgrade Metropolitan Region in the context of European Spatial Development. *Urbani izziv* 15:17-24 (in Slovenian)

Stojkov B, Vujošević M, Subotić S (1998) Neue Ansätze för die Raumplanung des Donauraums in Jugoslawien. *EUREG* 7:60-65 (in German)

Sýkora L (1995) Prague. In: Berry J, McGreal S (eds) European cities, planning systems and property markets. E & FN Spon, London

Sýkora L (1999) Transition states of East Central Europe. In: Balchin P, Sýkora L, Bull G (eds) Regional Policy and Planning in Europe. Routledge, London

Thomas MJ (1998) Thinking about planning in the transitional countries of Central and Eastern Europe. *International Planning Studies* 3:321-333

Vujošević M (2004) The Search for a new development planning/policy mode: Problems of expertise in the transition period. Proceedings of the 3rd Swedish-Serbian Symposium Belgrade and Stockholm at the End of XXth Century. Serbian Academy of Sciences and Arts and The Royal Academy of Letters, History and Antiquities, Stockholm, Belgrade, pp. 1-13 (in Serbian)

Vujošević M (2003) Planiranje u postsocijalističkoj političkoj i ekonomskoj tranziciji/Planning in the post-socialist political and economic transition. Institut za arhitekturu i urbanizam Srbije, Beograd (in Serbian)

Vujošević M (2002a) Novije promene u teoriji i praksi planiranja na Zapadu i njihove pouke za planiranje u Srbiji-Jugoslaviji / Recent changes in the Western planning theory and practice and the lessons for planning in Serbia-Yugoslavia. Institut za arhitekturu i urbanizam Srbije, Beograd (in Serbian)

Vujošević M (2002b) Komentari *Nacrta Zakona o planiranju i izgradnji* / Comments on the *Draft of the Planning and Construction Act.* Unpublished paper. Institut za arhitekturu i urbanizam Srbije, Beograd (in Serbian)

Vujošević M (2001) Geography lost and found - Integrating six Balkan countries through the co-projects ESTIA and OSPE, Early experience. Institute of Architecture and Urban & Spatial Planning of Serbia, Belgrade

Vujošević M (1996) Uloga prostornog planiranja u odnosu na druge instrumente razvoja / The role of spatial planning relative to other development tools. Doctoral dissertation. Faculty of Geography, University of Belgrade, Belgrade (in Serbian)

Vujošević M, Filipović M (2002) Serbia at the turn of the XXI century – The spatial and urban development planning policies of the 1990s failed and a "new beginning"? Presentation at EURA Conference, Urban and Spatial European Policies: Levels of Territorial Government, Torino

Vujošević M, Spasić N (1996) Opšti principi održivog razvoja i perspektive planiranja / General principles of sustainable develpoment and planning perspectives. Posebna izdanja / Special Issues (3) Korišćenje resursa, održivi razvoj i uredjenje prostora / Use of resources, sustainable development and arrangement of space. Institute of Architecture and Urbanism of Serbia – IAUS, Belgrade (in Serbian)

Vujošević M, Spasić N, Petovar K (2000) Reintegrating Yugoslavia into European Development Schemes – The Urge to Reform the Planning System and Practice. Posebna izdanja / Special Issues (5) Korišćenje resursa, održivi razvoj i uredjenje prostora / Use of resources, sustainable development and arrangement of space. Institute of Architecture and Urbanism of Serbia – IAUS, Belgrade (in Serbian)

Wu F (2003) Transitional cities, commentary. *Environment and Planning A* 35:1331-1338

Yiftachel O (1998) Planning and social control: exploring the dark sides. *Journal of Planning Literature* 12:395-406

Zakon o lokalnoj samoupravi/The Act on Self-governance, Службени гласник Републике Србије, 9/2002 (in Serbian)

Zakon o planiranju i izgradnji/The Planning and Construction Act, Службени гласник Републике Србије, 47/2003 (in Serbian)

Žegarac Z (1999) Illegal construction in Belgrade and the prospects for urban development planning. *Cities* 16:365-370

15 Entrepreneurial governance and the urban restructuring of a Slovakian town

Brian Schwegler

Introduction: Normative post-socialist urbanism?

As we were driving through the southern Slovakian town of Komárno in December 1998, Panni Cséh, a local lawyer, pointed out a newly renovated building that housed a major domestic bank, on a street corner dividing the central historic district from socialist-era constructions. The building, in a millennial revision of *Jugendstil* origins, merged green reflective glass with plasterwork. For Ms. Cséh, the bank and similar (re)emerging structures made the central district "a pleasant place for a stroll," a radical contrast to the "ugly communist buildings" in the surrounding ring.

Months later a local planning official, sitting beside a poster of new zoning designations, told me about a development project that would replace squatter structures and piles of garbage with a contemporary urban core. The unprecedented scale and innovative design, she insisted, would demonstrate the regional importance of Komárno and would create jobs both during and after construction.

In the time between my encounters with these optimistic readings of the emerging townscape, a local nurse and lifelong Komárno resident complained to me about uncollected trash and broken lights in her 1970s panel apartment building: "The landlord, the town government, keeps raising the rent on this place, but something else is always broken."

Those three moments echo familiar perspectives on urban life in east-central Europe during the late 1990s. Each one points to an aspect of capital: its ability to make the old appear new; its role in renovation as social transformation; and its tendency toward the deterioration of public services through privatization of urban administration. Taken together, however, the three moments raise a normative question: "What should the post-socialist city look like and how should it be managed?"

Across southern Slovakia, the responses by both municipal authorities and local residents to the challenges of post-socialist urban management have revealed a yearning for models of urban space that might of construct social, aesthetic, and economic values consistent with the ascendant ideals of liberal-democratic states populated by citizens in a global economic order. The search for such models took place among the "modernist ruins" (Jaguaribe 1999) of state socialist teleology—degraded infrastructure, abandoned urban cores, and economies with national, not global, focus. Although the pressures now to realign post-socialist cities with the global order cannot be attributed solely to external market influence

(Bodnár 2001), municipal authorities have increasingly sought inspiration from post-Fordist development models. Using Komárno as a case study, this essay draws on theories of "entrepreneurial" governance (Brenner and Theodore 2005; Harvey 1989; Hubbard and Hall 1998; Ward 2003) to examine the concerns endemic to neoliberal restructuring in post-socialist contexts.

15.1 "Neoliberalizing" management in a Slovak regional town

15.1.1 From dirigiste government to post-Fordist Millennial governance

Komárno is a town of 40,000 on the Danube River, half-way between Bratislava and Budapest. In the 1990s, local authorities faced problems typical of regional post-socialist towns: rising unemployment, postindustrial economic reorganization, and aging infrastructure. In 1990, responsibility for urban administration (budgeting, maintenance, and service provision) had transferred from the *dirigiste* state socialist national government to municipal authorities; the newly autonomous local government faced serious problems.[1] To cope, local authorities adopted strategic plans (Hollý et al. 1993; Hollý and Kostovský 1993) for redevelopment initiatives and endeavoured to attract external capital. This essay traces how those management initiatives plotted a transition from socialist urban government to post-Fordist governance— i.e., from state control over resource allocations for urban development (Szelenyi 1996; Marcuse 2002) to the situation in which authority for decision-making and capital investment was distributed among market actors, institutions of civil society, and government (van Kempen 2002; Marcuse 2002).

The essay also problematizes the economic logics animating the new development plans and subsequent initiatives (Ward 2003). Freed from redistributive, service-providing tasks and deterministic comprehensive planning, local officials devoted their energies to long-term growth initiatives. To secure mobile or contingent capital, Komárno's municipal authorities embraced "weak entrepreneurial" governance initiatives (Jessop 1998), including tourism-oriented image-making, competitions for structural improvement grants, and the sale of municipal property assets. The dispersion of state authority over the urban landscape had brought

---

[1] Law 369/1990 'Zákon Slovenskej národnej rady zo 6. septembra 1990 o obecnom zriadení' established municipalities as self-governing entities authorized to enact local statutes and to develop independent financial resources (e.g., taxation, fees for permits, etc.). It also transferred ownership of properties (including municipal buildings, cultural monuments, and housing complexes) not controlled by state authorities or independent corporate entities to municipalities.

flexibility to development priorities. A mode of "contingent governance" (Wigmans 2001) had empowered local authorities to shift resources fluidly to support public-private development projects. At the same time, such strategies using limited resources to acquire ephemeral capital -- tourism revenue, development grants, and limited foreign direct investment (FDI) -- tied the long-term viability of urban management to uncertain market forces. By their "neoliberalization of the city" (Ward 2003), local governments create attractive sites for investors and consumers but limit the possibility of ameliorating economic and social segregation or pursuing comprehensive economic restructuring. Such an interplay of (dis)empowerment is central to the "millennial" character of neoliberal capitalist restructuring (Comaroff and Comaroff 2000) and its uneasy dependence on state structures for market regulation (Brenner and Theodore 2005; Sassen 2000).

15.1.2 Essay structure

This essay identifies four challenges to the adoption of entrepreneurial strategies in east European post-socialist cities and then examines how each was addressed in Komárno during the 1990s. Section two examines strategies pursued by the urban actors (local bureaucrats, elected officials, developers, and residents) reframing the urban landscape in response to exigencies ranging from localized revitalization to increasing economic segregation. Section three analyzes Komárno's development plans, isolating their neoliberal logics and identifying the spaces for innovation and contingency that they enabled. Section four traces the emergence of urban heritage marketing and place-making strategies which initially took advantage of the flexibility in the governance model but ultimately were constrained by their dependence on shifting market demands capital interests, and structural determinants beyond local control. The analysis suggests that the freedom and flexibility offered by the governance frameworks could not alter the fundamental uncertainty of neoliberal urban restructuring.

15.2 Challenges for smaller post-socialist entrepreneurial cities

The newly established, post-socialist local authorities were challenged by the contradictions between the organizational structures of socialist cities and global capitalist expectations. Although somewhat similar to the experiences of capitalist cities during post-industrial restructuring, these challenges differed in substantive ways because of the orientation of rights, expectations, and productive energies toward the state that had characterized socialism. Fundamental questions of ownership, management, production, and consumption required a reframing of management strategies and of the social and economic models for organizing urban space. The resulting challenges can be formulated as follows:

- **Fragmented Cityscape**—transformations in ownership, control, and responsibility driven by competing spatial claims: individual, public, and commercial.
- **Economic and Social Reframing**—the need to translate the legacies of state socialist government into problems and solutions defined in neoliberal terms.
- **Orientation and Visibility**-- the redirection of urban development strategies from the non-competitive command economy to the global market.
- **Managerial Flexibility**—market-responsive policies' need for "post-postsocialist" administrative capacity.

15.2.1 Fragmented cityscape

Conflicting ownership rights, decades of neglect and uneven investment all had contributed to the fragmentation of post-socialist cityscapes. Neoliberal urban governance required clear ownership rights for property and transparent procedures for transfer. For development projects and revitalization zones, control over buildings and neighbourhoods had to be shifted to individuals or to partnerships. However, in doing so, post-socialist cities contended with the overlapping property claims from decades of conflicting individual and state rights over land and its use (Marcuse 1996). As a result, the investment in urban cores neglected under state socialism, now created patchwork redevelopment—part of the "immature aesthetics" of post-socialism (Enyedi 1998). Since the success of urban marketing campaigns depends on controlling urban imagery, such cityscape fragmentation must be restricted.

15.2.2 Economic and social reframing

The initiatives of entrepreneurial governance explicitly abjure paternalistic, high-modernist, and teleological urban structuring. They nonetheless demonstrate an ideological structuring, a "common rhetoric and narrative of 'entrepreneurialism'" (Jessop 1998, p. 79). Jessop argues that although few such initiatives display "strong" innovative entrepreneurialism—in the Shumpterian sense of providing new methods or objects of production and consumption—the ideological pressures on municipalities do encourage authorities to frame management strategies in terms of market competition (Jessop 1998). In the post-socialist context, that inclination is manifested in the heuristic value and public role of strategic development plans, which serve both as outlines of normative urban transformation and as touchstones for the embodiment of local concerns in terms of neoliberal market demands and solutions. Public statements of the transparency of governance as well, these plans are key artefacts of post-socialist narratives. They demonstrate the "internal discursive logic" of local authorities' engagement with the market-oriented "discourses of modernization" (Smith 1993, p. 216).[2]

---

[2] In Komárno, these plans were public artefacts of urban governance. Their zoning designations adorned the offices of town bureaucrats and local functionaries referenced develop-

15.2.3 Orientation and visibility

Capital and major regional cities excepted, post-socialist urban centres struggled with orientation and visibility as they tried to shift development priorities from centralized state economies to the global market. Centralized state planning with its specialized economic modernization (often mono-industrialization) had constrained workforce and infrastructure flexibility, thereby increasing redevelopment costs for regional city governments as well as for private investors. The nodal cities lack the density and flexibility of natural and human resources found in larger urban areas; consequently, they have generally had lower rates of initial direct investment. Lower investment rates, in turn, have compounded revenue and employment crises, thus adding to the impetus for developing entrepreneurial strategies. At the same time, however, those cities lacked profiles beyond their regions to attract investment and entrepreneurial interest (Herrschel 1998). As Herrschel (1998) demonstrates in the case of East Germany, the relative economic disadvantage of smaller regional cities is reflected in their lack of coherent strategies for long-term development and their reliance instead on opportunistic or "experimental" initiatives.

15.2.4 Managerial flexibility

Transition from a government to a governance model requires changes by both institutions (bureaucratic and administrative) and individuals. Painter (1998) argues that the success of an entrepreneurial governance regime depends on local institutions' support for managers' efforts to recognize and maximize growth opportunities. An entrepreneurial climate can be nurtured through strategies such as hiring external consultants, establishing managerial training initiatives, creating adaptive public-private partnerships, and cultivating knowledge networks (Painter 1998). For smaller post-socialist cities, the development of managerial flexibility has been an incremental process beginning with rethinking the local context in market terms and accepting proactive approaches to development (cf. Herrschel 1998). Gradually becoming families with new structures, governance agents have progressively internalized the vocabularies and comparative experiences characteristic of European urban cosmopolitanism (cf. Borneman and Fowler 1997). Managerial flexibility has thus been acquired, through technologies, practices, and heuristics that enabled "post-post-socialist" (Sampson 2002) governance practices. The terms of transition have been demystified and "the larger structures of the global order embedded in people's consciousness" (Sampson 2002, p. 298).

---

ment projects in the language of the plan's dictates. The 1993 plans are still available on the town's public administration webpage:
(http://www.komarno.sk/samosprava/default_svk.asp?prg=uzemny_plan accessed on August 18, 2005).

15.3 Parsing space, post-socialism and heritage marketing in Slovakia

15.3.1 Competing claims in a fragmented townscape

15.3.1.1 Uneven development

The competing legacies of spatial administration are readily visible from the roads leading into Komárno. Entering the town from the west, drivers encounter a welcome sign in the languages of the town's inhabitants, Slovak and Hungarian (30:70 ratio). Nearing the town centre, the road passes clusters of family homes built during the later years of socialism and the more recent suburbanization. These give way to fenced garden plots, rows of private garages, and an industrial complex with a massive shipyard and rail depot—the centrepiece of socialist industrial modernization.[3] Farther along, the road enters the town centre, encircled by the largest fortification system in central Europe, a reminder of the town's origins as a defensive outpost at the confluence of the Váh and Danube rivers. Finally, arcing through housing estates from the 1950s to the 1980s, the road retraces its earlier path in reverse.

National disparities in post-socialist development are highlighted on the approach to the town from the M-1 highway in Hungary, the region's major transportation artery. The highway access road passes through Komárom, Hungary, formerly a district of Komárno which is the frame of reference for municipal officials and Komárno residents in their evaluations of urban development. The divergent approaches to FDI initiatives taken by Slovakia and Hungary in the 1990s are displayed in the contrast between Komárom's contemporary industrial park (anchored by a Nokia plant) and Komárno's underutilized, socialist-era industrial quarter. The difficulties posed by scarcities of restructuring funds appear as one

---

[3] Founded in 1889, the shipyard was alternately controlled by a Hungarian joint-stock company and the Škoda conglomerate (as the town shifted between Hungarian and Czechoslovak administration) until nationalization in 1947 (Holka 1969). The town's main employer, the shipyard's peripheral ties encompassed the local economy from rail yard workers to the staff of local technical school's shipbuilding program. Although globally competitive the privatized shipyard shed jobs throughout the 1990s. Systemic problems became public in 1999 after management claims that N.A.T.O.-generated blockages of Danube rendered the company unable to complete its orders. Subsequent layoffs led to protests by workers and increased attention from state regulators, who discovered that the company had been 'tunnelled' by management (Zachovalova and Santur 2001). Control of the shipyard was acquired by the Slovak National Property Fund; under its management, the shipyard secured new orders and re-hired some employees, but overall employment remained well below mid-1990s levels. Controlling interest in the shipyard was acquired by an Austrian investment company in December 2003 (Balogová 2003).

crosses the Danube into Komárno and Slovakia along a north/south axis road dividing historical and "communist" Komárno. Throughout the 1990s, renovation on both sides of this line followed uneven patterns of investment and management. The historic centre is a patchwork of restoration and deterioration, with renovated private commercial buildings abutting decaying municipally owned properties that lack buyers or funds for maintenance. The "communist" side contains crumbling housing estate towers with eclectic curvilinear shopping centres built in their shadows. Fully privatized apartment blocks have new landscaping and coats of paint paid for by homeowners associations, while partially privatized buildings under municipal administration are strewn with trash and display only structurally necessary maintenance.

15.3.1.2 State socialist urbanism—Legacies of an "unrecognizable" townscape

State socialist planning and development in Komárno followed the 'concentric zone' model of 'microregion' development (Smith 1996; cf. Hruška 1966, Švidkovskij 1966). The town was divided into districts with specialized functions in the local economy: a historic central business district ringed consecutively by housing estates, recreational spaces (e.g., garden plots), industrial quarters, areas of private homes and agriculture. In the early 1950s, the modernist functional reconstruction of the town began in earnest when the pre-socialist buildings were razed and replaced with housing estates. Rural immigration, by increasing the pressures on housing stock spurred the pace and scale of modernization. From 1960 to 1990, the town population's rise from 23,000 to 37,000, resulted in the construction of 5,000 new housing estate apartments (Okresné oddeleneie Slovenského Štatického úradu Komárno 1992, 1982). To this day, residents track the town's demographic transformation through the height of apartment buildings—from 1950s' three-story buildings to ten-story towers from the 1970s and 1980s.

Outside the central district, socialist redevelopment of the town was nearly total, leading a local Party official to comment in 1986:

> Through the forty years which have passed since liberation [the start of socialist rule], the look of the town has changed so as to be unrecognizable. On the town's zigzag streets with single story houses grew modern housing estates, on sunken, bog-covered, unused surfaces new living quarters and industrial plants were built. Everyday life for the inhabitants of the town changed as well. Already today the predominant majority of Komárnoers live in comfortable, well-equipped apartments; many more own their own car. The right to work, free health-care, and educational opportunity are already taken for granted. Newly-constructed cultural institutions and sport areas have created conditions for active after-work relaxation for the residents of the town. (Škreko 1985, p. 3)

Urban formations that had rendered the town 'unrecognizable' created challenges for officials when they attempted to encourage economic growth within the urban centre. Although Czechoslovak socialist urbanism had emphasized town centres as *loci* of social and administrative life (Hruška 1966), in Komárno adequate resources had not been allocated for maintenance of that district. Development funds had been distributed outward toward the housing estates, whose services had progressively replaced those in the central district (Szelenyi 1996). Decades of neglect and lack of interest by state authorities had left the municipal government with a severely degraded central district and without the short- or long-term resources to maintain or to market it effectively.

15.3.1.3 "Immature aesthetics"

Construction within Komárno's 'unrecognizable' townscape of the 1990s reflected post-socialism's "immature aesthetics": "a peculiar blend of obtrusive American shopping centres, newly rediscovered Central European elegance, elements of a national style and the architectural insipidity of the state socialist period" (Enyedi 1998, p. 29). Local developers capitalized on revised and uneven zoning to construct clusters of shops and offices on the underutilized inner spaces of housing estates (Fig. 15.1.). Visually jarring, these buildings interrupted the familiar visual "figure/void" relationships of the modernist urban plan (Holston 1989). The higher relative costs of renovating inefficient socialist-era structures for flexible commercial uses (Bodnár 2001) encouraged local developers to build new shopping centres next to abandoned socialist-era commercial buildings. Thus, the duality of post-socialist gentrification—simultaneous renovation and deterioration—left a patchwork of spaces engaged, avoided, lauded, and lamented. As Bodnár has noted, the "logic of privatization" at work in post-socialist urban renewal is not concerned with comprehensive renovation except as it affects profitability. An endemic symptom of resource scarcity, townscape fragmentation emerges as control of urban space is ceded to the market; its long-term abatement, however, relies on local, structural government conditions.

15.3.1.4 Competing spatial claims

Increasing disparities of wealth, unstable employment conditions, and uneven property values in the 1990s exacerbated the fragmentation of social and economic townscape in Komárno. Local developers began partial gentrification of degraded pre-socialist and early socialist neighbourhoods by building townhouses in trendy neo-historicist and Organic styles. More expensive than socialist-era housing, these projects catered to the desire of the emergent professional class for residential "normalcy" through ownership of fashionable domestic space (Féhervári 2002). The appeal of these projects and styles, Féhervári (2004) argues, came from their radical break with socialism's modernist material culture; ownership symbolized post-socialist sensibilities and political identities. Even with broad support from local officials, however, their small scale and limited customer base precluded comprehensive gentrification. The resulting neighbourhood landscape was visually and economically fragmented. Whatever the appeal of post-socialist styling, unequal access as well as gentrification's insertion of new

15 Entrepreneurial governance and the urban restructuring of a Slovakian town 303

Fig. 15.1. Fragmenting the modernist urban landscape—a late 1990s commercial structure built within a 1970s housing estate

structures into degraded neighbourhoods emphasized the staggered pace of revitalization.

Eclectic shopping centres, property speculation, and luxury townhouses projected an idealized image of an entrepreneurial townscape. Everyday inequities in the pace of renewal, however, generated spatial counter-claims. To avoid high prices in the new shopping centres, many Komárnoers shopped at open-air markets and hypermarkets in Hungary, where prices were significantly lower in the 1990s and early 2000s. That cross-border commerce reduced Komárno's municipal revenues and its hampered entrepreneurial commerce, and local officials attributed their vacant storefronts to Hungary's booming discount market. At the same time, garden plots from the socialist era became increasingly appreciated as sites for the production of fruit and vegetables with a social value exceeding that of store-bought equivalents (Czegledy 2002). Rather than declining in importance in the face of emergent discount markets and hypermarkets, such peripheral landscape features became firmly entrenched as sources of additional income and *loci* of household investment.

Further, high prices and interest rates excluded many Komárnoers from new housing and prevented some long-time housing estate residents from purchasing their apartments.[4] Uneven participation in the real estate market had broad and diverse effects. Below-market rents and the rising maintenance costs for unsold apartments constrained the municipal budget, while homeowner associations in partially privatized buildings struggled with the diverging interests and capabilities among owners and renters.

Individuals on the margins of the land tenure transformation occupied land in semi-legal or illegal ways to circumvent the increasing private control of space. Under socialism, quasi-legal building activities, from the use of purloined materials to squatting on ambiguously controlled land, had been glossed as 'black constructions' (*fekete építkezések*). In the 1990s, local officials applied the term to new claims on the increasingly privately controlled landscape, from clandestinely built garages to squatting by disenfranchised Roma families. Despite some efforts to purge such activities from commercially valuable land, 'black constructions' persisted at the margins of commercial and municipal authority. Bureaucrats traded stories of outrageous violations of zoning and occupancy laws, yet 'black constructions' continued, displaying an "ambiguous persistence" rooted in the "informal social legitimacy" granted people's efforts to surmount systemic economic challenges (Smart 2001, p. 32).

15.3.2 Millennial governance and economic restructuring

This section of the essay examines documents that served as heuristic blueprints for neoliberal governance in Komárno: *Territorial Plan for Residential Development* (Hollý et al. 1993) and *Territorial Plan for Residential Development: Proposal for the Regulation of Territorial Development* (Hollý and Kostovský 1993). These two management studies became touchstones for urban policy into the 2000s. Discussion by discussion and district by district, they reframe socialist urban government in terms of capitalist urban management. The documents' neoliberal logics emphasize municipal responsibility for fostering capital growth while at the same time undermining municipal control over urban economic outcomes. Their logic casts development initiatives as dependent upon market whims for their success (Brenner and Theodore 2005).

---

[4] Slovakia did not have a deadline for the completion of sales of former state-owned apartments; municipal authorities acquired responsibility for these units in 1990 and rented them at subsidized rates to long-term occupants during the 1990s (see Marcuse 1996: 164). Although the completion of housing privatization was a priority for Komárno's municipal government, it was not achieved by the end of the decade.

15.3.2.1 Neoliberal governance's Millennial logics

Describing the "millennial" features of neoliberal capitalism, Jean and John Comaroff isolate a number of contradictory themes within the ideal of global transformation through market consumption. Neoliberalism's central tenets merge "libertarian" and "legalistic" ("constitutionality with deregulation") themes, production and consumption, and the fantastic and the mundane in a teleology of accumulation (Comaroff and Comaroff 2000). In the context of institutional governance, neoliberalism's "binary complementarity" (Comaroff and Comaroff 2000) emphasizes reliance on abstract market forces that use the structures of the state to foster stable economic conditions while at the same time erasing the vestiges of state control over economic activity. Neoliberal governance logics are thus built on uncertainty: whatever efforts are made to structure local economic activities according to perceived market demands, municipalities are not guaranteed returns. Despite the attribution of occasionally spectacular failures of neoliberal strategies to local failures to embrace market conditions, local agency is in fact partial and fleeting. Neoliberal capitalism's "millennial" character is rooted in its interplay of control and acquiescence. Local authority is vacated in the hope that this will bring positive returns.

At the level of practical governance, markets require safeguards and institutions to regulate and protect transitory capital (Comaroff and Comaroff 2000; Sassen 2000; Brenner and Theodore 2005). Restrictive regulation, however, constrains the free movement of capital and its ultimate replication, which is the fundamental promise of the system. The challenge for neoliberalism then is to develop strategies and approaches toward governance that respond to market conditions without limiting growth. A flexible managerial regime must frame social goals in terms of problems with clear input and limits for regulating agencies. The process relies on mediating mechanisms to translate social problems into managerial challenges.

15.3.2.2 Managing the transformation of the neoliberal townscape

The 1993 strategic plans transform the socialist urban legacy into objects of managerial action. On one hand, they express widely-held ideas about postindustrial urban change. They divide Komárno's urban development into three stages (pre-1990, 1990-2000, and 2000-2010) and provide a managerial baseline for contingent projections. They catalogue the existing housing stock by type, building material, and age and estimate housing needs based on population projections.[5] They recommend changes in zoning, infrastructure, and social institutions in each of the town's districts. They examine the labour market, projecting transformations in secondary and tertiary sector employment and the types of companies required for optimal employment conditions. In short, they comprehensively outline what the town did and should look like.

---

[5] The impact of socialist urbanization is reflected in these reports--Komárno's population doubled during the socialist era and socialist-era housing comprised 91.5% of the housing stock (Hollý et al. 1993).

Beyond their specifics, the totality of the recommendations charts an ontological shift from socialist government to neoliberal governance. As the *Proposal for the Regulation of Territorial Development* notes:

> The purpose of processing changes and additions for the territorial plan for residential development for Komárno was the establishment of the optimal hypothesis for the overall urban organization of settlement in the changing political and socio-economic conditions of the transformation to a market economy for the contemporary maintenance of its functioning and importance as a district town (Hollý and Kostovský 1993: 21-22).

The contingent character of the plan's mandate is central to its neoliberal logic, which authorizes directives for how urban space should function without articulating the mechanisms for realizing the projected goals.

The plans consistently frame social issues in terms beyond local control. They describe labour market transformation, for example, as a comprehensive structural phenomenon: "unemployment is a phenomenon that accompanies the transformation to the market economy in Slovakia that expresses itself in different intensities throughout Slovakia and also in regions of the district and town of Komárno" (Hollý et al. 1993, p. 40). The strategies presented for overcoming unemployment are partial, shifting ultimate outcomes to forces beyond the control of local authorities:

> Unemployment is a serious economic and social problem that requires a wide ranging approach to its solution. The consequences of economic reform, new trends in the development of the national economy and structural changes caused marked decreases in the number of employment opportunities most of all in the manufacturing branches. A shortage in the creation of new employment opportunities in the private sector will not alleviate this decrease. This is all expressed in extensive unemployment (Hollý et al. 1993, p. 40).

The didactic framing—surprising because the report was written three years after these 'changes' when the town was facing 16% unemployment—removes the labour market from direct local intervention. It also demonstrates the extent to which the plans were as much efforts to restructure conceptions of the roles of government and citizens as they were blueprints for solving urban challenges. Though the plans do not allow for certitude, they do suggest incremental steps for workforce restructuring to alleviate unemployment and its economic consequences: shifts from secondary to tertiary sector employment, job-training programs to create a highly- and flexibly-skilled labour force, and support for small- and mid-scale entrepreneurial activity (Hollý et al 1993). The larger development plan predicted a short-term downturn in industrial employment and the long-term growth of a mixed industrial-service economy that would merge local entrepreneurial activity with moderate levels of foreign direct investment, a standard strategy in the region (Enyedi 1998).

Similar logics describe the restructuring of housing markets, zoning and land use, and social service and cultural institutions. Each plan calls for the reduction of direct municipal authority over the economy and urban management. Although not strictly supply-side economics (as the mechanisms of significant fiscal control rest largely at the level of the state), their supply-side logic of urban management directs local governance toward reducing investors' secondary costs (Ward 2003). In this model the energies of local government actors would go to attracting external capital investment. By fragmenting the local workforce, emphasizing diverse corporate scales, and directing local resources toward infrastructure development, the town would be actively shaped as an attractive site for capital investment, a common development strategy for post-socialist local economies (Enyedi 1998).

The interplay of (dis)empowerment is at the core of these plans, as of other entrepreneurial or neoliberal governance models. The newly enfranchised local authorities face structural problems they cannot solve (radical social transformation). The measures proposed to encourage the capital investment that could accomplish such restructuring, however, presuppose the uncertain cooperation and resources of private sector actors. The foundational documents of Komárno's post-socialist restructuring are thus rooted in neoliberalism's millennial conundrum—the mandated direction of limited local resources toward uncertain capital growth strategies.

15.3.3 Scale, visibility, and flexible planning

15.3.3.1 Urban restructuring and the "multifunctional social space"

Private and public-private development initiatives in Komárno in the 1990s were generally restricted to the 'local private economy' (Enyedi 1998, p. 20) dominated by local entrepreneurs, manufacturing and service firms catering to the domestic market, and smaller foreign retail establishments. In the 1990s, the FDI funds for economic restructuring in Slovakia were lower than those in other areas of east-central Europe.[6] Residents and local officials charted this unequal regional development in comparisons between the shipyard, which was shedding jobs amid allegations of mismanagement, and the expanding presence of multinationals (including Nokia and Amstel) in neighbouring towns in Hungary. Attributable primarily to state-level problems with attracting FDI during the 1990s, Komárno isolation from the circuits of the global economy placed both fiscal and administrative burdens on local officials. Lacking external investment to support its labour market and industrial restructuring, Komárno's officials developed small-scale strategies to foster local economic growth. Using the flexibility afforded within the strategic plans, they undertook to develop a local service economy under the rubric of urban heritage marketing.

---

[6] During the 1990s, levels of FDI in Slovakia were roughly 1/10th of those in Hungary and the Czech Republic (Marcinčin 2000).

The general framework for urban restructuring outlined in the strategic plans did not identify the actors responsible for targeted renewal projects. To maximize their opportunities for entrepreneurial or "contingent governance" in the face of market uncertainty (Wigmans 2001), local officials turned to sources of funding and aesthetic inspiration unforeseen in the development plans and embarked on revitalizing the town centre as the centrepiece of a nostalgic Austro-Hungarian imaging campaign. Komárno's strategic planning documents had identified the historical town centre as the primary site for commercial and residential redevelopment. The general contours of the plans called for renovating pre-socialist structures, replacing single-use buildings with multi-use structures, and encouraging a transformation from a marginalized, socialist central commercial district to a "socially important, multifunctional social space" (Hollý et al 1993, p. 18) at the heart of the local economy. The revitalized centre was to offer cosmopolitan amenities and possibilities in the form of luxury condominiums, restaurants, hotels, "artistic coffee shops," and "cultural equipment" for civic organizations organized according to "opinion, politics, ideology, religion, nationality, ethnicity, social age, professional field, department, etc" (Hollý et al. 1993, p. 18).

While thus functionally comprehensive, the strategic plans neither targeted specific investment capital funds nor outlined aesthetic themes for renewal. From their strategic standpoint, townscape aesthetics were secondary to urban function and a detail to be determined by external developers. Such normative relegation of aesthetic form to capital interests is of the target of critiques of post-socialism's 'immature aesthetics' and lies at the core of controversies over the local suitability of such buildings as Prague's Nationale Nederlanden "Tančící Dům." Commercial landmark constructions became "postsocialism's symbolic buildings" because of their ubiquity and their reordering of urban landscapes with no consideration of local aesthetic history or specificity (Bodnár 2001, p. 92). The transfer of control over form to external developers rendered comprehensive contextual aesthetics impossible, resulting in a "new landscape of urban consumption" that displayed "blatant disregard of the traditional scales of the architectural environment" (Sármany-Parsons 1998, p. 209).

15.3.3.2 Flexible management and the 'genius loci'

The limited private development funds posed challenges but also opportunities for local governance mechanisms. With the success of restructuring resting upon the revitalization of the central district, local officials had to establish both a guiding image and funding for its renovation. Acting as direct agents of investment, they channelled the funds acquired through property sales and public credit initiatives toward small renovation projects intended to recast the central district as a revenue-generating tourist attraction. Charged with administering services and generating revenue streams, local officials developed flexible managerial strategies to capitalize on contingent funding opportunities. Support for entrepreneurial initiatives within municipal departments and the town council allowed managers to concentrate on raising the town's profile in governance networks outside the local capital markets and the Slovak state. By the end of the 1990s, managerial flexibility was routinized: bureaucrats regularly attended regional management seminars, where they acquired networks and the expertise to cast local needs in terms commensurate with the development priorities of grant agencies. Grant-writing became commonplace at the department level, and managers regularly shared the information about funding competitions and opportunities for cooperation with other towns that they acquired through burgeoning regional networks.

Thus, pressed by unfavourable market conditions, managerial entrepreneurship maximized strategic flexibility to empower local government structures as active development agents. It further authorized urban heritage marketing efforts by municipal officials. Local imaging strategies were developed to replace the public prominence of socialist modernization's "unrecognizable" and unsustainable landscape with postmodernist nostalgic historicism. Cracked streets became cobbled pedestrian zones. The European Union's PHARE development grant underwrote the renovation of a 19th-century Austro-Hungarian officer's barracks for multi-functional use as a concert hall, café, and office building. An 18th-century palace was restored to house a museum of local history, whose displays cantered on the town's role in the 1848 Hungarian Revolution and its pre-socialist bourgeoisie. The *genius loci* articulated through these entrepreneurial management initiatives merged Austro-Hungarian cosmopolitanism and Magyar liberal nationalism into a fantastic petit-bourgeois landscape of boutiques, coffeehouses, and noble sacrifice (Figs. 15.2. and 15.3.).

Fig. 15.2. Imaging Magyar Liberal Nationalism: 1990s postcard featuring György Klapka, local hero of the 1848 Hungarian Revolution

Fig. 15.3. Nostalgia for the present—1990s postcard featuring Austro-Hungarian town centre renovated under municipal direction

Strategic and managerial flexibility enabled local officials to orient renovation projects toward a coherent image of place. Despite the increasing strength of quasi-market mechanisms and officials' network ties to European development and governance agencies, however, long-term economic stability required market and governance diversification. Shrinking grant funds and revenue crises prompted greater efforts to involve private sector actors in the development of service and tourist commercial opportunities. Thus, although contingency and flexibility in strategic planning allowed local officials to maximize fleeting investment and development opportunities, successful restructuring required other governance actors.

15.3.4 European nostalgia as development project

15.3.4.1 Nostalgia for the New Europe

As a development strategy, self-referential nostalgia risks creating products whose buyers are its makers. To avoid infinite regressions of memory, as Boym notes, commercial historicism must package nostalgia's "retrospective" and "prospective" aspects into a product that unifies intimately local visions of the past and broadly compelling aspirations for the future in a "local cosmopolitanism" (Boym 2001, pp. xvi-xviii). Tourism marketing based on such commercialized nostalgia is a central feature of development programs and place-making campaigns (Kearns and Philo 1993). Towns across Europe have turned to their pasts as tourism magnets, constructing imagined practices of earlier townscapes resonant with images of once and future European or petit-bourgeois subjectivities (Johler 2002; Borneman and Fowler 1997). Since towns across the continent were competing to become old in new ways to attract tourists, Komárno's urban heritage marketing initiative did not guarantee escape from neoliberal millennial uncertainties. Given the centrality of place-making in entrepreneurial governance regimes, successful entrepreneurial place-making depends on themes and spaces that can compete against other towns with similar demographic and historical profiles. In short, Komárno needed a unique marketable image.

That image was presented in a public-private development project proposed by a consortium of local developers and architects for an underutilized property in the town centre. In its public presentation, the initiative was a nearly textbook example of urban neoliberalism's emphasis on discrete development projects that "captur[e] a segment of the city and tur[n] it into a symbol of the new restructured/revitalized metropolis cast with a powerful image of innovation, creativity, and success" (Swyngedouw et al. 2002, p. 215). Entrepreneurial governance tenets of public-private partnerships, townscape commodification, and market restructuring were to be realized in a project that Slovakia's Vice-Premier for European Integration called "one of the symbols of Slovakia's belonging to Europe in historic, cultural, and political fields" (Vás 1999, p. 14). The New Europe was to be built in Komárno by a project entitled *Europe Place*.[7]

Described in broad strokes, the project, proposed in 1998, would create a self-contained residential and commercial centre emphasizing the European past and future of Komárno. A run-down section of the central district filled with municipal poverty's detritus (mounds of trash, dilapidated buildings, and 'black constructions') would be replaced by a complex of neo-historicist structures, each built in the architectural tradition of one of Europe's historical regions or nations. The complex would construct the strategic plans' "multifunctional social space" through multiuse commercial and residential structures. An attempt to inscribe the "architectural symphony that sounds in certain areas of Europe when we look at them" (Vás 1999, p. 14), the project would create what one local university student called "a town within a town"—an apt description of the economically segregated "urban islands" that neoliberal development projects characteristically produce (Swyngedouw et al. 2002, p. 224). Surpassing local standards in its physical scale and financial scope—300 million SKK (Klesnilová 2000)—*Europe Place* was publicly embraced by local officials as the centrepiece of local development.

---

[7] *Europe Place* is the project's English name. Publicity materials were produced Slovak, Hungarian, German, English—with corresponding titles *Nádvorie Európy, Európa Udvar, and Europa Platz.*

Overall, *Europe Place* was an exemplar of the process of Europeanization in Komárno, replete with fantasies of market salvation through job creation and controversies about experiences of economic segregation (Schwegler 2003). From planning to publicity, the project displayed the hallmarks of a governance initiative. Local developers designed the project and acquired funding from regional investment corporations; local authorities negotiated conditions for the sale of the property and for the development of infrastructure and developed strategies to sell the project to local citizens (some of whom it displaced) and the wider tourist public; national and international institutions ideologically aligned with the project's themes provided it with financial and marketing support. The Vice-Premier for European Integration was named the project's spiritual patron (*védnek*), and the European Union sent monies and representatives whose presence lent ideological legitimacy to the project's groundbreaking and opening ceremonies. Local nongovernmental institutions were founded in association with the project (and funded in part by the European Commission) to "contribute to the development of the civic society, to the dissemination of ideas of democracy and cooperation, and support of knowledge and development of the European social and cultural values [. . .] and to the support of European integration" (Litomericzky 2001, p. 91). Neither a wholly independent capital initiative nor a self-contained municipal project, the work demonstrated managerial governance's idealized plurality of agents and interests.

Europe Place displays a nostalgia for the New European ideal that resonates with the historicism of Komárno's urban heritage marketing. In contrast to the place-less aesthetic of post-socialism's symbolic commercial buildings in the town centre, *Europe Place* aimed to be "considered Komárno as much as European" (Szabad Újság 1999) through a Romantic neo-historicism that complemented the town centre's baroque styling (Fig. 15.4.). As part of the reinscription of the pre-socialist past in the revitalized town centre, *Europe Place* promised to return the vibrant urban past to the town's future: "In the confines of the architectural complex a cosy environment will arise in the centre of town—an environment of urban petit-bourgeois [Slovak. *meštiansky*; Hungarian. *polgári*] sensation that forty years of censorship erased from the lives of two generations" (Mácza et al. 1999). Reconstructing space and sensation, *Europe Place* was simultaneously nostalgically anti-socialist and anticipating a European future that would emerge within Komárno.

Fig. 15.4. *Europe Place's* **(foreground) merger of architectural heritage (background) and present/future European visions**

15.3.5 Ephemeralities of the present

Europe Place's 'multifunctional social space' was completed in 2000 and is the centrepiece of municipal celebration. The promise and excitement of being (EU)ropean has been channelled through recent festivals at the complex that have celebrated Europe, its artists, and its traditions. *Europe Place*'s success in revitalizing the larger urban landscape, however, has been mixed. Lease prices for condominiums and commercial space in the complex are significantly higher than in other parts of town, leading to high vacancy rates and dissatisfaction over socio-economic stratification. Many of the residents of this little New Europe are immigrants from Western Europe (Klesnilová 2000). Komárno residents who emphasized to me the importance of the project admitted that the anticipated crowds of tourists have yet to arrive. Further, since most of east-central Europe is now part of the E.U., *Europe Place*'s future vision (and commercial appeal) is yesterday's news.

Despite its success as an entrepreneurial governance project, *Europe Place* points to the ephemeral nature of neoliberal capitalism and governance. The project did realize the optimistic messages sent by Slovakia's leaders at the opening of the project, in that it did, as Slovak President Rudolf Schuster noted, "symbolize the 'place' from where we [Slovakia] will enter under the common roof of the

European Union" (Schuster 2001). It was worthy of praise "because of the fact that it meant the investment of the amount of several hundreds of millions [of SKK] in the period difficult for the [sic] new entrepreneurial activities, as well as the establishment of the new social, commercial and residential centre, important for the whole region" (Litomericzky 2001, p. 10). Nonetheless, even singularly successful development projects simply shift the timeframes of neoliberal restructuring. To achieve comprehensive long-term growth, new entrepreneurial initiatives are required to continuously remake the townscape to survive as a competitive location and concept

Europe Place was a simulacrum of the New European ideal in its east-central European guises: an inhabitable past, a prospective future, a political ideal, and a fantasy of prosperity. Like other postmodern developments, *Europe Place* required mastery over form and function. Although multifunctional by design, it is neither interactive nor multivocal—space use and social interactions are scripted, managed, and enforced by the nature of the structure. It was a successful vessel for capital attraction, but remains constrained by 'millennial' concerns. Its very success as a fixed commodity-image is its liability in a shifting market. As the developer noted, the "basic idea of establishing the Europe Place [was] linked closely to the Millennium and to the pursuit of our country to accede to the European Union" (Litomericzky 2001, p. 26). As these moments recede into the grey space between present and nostalgized past, *Europe Place's* ability to contribute to long-term economic restructuring recedes as well.

Conclusion

Komárno's experiences with the transformations of neoliberal and entrepreneurial governance highlight the strengths and the challenges of urban restructuring in the post-socialist context. By maximizing contingency and flexibility in strategic goals and management practice, municipal authorities were able to compete for development funds that directly supported urban renovation projects. Cultivation of public-private partnerships and careful management of urban heritage marketing contributed to a consistent imaging strategy and a large-scale urban development project that revitalized underutilized sections of the town centre.

At the same time, restrictive financial conditions, the structural legacies of socialist modernization, and emerging socio-economic stratification helped to ensure the endurance and expansion of townscape fragmentation. The immediate benefits of the new urban centre were not felt by housing estate residents, and *Europe Place's* grand vision of returning the vibrant urban past to the town's future has largely failed to materialize. Although levels of FDI in Slovakia are among the highest in the region since the early 2000s (in accordance with the pro-market stance of the current government), the institutional challenges of urban restructuring remain. Despite current upswings in employment and investment, those modes of spatial appropriation that resist market fluidity are likely to remain entrenched. Presented with cafes and restaurants they could not afford, Komárno residents retreated to their garden plots and built 'illegal constructions' at the margins of governmental authority: patterns of accommodation that mark the dissonance between visions of the town as commodity and as social environment.

Comparing the entrepreneurial restructuring in Komárno to the logic of market transition outlined in its strategic plans highlights the post-socialist path-dependent and market-dependent exceptions to standard governance frameworks. Although Komárno's experiences constitute a mostly positive example of coping with problems of market orientation, visibility, managerial capacity, and network density, they also underscore the extent to which neoliberal governance is a continuous process of economic crisis management. The dependence on the competitive urban market for economic growth and social wellbeing is an interplay of the (dis)empowerment of local public and private agents. While singularly successful development projects like *Europe Place* pay short-term rewards, they do not address the fundamental, millennial insecurities of neoliberal governance.

Acknowledgements

This paper draws from ethnographic fieldwork conducted in Komárno in 1997 and 1998-99. The generous support of the Spencer Foundation and the USIA-IIE Fulbright program for the field research and of the American Council of Learned Societies—East European Studies Dissertation Fellowship program for the analysis of the research data is gratefully acknowledged. I thank the local officials and residents who donated their time and energies in support of this research, particularly Nándor Litomericzky, Katalin Besse, and Ľubomír Augustín. Petra Bohílová and Dr. Joseph Ungvari provided invaluable research assistance. Finally, I thank John Comaroff, Robert Schwegler, Tara Schwegler and the participants in the "Winds of Change" conference for their insights on early versions of the essay. Special thanks go to Zorica Nedovic-Budic and Sasha Tsenkova for guiding these discussions from their conference origins to print.

References

Balogová B (2003) Euram to take over majority in Slovak shipyard. The Slovak Spectator, December 12. http://www.slovakspectator.sk/clanok.asp?vyd=online&cl=14638
Bodnár J (2001) Fin de Millénaire Budapest: Metamorphoses of urban life. University of Minnesota Press, Minneapolis
Boym S (2001) The future of nostalgia. Basic Books, New York
Borneman J, Fowler N (1997) Europeanization. Ann Rev Anthropology 26: 487-514
Brenner N, Theodore N (2005) Neoliberalism and the urban condition. City 9:101-107
Comaroff J, Comaroff JL (2000) Millennial capitalism: First thoughts on a second coming. Public Culture 12: 291-343
Czegledy A (2002) Urban peasants in a post-socialist world: Small-scale agriculturalists in Hungary. In: Leonard P, Kaneff D (eds) Post-socialist peasant? Rural and urban constructions of identity in Eastern Europe, East Asia, and the former Soviet Union. Palgrave, New York, pp 200-220

Enyedi G (1998) Transformation in Central European post-socialist cities. In: Enyedi G (ed) Social change and urban restructuring in Central Europe. Akadémiai Kiadó, Budapest, pp 9-34

Fehérváry K (2002) American kitchens, luxury bathrooms and the search for a 'normal' life in post-socialist Hungary. Ethnos 67:369-400

Fehérváry K (2004) The political logic of state socialist material culture. Paper presented at the Anthropology of Europe Workshop, University of Chicago, April

Hubbard P and Hall T (1998) The entrepreneurial city and the 'New urban politics.' In: Hall T, Hubbard P (eds) The entrepreneurial city: Geographies of politics, regime, and representation. John Wiley and Sons, Chichester, pp 1-26

Harvey D (1989) The condition of postmodernity: An enquiry into the origins of cultural change. Blackwell, Cambridge

Herrschel T (1998) From socialism to post-Fordism: The local state and economic policies in Eastern Germany. In: Hall T, Hubbard P (eds) The entrepreneurial city: Geographies of politics, regime, and representation. John Wiley and Sons, Chichester, pp 173-198

Holka F (1969) Slovenské Lodenice Komárno. Vydavateľstvo ROH, Bratislava

Hollý J, Kostovský D (1993) Územný plan sídelného útvaru Komárno: Aktualizácia územného plánu sídelného útvaru Komárno: Návrh regulatívov územného rozvoja. Study by AUREX, spol.s.r.o., Bratislava

Hollý J, Kostovský D, Kantorová K, Šugárová V, Vaníček M, Pavlovkinová M, Cambel B, Zhorela J, Vágner M, Vágnerová S, Kučerová M, Blanárová T, Fickuliaková G, Suchárová M, Lehocký R, Grznárová J, Kostka M, Gašparovičová M, Nováková A, Kadenová J, Hvožďárová T, Vrátna E, Regecová B (1993) Územný plan sídelného útvaru Komárno: Aktualizácia územného plánu sídelného útvaru Komárno. Study by AUREX, spol.s.r.o., Bratislava

Holston J (1989) The modernist city: An anthropological critique of Brasília. University of Chicago Press, Chicago

Hruška E (1966) Problémy súčasného urbanizmu. SAV, Bratislava

Jaguaribe B (1999) Modernist ruins: National narratives and architectural forms. Public Culture 11: 294-312

Jessop B (1998) The narrative of enterprise and the enterprise of narrative: Place marketing and the entrepreneurial city. In: Hall T, Hubbard P (eds) The entrepreneurial city: Geographies of politics, regime, and representation. John Wiley and Sons, Chichester, pp 78-99

Johler R (2002) Local Europe: The production of cultural heritage and the Europeanisation of places. Ethnologia Europaea 32:7-18

Kearns G, Philo C (1993) Selling places: The city as cultural capital, past and present. Pergamon Press, Oxford

Klesnilová A (2000) Nádvorie Európy otvoria na budúci týždeň. Národná Obroda, December 9

Litomericzky N (2001) Európa Udvar-Nádvorie Európy-Europa Platz-Europe Place. Palatinus Civic Association, Komárno

Mácza M, Fülöp A, Litomericzky N, Méhés A, Mester P (1999) Katalóg Nádvorie Európy. Atelier Europa, Komárno

Marcuse P (1996) Privatization and its discontents: Property rights in land and housing in Eastern Europe. In: Andrusz G, Harloe M, Szelenyi I (eds) Cities after socialism: Urban and regional change and conflict in post-socialist societies. Blackwell, London, pp 119-191

Marcuse P (2002) The partitioned city in history. In: Marcuse P, van Kempen R (eds) Of states and cities: The partitioning of urban space. Oxford University Press, Oxford, pp 11-34

Marcinčin A (2000) Enterprise restructuring. In: Marcinčin A, Beblavý M (eds) Economic policy in Slovakia, 1990-1999. Slovak Foreign Policy Association, Bratislava, pp 321-358

Okresné oddeleneie Slovenského Štatického úradu Komárno (1992) Sčítanie ľudu, domov a bytov k 3. marcu 1991 v okrese Komárno

Okresné oddeleneie Slovenského Štatického úradu Komárno, Komárno (1982) Sčítanie ľudu, domov a bytov k 3. marcu 1981 v okrese Komárno. Okresné oddeleneie Slovenského Štatického úradu Komárno, Komárno

Painter J (1998) Entrepreneurs are made, not born: Learning and urban regimes in the production of entrepreneurial cities. In: Hall T, Hubbard P (eds) The entrepreneurial city: Geographies of politics, regime, and representation. John Wiley and Sons, Chichester, pp 259-274

Sampson S (2002) Beyond transition: Rethinking elite configurations in the Balkans. In: Hann CM (ed) Postsocialism: Ideals, ideologies, and practices in Eurasia. Routledge, New York, pp 297-316

Sármány-Parsons I (1998) Aesthetic aspects of change in urban space in Prague and Budapest. In: Enyedi G (ed) Social change and urban restructuring in Central Europe. Akadémiai Kiadó, Budapest, pp 209-232

Sassen S (2000) Spatialities and temporalities of the global: Elements for a theorization. Public Culture 12:215-232

Schwegler B (2003) Building the New Europe(an): Place, architecture, and history in Slovakia. Conference Paper "EUtopia: Enlargement and the Politics of European Identity," University of Illinois, Urbana-Champaign, 10-12 April

Schuster R (2001) Nádvorie Európy. In: Litomericzky N (ed) Nádvorie Európy-Európa Udvar-Europa Platz-Europe Place. Palatinus Civic Association, Komárno, pp 5-6

Smart A (2001) Unruly places: Urban governance and the persistance of illegality in Hong Kong's urban squatter areas. Amer Anthropologist 103:30-44

Smith DM (1996) The socialist city. In: Andrusz G, Harloe M, Szelenyi I (eds), Cities after socialism: Urban and regional change and conflict in post-socialist societies. Blackwell, London, pp 70-99

Smith S (2003) Conclusion: The narrativisation of social transformation. In: Smith S (ed) Local communities and post-communist transformation: Czechoslovakia, the Czech Republic and Slovakia. RoutledgeCurzon, London, pp 206-220

Swyngedouw E, Moulaert F, Rodriguez A (2002) Neoliberal urbanization in Europe: Large-scale urban development projects and the new urban policy. In: Brenner N, Theodore N (eds) Spaces of neoliberalism: Urban restructuring in North America and Western Europe. Blackwell, Oxford, pp 195-229

Szabad Újszág (1999) Áprilistól Európa-Udvar épül Komáromban. April 7, pp. 14-15

Szelenyi I (1996) Cities under socialism—and after. In: Andrusz G, Harloe M, Szelenyi I (eds) Cities after socialism: Urban and regional change and conflict in post-socialist societies. Blackwell, London, pp 286-317

Škrejko F (1985) Predslov. In: Mácza M (ed) Vývoj Komárna v obrazoch Oblastné Podunajské Muzeum, Komárno, p 3

Švidkovskij OA (1966) Urbanismus socialistického Československa. Academia, Praha
van Kempen R (2002) The academic formulations: Explanations for the partitioned city. In: Marcuse P, van Kempen R (eds), Of states and cities: The partitioning of urban space. Oxford University Press, Oxford, pp 35-58
Vás G (1999) Európa udvar Révkomáromban a harmadik évezred jegyében. Szabad Újság March 24, pp 14-15
Ward K (2003) The limits to contemporary urban redevelopment: 'Doing' entrepreneurial urbanism in Birmingham, Leeds, and Manchester. City 7:199-211
Wigmans G (2001) Contingent governance and the enabling City: The case of Rotterdam. City 5: 223
Zachovalová K, Santur R (2001) A leaky vessel. Transitions Online, August 23

16 Urban redevelopment programmes in Kazan, Russia

Nadir Kinossian

Introduction: Rationale and analytical framework

The recent Russian political transition controversial since 1991, is not yet complete, nor is it clear whether Russia will firmly reincarnate itself as a market economy (Lowenhardt 1995) or, eventually, as an authoritarian state (Brown 2004; Politkovskaya, 2004). Some of the continuing political controversies at the national level are reflected at the city level as well. Russian cities have experienced both political and socio-economic changes: development of land and real property markets, deregulation of urban services, and growth of the trade and service sectors (Andruzs et al. 1996). Since the collapse of the centrally planned system the cities have had to rely on more fluid sources of funding and have become responsible for their development policies. Russian cities, like other in the West, have adopted entrepreneurial urban policies that, while innovative, have questionable effects on socio-economic sustainability (Harvey 1989; Hubbard 1996; McLeod 2002).

Those changes and uncertainties stimulate interest in studying the politics and policies of post-socialist cities. Why are particular policies adopted? What are major factors that can explain the development outcomes? Which theories are useful as explanatory tools?

Responses to such questions are hampered by the lack of relevant theoretical and conceptual frameworks in the literature. Socialist urban theories became largely obsolete given the new conditions; at the same time, Western urban theories have little application to post-socialist cities and their political, economic, spatial and cultural transformations. The present research attempts to bridge that gap. Its theoretical ambition is to apply Western urban theories to the analysis of a Russian city in transition—Kazan—and to its post-socialist urban development. Its analytical framework draws on urban regime theory (Ferman 1996; Savitch and Kantor 2002; Stone 1989).

Stone (1989) conceptualizes urban regimes as a product of politicians' will and shows how different regimes arise under different political leadership. His main argument is that in cases of the "absence of comprehensive planning and system of command" urban development outcomes can be explained by cooperation between the public and private sectors rather than by coercion. Thus urban regime is a mode of cooperation created by politicians. The author suggests that it is therefore more important to explain informal cooperative arrangements than formal ones. The regime, according to Stone (1989), comprises "the informal arrangements by which public bodies and private interests function together in order to make and carry out governing decisions. There are three elements of this definition: i) a capacity to do something; ii) a set of actors to do it; and iii) a relationship among the actors that enables them to work together" (p. 179).

Savitch and Kantor (2002) introduce the concept of bargaining between the public and the private sectors. In that bargaining process the public sector should use its assets wisely to maximize public benefits. In terms of urban bargaining theory, intergovernmental support seems particularly applicable to the policy-making process in post-socialist cities. Intergovernmental support refers to the practices through which city, regional, provincial, or national authorities intervene in the marketplace to strengthen public control over development. The support mechanisms include planning, land-use controls, fiscal support, differential tax policies, and infrastructure and housing construction. A combination of qualitative assessments and quantitative indicators can be used to analyze intergovernmental support. The analyses can describe intergovernmental institutions and their impact, as well as intergovernmental cooperation in planning and development; explain housing policies; assess housing subsidies; and investigate of intergovernmental aid.

The analytical framework of this study is based on the following elements of regime theory:

- intergovernmental support
- the role of the political actors
- cooperation between the public and private sector.

The study focuses on those conceptual elements in analyzing two urban redevelopment programmes implemented in Kazan during the last decade. Data were derived from legal documents, official reports and information published in the local press. One programme, *Slum Clearance and the Modernisation of Slum Blocks in Kazan* (1995-2004), aimed to relocate people from slums to new housing. The other programme, *Preservation and Development of the Historic Center of Kazan* (2001-2005), supported the construction of several showcase projects linked to Kazan's Millennium celebration in 2005. This programme served the goal of enhancing Kazan's competitiveness in "episodic markets" (Turok et al. 2004). Both urban redevelopment programmes have been implemented with strong governmental support and coercive administrative methods. They have been characterized by formalized and minimal public participation and the government's dominating position. Moreover, in Kazan's case there is scarce evidence of "bargaining" between the public and the private sector. Therefore, to understand both the implementation of the two redevelopment programmes and their results, one must study the interaction between government agencies and the role of leadership.

16.1 Kazan's institutional setting

Kazan city is located in the Central European part of Russia, 797 km east of Moscow. In 2004 its population was just over 1,100,000. Kazan is the capital of the Tatarstan Republic of the Russian Federation, having declared its sovereignty after the break-up of the Soviet Union in 1991.

To preserve national unity, the federal center had to relinquish the historical union of the republics with Russia and allow regional leaders to be as independent as they might wish: in the famous words of Boris Yeltsin, "Take as much sovereignty as you can swallow!" (Tatarstan Republic 2003). According to the political bargaining concept, when the center cannot exercise full control over the country but is still strong enough to "punish" explicit disobediences (e.g., in Chechnya), it has to bargain with the other sub-national units to sustain its power (Solnick, 1998). President Vladimir Putin uses both "stick" and "carrot" approaches. In 2001, for example, all taxation privileges that had been granted initially to Tatarstan were taken back. The president of the Tatarstan Republic Mintimer Shaimiev, claimed that Tatarstan had not surrendered its privileges for nothing – a large federal grant was given to modernize Kazan's historic center (Tatarstan Republic 2003). When in 2005 President Putin abolished gubernatorial elections in the Russian Federation, Tatarstan's first president, Shaimiev, started his fourth presidential term as Putin's appointee.

Kazan city has a unitary authority, that is, a single jurisdiction, government and budget. Kazan's Soviet of People's Deputies has 120 representatives elected at the city level. The Chair, who is elected among the Soviet's deputies presides over the Soviet. The executive branch of government, or Kazan City Administration, is led by the Head (city mayor), who is appointed by the president of the Tatarstan Republic.[1] *De jure,* Kazan City Administration is subordinated to the Soviet and responsible for implementing the Soviet's decisions. *De facto,* the administration dominates the decision-making process, while the Soviet plays the ceremonial role of a voting machine that legalizes documents produced by the bureaucrats. While the members of the Soviet are political volunteers and "amateurs," the administration comprises civil service professionals. The administration's institutional capacity, if measured by the number of staff, offices, equipment, and funds, exceeds that of the Soviet By far. However, as in the former USSR, the Soviet and the administration mechanisms are interlocked (Frolic 1970; Taubman 1973). For example, Mr Kamil Iskhakov serves as the Chair of the Soviet and the Head of the administration at the same time. This creates a Kafkaesque situation when Mr. Iskhakov as the Chair of the Kazan Soviet adopts directives from the Soviet to the administration, and then as the administration's Head promises the Soviet to carry them out.

---

[1] This was practiced until 2005, when according to new Russian municipal legislation mayors can be either elected directly or elected by the representative body of power (Федеральный, 2003). In Kazan, due to a lack of democratic traditions, it was decided to avoid direct elections and follow the second option, so that people elect the soviet and then soviet elect the mayor.

More recently, after the Communist party and its local committees exercising real power at the city level had ceased to exist, the administration has expanded its role from an instrumental to a political one; it now functions as the decision-making center. The administration controls the budget, manages access to land and infrastructure and provides services to the city residents. Since the mid-1990s the administration has been proactive in tackling local problems and trying to add some European gloss to the city appearance. As the result of these proactive initiatives Kazan received three loans from the World Bank (the last one worth 125 million dollars), obtained funding from the government of Tatarstan Republic under the *Slum Clearance and the Modernization of Slum Blocks in Kazan Programme*, and from the federal government for the *Preservation and Development of Kazan Historic Center Programme*. These programmes are described and analyzed below.

16.2 The Programme for Slum Clearance and the Modernization of Slum Blocks in Kazan (1995-2004)

16.2.1 Programme objectives

On October 23, 1995 Tatarstan's president, Shaimiev, issued a decree aimed at solving the problem of slums across the republic. At that time of economic stagnation housing construction had declined and the free provision of flats had decreased considerably. Yet only a small proportion of the population could afford to buy real estate on the market. Hence government intervention was seen as the only way to improve the housing for many people who lived in deteriorated residential areas. A State Off-Budget Housing Fund was established to finance slum clearance, modernization of slum blocks and management of the funds allocated for those purposes. Talgat Abdullin, a former banker, was appointed by the president as the Fund's executive director. The Fund along with the local administration was obliged to "implement modernization of slum blocks in accordance with comprehensive development and heritage protection requirements" (Указ 1995, clause 6). The decree identified the following sources for the Fund:

- a special slum clearance tax paid by enterprises and calculated as one percent of their sales
- an excise duty tax on sales of crude oil produced in Tatarstan
- funds raised from sales of real estate located in slum blocks
- investments and credits (Указ, 1995, clause 3).

On November 1, 1995 the Kazan Soviet adopted *The Programme for Slum Clearance and the Modernization of Slum Blocks in Kazan*. According to the program, 31,907 families, registered in 8,001 dilapidated homes, with total living space of 1,211 thousand sq. meters, were entitled to receive new accommodation free of charge and with the right to privatize and sell the new units. The Programme had two objectives: 1) to eliminate poor housing conditions in Kazan and 2) to modernize the city center with commercial functions and high quality housing. Even though the Programme declared rehabilitation of historical areas and preservation of their urban scale to be program priorities, it was set to demolish 6,424 (80.2%) of 8,000 dilapidated buildings and refurbish 1,577 (19.8%).

16.2.2 Programme results

By 2005 the Programme was complete and 33,372 families had been relocated from slums to new flats (Table 16.1.). To accommodate about 100 thousand people, 315 high-rise blocks of flats with the total living space of 2,07 million sq meters had been built (Решение 2005). The largest financial contribution to the program was made by an oil company, Tatneft—the equivalent of $276,2 million; the second largest by a petrochemical plant, Nizhnekamskheftekhim—$46.6 million; and the third largest by an electrical company, "Tatenergo"—$23.6 million (Дурницина 2004). Between 1996 and 2004 as much as $759.4 million was collected from 35,000 enterprises.

Table 16.1. New housing construction funded through *The Programme of Slum Clearance* **and** *Modernisation of Slum Blocks* **in Kazan**

Year	Living space allocated (sq m)	Number of families relocated from the dilapidating housing
1996	152,379.1	3,003
1997	170,818.6	3,207
1998	213,812.0	4,032
1999	257,172.9	4,040
2000	217,176.7	4,000
2001	229,340.7	4,000
2002	201,974.6	3,506
2003	186,584.7	3,500
2004	-	4,018
Total	2,070,442.0	33,306

Source: Kazan City Soviet (Решение, 2005; Программа, 2004).

Despite the impressive numbers, the Programme's accomplishments are open to question: while the first objective, slum clearance, has been generally met, achieving the second objective, reconstructing the city center has not been. The city's Soviet reported that "redevelopment of the city center, has not been finished, the tasks of construction of urban amenities and heritage restoration have not been fully accomplished" (Решение 2005) In the newly built neighbourhoods the Programme "failed to create adequate provision of social services" (*ibid*) It proved to be very difficult to attract investments in the half-ruined historic area. In the late 1990s very few private investors would take the risk of reconstructing dilapidated structures when it was cheaper to build a new structure of comparable size. After being abandoned for years, many buildings including listed monuments and unique examples of wooden architecture were destroyed by severe weather conditions, arson, or illegal demolition. In 2003 there had been about 1,000 such old houses waiting for reconstruction. Ultimately, there was no choice but to tear them down; whole city blocks were wiped from the city map.

After the Russian economy recovered from the stagnation of the mid-1990s, private development resumed in the city. Some locations became very profitable, with sale prices exceeding US$1,500 per square meter,[2] but other, less attractive locations stayed in ruins. Now the urban environment of the historic center presents a combination of new commercial and residential projects erected between empty sites, and crumbling buildings that have survived the slum clearance. Because of poor planning and development controls, new, 4-5-story buildings are squeezed into historic subdivisions suitable for 1-2-story buildings. No space remains for parking and playgrounds.

Furthermore, the Programme did not always go smoothly. Apartments were distributed free of charge according to the "social norms," regardless of the size of the occupants previous properties. For that reason privatization of old properties (many of which, though in slum areas, were not dilapidated) was banned by the administration. Some tenants did not want to surrender their spacious homes for smaller flats. The strategy was soon adopted of convincing some tenants to move out by cutting off their electricity and gas supplies. Other tenants did not like the distant new locations. And it was soon realized that construction of schools, hospitals and shops had lagged behind the housing construction, so the daily needs of the newly built up areas were underserved. In 2001 a sewerage collector that had been built in a rush leaked and caused an outbreak of cholera. The redevelopment of the historic center too, was inhibited by inadequate capacity of the infrastructure to handle new projects. Altogether, coercive relocation practices,[3] unequal exchange between the old and the new properties, inconvenient locations and unreliable infrastructure[4] — all gave a rise to numerous disputes between citizens and the administration.

There were problems on the financing side, too. Some enterprise managers tried to avoid paying the "voluntary" donations imposed by the presidential decree. However, after the president pointed out that those who did not pay had better move their businesses from the republic, all enterprises complied. Additional reasons for the Programme's failure were the lack of understanding of market mechanisms, outmoded construction technology, the pursuit of narrowly defined

---

[2] In 2005 minimum housing price on the primary locations reached an equivalent of US$550 per square meter.

[3] Вечерняя Казань reports, that the methods the administration uses to convince people to move into new accommodation if they refuse to do so have little in common with legal procedures. The practice of threatening to switch off heating and electricity is reported by Вяткина and Толмачева (2001) respectively.

[4] Вечерняя Казань reported that residents of a newly constructed Azino district suffered from sewage flooding in the yard. The smell was so bad that in some premises people could not open windows. Communal services failed to fix the problem. (Вяткина 2001).

departmental interests by local officials, an unclear regulatory framework, and lack of development incentives.

No doubt the Programme was a socially important government action. Nevertheless, it could have been implemented in any of many ways, and not necessarily in the way most convenient for the construction industry. The alternative solutions often were discarded for the sake of the speed of construction. That is why massive numbers of residential blocks were constructed on greenfield sites instead of in central areas that would have required more elegant and complex solutions.

16.2.3 Programme analysis

Understanding the outcomes of the slum clearance and housing program, i.e., relocation of about one hundred thousand people from slums to new and free apartments, requires examination of both the policy as formulation and its implementation. During the economic stagnation of the 1990s, government intervention was seen as fuelling regional economic growth. Thousands of families could not have been accommodated fast enough if the city revitalization approach, as opposed to greenfield development or in the case of Kazan urban sprawl, had been adopted. Neither planners nor contractors could have switched to a new technology in the rush of the Programme's start. It would have taken too much time to deal with the complicated conditions in the city center, bad infrastructure and planning restrictions. The construction industry delivered what it was able to produce fast and in huge volumes: mass-built blocks of flats. One may argue, however, that the Programme removed from the center not only slums, but the "social pollutants" too, in order to make the center more attractive. That aspect of the Programme fits very well with the notion of converting Kazan into the spiritual capital of all Russia's Muslims and the third major center after Moscow and St. Petersburg.

16.2.3.1 Intergovernmental support

The Programme has partially met its objectives in terms of new construction, but failed in redeveloping the historic parts of the city. According to the Housing Fund's executive director Talgat Abdullin, the latter effort "was [simply] buried" (Таран 2003b). The debacle happened partly because two main parties -- the Housing Fund, which had money but no development rights in the city center and the Kazan City Administration, which had development rights but no money -- never reached an agreement as to who would do what. The Housing Fund bore alone the financial burden of relocating people from the slums to free housing on the city's outskirts. The Fund accumulated significant financial recourses and intended to redevelop vacant sites in the city center for commercial projects. The Fund expected to obtain titles on those sites free of charge. However, the Kazan City Administration rejected the Fund's claims in order to protect its own future profits from land sales and development, though it had neither the finances nor the investment offers to manage that. As a result, the land market in the center remained "frozen" for several years.

The Housing Fund redirected financial flows from the donors to the contractors. But payments in kind were accepted too, and that is why the Fund had a stock of construction materials that were not necessarily what was needed on many of the constructions sites that the Fund was managing. In a private conversation, one construction engineer complained that when they needed blocks to lay the foundation of the building, the Fund supplied them with roof elements and vice versa. Inefficiencies and delays arose because contractors had to sell the parts that they did not need, to buy parts they were lacking – all in the tense circumstances of urgent deadlines and limited cash flow.

16.2.3.2 Role of the political actors

The political commitment of the President of the Tatarstan Republic was essential for the Programme's initiation and implementation. President Mintimer Shaimiev's primary interest, however, was to be re-elected; the image of a socially oriented politician was expected to help. The populist slogans of "socially oriented reforms" and "soft entrance into the market" helped Shaimiev to gain national publicity. After the election, in his address to the Kazan Soviet of People's Deputies on March 25, 2004, Mintimer Shaimiev directly related the election results to the urban development programmes implemented in Kazan: "Because of all the work that is being done and that has been positively evaluated by the absolute majority of people, Kazan residents demonstrated unprecedented turnout at both the December and March elections; both parliamentary and presidential elections. They supported President Putin and "United Russia." Overall – this is too the result of our work" (Tatarstan Republic 2004).

President Shaimiev has been promoting his image as a "builder" of Kazan. Like many other Tatarstani politicians, Minimer Shaimiev started his urban life as a student at the Agricultural Institute. Interestingly, lack of urban background and experience has not restrained his appetite for initiating grandiose urban projects. He has also been closely involved in launching construction of the Metro and in other flagship projects such as Kul-Sharif Mosque and the Basketball Arena.

16.2.3.3 Public/private cooperation

On October 31, 2001 the Supreme Court of the Tatarstan Republic, acting in conjunction with new Russian legislation, declared invalid the slum clearance tax that had been the main source of funding for the *Slum Clearance Programme* (Указ 2002). Entrepreneurs and industrial directors hoped that the financial burden imposed by the President's decree would now be removed, but their hopes proved to be premature. The Tatarstani Minister of Construction and Housing Services and the executive director of the Housing Fund, at a joint press conference, stated that "even though the situation in the taxation legislation had changed, the republican government has come up with a new financial scheme to attract funds from enterprises" (Таран 2002). The "new financial scheme" was in fact the old state racket in a new form. A week before the Supreme Court decision, invalidating the tax, on October 25, 2001, the Tatarstani Gossoviet (regional assembly) adopted a new

Law on Slum Clearance Transfer which replaced the tax by voluntary transfers of the same size.

How could the government be sure that the voluntary contribution would be collected as effectively as a tax? Amazingly, the "voluntary" transfers came in even more promptly than the compulsory tax had. According to the local press, the revenue authorities explained that phenomenon by "the good job that was done among the enterprise managers" (Прокофьев 2002). By no means could the willingness to pay have been explained by healthy state of the Tatarstani economy, given that in 2003, 45% of large and medium-size enterprises in Tatarstan finished the fiscal year with losses (Etatar 2004).

What did happen was that Tatarstan's President made it clear to the enterprise managers that the *Slum Clearance Programme* was one of the government's main priorities and the "common cause." The methods he used were direct. For example, after a year's application of the new rules the President addressed the topic at a government meeting in order to remind disobedient industries of their duties. The case in point was a Moscow-based company with an outstanding debt (about $1 million) to the Housing Fund. President Shaimiev commented that "[t]he oligarchs came over here by mistake. They still do not know Tatarstan well. We will do everything to make sure the housing is being constructed . . . You will be paying to the Housing Fund until the moment I tell you it is enough" (Таран 2003a).

In contrast to the funding and implementation of slum clearance in the center and the new housing construction on the periphery, no realistic planning idea existed to bring private investments to the reconstruction of the historic neighbourhoods. Preparation of those planning documents did not coordinate with *The Slum Clearance Programme*. In fact, the city center's detailed master plan was prepared after the programme had mostly ended.

16.3 The Federal Programme of Preservation and Development of Kazan Historic Center (2001-2005)

16.3.1 Programme objectives

In March 2001 the Russian federal government adopted the programme for "Preservation and Development of the Kazan Historic Center" (2001-2005). The programme was directly related to Kazan's millennium celebration in 2005. While the *Slum Clearance Programme* was fully funded from republican sources (through "voluntary" transfers), the *Programme for Preservation's* funding was planned to have four sources: federal (30,42%), republican (30,58%) and city (9,36%) budgets, and an off-budget source through private investments and credits (29,64%). The total projected budget was as high as 64,93 billion roubles (approximately $US 2.19 billion). The city's Administration had very high expectations for the Programme's support of the regeneration of Kazan's center, as the *Programme for*

Slum Clearance had left entire blocks abandoned and in ruins after people were relocated. The *Programme for Preservation* was expected to help refurbish the abandoned buildings and restore architectural monuments.

The Programme had three main goals: 1) to restore the unique Eurasian cultural, historical and architectural heritage of the peoples of the Central European part of the Russian Federation; 2) to modernise infrastructure in the city's historic area; and 3) to develop inter-regional and international cultural and business links with other countries in Europe and Asia. The goals were to be accomplished by a set of distinct tasks, among others: historical preservation and restoration of architectural monuments, elimination of the negative environmental effects of industrial enterprises, reducing the transportation pressures in the historic center and developing modern transportation infrastructure, and enhancement of urban amenities and overall improvements of the quality of life (Постановление 2001).

The Programme was to be implemented through 131 projects -- 82 focusing on heritage protection, 6 on transport infrastructure, 8 on community facilities, 3 on landscape and recreation amenities, and 32 on tourist and business development. The anticipated results included the restoration of the historical, cultural and architectural heritage of Kazan's center on 13 sites; construction of a metro line and 30 km of ring and radial roads; improvements in the quality of life for the residents of the historic center; restoration of the ecological balance; turning Kazan into an inter-regional business and tourist center; and creation of 15,000 new jobs (Постановление 2001). All the projects were to be completed by the Millennium celebration in August 2005.

16.3.2 Programme results

Although the official report on the Programme has not been issued yet, fragmentary data that are currently available allow for some preliminary and general conclusions. In June 2005 the deputy mayor reported at a session of Kazan's Soviet that the Programme had received only half of the expected funding (Intertat 2005). The total funding secured was only 32,52 billion roubles: 7,1 billion roubles (35,9%) from the Federal budget, 18,07 billion roubles (91%) from the Tatarstan Republic's budget; and 7,51 billion roubles (39%) from off-budget sources including credits and private sector investments. Table 16.2. provides a summary of total funding received by 2004 and compares the planned versus the actual contributions.

The smaller than expected funding forced the city administration to reshuffle the original list of 131 projects. In September 2003 it was announced that because of the shortfall in funding, the number of projects would be substantially reduced (Корнеева 2004). The local press reported that the city administration had decided to drop 50 projects but add 26 new projects -- making the total of 106 implementation projects (Тихонов 2003). By 2005 it had become clear that only a fraction of what was planned has been achieved. The official web site for the Millennium Celebration listed 41 projects to be completed before the celebration, of which

Table 16.2. Budget for *The Programme for Preservation and Development of Kazan Historic Centre* in **2004**

Funding Sources	Planned	Collected	% of funding resources secured
Russian Federation Budget	4 687,5	2 200,0	46.9
Tatarstan Republic Budget	5 222,1	5 417,3	103.7
Off-Budget Sources	1 966,5	1 624,6	82.6
Total (millions of roubles)	11 876,1	9 241,9	77.8

Source: Tatarstan, 2005. As a reference in 2004 an average exchange rate was 28,8 roubles for $US1.

over 20 have been completed. Among the completed projects were 5 metro stations on a 7 km long line at a cost of 14.3 billion roubles (about $US482 million), Horse Racing Complex, an Ice Ring, and an up-scale housing development for VIP guests during the celebration. That housing project's new buildings were unrelated to heritage restoration.

As the administration faced giving priority to the most important projects and freezing the others, it became evident that the flagship projects were prioritized over the socially valuable ones. For example, the Horse Racing Complex was completed, but the Kazan Oncologic Hospital, with over 10 patients squeezed in each of its small wards, did not receive funding for a new building (Мачнева 2005).

16.3.3 Programme analysis

16.3.3.1 Intergovernmental support

The major reason that the intended Programme goals were not met was the serious difficulty with funding. Even though monies were transferred in time, the city administration failed to spend them as scheduled because the construction plans had not been approved. Federal financing could be stopped if the money was not spent within the designated time. In April 2002 the Deputy Head of Kazan's city administration announced that the reconstruction was going more slowly than expected, and that the deadlines might be missed (Пахомова 2002а). The main reason for the delays was the same as in the previous year – unapproved site development blueprints. The treasury did not pass the money to the contractors, and the 2002 budget was reduced to $US150 million. In 2004 the Russian federal agency reported that "due to insufficient funding the construction and restoration of 48 projects listed in the Programme has not been initiated. In 2002 there were no construction works on 62 sites and in 2003 this increased to 131 sites" (Accounts Chamber of Russia 2004).

In 2001 the Head of the Kazan city administration decided unofficially to stop selling empty land plots at auctions, as required by the Federal Land Code, because the distribution of that sales revenue between different tiers of budget that was imposed by the new federal Tax Code was unfavourable to the city. As a result, the subsequent transactions on the primary land market were in the form of either a lease from the government or a developer's purchase of an existing building on a plot. There was no direct financial support, given to developers, but preferences were given to particular firms or people in granting access to land. According to the local press, out of 250 land plots sold in Kazan during two years, only 25 were sold through auctions. The rest were "secretly passed to insiders" (Пахомова 2002b) The land in the city center was becoming increasingly inaccessible, and the procedures for acquiring development rights, approval of a project and permission to connect to infrastructure were becoming complicated and legally obscure.[5]

16.3.3.2 Role of the political actors

The Russian President agreed to be the chair of the State Commission preparing for the celebration of the 1000-year anniversary of Kazan. In January 2001 President Vladimir Putin noted that this anniversary should become an event of "international importance and a national holiday. He emphasized the goal not only to preserve and reconstruct the historic center of Kazan and its monuments, but to create a living environment that meets the standards of the 21st century. The Tatarstan President, Shaimiev, was optimistic, too as he confirmed that "[t]he whole Republic is involved in the preparation process. All financial resources are mobilised including the city budget and extra-budget sources. The republic relies on credits, given under the Russian government guarantees. It takes a lot of effort, but we have a unique opportunity to revitalize Kazan, to learn how to build nicely and quickly, in order to reach a final result with which that people in the capital of Tatarstan feel comfortable" (Tatnews 2001).

16.3.3.3 Public/private cooperation

The city administration had only limited knowledge of how an urban development process works in a market economy. The city's development plans did not suggest investment priorities so that the private sector could know what to expect and have guidelines. The administration had a clear vision of the long-term goals, but was not sure which of the many projects to pursue in the short run. It also kept changing the list of projects. Thus, the foundations for any joint initiatives between the public and the private sector were shaky.

The participation of private investments in the Programme was not substantial. "Off-budget sources" contributed 17.6% to the Programme's funds for 2004 (Table 16.2.). Private investments were probably even less, since the "off-budget sources" rubric included government borrowing from banks and private investors.

---

[5] Вечерняя Казань reports that the secretary of Kazan chief architect has been detained on suspicion of receiving a 100 000 roubles bribe that was paid to smooth the process of obtaining land development approval. Next month the chief architect himself resigned and the deputy chief architect got under investigation (Вечерняя 2004).

This time, the methods used in the *Slum Clearance Programme* to extract funds from the private sector were not exercised. Nevertheless, industries were strongly encouraged to participate in the Programme. For instance, a local distilling company contributed 2 billion roubles for the Horse Racing Complex, and the oil company Tatneft spent 570 million roubles on housing for VIP guests during the jubilee (Чудодеев 2005). Officially, 314 industrial enterprises donated an equivalent of US$ 5 million as "assistance for preparation" for the millennium celebration (Циунчук 2005).

An additional major obstacle to the regeneration of the city's center has been the inadequate technical capacity of urban services. Water and sewage lines in the central city are crumbling. Private developers, meanwhile, have used all possible ways to get access to the existing networks at minimal cost. Hooking up to the infrastructure lines is always an exhausting bargaining game between the developers and the government-owned company that provides the services. Sometimes that bargaining has a tragic conclusion. In February 2004 the director of the Kazan municipal water supply and sewage company was shot dead at his apartment block entrance. Some journalists speculated that the unfortunate director had not accepted any compromises with developers and had used under-the-table payments in financial settlements (Шебалова and Билалов 2004).

When the government does try to provide new infrastructure, it is not always at the right location. A large area in the city center that was recently serviced has attracted only a few private developers, as it is not an attractive location and land prices there are high.

Conclusion

This chapter has emphasized how urban politics influence urban development outcomes in post-socialist cities. To explain why certain policies receive priority and why public resources are directed towards particular projects whereas others remain neglected, we analyzed the implementation of two urban redevelopment programs in the city of Kazan. The analysis is placed within the specific political, economic and institutional circumstances in the city. The analytical framework draws on urban regime theory and tests its applicability to post-socialist cities. We focus on intergovernmental support, the role of political actors, and public/private partnerships as they define the urban governance and the circumstances of programme implementation. The two case studies show that, with some limitations, the major concepts of urban regime theory can be used in the new socio-political and cultural context of post-socialist cities.

Table 16.3. presents a matrix comparing the two programs in three areas: intergovernmental support, political actors, and private/public cooperation. The results highlight A- main characteristics, and B-impact. In the case studies there is ample evidence that intergovernmental support as proposed by Savitch and Kantor (2002) was an important factor in explaining the outcomes of urban programmes and policies. Both redevelopment programmes in Kazan suffered from poor organization and inadequate institutional capacity. Modernization of Kazan's center was delayed for years because the Head of the Kazan City Administration and the Executive Director of the Housing Fund could not agree on how the two major organizations should participate effectively. Planning documents prepared by the city's administration were incomprehensible to the business sector in that they did not provide a clear message about investment priorities.

The role of political actors was significant, too. *The Programme for Slum Clearance and Modernization of Slum Blocks* connected with the widely held perception of housing as welfare/right and the political advantages that could be gained by politicians who demonstrate their personal commitment to that basic human need. As both case studies showed, Tatarstani politicians had a key role in creating Kazan's urban regime. They shaped the redevelopment programmes to suit their individual political interests and used coercive methods to force the private sector to contribute financially. Major development programmes are helpful in gaining national publicity or in securing political appointments. In such political games, however, the substance is often neglected. While the showcase projects create an image of prosperity, promote economic development, and stimulate private investments, they also have negative social and environmental consequences.

The results of this empirical study also demonstrate the need to revise some fundamental assumptions of the urban regime theory when applying it in a post-socialist context. Even though the government in a post-socialist country has surrendered some of its urban development functions to the private sector, it still directly provides many goods and services, does planning and enforces development regulations. The control over urban development can be exerted through both *formal* arrangements (including comprehensive development planning) and *informal* arrangements (including coercion and deal-making). The implementation of the *Slum Clearance Programme* illustrates how the development outcomes depend on government policy enforced through informal coercion. That strong role for government diverges from the regime theory's focus on the informal agreements between politicians and businessmen as the major explanatory factor. The major difference from cities in developed market economies is that creation of an urban regime through coercion rather than through cooperation between the public and the private sectors. Nevertheless, the mode of cooperation in both market and post-socialist contexts seems to be shaped by politics.

The case studies also reveal that the state has a much more influential role as a direct provider of development than the regime theory assumes. That is why in post-socialist contexts the bargaining along the bureaucratic channels of power is as important as the bargaining between the public and the private sectors. Both urban redevelopment programmes explored in this chapter have had a most profound impact on urban conditions in Kazan in the last decade. Both programmes were funded predominantly by the federal government budget, indicating that the implementation. In Kazan, the decisions about urban development remain almost

Table 16.3. Programme outcomes (A – characteristics, B - impact).

Case Studies Programmes		Intergovernmental support	Role of political actors	Public/private cooperation
Slum Clearance and Modernisation of Slum Blocks in Kazan (1995-2005)	A	Tensions between the City administration and the Housing Fund over development rights in the city centre.	Politicians wanted to demonstrate personal commitment to basic human needs and used coercive methods in implementation.	The state enjoyed the role of a direct provider of housing and forced industrial enterprises to contribute financially to the programme. No cooperation was established.
	B	Delays led to failure of the modernisation component of the programme.	The scope of the programme (9% of a city of 1,1 million people have been relocated) and planning solution to accommodate such scope.	Private sector expressed much less enthusiasm for modernisation of slum blocks than it was anticipated; slow pace of modernisation; patchwork approach to regeneration efforts.
Preservation and Development of Kazan Historic Centre (2001-2005)	A	Lack of coordination between different tiers of government caused delays in funding.	Politicians were motivated by gaining national publicity helpful for both city/region competitiveness and securing political appointments for themselves.	Almost all projects belong to the non-commercial category; the list of projects was constantly changed.
	B	Initial list of 131 projects has been reduced to 41.	Selection of projects served its main goal - to impress VIP visitor and create an image of prosperity and smart governance. Very few actually involved preservation of historic heritage.	Projects serving the goal of episodic city marketing may not find their niche in the real economic context and will continue to be a burden for the budget.

Source: Compiled by the author.

entirely within the bureaucratic structures, and Kazan's urban future is shaped by major redevelopment projects initiated by the government. Success in competing for federal funds is largely politicized and depends primarily on the ability of the local politicians to negotiate and bargain with Moscow. Furthermore, to secure the private sector's participation in development programmes, the government uses coercive methods. The programme outcomes can therefore be better explained by bureaucratic procedures, politics and the rational behaviour of the local political elites rather than by cooperation between the public and private sectors.

References

Andrusz G, Harloe M and Szelenyi I (eds) (1996) Cities after socialism: urban and regional change and conflict in post-socialist societies. Blackwell, Oxford; Cambridge, MA

Brown F (2004) Fear factor. In: Vladimir Putin's Russia, worries about what comes next are stifling business. Newsweek International, October 25, 2004

Ferman B (1996) Challenging the growth machine. University Press of Kansas, Lawrence, KS

Frolic M (1970) The Soviet study of Soviet cities. The Journal of Politics 32: 675-695

Harvey D (1989) From managerialism to entrepreneurialism: the transformation of urban governance in late capitalism. Geografiska Annaler 71(B):3-17

Hubbard P (1996) Urban design and city regeneration: social representation of entrepreneurial landscapes. Urban Studies 33:1441-1461

Lowenhardt J (1995) The reincarnation of Russia. Longman, London

McLeod G (2002) From urban entrepreneurialism to a "Revanchist City"? On the spatial injustices of the Glasgow Renaissance. Antipode 34:602-624

Politkovskaya A (2004) Putin's Russia. The Harvill Press, London

Savitch HV, Kantor P (2002) Cities in the international marketplace. Princeton University Press, Princeton

Solnick S (1998) Will Russia survive? In: Rubin B, Snyder J (eds) Post-Soviet political order. Conflicts and state building. Routledge, London and New York, pp. 58-80

Stone C (1989) Regime politics. University Press of Kansas, Lawrence, KS

Taubman W (1973) Governing Soviet cities: Bureaucratic politics and urban development in the USSR. Praeger: New York Washington, London

Turok I, Bailey N, Atkinson R, Bramley G, Docherty I, Gibb K, Goodlad R, Hastings A, Kintrea K, Kirk K, Leibovitz J, Lever B, Morgan J, Paddison R (2004) Sources of city prosperity and cohesion: the case of Glasgow and Edinburgh. In Boddy M, Parkinson M (eds) Competitiveness, cohesion and urban governance. The Policy Press Bristol, UK, pp. 13-31

Accounts Chamber of Russia (2004) Отчет о результатах (Report on the results), Bulletin 11(83)/2004. <http://www.ach.gov.ru/bulletins/2004/11-7.php>

Вечерняя Казань (2004) Из главных архитекторов – в главные архитекторы (From chief architects to chief architects). Вечерняя Казань, No. 174, October 20, 2004.Вяткина Н (2001) Квартплата… за проживание на улице (Rent… for living on the street), Вечерняя Казань, No. 113, July 17, 2001

Дурницина И (2004) Татарстану не привыкать к масштабным задачам (Tatarstan does not need to get accustomed to big tasks). Республика Татарстан. No. 259-260, December 31 2004

Intertat.ru (2005) Казанские депутаты обсудили ход выполнения (Kazan Deputies discussed the implementation). Posted June 30, 2005 <http://www.intertat.ru/index.php?cat=r&bigoffset=0&microoffset=0&id=68188> [Accessed September 22, 2005]

Корнеева Т (2004) Казань займет 1 млрд. рублей (Kazan will borrow 1 billion rubles). Коммерсант, No. 94 (2933) May 27, 2004

Мачнева О (2005) К 1000-летию - все что угодно, только не больницы (For the Millennium – whatever, but hospitals). Вечерняя Казань, No. 39, 15 March 2005

Official Millennium Server (2005) List of Development Projects, <http://www.kazan1000.ru/rus/built/kazan.htm> [Accessed September 22, 2005]

Пахомова В (2002a) То денег нет, то документации (At one moment no money, at another no blueprints). Вечерняя Казань, No. 64, 9 April 2002

Пахомова В (2002b) Президент опоздал с деловым советом мэру (The president was late with his business advice to the mayor). Вечерняя Казань, No. 115, 12 July 2002

Постановление Правительства РФ (2001) О Федеральной целевой программе Сохранение и развитие исторического центра г. Казани (About The Federal Programme for Preservation and Development of the Historic Center of Kazan City), No 180, March 14 2001

Программа ликвидации ветхого жилого фонда и реконструкции кварталов ветхого жилья в г. Казани (2004) (Programme for Slum Clearance and the Modernisation of Slum Blocks in Kazan). Kazan City Soviet, Kazan

Прокофьев Ю (2002) Ликвидация ветхого жилья: суд вынес решение, которое ничего не решает? (Slum clearance: the court made a ruling that does not mean anything?). Время и Деньги, February 21 2002

Решение №39-23 (2005) Итоги выполнения программы Ликвидации ветхого жилого фонда и реконструкции кварталов ветхого жилья в г. Казани (Slum Clearance and the Modernisation of Slum Blocks in Kazan Programme Evaluation). Kazan City Soviet, May 25, 2005, Kazan

Таран Е (2002) Программа ликвидации ветхого жилья будет выполняться в любых условиях (Slum Clearance Programme will be implemented under any circumstances), Республика Татарстан, No. 85, April 26 2002. Available on-line at <www.rt-online.ru>

Таран Е (2003a) Работа над ошибками, Республика Татарстан, No. 144, July 18, 2003

Таран Е (2003b) Деньги следует тратить с любовью, Республика Татарстан, No. 14-15, January 23, 2003

Tatarstan Republic (2003) Минтимер Шаймиев: Права регионов будут расширяться (Minimer Shaimiev: Regions rights will be expanding) Interview with BBC diplomatic correspondent Bridget Kendall, November 17, 2003, Tatarstan Republic Official Web Server <http://www.tatar.ru> [accessed April 10 2003]

Tatarstan Republic (2005) Тезисы доклада министра (Minister's report summary). February 24, 2005 Tatarstan Republic Official Web Server <http://www.tatar.ru> [accessed 5 April, 2005]

Tatarstan Republic (2004) Выступление Президента РТ на сессии Казанского городского Совета народных депутатов (Official Address of the Tatarstan Republic President at the Kazan Soviet of People Deputies Session). Tatarstan Republic Official Web Server, March 24, 2004. <http://www.tatar.ru> [Accessed September 8, 2005]

Tatnews.ru (2001) Казань встретит юбилей достойно (Kazan will decently meet the jubilee). <http://www.tatnews.ru> [Accessed: November 11, 2001]

Тихонов Д (2003) А как же уважение к общественности? (What about respect to the public). Республика Татарстан, No. 227-228, November 14, 2003

Толмачева Л 2001 Собственность есть, и её вроде нет (The property is there, but it is like there is no). Вечерняя Казань, No. 88 (2195), 2 June 2001

Указ Президента РТ № УП-720 (1995) О мерах по улучшению жилищных условий граждан (On Measures for Improving Housing Conditions of Citizens). President Decree No. УП-720, October 23, 1995, Kazan

Указ Президента РТ N УП-47 (2002) О внесении изменений в Указ Президента (On changing president's decree) President's Decree No УП-47 January 16, 2002

Федеральный Закон N 131-ФЗ (2003) Об общих принципах организации местного самоуправления в Российской Федерации (On General Principles of Local Self-Governing in Russian Federation) Federal Law No. 131, September 16, 2003

Циунчук Т (2005) 314 предприятий республики окажут шефскую помощь. Posted on 03.30.05 16:11 <http://www.tatarinform.ru/news/kazan/?ID=4347> [Accessed 31 March, 2005]

Чудодеев А (2005) Даешь миллениум! Итоги, September 5, pp. 20-22

Шебалова Л, Билалов Р (2004) Губит людей вода. Восточный Экспресс, February 6-12, 2004

17 Urban policies and the politics of public space in Bucharest

Augustin Ioan

Introduction

Bucharest today reflects the legacy of city planning policies spanning more than thirty years of communism, as well as the new interventions of the 1990s that transformed the city's economy, society and urban politics. Some time after the devastating 1977 earthquake, President Ceauşescu led a campaign to change Bucharest from the ground up. Major operations of urban "renewal," including construction of the House of the Republic (then the second largest building in the world, which became the Parliament Building after 1989) and the Boulevard of the Victory of Socialism (which became "of Union" after 1989), have changed the fabric of the capital city of Romania (Fig. 17.1.). This chapter deals with the changes that the demolition and rebuilding over the last two decades made in the core of downtown Bucharest.

Several attempts to reinvent the area were doomed by bad politics and by the lack of research and definition concerning what public space is and might be. As a spectator, a critic, and an actor in the process, I can offer not only its story but, I hope, some unconventional insights on the future of Bucharest and the fate of post-socialist cities in Central and Eastern Europe. In the absence of any major social science literature on the pre- and post-socialist urban environment in Romania, this chapter draws primarily on *viva voce* (oral) history research and interviews with the architects and decision-makers involved in recent design competitions.

17.1 Change and the scars of urban renewal in Bucharest

Two major design competitions, one in 1991 and another in 1995-6, investigated the possibilities for healing the scars of urban renewal, but never achieved realization of the proposed ideas. The 1996 winning project, a master plan of the demolished area by Meinhard von Gerkhan and Joachim Zeiss, ended up as a beautiful wooden model in Bucharest City Hall. Two more design competitions, in 1999 and in 2002, were dedicated to implanting an alleged source of sacred healing -- the Orthodox Patriarchal Cathedral. That proposal stirred so much debate that major political actors intervened, and decided against the envisioned placement of the cathedral in order to reserve the site for a "major real estate investment." On other derelict sites in downtown Bucharest, buildings await conversion into *objets singuliers* (Baudrillard and Nouvel 2002). For example, the national library was to become the government headquarters in 2003, but the change of government in 2004 interrupted the process; the "Junior" building - a former supermarket dating back to socialist days–was turned into the new Palace of Justice; and the Communist Party Museum is to become a hypermarket in 2006 – quite telling of the new dominance of consumerism across the social sphere.

Fig. 17.1. Boulevard "Victory of Socialism" created during the Ceauşescu years and renamed to "Union Boulevard" in 1998

The past 15 years may be viewed as a continuation of the architectural history of the "civic centre" of Bucharest – that is, as the continued insertion of kitsch into the heart of the centre. That is not a new process. Back in 1947, Cantacuzino identified certain characteristics of Bucharest's urban texture – namely, that by destroying historical centres (the urban culture) and villages (the folk culture), the new projects created a unique, alternative reality that undermined old cultural forms, evading all relation to the urban or the folk culture (Ioan 1992). A good illustration of that bankruptcy is the House of the Republic (today the Parliament Building), which fails to integrate with the urban fabric. It is just as imposing and jarring in juxtaposition to the surrounding urban pattern as are the housing "blocks for commuters" built in the 1970s and 1980s in the centre of the old villages (Fig. 17.2.).

Bucharest's urban vernacular also is full of paradoxes. The eclecticism of the 19th and 20th centuries produced a random display of styles. For example, gothic inspired the neo-gothic of the last century, but only in terms of "mystery," expressed in sombre pointed-angled houses or cottages that are unsightly unless tricked out with ivy or pelargonia at the windows; moreover, the neo-gothic, like any parvenu, is excessive – "more Catholic than the Pope" (Baudrillard and Bunschoten 1998). In the inner city, the residential quarters built with stucco and bad plaster are eclectic as well, but "carnevalesque" reflections of the original French eclecticism (Ioan 2003).

Fig. 17.2. The House of the Republic, home of the Romanian Parliament in Bucharest

The historical importation of inferior models from the periphery of culture and authentic art into the architecture of power continued during the communist and post-communist periods, for example, in the eclecticism of The House of the Republic/Parliament. This kinship line linking the kitsch to the vernacular, the official architecture of the Ceauşescu regime and the traditional small scale of the Lipscani neighbourhood in central Bucharest, might have been a salutary urban combination for assembling the "new civic centre." Scale aside, both Lipscani Street, the main commercial route of the historic district of downtown Bucharest, and the Victory of Socialism Boulevard are of the same picturesque, eclectic nature.[1]

Another recent example of the unbroken habit of Bucharest architecture was the proposed (but unrealized) project of the *America's Partners* group: building a Transylvania/Dracula Theme Park on one side of the House of the Republic/Parliament, together with casinos and commercial galleries. The investment group was to use Michael Jackson's money as well as those of several American native tribes. Perhaps it was no wonder, given the recent interest in theme parks, that one of the main projects of the 2000-2004 social democratic government was

---

[1] Both areas are diverse in their architecture, eclectic and picturesque, regardless of their different scales; also, both avenues have a chance to revive as commercial routes in the future city of Bucharest.

to build a Dracula Theme Park outside Bucharest.[2] This project also has not been implemented so far.

17.2 Remaking the civic centre – the "Bucharest 2000" design competition in 1995-96

After the massive demolition in the 1980s (approximately 485 hectares, that is about the surface of Venice), followed by reconstruction along the lines envisaged for the boulevards, the 1990s brought their own urban revitalization solutions. Those solutions were sought through several design competitions. Unfortunately, the approach, the programme requirements and the political climate, with former communists -- many of whom had contributed to the demolition and reconstruction in the 1980s -- in the key posts, triggered dismal results. Some utopian schemes, such as those in 1991; some unrealistic ones, as in 1995-6 – the design competitions constrained and delayed the urban development of the city. The story of the making-by-demolition and then the unmaking-by-building of this Romanian "ground Zero" is a remarkable one, not only entangling urban design and architectural arguments, but illustrating the working of state and city politics and what can happen when urban policies and expertise are lacking.

The "Bucharest 2000" International Design Competition was in many ways the first test for Romanian architects in the post-1989 period; a few researchers saw it also as a crash test for foreign architects facing post-socialist urbanism (Bucharest 2000 International Urban Planning Competition 1996). As stated by Roann Barris in her article "The Rape of Bucharest" (2000), despite expectations that it would generate a "healing plan" for the renewal of Bucharest, the design competition was a great disappointment to the guild of architects. In particular, none of the design entries advanced a solution to the lack of public space (as opposed to the existing wasteland), except for the rejected project by Richard Rogers Partnership. That entry was allegedly a follow-up to his entry in another competition in Beijing that was not awarded a prize (Barris 2000). Richard Rogers proposed an intricate design with ovoid squares and low but dense residential units at the neighbourhood scale, which probably would have woven Bucharest's urban tissue precisely where it was broken.

Another entry, by Amy Christie Anderson of the U.S., included a "democratic forest" that, according to Barris, was perceived by the jury as "the image of open democracy" (Barris 2000, 10/11). In fact, this entry's focus on landscaping and ecology in a place of dereliction, political charge and violent disputes among former owners, city hall, government and intellectuals was far distant from the "crea-

---

[2] The project was initially located in Transylvania at Sighisoara, a Saxon fortress, where, allegedly, Vlad the Impaler (the historic figure behind the legend of Dracula), lived for short periods. Bucharest lacks the infrastructure required to service this colossal project (airports, hotels, highways, services).

tion of a virtual palimpsest of memories, actualities, and visions" (Barris 2000, 8/11). A few other proposals entertained the idea of public place, such as one by Federico and Domenico Fiorani (Italy) and another by Pierre Sicard Gillot and Mariano Marcos (France). However, the former entry conceptualized public space as administrative offices placed in a government campus, while the latter envisioned three Versailles-style spaces added to the existing square in front of the House of Republic/Parliament. An interesting final entry by Florin Biciusca (Romania) included a concrete burial slab surrounding the House of the Republic, a proposal more meaningful as a memorial than as an urban renewal strategy. The competition jury was unsettled by that proposal, being, according to the catalogue of 2000, "shocked by the radical nature of this entry, but [feeling] that its ideated force is inadequate to become an urban development strategy"(Bucharest 2000 International Urban Planning Competition 1996, p. 76).

However, even the commercially-oriented entries, like the winning design by von Gerkhan and Zeiss, were devoid of economic criteria and too utopian to guide the development of the central area of Bucharest (Fig. 17.3.). At 1999 costs, the implementation demanded 18 billion dollars of investment, primarily in infrastructure -- a sum larger than all foreign investment in Romania since 2000. Von Gerkhan and Zeiss' idea of having a Bucharest financial/business city district rise – huge office towers with the purely aesthetic function of camouflaging the House of the Republic/Parliament – was sabotaged by the country's political instability and the inability to attract sufficient foreign investment. At present, there are 70,000 square meters of office space available. The winning entry's core idea of turning the Unirii Plaza into a lake with two subway lines and the artificial bed of the Dâmbovița River running below it also resoundingly affirms the counter-economic nature of its master plan.

The unfortunate outcomes of the "Bucharest 2000" design competition may be traced to the political environment that promoted the process. The competition was supported by a group of well-intentioned people who lacked experience formulating in urban policies fit for a market economy. They felt it was important to have an international contest as a sign of the country's and city's opening to the world. Indeed, the competition was a splendid and prestigious process, yet so far it has done nothing but add ten more years to the city's development drama (Ioan 2003). It has also engendered a major problem: the reluctance of British and German investors to consider Bucharest as a potential investment opportunity because of its dysfunctional city development guidelines, absence of clear regulations for specific areas, and growing prejudice against architects.

Then the local and general elections again changed players in the local government and the mayor. The new government appointed the director of the 1995-6 competition as secretary of public works. He immediately stopped the activity of the Central Bucharest Consortium Ltd., under the pretext that von Gerkhan, having won the design competition, had to undertake the study. A visit paid by von Gerkhan to Romania two years later to be decorated by President Ion Iliescu, official patron of the 1995-6 contest, did not change much. The complete

Fig. 17.3. Bucharest 2000 Design Competition: von Gerkhan and Zeiss winning design

lack of action on implementation left the huge central area of Bucharest empty. The dwarfed vision, the lack of urban practice in market economy conditions, the excessive rigor of architects and city planners that stalled negotiations with the actual actors in the public space, the politicians' lack of interest – all contributed to the inaction and lethargy about reviving public space in central Bucharest.

17.3 Public spaces as places of worship, memories and symbols

After the events of 9/11 American researchers like Barris may have a better (because closer to home) view of the role of working through the trauma that memorials and monuments, or even mere for-profit building may have in dealing with the violent loss of monuments or meaningful places. In Sorkin's (2003) words reflecting on the site of the former World Trade Center's twin towers:

> The clearing of the site was accompanied by widespread claims for its sanctity. Everyone recognized that this was sacred ground, a gravesite, a place permanently marked by tragedy. In those first days, many of us called for the preservation of the entire fourteen acres as a memorial to the three thousand victims of the horrendous attacks...It is clear that most consider the site permanently saturated with solemnity and therefore entitled to special consideration, some exception from business as usual (p. 66).

Although one perhaps cannot claim a similar status for the central area in Bucharest, I believe that its present catastrophic dereliction and the state of disrepair of its "second skin" (i.e., its built environment, Bunschoten 1998), calls for a memorial approach. That would honor those who lost their homes and churches, who died because of trauma caused by demolition or by forced labor at the House of the Republic site itself, and who were unaccounted for after 1989. Another design competition in 2002, for the Orthodox Patriarchal Cathedral, was an invitation to revisit those memories. It was based on the premise that government offices would be established in the unfinished building of the National Library on the left bank of the Dambovita River, and the Ministry of Justice would be located in the converted Junior supermarket. However, new uses for these structures associated with Ceausescu's regime triggered criticism of the symbolism. The possible construction in that neighborhood of the Patriarchal Cathedral of the Romanian Orthodox Church, the country's most practiced religion (by 85% of the population) and a strong political force, would have done little to improve the urban situation.

Fig. 17.4. Ioan's winning design in The Orthodox Cathedral Competition: a collaborative effort with a team of professors and students from the University of Architecture and Planning in Bucharest.

The location of the Catheral was considered in the context of the von Gerhan and Zeiss master plan, which had won the Bucharest 2000 competition. After a year of procrastination, a decision in 2003 planned to move the Cathedral site from the Unirii Plaza to a peripheral park adjoining an elegant mausoleum of communist heroes erected in 1959. Thus, the winning project was removed from the plaza where it could have made a structural and memorial contribution to the public space that needed most attention.[3]

The beginning of 2004 saw fresh political discussions and protests, because the park is a protected historical site, as is the mausoleum. Despite the clear public importance of the cathedral, the Romanian Orthodox Church refused to share a location with the funerary monument. Although a variety of designs were presented, the Church continued to push for the obliteration of the mausoleum, the witness of a past (yet impossible to ignore) historical epoch.

In 2004, the site for the future cathedral was changed once more, to none other site than the courtyard of Ceausescu's House of The Republic/Parliament. While filling the derelict space behind that building was not necessarily a bad idea, public debate revived this time on whether it was appropriate to bring together two major buildings with such opposite meanings. After all, the House had replaced, among many other demolished edifices and common houses, several churches and the major Mihai Voda Monastery. In 2005, rumors were heard in the Parliament that the location was not yet definitive, as apparently it was situated on top of a "secret,": quite possibly imaginary tunnels connecting the House with the Ministry of Defense across the street.

All those *faux pas*, materializing in several contradictory government resolutions and five different site locations in less than five years, stemmed from the inability to produce and support consistent city planning policies transcending an electoral calendar or individual passions. The inadequate training of architects and city planners, the lack of decision-making experience within the public works administration and the monument conservation commission, and the absence of public accountability (shown, for instance, by the meddling with the results of the national contest) are a few of the many impediments to urban development policy for the public space in the centre of Bucharest. It seems that the wind of change has barely touched the Romanian capital.

17.4 Reinventing public spaces and neighbourhood centres

At the time of its construction during the 1970s, the Drumul Taberei neighborhood represented a civilized example of the way the modern urbanistic principles of the Charter of Athens could be put into practice: collective dwellings scattered about, commercial centers in isolated groups, alleys freely undulating amid the blocks that varied in shape and height. The neighborhood was built at the outskirts of the

---

[3] Following the logic of theme parks, the original location of the Patriarchal Cathedral was changed in 2003 to allow a private company to redevelop the site for commercial real estate with a strong entertainment touch (shopping mall, hotels, multiplex, high end housing).

city, so that it spared the older buildings from demolition. However, as the communist regime had more blocks built, the verdure spots were done away with, the tenants' intimacy was intruded upon, the various networks were over-used and traffic congested. To reach the city center from this area is now an irksome undertaking. Improvised market places have popped up wherever the need was felt, mocking the architects and urbanists of thirty years ago.

The center of Drumul Taberei neighborhood is opposite to the "Alexandru Moghioroș" market place. For a fierce stalinist leader of Romania to have his name outlive him in a space of free negotiation, against which he fought, is an ironic fate. On the other side of the post office, located opposite an open air market, in the very center of the new neighborhood a waste ground exists where a neighborhood center was once planned to rise, one that would have hosted spaces for commerce, administration, and public services. However, the center was never completed.

After the 1989 revolution, the residents were alerted from time to time that the place was to become a small-scale Luna Park. But it remains the same old waste ground with its iron plate pubs where, beside meat rolls and fake rum, *SC Tradiția srl* sells furniture. A workshop for plastic processing functions in a plank shack. Several electric cars –the closest thing to the idea of a Luna Park -- ramble around, as if bewildered, just like the whole nation. Iron plate, undulated plastic, forged fences, Gypsy music, vomit and mud – all is there to stay. A huge *bidonville*, nourished there by the carelessness of the former local administration and of the district and city offices for good urban environment. The authorizations for the locations of the shanties, if any, are either provisional or fraudulent. No one exhibits any intention, however feeble, of getting things in order.

Meanwhile, since the late 1990s, several signs have emerged indicating intensions of future develoment. The German chain of supermarkets, BILLA, opened a store in the area of the envisioned neighborhood centre, accompanied by a Shell gas station and, lately, next to a proud Orthodox church built via pious telethons. The empty wasteland has turned into a market place of household goods, of gasoline and of religion. Unfortunately, moreover, there is no sign of any parking provided for the ever-extending market place. These developments illustrate the vernacular way of realizing a retail centre, which then becomes the preferred land use for both local authorities and private investors in the unresolved places of downtown Bucharest. The empty land of Drumul Taberei was changed from civic to commercial, from designed by authority on behalf of the public interest to vernacular patchwork appropriation. No clear vision ever appeared.

Similar transformations are taking place on the former Constitution Square placed in front of the House of the Republic/Parliament. Almost weekly, beer festivals, auto shows, open air concerts replace the original civic nature of such squares. Here as elsewhere in Bucharest, the public place has become a void, an empty *maidan* (a word of Turkish origin, originally meaning square), waste ground and space leftover from previous building operations.

Conclusion: Bucharest as an unfinished project

For the time being there is no immediate solution for Bucharest. The city lacks *public spaces* dedicated to such shared functions as meeting and recreation, but instead has been flooded with huge, inward-looking consumption spaces, like supermarkets. They are located in strategic positions downtown, and as a result of their very presence and success, the surrounding exterior public realm is scorched. If there is really such thing as the Bucharest *midan,* which the Turkish original word *meidane* for square does not sustain, then it exists right at the centre of the city. The focus on individual edifices to the detriment of the overall urban structure still prevails among urban designers, city planners and politicians, alike. With the probable exception of the urban square of the Palace Hall (a 1959-60 addition to the 1935 Royal Palace, turned into the National Art Museum), which imposed some degree of control over the demolitions and additions in the surrounding urban space, the scarce and random presence of regulating principles elsewhere in central Bucharest indicates only inconsistent and interrupted future intentions rather than projects turned into actual reality.

To maintain that contemporary Bucharest lacks public places and space as a result of the historical influence of Ottoman urbanism is dubious, a way of avoiding the responsibility borne by the more recent decisions made about the city during the 20th century. Harhoiu (1997) claims, however, that the urban look of the city today is largely a *post-Ottoman* product of heavy French influence in the 19th century. The residual, leftover public spaces are the outcome of the clash between the unassimilated, post-Enlightenment urbanist models and the "organic" reality of the town. All subsequent adjustments, including those made during communism, have tried to "straighten," "regularize," "bring to a logical shape," or "modernize" the city. However, many such interventions, like the unabashed cut of the Victory of Socialism Boulevard, uniting the pre-existing points of the urban texture, actually create spatial conflicts. In close proximity to these areas of conflict are the empty spaces – the derelict outcomes of urbanistic violence.

There are various ways of engaging in a dialogue on how to deal with the residual spaces in Eastern European post-socialist city that were born out of architectural and political repression. The Romanian politicians and architects opted for international urban design competitions, yet failed to consider ideas that might redress the painful memories in post-socialist public space. The Master plan for Bucharest downtown is still subject to controversy and political agendas of changing governments, but in any case the core of the city is being used for commercial developments (malls and theme parks), rather than for the civic and cultural uses found in the centre of an European city such as Bucharest once was. The lack of effective public administration and consistent urban policies has delayed the realization of winning urban design projects from several competitions, leaving downtown Bucharest as a vacant playground for consumerism. A few alternative projects do take place in Bucharest, far from the grip of the political administration, and with European financing that cannot be controlled by the power magnates or simply though the dedication of a handful of architects countering the mainstream trends. The other Eastern European capitals probably fare better with regard to urban policies as a means of guiding urban reconstruction and new developments. The gap in the case of Bucharest may be due to a lack of awareness or backing of urban policy by the local administrators, as well as the failure to translate policies into feasible urban projects.

Much remains to be done to grasp the dynamics of public and private spaces, the local examples of "other spaces" (Foucault 1984) and the interplay among the social production, appropriation and use of the public built (or unbuilt) environment. The real (re)working of Bucharest and its spatial structure is yet to come. And it would be well for it to be preceded by a serious (re)thinking of Bucharest as a contemporary European city, in a moment when the very meaning of what a contemporary city is, or will be in times of public violence, shifts rapidly. Not an easy task, but nevertheless one long overdue.

Acknowledgement

I am very grateful for the insightful comments on earlier drafts provided by Dr. Nedović-Budić and Dr. Tsenkova. Their constant support and assistance was instrumental in defining the framework of analysis in this chapter.

References

Bucharest 2000 International Urban Competition (1996) Bucharest 2000 Urban Competition catalogue. Simetria Press, Bucharest

Baudrillard J, Bunschoten R (1998) Metaspaces. Black Dog Publishing Ltd/CHORA and Joost Grootens, London

Baudrillard J, Nouvel, J (2002) The singular objects of architecture. University of Minnesota Press, Minneapolis, MN

Barris R (2000) The rape of Bucharest, www.artmargins.com/content/feature/barris.html

Bunschoten R (1988) Metaspaces. Black Dog Publishing Ltd/CHORA and Joost Grootens, London

Cantacuzino GM (2002) Pentru o estetica a reconstructiei (Towards an aesthetics of reconstruction, in Romanian). Romanian reprint of the original edition of 1947, Paideia Press, Bucharest

Foucault M (1984) Of other spaces. Translated in Romanian. In: Ciprian M (ed) (2003) Altfel de spatii – Studi de heterotopologie. Paideia Press, Bucharest, pp. IX-XXV

Harhoiu D (1997) Bucharest: A city between orient and occident. Simetria Press, Bucharest

Ioan A (1992) Arhitectura si puterea. (Architecture and power) (in Romanian) Agerfilm Press, Bucharest

Ioan A (1999) Power, play and national identity. Romanian Cultural Foundation Press, Bucharest

Ioan A (2003) Arhitectura sacra contemporana (Sacred Architecture Today) (in Romanian). Noi Media Print, Bucharest

Potrč M (2003) Urban negotiations. IVAM Institut Valencià d'Art Modern, Valencia.

Sorkin M (2003) Starting from zero - Reconstructing downtown New York. Routledge, London, N.Y.

18 The post-socialist urban world

Sasha Tsenkova with Zorica Nedović-Budić

Introduction: Dimensions of urban change

Post-socialist cities and societies are undergoing a dramatic economic, social and cultural change. Currently several key forces are affecting urban planning and policy in the countries of transition: political and economic transformation, restructuring of state enterprises on market principles, privatisation, and social change. Other forces behind the dynamics of urban change are land and housing reforms, property market differentiation and fragmentation, and the increased flow of domestic and foreign investments (UNECE 1997; Tsenkova 2005). The impact of those factors should be considered against the background of rapidly changing roles of traditional institutions, actors and relationships in the urban development process. Within the new market reality, urban development is associated with a wave of investment in land uses offering opportunities for higher return, selective inner city redevelopment by the private sector and gentrification of the inner city neighbourhoods (Hamilton et al. 2005). These phenomena are explored in a series of case studies included in the book. The compelling narratives demonstrate the impact of these general mega trends and processes of urban change highlighting the importance of the richness and uniqueness of the local context. The local responses are equally important for the understanding of the manifestations of urban change in individual cities as are the general regional and global drivers of change. Although the book does not use a rigorous comparative approach to explore the urban experiences in the post-socialist cities, it contributes to our understanding of the interrelated nature of economic, social, institutional and spatial transformation, presenting a *mosaic of diverse urban experiences* across Central and Eastern Europe (CEE) and the Commonwealth of Independent States (CIS). While it may be too early to develop a convincing theoretical account of the transition process in post-socialist cities, insights from different countries and cities across the region may nonetheless test the capacity of theoretical concepts to generate explanations of the trajectories of change, and may provide empirical material for further theoretical development (see Tsenkova - Chapter 2).

New challenges arise from the profound structural changes in the economy as a result of transition from planning to markets. The pressure of national and international economic forces, and the opening up of previously sheltered sectors to the growing competition in the global marketplace, requires urgent adjustment of industries, services and other economic activities (The World Bank 2000; Adair et al. 1999). Further privatisation leads to the increasing importance of the private sector in economic development; a new industrial mix is likely to emerge; the small businesses, mostly service oriented, will demand new production spaces. The contributions to this book demonstrate that the urban change in post-socialist cities has several principal dimensions: a. globalisation and economic restructuring within the hierarchy of cities, affecting their economic base and labour markets; b. social transition, including social differentiation, inequality and the emergence of urban poverty; c. transformation of private and public institutions; and d. the spatial restructuring processes in the built environment (see Taşan-Kok - Chapter 3, Andrusz - Chapter 4 and Tsenkova – Chapter 2, in this volume). This classification suggests the complexity of economic, social and institutional challenges that shape the context for effective urban planning and policy intervention in post-socialist cities. The dimensions of urban and institutional change will be explored in more detail in this concluding chapter. The discussion will incorporate the major findings of the analyses presented in the book, outline major trends and urban policy challenges and reflect on the post-socialist urban future.

18.1 Major trends and local nuances

Major trends in post-socialist cities are driven by a series of interrelated processes of change: economic, political, technological, demographic, social and cultural (UNCHS 2001b). The sequence and rhythm of these changes reshapes existing urban systems and urban forms, transforms the social and demographic composition of neighbourhoods and leads to new urban life styles (Knox 1994). In this context of dynamic change, globalisation and economic restructuring, social differentiation, and changes in the institutional landscape are powerful contextual determinants of the transformations in the built environment and in urban policy development and implementation (Giddens 2001; Hall 1993; Marcuse and van Kempen 2000).

18.1.1 Globalisation and economic restructuring

National economies in the post-socialist world have become increasingly integrated within a global system of production, distribution and exchange. The liberalization of trade, international flow of capital, the growing influence of transnational corporations are well known developments which have led to fundamental economic restructuring, particularly visible in the post-socialist cities (Castells 1992; Giddens 1990). The transition from a centrally-planned industrialized system of mass production to a system of flexible accumulation has been accompanied by restructuring of the welfare state and a transition to pluralist, democratic governance. The role of the state, local governments and public sector institutions has been redefined with an emphasis on deregulation, privatisation and competition in the delivery of urban services and overall urban economic development (Buckley and Mini 2000; van Kempen et al 2005).

Globalisation has a deep impact on the restructuring of cities and localities involved in the process. The performance of cities and regions is increasingly affected by processes and forces external to their geographical areas, and even to boundaries of their national states (Sassen-Knoob 1987, 1994). Urban restructuring in the post-socialist world is marked by the following trends:

- increasing internationalisation of metropolitan areas in terms of both capital and labour;
- deindustrialisation and growth of command and control functions in capital cities;
- increasing social and economic polarization within cities;
- changing power relations between the public and the private sector mirrored in deregulation of planning and the emerging competition to attract foreign investment;
- emergence of post-modern urban landscapes, emphasis on place promotion and city marketing in the context of growing competition for investment and jobs (see Andrusz – Chapter 4, Tosics – Chapter 7 and Tsenkova – Chapter 2, in this volume).

18.1.2 Social differentiation

Transition economies have experienced profound social and economic differentiation in the last fifteen years, resulting in escalating unemployment, degradation in living standards, and growing social problems. The social cost of the transition from planning to markets has been particularly high, as demonstrated by Buckley and Tsenkova (Chapter 9), and particularly so in the cities of the Former Soviet Union, where the socialist legacy has left a much more powerful imprint on the cities' economies, societies and spatial structure.

Social problems in post-socialist cities are related to labour market restructuring and to the growth of long-term unemployment (Buckley and Mini 2000). Lack of political commitment to address problems such as structural unemployment or rising homelessness in a comprehensive manner, as well as the reduced expenditures on social welfare further aggravate the situation (see Andrusz in this volume for further discussion). Economic restructuring and prolonged recessions have been marked by:

- decline of manufacturing industries, the loss of skilled manual middle-income jobs;
- growth of highly skilled and well paid professionals managing the new post-industrial, service-driven urban economy;
- parallel development of low-skilled and low-paid service jobs, often part of a city's informal sector.

Economic recessions, cut-backs in social welfare and reduced spending on social programs contributed to the growing income and social inequalities (Tsenkova 2003). The impact of increasing polarization resulting from rapid economic and social change has become visible in the growing social problems in the inner cities and peripheral public housing estates, equally dramatic in Budapest, Moscow and Sofia explored in the book. These trends of social polarization and deprivation underline the pattern of poverty concentration in run down neighbourhoods as well as peri-urban areas with illegal settlements (see Deda and Tsenkova for an indepth discussion of the problem of urban poverty in Greater Tirana). Growing social polarization and the elimination of state funded housing programs coupled with the high cost of urban services and housing, jointly contribute to homelessness and social marginalisation, which Andrusz (see Chapter 4) discusses in the case of Russian cities. In addition to social marginalisation, the author also turns our attention to ethnic conflicts stemming from historic tensions as well as new immigration dynamics in post-socialist cities.

18.1.3 The new institutional context of urban development

Urban planning and policy in post-socialist societies are driven by the transition from the stability of socialism towards the instability of post-socialist, post-industrial and perhaps post-modern society (Simpson and Chapman 1999). In the aftermath of the economic and political crisis of socialism, followed by the erosion of nation-states and the welfare state, powerful urban effects have been generated. These urban effects have occurred in the context of rapid institutional transformation, where many new institutions are established but they tend to be immature and in a state of flux. This institutional incompleteness characterizes local entrepreneurialism, city image building, and strategic planning in post-socialist cities, as argued by Taşan-Kok (see Chapter 3). The institutional transformation is path-dependent and does influence the success and speed of the transition in urban governance, as Kim (Chapter 11) and Kinossian (Chapter 16) demonstrate. Kim's study of Warsaw's housing market highlights the importance of strong legal and social norms that facilitate a more effective operation of private institutions.

Political changes are also an important determinant of urban development. Post-socialist urban and regional policy in the 1990's has undergone pronounced decentralization in public administration and a shift of decision-making power from the central to the local level (Tsenkova 2005; UNECE 1997). The ideological shifts in urban planning and policy have marked new relationships between the 'private sector' city and the 'public sector' city. Public-private partnerships have emerged as leading instruments in urban development, especially in the recycling of urban areas. The role of the market in creating and managing urban infrastructure is being reconsidered in urban management (see Tsenkova – Chapter 2, Vujošević and Nedović-Budić – Chapter 14 and Schwegler – Chapter 15 in this volume).[1] Privatisation of urban services, private enterprise and capital take over traditionally 'public' intra-urban and inter-urban infrastructures.

---

[1] In transition economies budget constraints and new fiscal realities reduce the flow of funds in the urban and regional economies. Central and local governments are unable to provide adequate infrastructure investment, while the emerging private sector is still finan-

Within the new realities, regional and urban planning has been transformed into a democratic participatory process, and the legacy of socialist top-down approach has been abolished. The process has been embedded in the overall institutional transformation in post-socialist societies driven by efforts to decentralize political and economic decision making. It has created numerous political and economic actors endowed with generally weak planning and coordination instruments. The planning system is forced to redefine itself and search for new mechanisms to stimulate investment, encourage efficient land use and enable the operation of land and property markets. The system so far has produced rigid documents that do not take advantage of, or account for the new socio-economic circumstances; at the same time, the system has been deemed as too opportunistic and too flexible in implementing urban development projects, and particularly careless about preserving the public spaces. Interestingly, some of the case studies included in this volume demonstrate a continuing strong role of state and local government in urban redevelopment (see Kinnosian - Chapter 16 and Schwegler - Chapter 15).

Recent urban planning initiatives in post-socialist cities are characterized by their neo-liberal orientation, inspired by the desire to streamline and deregulate the excessively bureaucratized, slow and complicated process of urban approval. The comprehensive planning during socialism has been subject to a devastating critique on the basis that comprehensive plans were neither practically feasible under market conditions, nor politically viable. The 'incremental approach' has gained importance. Master plans, or urban general plans, approved to guide urban development are often revised on the basis of short-term bargaining rather than long-term goals and objectives. All this still does not mean that the processes and initiatives for urban development and revitalization are depoliticized or unchallenged by the variety of interests and views. The conflicting situations often arise around the new visions for the public spaces, as Ioan (Chapter 17) tells us in the fascinating story of the design competitions for the civic centre of Bucharest. Tosics (Chapter 7) also offers additional examples of conflicts in Budapest's areas of newly acquired prestige as well as in the areas of competing development needs.

18.1.4 Spatial restructuring: decentralization and revitalization

Despite the high levels of urbanization in post-socialist countries, recent developments have led to two diverging scenarios. Most CEE countries have experienced significant population decline and demographic shocks, leading to slow urbanization in the last fifteen years, while in several of the CIS countries substantial urban growth has led to rapid urban change and expansion of cities (UNECE 1997; UNCHS 2001a). To some extent, the different patterns of urban development may be attributed to different stages in the urbanization process, reflecting the level of economic and industrial development in the country or sub region (see Andrusz et

---

cially very weak to fill in the gap. Those processes have a significant impact on spatial dynamics of post-socialist cities.

al. 1996 and Buckley and Tsenkova – Chapter 9 - for elaboration on this point). These differences are a defining element in the pattern of general spatial restructuring of economic and social activities, which shapes the diverse mosaic of post-socialist cities.

Urban development in the 1990s in most of the post-socialist world, particularly in the capital cities, has been characterized by spatial expansion of urban areas. A number of factors including economic growth, demographic changes, higher purchasing power of the population, and increased mobility have facilitated the tendency of high area consumption per capita.[2] Suburbanization has been boosted by consumer preferences for suburban lifestyles. Decentralization trends have been even more pronounced for new retail and industrial development. Suburban locations have offered cheaper land, access to major transport networks, and ample parking for wholesale and retail businesses, as well as recognized economies of scale for new office parks (see Kreja – Chapter 13 and Hirt and Kovachev – Chapter 6). Cities have expanded into low density areas, while some inner city areas have experienced decline. Hypermarkets and malls have become the key manifestations and symbols of the new consumerism, as Kreja (Chapter 13) suggests in the case of Warsaw and Andrusz demonstrates in his analysis of retail formations in Moscow (Chapter 4). Garb and Dybicz in their empirical study of Warsaw and Prague (see Chapter 12) find a close relationship between the decentralization of retail and increased motorization. They also discover the emerging creativity of this sector in meeting demand from various population segments as well as its ability to capitalize on the existing, reliable public transit.

The provision of urban housing has been a consequence of population growth, limited investment and ad hoc responses to urban housing shortages. As several authors demonstrate (Kim – Chapter 11, Golubchikov and Badyina – Chapter 10 and Buckley and Tsenkova – Chapter 9), the market demand for high-rise apartments in post-socialist cities declined sharply in the 1990s. It might be expected that increasing consumer affluence will sustain a tendency towards a higher proportion of low-rise and single-family dwellings in the future, often in prime urban locations. The process of gentrification of older neighbourhoods is a by-product of the demand for high-end urban living visible in some cities (e.g. Moscow, Budapest and Sofia).

While the new housing developments improve the neighbourhood, they are also accompanied by a controversial process of displacing the original residents, as vividly described by Golubchikov and Badyina in the case of the Ostozhenka district in Moscow (see Chapter 10). A considerable growth in the construction of single family dwellings and other low-rise housing could be expected, as housing will be provided by decentralized suppliers, often in the periphery as Tosics (Bu-

---

[2] In many post-socialist cities population densities show some distinctive features: residential densities are low in the city centre which is counterbalanced by a high commercial density, then densities peak in the peripheral housing estates and fall gradually towards the urban fringe. Such patterns, as argued by Bertaud. are not in line with the standard economic model assuming intensity of land use to be highest in the locations with the highest transport accessibility and highest locational value.

dapest – Chapter 7) and Hirt and Kovatchev (Sofia – Chapter 6) demonstrate (see Fig. 18.1.). Increased car ownership and mobility in post-socialist cities has made suburban locations more accessible, compared to the urban cores. The intra-urban decentralization of both people and jobs implies that the density gradient from downtown core to the urban fringe is becoming less steep (Bertaud – Chapter 5).

Fig. 18.1. New single family housing in the suburbs of Sofia[3]

---

[3] Photographs in the chapter by Sasha Tsenkova

Notwithstanding suburbanization pressures, the new market-based economy is the driving force behind the reorganization of city centres. As development pressure on traditional central areas continues and their density increases, the cluster of service, financial and highly profitable urban functions continues to expand, replacing economically less viable activities such as housing and public open spaces. The vitality of the central city core in most capital cities has been re-emphasised. Themes such as quality of urban living (gentrification, new retail and sophisticated entertainment), and enhanced social control over both public and private spaces within the city have become significant. This post-socialist restructuring of urban spaces is often associated with foreign investment, private sector driven development for affluent consumers, corporations and multinational companies, and growing emphasis on retail consumerism (see Andrusz – Chapter 4, Kreja – Chapter 13 and Schwegler – Chapter 15). Urban governments have become more innovative in their efforts to mobilize investment and make their cities more attractive as business and cultural centres, although in some cases the marketing of nostalgia and 'commercial historicism' is used to reinforce the European identity (as suggested by Schwegler in the case of Komarno). Bertaud (Chapter 5) claims that a strong and prestigious historical centre served by public transit reflects the European urban character of post-socialist cities, particularly in CEE, which is rediscovered today and reinvented in response to market demand.

18.2   The future of post-socialist cities: rethinking urban hierarchy

The transition from planning to markets is a process of economic adjustment in which economic functions are specializing and concentrating. Internationalization is leading to a hierarchy of functions and a hierarchy of location environments. A number of functions such as command and control functions of multinational corporations, the top management of services, media, and culture are grouped in capital cities. Other functions, mostly large-scale industry and services, are looking for specialized environments. This trend towards concentration is also occurring in the international trade and transportation sectors so that flows are bundled in main ports and destinations. Accommodating those trends in the urban environment through optimal locations for all these functions and through preserving and developing the existing capacity is a major challenge during the transition.

The overall level, size, and significance of this spatial transformation will depend on differences in the position of post-socialist cities and the differences in their support base. A distinct hierarchy of cities will be the unavoidable result of these developments. Post-socialist cities and specialized regions will be increasingly competing with each other on European and global levels.[4] Cities with an in-

---

[4] The process of spatial transformation is *regionally differentiated*. An increasing polarisation between rapidly advancing regions in CEE and CIS and those affected by severe economic recession and unemployment has been observed. The old industrial regions have

sufficient support base of retail and services, and obsolete industrial capacity, will become of secondary importance in the new urban network. Future urban policies might selectively focus on strengthening the existing capacity of urban centers and on identifying their competitive edge. This spatial approach promotes the efficient use of resources and investments in a specific location, its labor force, benefits from economic, social and environmental diversity, and connections.

A new spatial hierarchy has emerged in the post-socialist world of cities—with centres of new development and peripheries. The globalisation of urban economies, reinforced by the political and institutional integration in Europe, has created an atmosphere of growing competition among cities (Hall 1993). The capital cities have attracted human resources, driven the growth of employment, mainly in the tertiary sector, and reorganized production and residential activities into new metropolitan models of urban space, as Tsenkova's comparative overview in Chapter 2 demonstrates.

The first category is that of capital cities and large metropolitan centers. The largest cities have a leading edge in the competition for top functions. These activities are already concentrating there, and related requirements—labour market, production services, and communications—are adjusting very quickly to this process. In addition, the metropolitan environment with its banking and financial institutions, government bodies, business climate and a variety in cultural and recreation facilities, has distinctive advantages. Differences among metropolis and capital cities are decisive in the competition among cities for top functions and economic activities. The urban structure with its inadequacies: backlogs in the supply of office and retail space, transport problems, congestion, environmental pollution, deteriorating neighborhoods etc. affects the location choices and investment decisions.

The second group is that of cities with population over 300 000. This category includes a range of cities with different sizes of the population, strong industrial and manufacturing capacity, trade, education and research facilities. They will be struggling to attract new businesses, international companies' head offices, important financial institutions, trade fairs, cultural events, etc. Some of these attempts will be successful, depending on the quality of urban environment, the location advantages and economic/tax incentives to make investments viable. Currently some of those cities may lose the position of relatively independent urban centers due to inefficiencies in urban management, overall economic decline in the support base and considerable lack of resources to address growing needs for infrastructure investment and social inequalities. Some functions—banking, retail, office development—in these cities are lagging behind thus contributing to the

---

been affected by the elimination of non-efficient economic enterprises and branches. On the other hand regions with good communication networks and technological potential have experienced a flow of investment for the modernisation of infrastructure and transportation. Foreign capital has contributed to the improvement of the economic prospects of these areas. Under the impact of market economy and the integration with the European Union, the greatest stimulus to development has occurred in regions along the newly opened frontiers (see Buckley and Tsenkova – Chapter 9 - in this volume).

inadequacy of the urban support base. Large cities often have a particular specialization as: old industrial cities, cultural and tourist centers, distribution centers, ports, traffic and transportation intersections, and centers with government functions. Since this group of cities is very diverse, future urban policies might focus on enhancing the competitiveness of existing functions. In addition, attention to the urban living environment and its general attractiveness is very important. This is particularly true for the old industrial and port cities.

The third category includes a large number of smaller cities which can be divided into cities experiencing economic growth, and declining cities. The first group of cities scores high in the area of economic structural adjustment and new business development. The latter will need considerable efforts and resources to improve their urban quality. For both groups, economic developments and local economic strategies to stimulate modern industry, retail, and services are necessary together with an emphasis on improvement of the living environment and infrastructure. In some cases those cities will continue to be dependent on existing capacities for large-scale industry—steel, basic chemical industries, oil refineries, power production, and waste processing. Port locations and other intersections of heavy infrastructure also fall into this category. Questions of environmental protection will be of paramount importance.

An alternative urban hierarchy in the European context is likely to emerge. The *European Spatial Development Perspective* introduced a classification of European cities by level of influence, making distinctions among three categories: international level, national level and regional level (Faludi 2002). It singles out three policies of particular importance – regional policy, the development of trans-European networks and environmental policy. Policy options are grouped under three spatial development guidelines: 1. Polycentric urban development and a new urban-rural partnership; 2. Parity of access to infrastructure and knowledge; and 3. Sustainable development and wise management and protection of the natural and cultural heritage. The underlying values include economic and social cohesion and balanced competitiveness. A fair number of post-socialist cities, particularly in the new accession states have joined the trans-European economic space and have become a springboard for international investment in their local and national economies (see Fig. 18.2.). While it is difficult to predict the competitive position of post-socialist cities in the future European urban hierarchy, some winners have emerged—Prague, Budapest, Warsaw, Bratislava and St Petersburg. It is reasonable to expect that policies embedded in the *European Spatial Development Perspective* will translate into local opportunities and activities generating local trajectories in post-socialist cities, which would be as diverse and unique as the ones characterizing the transition from state socialism to market economies.

18.3 A new role for urban policy and planning

Local government efforts in directing and facilitating the process of economic, social and spatial restructuring in post-socialist cities have been relatively weak due to constraints in resources, jurisdiction and powers. The analysis of various policy initiatives in this book indicates that a variety of sectoral policies are introduced to overcome the existing urban conflicts: pollution, over development in the central business district, decay in other parts of the city, lack of adequate provision of transport and social infrastructure, the imbalance of employment opportunities, housing and services, etc. The effect so far has been marginal and the commitment inadequate (see Tosics – Chapter 7, Buckley and Tsenkova – Chapter 9, Andrusz – Chapter 4, Deda and Tsenkova – Chapter 8).

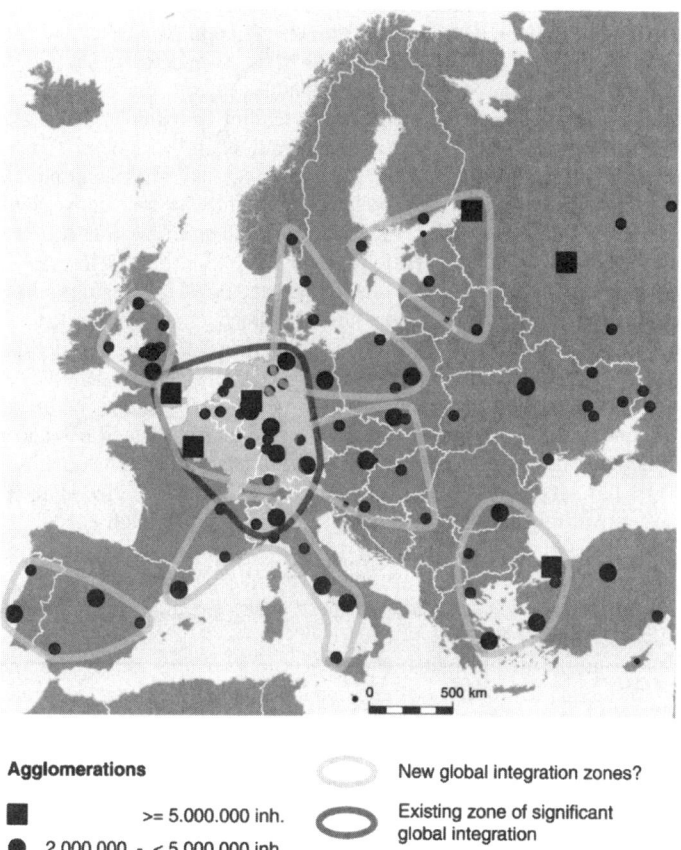

Fig.18.2. Metropolitan areas for future cooperation in Europe
Source: Faludi (2002), adopted from Mehlbye (2000, p. 759)

Urban reforms have taken a back seat in the overall process of economic and social transition (The World Bank 2000; van Kempen et al. 2005). Further, the cooperation and participation of a variety of groups that the concept of 'governance' implies, is limited; in fact the socialist urban management has been replaced by entrepreneurial rather than participatory governance. The flexible and largely neo-liberal approach by the local governments is far from neutral; it creates new winners and losers, and promotes elitists environments. The experiments with place-making in some cities (e.g. Bucharest, Budapest and Moscow) have produced fragmented environments—mixtures of glamour and deterioration.

In sum, urban planning and policy have promoted economic opportunities and, in the neo-liberal spirit, have not paid much attention to social outcomes. The price is often paid by neighbourhoods like Moscow's Ostozhenka. The full engagement in much-needed economic growth and recovery is often substituted with image building and place-making exercises, resulting in immature and fragmented environments—a mix of glamour and deterioration. In the context of rapid economic, social and political transition, local and regional administrations compete to attract economic activities and foreign investment, and frequently lower their development standards or change their land use plans to become the "winners" (sometimes, losers in this competition) (Dear 2000; Soja 2000). Inscribed within the frame of urban and territorial marketing strategies, place promotion in the post-socialist world of cities acquires new significance (see Schwegler – Chapter 15 and Taşan-Kok – Chapter 3). It refers to the diffusion of the appropriate information about the main resources, products, spaces, services, etc. that a city or territory offers, and their degree of adequacy to the demands of their potential users. Fig. 18.3. presents the attractive historical centre of Riga which has become the hub of international and domestic investment and business interaction in the Baltic States. Emphasis by proactive local governments is placed on "inward investment" strategies—investments attracted by a city or a region through specific policies (e.g. Budapest, Warsaw and Komarno). Regions and cities compete for inward investment; however, if minimum guarantees are not established, the extreme mobility of "global firms" and capital may result in abandonment of premises and major infrastructure (Buck et al. 2005; UNECE 1998).

Despite significant constraints with respect to resources and powers, there is a considerable scope for locally designed and implemented policies to manage the process of urban restructuring (Thorns 2002; Marcuse and van Kempen 2000). Several strategic options and policy choices exist: 1) selective restructuring, 2) strategic urban management and 3) non-interventionist approach. Selective restructuring implies a commitment to efficient management of urban change through limited support for key sectors. Programs of economic transition might promote the advancement of specialized industries and/or services production. Investment in key urban components might include infrastructure development, selective urban renewal, and management of urban growth (e.g., the strategic planning efforts in Riga, Prague, Sofia and Budapest). The approach offers a lot of advantages under fiscal austerity.

18 The post-socialist urban world   361

Fig. 18.3. Riga has become the centre of banking, foreign investment and technological innovation for Latvia and the Baltic States.

The non-interventionist approach is based on the notion that markets would automatically provide solutions to the growing number of unresolved urban problems and crises. This policy alternative is becoming the choice for some local governments due to budget constraints, lack of capital and inability to facilitate the adjustment process and to pursue local economic development strategies (e.g., Bucharest and Tirana). Some local authorities, however, resort to this approach due to general opposition to economic restructuring and the difficulties imposed on traditional industries and labour markets. The strategic urban management approach, based upon ecological and social principles, reflect a deep concern about economic restructuring and the economic vitality of cities. This comprehensive approach might address urban challenges within an integrated framework emphasising the importance of economic, social and ecological aspects of urban development. In this context, a critical task for urban and regional planning is to accommodate and facilitate the profound structural adjustments in the economy, as well as the urban and social change in the most rational and economically efficient manner. This complex process involves both short-term and long-term measures and initiatives.

There is hope that urban planning and policy will regain its status. The challenges and opportunities for improvement exist in all areas of planning and policy interventions, as well as in the planning and policy implementation processes. With respect to urban planning, most post-socialist countries have sought a new planning and policy model that supports the development of a civic society and is grounded in the authority of law and traditional social rules, as well as in the past or current planning practices. The evolving model generally encourages the planning and policy processes that are open, transparent, fair, participatory and accountable (Hamilton et al, 2005; Simpson and Chapman 1999). In practice, the implementation and the attempts to replace the so-called 'technocratic' with 'sociocratic' planning and policy might be at different points of institutionalisation (see Vujošević and Nedović-Budić – Chapter 14). The contributions to this book call for improvement of urban planning and policy implementation in areas of urban revitalization, provision of affordable housing, protection of public spaces and more effective infrastructure investment.

Finally, in the process of establishing new planning and policy systems and solving urban problems, the CEE countries have the opportunity to take advantage of the current or prospective European Union (EU) membership that would assist the harmonization of planning legislation and institutional development.[5] It can also facilitate the infusion of new polices and programmes as well as provide much-needed funds for local investment. While it is difficult for such high level policies and programmes to be effective in providing local solutions, they might facilitate the development of an urban policy agenda that addresses the multiplicity of urban problems in post-socialist cities in a more coherent manner. However, this would also require more comprehensive and better formulated urban policies by the European Union, concentrating on the development of integrated public policies that address urban services, economic and social development as well as environmental issues.

---

[5] The question of European identity and convergence between the old and new members of the European Union remains relevant from several perspectives – economic integration, social integration/cohesion, and differentiation between local and common identities in the process of preservation and promotion of historic urban heritage. Exploring the opportunities for local adaptation and implementation of EU rules, procedures and projects would be useful in guiding further integration efforts, their direction and scope.

18.4 Research agenda

This edited volume provides rich evidence on trends and processes of change in post-socialist cities. It offers an in-depth view of urban challenges and local policy responses in ten cities—Warsaw (Poland), Komarno (Slovak Republic), Budapest (Hungary), Belgrade (Serbia and Montenegro), Tirana (Albania), Sofia (Bulgaria), Bucharest (Romania), and Moscow, St. Petersburg and Kazan (The Russian Federation). Several additional chapters provide a comparative overview of trends, similarities and differences among the post-socialist countries and cities, emphasizing the pattern of diversity. In drawing the trends together, what stands out is that transformation and change have been central to the post-socialist urban experience in the past fifteen years. Questions that focus on the speed and complexity of that change are central to the future research agenda as are the questions about the multiplicity of interrelated economic, social, institutional and spatial outcomes of the transition from state socialism to markets and democracy. Exploring and reflecting on these 'transitions' through the urban lens necessitates the development of theoretical frameworks that adequately capture the dynamics and the diversity of urban phenomena in post-socialist cities. While the dominance of Western European and North American urban theory is increasingly being challenged (King 2000; Jacobs 1996; Thorns 2002), the literature so far has failed to advance a theoretical approach that accommodates the needs of post-socialist urban analysis.

Urban analysis needs to recognise change and continuity; to acknowledge the importance of particular places and localities; to understand the complexity of everyday life in post-socialist cities; as well as to capture the institutional and policy mechanisms that are evolving. While urban analysis of past trends might be helpful in predicting the future, the nature of transformations in post-socialist cities and their constant adjustment to dynamic realities, makes the urban research agenda a lot more challenging. However, based on contributions in this volume, we feel that some issues are likely to remain central for future urban research.

The first cluster of issues relates to economic competitiveness and growth. As the post-socialist countries and cities are emerging from prolonged economic recessions and in some cases economic shocks, the need for appropriate policies and strategies to foster economic revival and growth is likely to benefit from research on the determinants of successful economic development. In the context of increasing regional and global competition, future research might be able to explore a variety of opportunities and approaches that are suitable for cities of various sizes, local resources and capacities. This requires rethinking of policies that promote urban competitiveness, social cohesion and better governance (Buck et al. 2005). A related set of urban policies that enhance the competitiveness of cities and ensure adequate quality of life pertains to the provision of urban services. While these services in post-socialist cities due to fiscal austerity have been rapidly privatised, the short and long-term effects of privatisation are not well known. Local governments are not capable of securing such services given their limited revenues and the privatisation is likely to lead to differentiated access and increased disparities between affluent and poor residents (Tsenkova 2005). Better insight into the fiscal impacts of urban development and its relationship to the supply of urban services may support hybrid solutions that would be more appropriate in the future.

The second cluster of issues relates to urban change that is caused by decline—economic, demographic, and social—as well as poverty (see Fig. 18.4.). What will be the implications for the provision of social services, urban infrastructure, public transport and the creation of wealth generating opportunities in post-socialist cites? How would people face the consequences of rapid economic adjustment, closure of state industries, escalating unemployment and deprivation? For those left behind, the new welfare state is offering less generous social safety net and support systems. The effects of urban poverty are visible, but not well documented and measured in their multidimensionality (i.e., homelessness, erosion of social capital, crime). More importantly, additional research on policies and programs to alleviate poverty would place it on the political agenda and mobilize more adequate public and fiscal support for new social policies (Jones and Ravenda 2000; Dear and Wolch 1987). In particular, exploring and evaluating the viability of various policy instruments to assist the urban poor with access to affordable housing is of great immediate value in the context of increased economic and social polarization.

Fig. 18.4. Refugee camp in Podgorica, Montenegro

The third cluster of issues focuses on the new role of planning in post-socialist cities and the spatial development outcomes it facilitates. Traditionally placed somewhere on the continuum between government and the market, urban planning and policy have yet to find the point of balance. While this point may (and probably will) differ across post-socialist counties in the region, it needs to reflect some level of optimality relative to the local circumstances and institutional setups. More importantly, this balancing point should find the middle ground between extreme flexibility (opportunism) and rigid and restrictive instruments of control to guide spatial development (Dear 2000; Soja 2000). While economic factors, including the viability of land markets and availability of capital for new investments in urban development on the supply side, and the ability to pay by the consumers on the demand side, are the main drivers of urban development, it is important to better understand the other players, their roles and actions, and the resultant urban patterns and forms. The relationship between the institutions responsible for urban planning and management and the spatial manifestations of urban change should be the focus of future research. Exploration of spatial planning documents (plan-making processes, plan content and implementation) in post-socialist cities would offer further insights into strategies to plan and manage urban change more effectively. For example, should compact urban form be promoted? What are the most effective ways to manage suburbanization of housing and retail? Complementary to this topic, the processes of urban revitalization, recycling and re-use of urban spaces and buildings require further study, with comparative and evaluative approaches.

In conclusion, post-socialist cities offer a world of complexity and increasing uncertainty with respect to the path of future urban change. Research and critical reflection upon the direction of that change, its diversity and opportunities to manage it more effectively, requires urgent attention if we want to ensure economic viability, improve the built environment and enhance social conditions and cohesion in these cities.

References

Andrusz G, Harloe M, Szelenyi, I (eds) (1996) Cities after Socialism, Blackwell Publishers Inc., Oxford

Adair A, Berry J, McGreal S, Sykora A, Ghanbari Parsa A, Redding B (1999) Globalisation of Real Estate Markets in Central Europe. European Planning Studies, 7: 295-305

Buck N, Gordon J, Harding A, Turok I (2005) Changing Cities. Rethinking Urban Competitiveness Cohesion and Governance. Palgrave Macmillan, Hampshire and New York

Buckley R, Mini F (2000) From Commissars to Mayors: Cities in the Transition Economies. The World Bank, Washington, D.C.

Castells, M (1992) European Cities, the Informational Society and the Global Economy. Centrum voor Grootstedelijk, Amsterdam

Dear M (2000) The Postmodern Urban Condition. Blackwell, Oxford

Dear M, Wolch J (1987) Landscapes of Dispair; From Deinstitutionalisation to Homelessness. Polity Press, Cambridge

Faludi A (ed) (2002) European Spatial Planning. Lincoln Institute of Land Policy, Cambridge, MA
Giddens A (1990) The Consequences of Modernity. Polity Press, Cambridge
Giddens A (2001) The Global Third Way Debate. Polity Press, Cambridge
Hall P (1993) Forces Shaping Urban Europe. Urban Studies, 30: 883-88.
Hamilton F, Dimitrowska-Andrews K, Pichler-Milanovic N (eds)(2005) Transformation of Cities in Central and Eastern Europe. Towards Globalisation. United Nations University Press, Tokyo
Jacobs J (1996) The Edge of Empire: Postcolonialism and the City. Routledge, London.
Jones C, Revenga A (2000) Making Transition Work for Everyone: Poverty and Inequality in Europe and Central Asia, World Bank, Washington D.C.
Marcuse P, van Kempen R (2000) Globalizing Cities: A New Spatial Order? Blackwell, Oxford
Mehlbye P (2000) Global integration zones – Neighbouring metropolitan regions in metropolitan clusters. Informationen zur Raumentwicklung, Special issue. Europäische Metropolregionen, 11/12:755-762
Saasen-Knoob S (1987) The Mobility of Labour and Capital. Cambridge University Press, New York
Saasen-Knoob S (1994) Cities in a World Economy. Pine Forge Press, Thousand Oaks, CA
Simpson F, Chapman M (1999). Comparison of Urban Governance and Planning Policy: East Looking West. Cities, 16:353-364.
Soja E (2000) Postmetropolis: Critical Studies of Cities and Regions. Blackwell, Oxford.
Thorns D (2002) The Transformation of Cities. Urban Theory and Urban Life. Palgrave Macmillan, Hampshire and New York
Tsenkova S. (2003) The Reform Path in Central and Eastern Europe: Policy Convergence? In Tsenkova, S. and Lowe, S. (eds.), Housing and Social Change in Central and Eastern Europe., pp.312-328, Ashgate Publishing Limited. Aldershot
Tsenkova S (2005) Urban Sustainability in Europe and North America. University of Calgary, Faculty of Environmental Design, Calgary
United Nations Centre for Human Settlements - HABITAT (UNCHS) (2001a) Cities in a Globalising World. Global Report on Human Settlements 2001. Earthscan Publications Ltd., London
United Nations Centre for Human Settlements - HABITAT (UNCHS) (2001b) The State of the World's Cities Report UNCHS, Nairobi
United Nations, Economic Commission for Europe (UNECE) (1997) Human Settlement Developments in the Transition Economies of Central and Eastern Europe. UNECE, Geneva, New York
United Nations, Economic Commission for Europe (UNECE) (1998) Major Trends Characterising Human Settlement Developments in the ECE Region. UNECE, Geneva, New York
van Kempen R; Vermeulen M, Baan, A (eds) (2005) Urban Issues and Urban Policies in the New EU Countries. Ashgate Publishing Limited, Aldershot
World Bank (2000) Cities in Transition. The World Bank Urban and Local Government Strategy. The International Bank for Reconstruction and Development/ The World Bank, Washington, D.C.

List of figures

Fig. 1.1. Conceptual framework..	5
Fig. 2.1. Conceptual framework for analysis of urban change in post-socialist cities..	24
Fig. 2.2. Patterns of urbanization and growth in socialist and middle income market economies, 1960-1990..	26
Fig. 2.3. Urbanization patterns in 2000..	27
Fig. 2.4. Growth in Gross Domestic Product, 2002...............................	32
Fig. 2.5. Unemployment in capital cities in selected transition economies, 2000...	37
Fig. 2.6. Waste water treatment, selected cities.....................................	41
Fig. 2.7. Small scale retail in Sofia's pedestrian zone...........................	43
Fig. 2.8. Home ownership in CEE and CIS capital cities........................	44
Fig. 3.1. Institutions, actors, and spatial development...........................	54
Fig. 3.2. Organizations, institutions, and property market......................	54
Fig. 3.3. Distribution of commercial complexes in Budapest (2002)..........	55
Fig. 3.4. Distribution of commercial complexes in Warsaw (2002)............	56
Fig. 3.5. Entrepreneurial capacity of municipal government systems in Budapest and Warsaw...	58
Fig. 3.6. Profiles of changing planning regimes in Budapest and Warsaw...	64
Fig. 4.1. Datchas in Moscow..	76
Fig. 4.2. Waiting to be gentrified – St Petersburg..................................	77
Fig. 4.3. Cardboard city in Moscow...	79
Fig. 4.4. Kazan Cathedral in 1992—the Museum for Religion and Atheism—as a backdrop for Salvation Army event in St. Petersburg..........	87
Fig. 5.1. Density in European cities...	96
Fig. 5.2. Comparative density profile between CEE cities and Western European cities..	98
Fig. 5.3. Budapest: Distribution of people by distance from the centre and densities..	99
Fig. 5.4. Land price and density profile in CEE cities and in a market economy...	100
Fig. 5.5. St Petersburg. Map of industrial areas.....................................	102
Fig. 5.6. Industrial land..	103
Fig. 6.1. Percentage change in dwelling units in the Municipality of Sofia by administrative district, 1992-2001...	119
Fig. 6.2. A 1987 aerial image of "Vitosha Collar" in the outskirts of mountain Vitosha..	120
Fig. 6.3. An image of the same area in 2002: City and country have "crawled" toward each other...	120
Fig. 6.4. Yet another imposing all-marble and gated residence in the Vitosha Collar..	120
Fig. 6.5. Location of Sofia's hypermarkets...	123

List of figures

Fig. 6.6. The gated entrance of "Green City".. 125
Fig. 7.1. The city of Budapest, the agglomeration zone, and the Central
Hungarian Region.. 137
Fig. 7.2. Case study areas of territorial conflicts in Budapest..................... 142
Fig. 8.1. Pyramid of poverty concepts... 154
Fig. 8.2. Spatial growth in Greater Tirana... 158
Fig. 8.3. The infrastructure in Bathore, one of the poorest neighbourhoods
in peri-urban Tirana, is upgraded through community-based partnerships... 165
Fig. 8.4. Mihal Grameno neighbourhood in peri-urban Tirana has the lowest
concentration of poor households but still lacks basic infrastructure.......... 167
Fig. 9.1. Density patterns in selected cities.. 182
Fig. 9.2. Population growth in European and Central Asian cities............. 184
Fig. 9.3. Housing estate on the outskirts of Riga, Latvia............................. 189
Fig. 10.1. Central Moscow and the location of the Ostozhenka district....... 198
Fig. 10.2. A restored historic building in the Ostozhenka district............... 200
Fig. 10.3. Building activity in Ostozhenka between 1994 and 2006........... 204
Fig. 10.4. The estimated number of residential houses (units) by
construction period in 1992 and 2006.. 205
Fig. 10.5. The same view photographed in June 2003 and September 2005.
The historic buildings wait for a new wave of investment........................... 206
Fig. 11.1. Housing completions in Warsaw, 1994 – 2003............................ 216
Fig. 11.2. Warsaw building permits by gmina, 2002.................................... 222
Fig. 12.1. Use of cars for food shopping - national level household survey
in the Czech Republic... 236
Fig. 12.2. The location of four surveyed malls within the Prague municipal
boundaries.. 238
Fig. 12.3. Factors influencing key trip parameters (after Garb, 2004)......... 239
Fig. 12.4. Summary of changes in travel patterns in the transition to
hypermarket shopping: arrival mode, monthly frequency and duration of
visits... 241
Fig. 12.5. Conversion of trip modes with the emergence of hypermarkets.... 242
Fig. 12.6. Breakdown of household car availability by travel mode of
arrival at the surveyed Prague malls... 243
Fig. 12.7. Trips from Zlicin mall, Prague; line width denotes volume of
trips to each destination zone.. 245
Fig. 12.8. Comparison of two malls in Warsaw: Centrum Janki, an
out-of-town mall, versus HIT Kabaty, a mall on a subway stop station in a
fairly dense residential area.. 247
Fig. 13.1. Development of shopping centres in Warsaw in sq m.   256
Fig. 13.2. Warsaw's modern shopping centres and the retail
corridor.. 259
Fig. 13.3. Typologies along corridor : 19 retail developments along the
Marszałkowska / Puławska corridor and three identified clusters.............. 262
Fig. 13.4. Solid-void analysis of case studies.. 266
Fig. 13.5. Land use comparison: before and after transformation............... 267
Fig. 14.1. Planning in the public domain: conceptual framework............... 276

Fig. 14.2. Location of former Yugoslavia and Serbia and Montenegro in the context of the Balkan Peninsula... 279
Fig. 14.3. The Regional Spatial Plan for the Administrative Area of Belgrade: land use and infrastructural elements.................................. 284
Fig. 14.4. The Master Plan of Belgrade: urban boundary and the metropolitan region... 285
Fig. 14.5. A sample of functional elements of The Master Plan of Belgrade: land use, green space and implementation priorities............................ 286
Fig. 15.1. Fragmenting the modernist urban landscape—a late 1990s commercial structure built within a 1970s housing estate....................... 303
Fig. 15.2. Imaging Magyar Liberal Nationalism: 1990s postcard featuring György Klapka, local hero of the 1848 Hungarian Revolution.................. 309
Fig. 15.3. Nostalgia for the present—1990s postcard featuring Austro-Hungarian town centre renovated under municipal direction.......... 310
Fig. 15.4. Europe Place's merger of architectural heritage and present/future European visions... 313
Fig. 17.1. Boulevard "Victory of Socialism" created during the Ceauşescu years and renamed to "Union Boulevard" in 1998............................... 338
Fig. 17.2. The House of the Republic, home of the Romanian Parliament in Bucharest.. 339
Fig. 17.3. Bucharest 2000 Design Competition: von Gerkhan and Zeiss winning design.. 342
Fig. 17.4. Ioan's winning design in The Orthodox Cathedral Competition: a collaborative effort with a team of professors and students from the University of Architecture and Planning in Bucharest........................... 343
Fig. 18.1. New single family housing in the suburbs of Sofia 355
Fig. 18.2. Metropolitan areas for future cooperation in Europe................. 359
Fig. 18.3. Riga has become the centre of banking, foreign investment and technological innovation for Latvia and the Baltic States........................ 361
Fig. 18.4. Refugee camp in Podgorica, Montenegro............................... 364

List of tables

Table 2.1. Major urban indicators in selected CEE countries..................	29
Table 2.2. Economic and social indicators in post-socialist countries.........	34
Table 2.3. The trajectory of urban change in post-socialist cities..............	47
Table 3.1. Analysis of post-socialist urban government, planning and property market institutions...	67
Table 7.1. New commercial investments in Budapest and its agglomeration, 1990-2004..	138
Table 7.2. Annual population change in and around Budapest, 1990-2003...	140
Table 7.3. Population in Budapest, the agglomeration zone, outer periphery and Hungary, 1990-2002...	140
Table 7.4. Conflicts in areas of newly acquired high prestige..................	143
Table 8.1. Comparison of poverty definitions in the context of Albania, 2002..	156
Table 8.2. Poverty and inequality in Albania...................................	157
Table 8.3. Population in Greater Tirana...	158
Table 8.4. Comparative indicators of unmet basic needs in Albania..........	159
Table 8.5. Profile of four neighbourhoods in peri-urban Tirana...............	162
Table 8.6. Comparison of household expenditures at the neighbourhood, city and national level..	164
Table 9.1. Household expenditures on urban services in market and in transition economies..	180
Table 9.2. The changes in the housing stock, income and population in selected countries, 1990 – 1999..	186
Table 10.1. Occupational profile of the working-age respondents, 1989......	201
Table 11.1. Description of firms studied...	217
Table 11.2. Residential eviction proceedings in the Mazowieckie Voivodship..	221
Table 11.3. The Polish residential mortgage portfolio, 1995-2001............	224
Table 12.1. Travel mode prior to the use of the surveyed facility by type of shopping—shoppers at 4 malls (n=1542)......................................	242
Table 13.1. Nineteen large-scale retail developments along Pulawska / Marszakowska corridor...	263
Table 16.1. New housing construction funded through The Programme of Slum Clearance and Modernisation of Slum Blocks in Kazan.................	323
Table 16.2. Budget for The Programme for Preservation and Development of Kazan Historic Centre in 2004...	329
Table 16.3. Programme outcomes..	333

Contributors

Gregory Andrusz is Emeritus Professor of Sociology at Middlesex University, an Honorary Research Fellow at the Centre for Russian & East European Studies, University of Birmingham, and a contributing member of the Russia-Asian programme at the Royal Institute of International Affairs (Chatham House). He has been involved in a variety of projects on homelessness, access to housing and the formation of civil society within the EU Tacis program, refugee projects in Russia funded by the UK Department for International Development, and, most recently, the British-Russian Development Partnership on poverty alleviation.

Anna Badyina is a PhD candidate at the School of Geography, University of Oxford. She holds her first degree from Khabarovsk State Technical University (Russia) and her MSc from the Royal Institute of Technology (Sweden). Earlier in her career, she served in several senior roles in Khabarovsk city and regional governments, and was lately a manager at a building corporation in Moscow.

Alain Bertaud is an urban planner with over 30 years of international professional experience. During his 20 years of service with the World Bank, he participated in the design and appraisal of large urban infrastructure and housing projects in Russia, China, Eastern and Central Europe and many countries of East and South Asia. Prior to his World Bank assignment, he worked with PADCO, a consulting firm in Washington DC and was a resident planner in Bangkok (Thailand), San Salvador (El Salvador), Port au Prince (Haiti) and with the United Nations Development Program, in Sanaa (Yemen).

Robert Buckley is Housing Advisor at the World Bank with project and urban policy experience in over 35 countries. He has published widely, including his recent studies From Commissars to Mayors, Housing Finance in Developing Countries, and Comparing Mortgage Credit Risk Policies: An Options Approach. Prior to joining the World Bank, he taught at the Wharton School and Syracuse University, and also was Chief Economist at the United States Department of Housing and Urban Development.

Luan Deda completed his MSc in Urban Economic Development at the University College London. He has an extensive planning and development work experience in social and infrastructure upgrading processes in a developing country context, including poverty alleviation, decentralization, housing for poor, legalization of informal settlements and citizen's participation in decision-making. He has provided consultancies for international organizations such as The World Bank, UNDP, UNCHS in Albania, Kosovo and Ghana and has recently joined Scott Brownrigg (UK) as Town Planner.

Tomasz Dybicz is a Lecturer at the Warsaw University of Technology, Transportation Engineering Division. He is responsible for research and teaching in the area of transportation engineering with a concentration on traffic studies, national and urban multi-modal transport network planning, and traffic engineering. He has a MSc degree in Transportation Engineering.

Yaakov Garb is a Visiting Assistant Professor in the Global Environment Program at Brown University's Watson Institute for International Studies and a Lecturer in the Jacob Blaustein Institute for Desert Research at the Ben-Gurion University of the Negev. He directed the Central European programs of the Institute for Transport and Development Policy (New York). After receiving his doctorate from Berkeley he studied at MIT and held postdoctoral positions at Harvard and the Institute for Advanced Studies at Princeton. His interests are in interdisciplinary analysis of a broad range of environmental issues and in the politics of mobility.

Oleg Golubchikov is a Clarendon Scholar at the University of Oxford pursuing his doctorate in human geography. He graduated from Moscow State University and holds an MSc from the Royal Institute of Technology (KTH) in Stockholm. He has recently been a visiting research fellow at the Division of Urban Studies at KTH, and is Director of an independent strategy consultancy, advising on Russia's regions.

Sonia Hirt is Assistant professor of Urban Affairs and Planning at Virginia Polytechnic Institute and State University. She holds a Ph.D. and Master's degrees in Urban and Regional Planning from the University of Michigan and a professional architectural degree from the University of Architecture and Civil Engineering in Sofia, Bulgaria. She has published articles on post-communist planning and on planning theory and history in the United States.

Augustin Ioan is Head of School of Research and Advanced Studies at the University of Architecture and Urban Planning in Bucharest. He holds MSArch degree from University of Cincinnati and PhD degree in History of architecture and philosophy. He has published extensively in Romania, Hungary and the US, including his latest book, Sacred Space (Etna, 2002). The same year he won the competition for the Orthodox Patriarchal Cathedral in Bucharest.

Annette M. Kim is Assistant Professor of Urban Studies and Planning at the Massachusetts Institute of Technology. She holds a Master's in Public Policy degree from Harvard University, and Master's of Arts in Visual Studies and Ph.D. in Urban Planning from the University of California Berkeley. She served as a consultant to the United Nations Centre for Human Settlements, the World Bank, African and Asian governments, as well as community-based NGOs in the United States and overseas in the areas of project evaluation, urban land market analysis, and institutional development in transition economies.